Advanced Placement*
Computer Science Study Guide

To Accompany Cay Horstmann's
Java Concepts
4th Edition

FRANCES P. TREES
Drew University

WILEY

JOHN WILEY & SONS, INC

ACQUISITIONS EDITOR	Bill Zobrist
MARKETING MANAGER	Frank Lyman
PROJECT MANAGER	Cindy Johnson
EDITORIAL ASSISTANT	Bridget Morrisey
COVER DESIGN	Susan Cyr / Harry Nolan

* AP and Advanced Placement are registered trademarks of the College Entrance Examination Board, which was not involved in the production of and does not endorse this product.

To order books or for customer service, please call 1–800–CALL–WILEY (225–5945).

ISBN 0-471-71861-0

Printed in the United States of America

10 9 8 7 6 5 4 3 2 1

Printed and bound by Courier Kendallville, Inc.

PREFACE

This Study Guide is designed to assist high school students preparing for the AP Computer Science Examination. It is organized and designed to accompany *Java Concepts, 4th ed.,* and *Big Java, 2nd ed.,* both by Cay Horstmann and published by John Wiley & Sons, Inc.

To the Student

Advanced Placement Computer Science is a college level course. As a student in an AP course, you are expected to understand college level material and to read college level textbooks. Because these texts may be used in multiple college courses, they contain material that is not tested on the AP Computer Science (CS) Examinations. This guide identifies and stresses the content that is tested on the AP CS Exams. This does not imply that you should skip the additional material in the text. Your teacher may include the additional material in your course and hold you responsible for that material. Some of the material that is not tested on the exam is extremely useful and may be included in your course. By following this guide, you will be able to focus on the topics included in the AP CS 2004-2005 Topic Outline and the elements of the AP Java subset that will be tested on the exam. You should visit the College Board Web site in the beginning of the school year to see if there are any updates or changes to the Topic Outline or AP Java Subset. Because the guide is designed for students taking either the A or the AB Computer Science exam, topics covered on the AB Exam are marked "AB only." If you are participating in an AP CS A course, this should not discourage you from reading these sections; it merely indicates that those topics will be tested on the AB Exam and not the A Exam.

Features of the Study Guide

This guide is organized to help students recognize and master those topics that will be tested on both the A and AB examinations. Where applicable, each chapter includes:

Topic Summary
This section parallels the material in the textbook, adding additional examples and explanation of topics presented in the text. Students will find special emphasis here on topics that are likely to be tested.

Expanded Coverage of Material That Is Not Found in the Text
Any topics in the AP CS Topic Outline or the AP Java subsets that are not covered in the text are presented in this section.

Topics That Are Useful But Not Tested

This section alerts students to sections of the textbook that present useful features of the Java language. Although these sections are not required for the AP Exam, they address features of Java programs that students are likely to encounter, or that they will need to progress in their programming ability. Although the student is encouraged to stay within the AP Java subset when writing solutions to free-response questions, a correct solution that implements Java features not in the subset will not be penalized.

Java 5 Issues

Java 5 is the most recently released version of Java (J2SE5.0). This newest version focuses on an "Ease of Development" theme. The many enhancements include generic types, auto-boxing, an enhanced `for` loop, enumerated types, and formatted input/output. This section will address the Java 5 enhancements as they may relate to the AP CS subset.

Any practice questions addressing Java 5 topics are clearly marked (Java 5) to alert the student and the teacher of the newest Java enhancements.

Things to Remember When Taking the Exam

Each chapter restates important concepts and provides specific suggestions for avoiding common errors.

Key Words

Vocabulary used in the chapter is listed alphabetically here for student review and reference. Each key word is accompanied by the page number(s) where it is defined and/or discussed in the text.

Connecting the Detailed Topic Outline to the Text

This listing links the topics presented in the guide to the pages in the text where the same topics are covered.

Practice Questions (Multiple Choice and Free Response)

A large number of practice questions, modeled after those on the AP exam, are included in each chapter. The questions use the multiple-choice and free-response formats that students will encounter on the exam. Answers to the practice questions are provided in Appendix A. In addition to the practice questions, there are cumulative reviews included after chapters 7, 14, and 18.

AB Examination Topics

Any sections (and practice questions) that cover topics that will not be tested on the Computer Science A Exam are clearly marked "AB only." Students who are preparing for the AB exam should be sure to complete these sections.

Web Resources

The reference materials that students may use during the AP Exam are available from the College Board's Web site at http://www.collegeboard.com/prod_downloads/student/testing/ap/compsci_a_ref.pdf (AP CS A) and http://www.collegeboard.com/prod_downloads/student/testing/ap/compsci_ab_ref.pdf (AP CS AB). These reference materials contain a listing of the classes, interfaces, and methods contained in the Java subset covered by the AP Exam and references and source code for the case study that are tested on the exam.

The AP Computer Science Topic Outline is available at http://www.collegeboard.com/student/testing/ap/compsci_a/topic.html?compscia. This Topic Outline and the AP Java subsets may be revised from time to time, so you are encouraged to check for the most current version of these documents in the AP Computer Science Course Description on the College Board site.

Web sites associated with this guide and with *Java Concepts, 4th ed.,* and *Big Java, 2nd ed.,* are another important resource for users of this guide. Cay Horstmann's site, http://www.horstmann.com, includes a section, *Help with Common Compilers,* that provides installation tips and getting started instructions for the most commonly used Java compilers and environments. You will also find source code for programs in the text(s), solutions to selected exercises in the text(s), frequently asked questions, a programming style guide, and more. Many of these same items are also available from the Wiley Web site for the text at http://www.wiley.com/college/horstmann. Also available at the Wiley Web site are instructor resources not available to students.

Acknowledgments

It has been a sincere pleasure and honor working with Cay Horstmann's material in developing this guide. Dr. Horstmann is truly a master computer scientist and teacher.

Many thanks to Cindy Johnson and her staff at Publishing Services for their hard work, support, and patience throughout. I am extremely grateful to Jennifer Turney and Joe Kmoch, whose reviews offered many valuable comments and suggestions.

My energy and enthusiasm for teaching computer science are constantly renewed by the many AP CS teachers that I work during AP CS workshops and summer institutes.

Finally, thanks to Eli for his patience, encouragement and support.

CONTENTS IN BRIEF

*Parenthesis indicates the corresponding chapter in *Java Concepts, 4th ed.*, and *Big Java, 2nd ed.*

CONTENTS

CHAPTER 1

Introduction

■ Topic Summary

1.1   What is Advanced Placement?

The Advanced Placement (AP) Program is a joint educational undertaking of the College Board, secondary schools, and colleges. This program provides a means by which secondary schools and colleges collaborate to develop college-level course descriptions and exams which are accessible to high school students. By participating in an AP course and taking the AP Exam, you have an opportunity to earn college credit, placement in higher-level courses, or both. You will gain confidence and develop skills that will be indispensable in college.

The AP Program currently offers 35 courses.
- *Art History*
- *Biology*
- *Calculus AB* and *Calculus BC*
- *Chemistry*
- *Computer Science A* and *Computer Science AB*

- *Economics: Macro* and *Economics: Micro*
- *English Language & Composition* and *English Literature & Composition*
- *Environmental Science*
- *European History*
- *French Language* and *French Literature*
- *German Language*
- *Government & Politics: Comparative* and *Government & Politics: US*
- *Human Geography*
- *International English Language*
- *Latin Literature* and *Latin Vergil*
- *Music Theory*
- *Physics B, Physics C: Electricity* and *Magnetism,* and *Physics C: Mechanics*
- *Psychology*
- *Spanish Language* and *Spanish Literature*
- *Statistics*
- *Studio Art*: *Drawing, Studio Art*: *2D Design,* and *Studio Art*: *3D Design*
- *US History*
- *World History*

Each offering is the responsibility of a development committee appointed by the College Board. The committee members include both high school AP teachers and college professors from the respective academic discipline. Committee members are appointed to three-year overlapping terms and represent a variety of types of secondary schools and colleges from various areas of the country.

1.1.1 Computer Science as an AP Subject

Although AP Exams were first offered in the early 1950s, the first Advanced Placement Computer Science (AP CS) Exam was not administered until 1984. The early 1980s were a time of significant change in the computer industry, with many companies manufacturing personal computers (PCs). PCs became more accessible and affordable; computer science departments flourished in universities; the number of college students interested in computer science increased rapidly. In response to this, the College Board added computer science to its list of Advanced Placement offerings. In 1984, a total of 4,263 students took the first AP CS Exam. In 2002, the number of AP CS Exams administered was close to 23,500, and in 2004, 20,600 AP CS Exams were taken.

Since 1984, Advanced Placement Computer Science has undergone many changes. These changes parallel the changes that have taken place in the computer science curriculum in colleges and universities. The most recent is the change in the implementation language from C++ to Java. The first AP CS Exam using Java as the delivery language was administered in May 2004.

1.2   Who Takes AP Courses?

In 2001, over 1,400,000 AP Exams were taken by 844,741 students worldwide. In 2003, more than 1,700,000 AP Exams were taken in more than 80 different countries. A variety of initiatives have been undertaken to make the AP Program accessible to all. The federal AP Incentive Program provides monies in the form of grants to encourage low-income students to participate in AP. Some states use their own resources to provide support by encouraging or requiring AP courses in high schools and assisting with students' AP examination fees.

There is no risk in taking an AP Exam and there are numerous benefits. In addition to experiencing the academic demands of a college-level course, students who succeed on multiple AP Exams could earn enough credits to enter college with sophomore standing. Any credits earned can free valuable course time so more electives can be taken or a dual major pursued. It is up to the specific college to grant placement or credit.

1.2.1   *Who Takes AP Computer Science?*

The intent of AP CS is to parallel the goals of the introductory sequence of courses for computer science majors in colleges. It is not expected that all students taking the AP CS Exam will major in computer science. In fact, AP CS can benefit students majoring in just about any area that involves problem solving and analysis.

Although AP CS is intended to be an introductory course, some secondary schools offer pre-AP courses that serve as prerequisites for AP CS. Students enrolling in AP CS should have skills in problem solving, writing, and algebra. The required prerequisite courses are usually designed to sharpen these skills and are taught in a variety of implementation languages.

1.3   What is the Difference Between AP Computer Science A and AB?

Advanced Placement Computer Science is intended to be an introductory course in computer science. The content of AP Computer Science A parallels that of most first-semester college courses. The content of the AB course more closely corresponds to the first two semesters of college computer science. Additional topics covered in AP CS AB include formal analysis of algorithms, advanced data structures and algorithms, and a more detailed design of classes and their relationships and responsibilities.

AP CS A covers less material but should not be considered an easier exam. Offering two separate AP CS Exams allows secondary schools to choose the appropriate course offering based on the school's environment and resources. Many schools do not have the time, resources, and/or enrollment to offer both AP CS A and AP CS AB. Others have an extended computer science curriculum offering multiple computer courses and including both AP CS courses.

1.3.1   *AP CS Course Organization*

There are two essential parts to any computer science course: lecture and lab. In the lecture portion, the course material is presented. In the lab portion of the course, you apply what you have learned to solving problems on the computer. Lab time is handled by different schools in different ways. Time on the computer does not have to be part of class time but is an essential element of successful completion of the course. You should spend as much time as possible working on AP CS lab assignments. The more experience you have, the more knowledge you will absorb.

1.4   Which Elements of Computer Science Are on the AP Exam?

The elements of computer science that will be tested on the AP CS Exams include basic programming concepts (branches and loops, method calls), object-oriented programming (classes, interfaces, inheritance), data structures, and algorithms. The focus of the exams is not the Java programming language. Java is a very large language and cannot be mastered in the AP course. The exams cover the elements of computer science. Object-oriented design is a major focus in the AP CS curriculum.

The tested materials are well defined in College Board documents. These resources are: the AP CS Topic Outline, the AP CS Java Subsets, the Quick References for the Java AP subset of classes, and the current case study documents. Before taking the exam, you should be familiar with the material contained in these documents.

1.4.1 Format of the AP CS Exam

The AP CS Exam is divided into two parts. Part 1 contains 40 multiple-choice questions which must be answered in 1 hour and 15 minutes. Part 2 contains 4 free-response questions with a time limit of 1 hour and 45 minutes. The two parts of the exam are weighted equally when determining the final AP score. The following documents are provided for use during both sections of the exam:

- Quick Reference for A Exam *or* Quick Reference for AB Exam
- Case Study Materials
  - Source code for visible classes
  - Index for the source code of the visible classes
  - Summary of class documentation for black box classes

1.5 Strategies for Taking the AP CS Exam

You first should decide which AP CS Exam you are prepared to take, A or AB. If you are enrolled in an AP CS A course and you are following that curriculum then there really is no decision and you should sign up for the A exam. However, if you are enrolled in AP CS AB, or if you are enrolled in AP CS A and doing additional work on the AB topics, you need to make a decision. The A exam is not necessarily easier then the AB exam but it does cover significantly less material. In order to feel comfortable with the AB exam, you need to be very, very comfortable with designing classes, and understand and be able to apply advanced data structures and algorithms.

You will be given supplemental materials that you may use during both parts of the exam. These materials are available to you throughout the entire year. Do not wait until the exam to become familiar with them. On exam day, briefly scan over these documents so that you are familiar with the official resources that you will be able to reference.

1.5.1 Strategies for Part 1

The first part of the exam contains 40 multiple-choice questions. Usually the questions are in a somewhat increasing order of difficulty but questions that are not difficult for one person may seem difficult to another.

- Read each question carefully. If you do not know the answer, circle the question, skip it for the moment and go on. Come back to that question later if you have time.
- Do not haphazardly guess on the multiple-choice questions. There is a deduction of one-quarter of a point for each wrong answer. Omitted questions do not add or subtract points from the total. If you can eliminate two of the possible choices, then your odds of choosing the correct answer are better.
- Review all possible answers before choosing one.

- If there is code in the question, read the entire question before reading the code.
- There may be several questions dealing with one code segment or problem specification. If you do not know the answer to the first question in a series, do not assume the following questions in the series are more difficult. Read them all.

1.5.2   Strategies for Part 2

The second part of the exam contains four free-response questions. Each of these four questions is weighted equally. Usually the questions are in a somewhat increasing order of difficulty but, as with the multiple-choice questions, what is difficult for one person may not be difficult for another. If the first question seems difficult, go on to another.

- Don't panic if the question seems extremely long. Read the question introduction and the comments in the code. Many times the comments outline an algorithm that solves the problem.
- Read the question carefully before you begin to write your answer. Read the question again after you answer the question to make sure that you satisfied the problem specifications.
- Most of the free-response questions have more than one part. If you do not know how to answer the first part, do not give up on the entire problem. Read all parts of the problem. Sometimes the last part of the problem is the easiest part to answer. In most problems, each part is graded independently from other parts.
- In a multiple-part free-response question, part (b) or part (c) may indicate that you may use a call to a method you wrote in part (a): "Assume that this method works as intended regardless of what you wrote for part (a)." This is usually a hint that the call to the method from part (a) will be useful. You may be able to answer this part of the question even if you skipped the previous parts.
  - Do not write code that you are told exists and works as intended. If your solution reimplements the functionality provided by methods given in the problem definition, or by methods written in previous parts of the problem, you will not receive full credit for your work. Rather than reimplementing these methods, you should appropriatcly invoke them.
- Do not worry about the efficiency of your algorithm unless explicitly told to do so.
- Do not include "extra" code in a solution.
  - Do not add `System.out.println` statements unless required by the problem. This is considered to be a side-effect and will probably be penalized.
  - Do not write code to check preconditions. Assume preconditions are satisfied.
- Though not an absolute rule, stay within the AP Java subsets when writing code.
- If you are told to justify your answer, you need to provide an explanation. The explanation need not be lengthy. Points will be deducted if you do not include a justification.
- Strive for clarity in your code.
  - Indent properly.
  - Use meaningful variables names that are distinguishable from class names by more than case differences. (Do not name a `String` variable `string` or a `Fish` variable `fish`.)
- Don't try to write overly clever code!
- Use braces where needed and for clarity. Comment only when absolutely necessary.
- The first solution on your paper is the solution that will be graded. If you rewrite a solution to a problem, be sure to cross out the unwanted solution. Do not waste time erasing.
- If you are running out of time, write as much code as you have time to write. Do not write comments on how you would solve the problem if you had time. No credit is given for comments!

- The exam answer booklet provides plenty of blank space for all of your answers. You should not run out of room. But, if you do, continue your work on a blank page in the back of the booklet. Clearly label the page with the problem number and indicate in the original space provided where the exam reader can find your answer. If there are no blank pages and you use additional paper, your paper has to be appropriately labeled. Your exam proctor should provide you with information on how to do this. Do not just include an unlabeled piece of paper in your answer booklet.
- Be neat! Real people have to read your answers!

1.5.3 Materials You Should Bring to the Exam
- Several #2 pencils.
- Erasers: Bring erasers that erase! Incorrect multiple choice answers need to be completely erased.
- A watch: If the start time and end time are not clearly stated on the board, take note of these on your exam booklet. Look at your watch frequently.
- Your social security number for identification purposes.
- A photo I.D. if you are taking the exam at a school other than your high school.

1.5.4 Last Minute Reminders
- Get a good night's sleep.
- Eat a good meal before your exam.
- Try to relax!
- Don't rush! If you are prepared, you should have sufficient time to answer all questions.
- Enjoy the exam. You worked very hard all year to prepare for this day!

1.6 How Are the Exams Graded?

The score on the multiple-choice part is equal to the number of questions answered correctly minus one-quarter of the number of incorrect answers. This part of the exam is graded by computer.

The free-response questions are graded by a group of experienced AP computer science teachers and university computer science professors. Each of the four questions is scored on a 9-point scale. A grading rubric is developed at the reading and used to insure that the student solutions are graded in a consistent manner.

The multiple-choice section and the free-response section are weighted equally when determining the composite score. A corresponding AP Grade (1–5) is then assigned.

Meaning of AP Grades

AP Grade	Possible Interpretation
5	Extremely Well Qualified
4	Well Qualified
3	Qualified
2	Possibly Qualified
1	No Recommendation

1.6.1   Special Recognition for Doing Well

The College Board recognizes excellent student performance on AP Exams through the AP Scholar Awards. In 2003, over 145,000 students were designated AP Scholars. This distinction is based on the student's average AP Exam grades (from that year and previous years) and the AP grade requirement for the specific award. There are 10 different AP Scholar distinctions including Scholar, Scholar with Honors, State Scholar, and International Scholar. You may cite the AP Scholar Awards among your achievements on college applications.

The Siemens Foundation recognizes America's most promising science and mathematics students by awarding monetary scholarships to 24 students, two females and two males in each of the six College Board regions. These awards are presented to the students who have earned the highest number of AP scores on the following AP Exams: *Biology, Calculus BC, Chemistry, Computer Science AB, Environmental Science, Physics C (Physics C: Mechanics* and *Physics C: Electricity and Magnetism* each count as half), and *Statistics.*

1.6.2   College Credit or Placement

The College Board AP Program offers high school students the opportunity to take college level courses while still in high school. More than 90% of colleges and universities have an AP policy regarding credit and/or placement for students receiving acceptable scores on AP Examinations. These policies differ among different universities. AP credit and placement policy information for many colleges and universities is provided through the College Board Web site, http://www.collegeboard.com/ap/creditpolicy.

1.7   How Should This Guide Be Used to Prepare for the AP CS Exam?

This study guide is intended to be used in conjunction with *Java Concepts,* 4th ed., or with *Big Java,* 2nd ed. (both written by Cay Horstmann and published by John Wiley & Sons, Inc.). Because these texts are college-level texts, they include material that is not tested on the AP CS Exam.

This study guide will lead you through the chapters of the text, focusing on the topics that will be tested on the AP CS Exams. The elements of each chapter are:
- Topic summary
- Expanded coverage of material that is not found in the text
- Topics that are useful but not tested (if applicable)
- Java 5 issues (where applicable)
- Things to remember when taking the AP Exam (if applicable)
- Key words (with references to the text)
- Connecting the topic outline to the text
- Practice questions

1.8   Where Can I Get More Information?

You can access general information about the Advanced Placement Program at:
http://www.collegeboard.com/ap/students/index.html

Information about the AP Scholar Awards can be found at:
http://www.collegeboard.com/student/testing/ap/scholarawards.html

Siemens Foundation Award information can be found at:
http://www.siemens-foundation.org/apawards/awards.htm

Specific information about AP Computer Science can be found at:
http://www.collegeboard.com/student/testing/ap/subjects.html

Information on university credit and placement policies can be found at:
http://www.collegeboard.com/ap/creditpolicy.

1.8.1   Where Can I Get the Text Ancillaries?
The student companion site for *Java Concepts,* 4th ed. can be found by clicking on the appropriate link at:
http://www.wiley.com/college/horstmann

Cay Horstmann's site for *Java Concepts,* 4th ed. is:
http://www.horstmann.com/javaconcepts.html

1.9   Are There Other Suggestions for Success in AP CS?

- The AP Computer Science Examinations will include questions based on the current AP CS case study. Chapter 19 of this guide describes why and how the case study is used in AP CS courses and on the AP CS Exam. Begin reading the case study documents early in the year so that the materials will be familiar to you *before* the day of the exam.
- Keep good notes of your teacher's lectures.
- Practice *writing* code. Actually writing code on paper is different than typing code into the computer!
- Keep your graded programming assignments and review your teacher's comments on the assignments. Don't just look at the grade on the paper and throw it away!
- Do not be afraid to ask for help on your assignments or to seek alternate solutions to problems.
- Volunteer to help your classmates debug their programs. Looking at someone else's code is not as easy as looking at your own code and may help you when exam time comes around.

CHAPTER 2

(Covers *Java Concepts* Chapter 1)

Introduction to Hardware and Software

■ Topic Summary

For the AP CS Exam, you are expected to have a working knowledge of major hardware components, system software, and responsible uses of computers. This chapter will review some commonly used vocabulary that may be included in multiple-choice questions.

2.1   What Is Programming?

Many people use computers for specific everyday tasks such as sending and receiving e-mail, conducting online banking activities, online shopping, playing games, and many other interesting and not-so-interesting activities. In order to attend to our every need, computers must be programmed. A computer program is a sequence of instructions that tells the computer how to complete a task. To use a program, you do not need to know how to design and develop the program. To develop a computer program, you need to attain a set of skills for which this course will provide a foundation.

2.2   The Anatomy of a Computer

The basic hardware components of a computer include
- the Central Processing Unit (CPU)
- primary memory (or storage)
- secondary memory (or storage)
- peripheral devices

The Central Processing Unit (CPU) is the "brain" of the computer. The CPU processes individual commands or statements of a program. The CPU consists of a chip or a small number of chips. Each chip contains transistors that send and receive electrical signals that control program execution, data transfer, and arithmetic operations. Processors execute machine instructions and processors from different companies (e.g., Intel Pentium, Sun SPARC, Motorola PowerPC G5) have different sets of machine instructions.

Primary, or main, memory stores software and data while it is being used. Primary storage, or Random Access Memory (RAM), loses its data when the power is turned off.

Secondary memory stores data in a permanent way. It is much cheaper and slower than primary memory. Some secondary storage devices popular today are the hard disk, the compact disc (CD), the digital video disc or digital versatile disc (DVD), the floppy disk (diskette), and the USB keychain memory device.

Input/Output (I/O) devices, or peripheral devices, enable us to communicate with the computer. Input devices such as the keyboard or the mouse are used to input data and programs. Monitors and printers are used to display information. Other computer peripherals include speakers, digital cameras, scanners, light pens, and barcode readers.

Many of us own single-user systems. A single-user system is a self-contained unit. Many computer labs are permanently connected to a local network. These computers are connected together so that information can be shared among them. The Internet is a world-wide network.

2.3   Translating Human-Readable Programs to Machine Code

A compiler translates a program written in a high-level language into machine code. An interpreter is similar to a compiler but translates and executes a small segment of code (perhaps one statement) at a time. Usually, a Java program is entered into the computer through an editor. It is then submitted to the compiler. The editor and compiler may be part of an integrated development environment (IDE). The compiler checks the program and reports any syntax or grammar errors such as missing semicolons. If the program is free of compilation errors, the compiler translates the Java program code into Java bytecode. The bytecode is written for the Java Virtual Machine (JVM). A JVM has been written for every major operating system. The JVM is like a simulated CPU that runs inside a particular operating system. The JVM is the reason that the same Java program will run on different operating systems such as Windows XP, UNIX, Linux, or Mac OS X. The JVM reads the bytecode and executes the program.

The operating system manages the computer resources. The operating system is software that automatically starts when the computer is turned on. Typical services provided by an operating system include deciding the priority in which programs are to run, loading the programs into memory, managing files, and printing. It is the operating system that makes the computer user-friendly (easy to use). *Random Fact 11.1* of your text discusses operating system tasks in detail.

2.4   The Java Programming Language

Java was designed so that a developer could create either stand-alone applications or programs that can be executed through the Internet using a browser. The programs that are executed using a browser are called applets. Java has many security features, including some that ensure that running an applet will not harm your computer. Because of Java's portability, the same program will run on various operating systems.

2.5   Compiling a Simple Program

Section 1.6 of your text introduces the traditional "Hello World!" program and explains the basic syntax of a trivial Java program. The program prints a string to the screen using the `System.out.println` method. You should enter and compile this simple program using the guidelines in Sections 1.6 and 1.8 in your text. By doing so, you will become familiar with the environment in which you will be programming. Example 2.1 below illustrates another simple Java program.

Example 2.1

```
public class TrivialProgram
{
   public static void main(String[] args)
   {
      System.out.print("This prints a line.");
      System.out.println(" This stays on the same line.");
      System.out.println("Now we are on the next line.");
   }
}
```

will print

> *This prints a line. This stays on the same line.*
> *Now we are on the next line.*

2.5.1   *Java Comments*

The two types of comments that you may see on the AP CS Exam are the single line comment

```
// This is a comment
```

and the multi-line comment.

```
/*
   This is a comment
   This is another comment
*/
```

These comments are discussed in *Advanced Topic 1.1* of your text.

2.6   Errors

Our first attempt in writing, compiling, and executing a program is not always perfect. Many of our errors can be classified as syntax errors. A *syntax error* is a violation of the rules of the programming language. The compiler will detect syntax errors. Missing semicolons and missing or unmatched braces and parentheses are examples of syntax errors. We may also have an error that causes a result other than the result that we originally intended. This is called a run-time or logic error. A *logic error* causes a program to take an action that the programmer did not intend. The program doesn't do what it is designed to do. The compiler does not detect logic errors. It is up to you, the programmer, to test your programs for logic errors. We will discuss this in detail in Chapter 10.

2.7   The Compilation Process

If you have typed a program into the computer, you may have experienced compile-time errors. After you correct all of your errors, the compiler is able to translate your Java program, your source code, into *bytecode*. The bytecode is stored in a `.class` file. The Java Virtual Machine loads the bytecode of your program and any other necessary library files and starts your program. The Java Virtual Machine is the reason that you can execute a compiled Java program on machines with different operating systems.

■ Expanded Coverage of Material That Is Not Found in the Text

- Included in the AP CS Topic Outline is "Responsible Use of Computer Systems." This topic is one that you deal with every time you access information on your computer.
  - The Association for Computing Machinery (ACM) has a Code of Ethics and Professional Conduct that every member of the ACM is expected to uphold. This Code of Ethics is accessible online at http://www.acm.org/constitution/code.html and best summarizes the issues related to this topic in the AP CS curriculum. Also included in this online document are Professional Imperatives and Leadership Imperatives. The General Moral Imperatives expected to be upheld include:
    - Contribute to society and human well-being.
    - Avoid harm to others.
    - Be honest and trustworthy.
    - Be fair and take action not to discriminate.
    - Honor property rights including copyrights and patents.
    - Give proper credit for intellectual property.
    - Respect the privacy of others.
    - Honor confidentiality.
  - The Computer Ethics Institute has written "The Ten Commandments of Computer Ethics" which can be accessed at http://www.brookings.edu/dybdocroot/its/cei/overview/Ten_Commandments_of_Computer_Ethics.htm.
  - The Computer Professionals for Social Responsibility is a public-interest group of computer scientists and others concerned about the impact of technology on society. General information about papers and projects can be accessed at http://www.cpsr.org/cpsr/about-cpsr.html.
- Documents and materials addressing privacy issues, legal issues, and intellectual property include:
  - The Fourth Amendment of the U.S. Constitution: The right of the people to be secure in their persons, houses, papers, and effects, against unreasonable searches and seizures, shall not be violated, and no Warrants shall issue, but upon probable cause, supported by

Oath or affirmation, and particularly describing the place to be searched, and the persons or things to be seized.

- The Privacy Act of 1974 is designed to be a "code of fair information practices" that attempts to regulate the collection, maintenance, use, and sharing of personal information by the federal government. More information is available at http://www.usdoj.gov/04foia04_7_1.html.
  The Computer Matching and Privacy Protection Act of 1988 amended the Privacy Act to include requirements for government agencies to follow when conducting computer-matching activities. More information is available at http://www.usdoj.gov/04foia/1974compmatch.htm.
- Copyright Law of the United States: The Congress shall have Power to promote the progress of science and useful arts, by securing for limited times to authors and inventors the exclusive right to their respective writings and discoveries. More information can be found at http://www.copyright.gov/title17/. Information about United States Copyright Law Limitations on exclusive rights regarding computer programs can be found at http://www.copyright.gov/title17/92chap1.html#117.

■ Topics That Are Useful But Not Tested

- Becoming familiar with your computer system and the Java compiler is the first important step toward a successful programming experience. Sections 1.5, 1.6, and 1.8 of your text guide you through writing, compiling, and executing your first Java program.
- *Productivity Hint 1.2* discusses how to develop a strategy for keeping backup copies of your work before disaster strikes. (The key word is *before*.)

■ Things to Remember When Taking the AP Exam

- Although points are not deducted for missing semicolons on the free-response part of the AP CS Exam, try to remember to write clear, correct code in answering all questions.
- Time is limited during the AP CS Exam. Do not spend time writing comments in your free-response answers unless your solution needs to be explained or you are specifically instructed to include comments.

■ Key Words

You should understand the terms below. The AP CS Exam questions may include references to these terms. The citation in parentheses next to each term identifies the page number where it is defined and/or discussed in *Java Concepts*, 4th ed., and *Big Java*, 2nd ed.

backup (15)

case sensitivity (17)

chip (4)

class (18)

comments (20)

compiler (9)

computer program (3)

Central Processing Unit
   (CPU) (4)

editor (25)

file (14)

integrated circuit (4)

Integrated Development
   Environment (IDE) (13)

Input/Output (I/O)
   devices (4)

Java Virtual Machine
   (JVM) (8)

library packages (12)

logic error (23)

main (19)

method (19)

network (4)

peripheral (6)

primary storage (4)

Random Access Memory
   (RAM) (4)

removable storage device (5)

run-time error (23)

secondary storage (4)

statement (9)

string (21)

syntax error (23)

transistors (4)

variable (9)

■ Connecting the Detailed Topic Outline to the Text

The citations in parentheses identify the pages where information in the outline can be located in *Java Concepts*, 4th ed., and *Big Java*, 2nd ed.

- What Is Programming? (2–3)
- The Anatomy of a Computer (3–8)
- Translating Human-Readable Programs to Machine Code (8–10, 433–434)
- The Java Programming Language (10–12)
- Compiling a Simple Program (17–22)
  - ■ Java Comments (20, 22–23)
- Errors (23–24)
- The Compilation Process (25–27)

■ Practice Questions

Multiple Choice

1. Every Java application contains a class with

   a. a `main` method
   b. a `System.out.println` statement
   c. a compiler
   d. a string
   e. comments

2. A syntax error is a violation of programming language rules. Syntax errors are detected by

   a. the operating system
   b. the compiler
   c. the Java Virtual Machine
   d. antivirus software
   e. the CPU

3. Which of the following is **not** a fundamental task carried out by the Central Processing Unit (CPU)?

   a. locating and executing the program instructions
   b. carrying out arithmetic operations such as addition, subtraction, multiplication, and division
   c. fetching data from storage and input/output devices
   d. sending data back to storage and input/output devices
   e. translating high-level programs to machine code

4. All of the following are examples of peripherals except

   a. mouse
   b. microprocessor
   c. keyboard
   d. printer
   e. monitor

5. A _____ translates programs written in a high-level language to machine code.

   a. CPU
   b. microprocessor
   c. compiler
   d. Java Virtual Machine
   e. storage device

6. What is printed as a result of executing the following Java program?

   ```
   public class Tester
   {
      public static void main(String[] args)
      {
        /*
           System.out.println("This is a test.");
           This is another test;
        */
      }
   }
   ```

   a. *This is a test.*
   b. *This is a test.*
      This is another test.
   c. *This is another test.*
   d. Nothing is printed. The compiler reports an error.
   e. There is no error reported but nothing is printed.

7. The hardware of a computer consists of all of the following except

    a. processor
    b. memory
    c. input and output devices
    d. storage
    e. operating system

8. Intellectual property rights refers to rights relating to which of the following:

    I.   literary, artistic, and scientific works
    II. scientific discoveries
    III. computer software

    a. I only
    b. II only
    c. III only
    d. I and II only
    e. I, II, and III

9. Refer to the Java statement:

    ```
    System.out.println("Hello");
    ```

    Which of the following statements is **not** true about the code printed above?

    a. `System` is the Java class that contains the `out` object.
    b. `out` is an object that represents the console window.
    c. `"Hello"` is a parameter to the `println` method.
    d. `System` is a string object.
    e. `println` is a method applied to the `System.out` object.

10. Which is the U.S. Government directive that requires government agencies to comply with legal norms for the collection, maintenance, and distribution of information in databases?

    a. The First Amendment
    b. The Fourth Amendment
    c. Copyright Law of the United States
    d. The Privacy Act of 1974
    e. Computer Matching and Privacy Protection Act of 1988

    (Note: It is not likely that the AP CS Exam will include questions referring to content of specific legal documents.)

CHAPTER 3

(Covers *Java Concepts* Chapter 2)

Using Objects

■ Topic Summary

3.1   Types and Variables

In the last chapter we introduced a simple Java program whose task was to print a string to the console window. Consider the Java statement below.

```
System.out.println("Hello");
```

`"Hello"` has the type `String` and `System.out` has the type `PrintStream`.

A variable is a storage location that has a type, a name, and contents.

```
String myFishy = "Nemo";
int testGrade = 92;
double hourlyPay = 15.25;
```

`myFishy` is the name of a variable of type `String` that refers to the string "Nemo". `testGrade` is a variable that holds the integer value 92 and `hourlyPay` is a variable that holds the floating-point number 15.25. Each of these three statements declares a variable and assigns a value to the variable when it is declared. After these declarations are made, the variables can be used anywhere in the program to refer to the assigned values. A variable can also be declared without explicitly giving it a value.

```
int quizGrade;
```

Before using the variable `quizGrade`, a value must be assigned to it. The combination of the above statement and the statement

```
quizGrade = 92;
```

would declare and initialize `quizGrade` for use in the program.

The compiler checks type mismatches and will report an error for the declaration

```
int number = "one";
```

You can not assign a `String` value to the `int` variable `number`.

There are rules and conventions used in naming variables. These rules and conventions are described in Section 2.1 of your text.

3.2 The Assignment Operator

Values of existing variables can be modified by using the assignment operator.

```
int testGrade = 92;    // testGrade has the value 92
testGrade = 94;    // testGrade now has the value 94
```

The compiler checks type mismatches and will report an error for the assignment

```
testGrade = "one";
```

3.3 Objects, Classes, and Methods

Object-orientation is an important approach in software development and design that supports the development of programs that are easy to understand, can be adapted to different situations, and can be reused in multiple contexts. *Objects* and *classes* are the central concepts of object-oriented programming and are a primary focus of the AP Computer Science courses.

You can think of a *class* as a factory for objects or a blueprint from which an object is created. Many objects can be created using the same blueprint. An *object* is an instance of a class that you can manipulate in your program. Each object has *behavior* and *state*. In Java, every object belongs to a class. The class defines the behavior and state of objects of that class. You access the behavior of an object by calling methods. Some methods may result in changes to the object's state. The statement

```
System.out.print("This prints a line.");
```

in Example 2.1 of this guide illustrates the `System.out` object being manipulated by its `println` method.

3.4 Method Parameters and Return Values

`String` objects can also be manipulated by methods.

Example 3.1

```
1     int numCharacters;
2     String myFishy = "Nemo";
3     System.out.println(myFishy);
4     numCharacters = myFishy.length():
5     System.out.println(numCharacters);
```

Line 1 declares the variable numCharacters that can hold an integer value.

Line 2 declares and initializes a String variable named myFishy whose value is the String "Nemo".

Line 3 invokes the println method on the System.out object. The object System.out has the type PrintStream. The println method has one explicit parameter, myFishy, which is of type String. The implicit parameter of the method call is System.out.

Line 4 calls (or invokes) the length method defined in the String class on the String object myFishy. The length method returns an integer value that represents the number of characters in this String object. Since "Nemo" has 4 characters, the integer *4* is the return value of this method call. This integer value is assigned to the int variable numCharacters. The length method has no explicit parameters. The implicit parameter of the method call is myFishy.

Line 5 invokes the println method on the System.out object. The println method has one explicit parameter, numCharacters. The println method does not return a value. Line 5 results in the number *4* being printed to the console window.

In the example above, the println method is called twice, once with a String parameter and once with an int parameter. When a class defines two methods with the same name and different explicit parameter types, we say the method is *overloaded*.

Lines 4 and 5 in Example 3.1 could be simplified to

```
String myFishy = "Nemo";
System.out.println(myFishy.length());   // 4 is printed
```

Some methods, such as the length method for a String object, *return* values. myFishy.length() returns the value *4* because the string "Nemo" has length 4. A method does not always return a value. The println method does not return a value. We will see later that a method that does not return a value has the return type declared with the reserved word void.

3.5   Number Types

Most Java programs require us to work with expressions and to define variables. Each expression and each variable has a type. These types can be primitive data types or class types. The primitive number data types that you are responsible for are int and double. Primitive types are not classes. Numbers are not objects. Numbers have no methods.

The objects that are tested on the AP CS Exam are strings, arrays (which we will cover in Chapter 8) and objects instantiated from existing classes (which are introduced in Chapter 3 of your text and Chapter 4 of this guide).

3.6   Constructing Objects

Up to now, we have only used the `System.out` object (of the `PrintStream` class) and the `String` class in our programs. Your text introduces the `Rectangle` class from the Java class library. Although the AP Exam will not ask you questions about this particular class, we will use it to discuss a few general ideas about objects and classes.

An object of type `Rectangle` describes a rectangular shape. The `Rectangle` object is not the rectangle itself. The state of the `Rectangle` object is defined by its width, its height, and the *x*- and *y*- coordinates of its top-left corner.

In order to manipulate an object, the object needs to be created by using the `new` operator. A *constructor* is called to create, or construct, a new `Rectangle` object.

```
new Rectangle(5, 10, 20, 30);
```

The top-left corner has coordinates 5 and 10; the width of the rectangle is 20 and the height is 30. Remember, these values are stored, not the rectangular shape itself. The four values (5, 10, 20, 30) are called *construction parameters*. The call

```
new Rectangle();
```

also constructs a `Rectangle` object. This constructor creates a new `Rectangle` object whose top-left corner has coordinates (0, 0), width 0, and height 0.

Because the `new` expression is not a complete statement, we usually construct an object and assign its value to a variable.

```
Rectangle box = new Rectangle(5, 10, 20, 30);
Rectangle anotherBox = new Rectangle();
```

Because we can construct a `Rectangle` object in different ways, we say the `Rectangle` constructor is *overloaded*.

3.7   Accessor and Mutator Methods

A class defines the behavior of its objects by supplying methods. A method either changes the state of the object or it does not. Methods that change the state of an object are called *mutator methods* or modifiers and usually have a `void` return type. An example of a modifier is the `Rectangle` method `translate`.

```
box.translate(15, 25);
```

The `translate` method moves the `Rectangle` object `box` a distance of 15 in the *x*-direction and a distance of 25 in the *y*-direction. This will result in changing the coordinates of the top-left corner.

The method `getWidth` returns the width of a `Rectangle` object without changing the state of the object.

```
box.getwidth();
```

returns the value 20. A method that accesses an object and returns some information about the object but does not change the state of the object is called an *accessor method*.

3.8   Implementing a Test Program

In order to test the behavior of an object, you can use an interactive development environment such as BlueJ or you can write a simple test program. Testing some objects requires us to import Java classes from packages. A package is a group of Java classes that are usually related in some way. The `Rectangle` class is contained in the `java.awt` package. In order to include a `Rectangle` object in our program, we need to import the `java.awt.Rectangle` class.

```
import java.awt.Rectangle;
```

This tells the Java compiler that the `Rectangle` class belongs to the `java.awt` package in the Java library. Without the `import`, we would have to use the fully qualified name for `Rectangle` by specifying the Java library package `java.awt` each and every time we refer to the `Rectangle` class.

```
java.awt.Rectangle box = new java.awt.Rectangle();
```

The steps you follow to write your test program, and the procedure used to import packages, are explained in Section 2.8 of your text.

3.9   Object References

In order to do anything with the object that we created, we must store a reference to the object in an object variable.

```
        Rectangle box = new Rectangle(5, 10, 20, 30);
or

        Rectangle anotherBox = new Rectangle();
```

The object variables `box` and `anotherBox` store references to `Rectangle` objects. There can be many instances of a class. Each object (or instance) has its own memory that contains specific information about it. An object variable stores the object's location. Every variable has a type that identifies the kind of information it can contain. `box` contains a reference to a `Rectangle` object; once declared as a reference to a `Rectangle` object, it cannot reference a `double`, a `String` object, or any other type of object.

```
        String student = "Anne";                   // This is OK
        Rectangle cerealBox = new Rectangle();      // This is OK

        Rectangle crate = "Davis";                  // WRONG!
        String csStudent = 4.35;                    // WRONG!
        double num = new Rectangle();               // WRONG!
```

You can choose any appropriate variable names for object variables. Rules for naming variables are discussed in Section 2.1 of your text. Object variables must be initialized before you access them. In the declaration,

```
        Rectangle box;
```

`box` is not initialized. The `new` operator creates a new object and returns its location.

```
        Rectangle box;
        box = new Rectangle(5, 10, 20, 30);   // Now initialized
```

You can have multiple references to the same object.

```
Rectangle anotherBox = box;
```

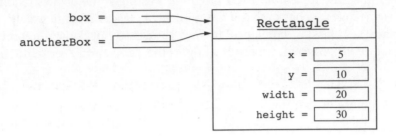

Because `box` and `anotherBox` reference the same `Rectangle` object, after the statement

```
box.translate(15, 25);
```

is executed, both variables, `box` and `anotherBox`, refer to the same object that has been moved.

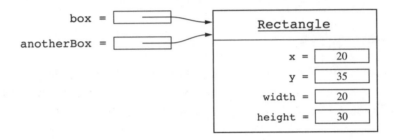

A variable with a number type stores a number, not a reference. This is illustrated in Section 2.10 of your text. You should understand that numbers are different from objects. Number variables are *not* created with new.

■ Topics That Are Useful But Not Tested

- The `String` methods `toUpperCase` and `replace` may be useful if your program deals with `String` objects. These methods are explained in Sections 2.3 and 2.4 of your text.
- The classes and methods of the Java library are listed in the API documentation. Although you are not explicitly tested on the Java API, you should be familiar with it. Navigating through the API documentation is explained in Section 2.9 of your text.

■ Things to Remember When Taking the AP Exam

- Initialize all objects and variables before you access them.
- When deciding on a variable name, choose a name that describes the purpose of the variable.
- Do not name the variable with the same word as the class name.

```
Rectangle rectangle = new Rectangle(5, 10, 20, 30);   // BAD
```

Although this would compile, it is very confusing to those grading your exam!

- Follow the Java conventions when naming variables, classes, and methods.
- Do not try to reset an object by calling a constructor. You cannot invoke a constructor on an existing object.

```
Rectangle box = new Rectangle(5, 10, 20, 30);
box(10, 5, 30, 20);   // WRONG
box = new Rectangle(10, 5, 30, 20);    // OK
```

This is explained in *Common Error 2.1* of your text.

- When calling methods from a test class (client program), include the implicit parameter in the call.

```
box.getWidth();   // This is OK
getWidth();   // WRONG! You need to supply an object reference
```

- Do not use a class name when an object name should be used.

```
Rectangle box = new Rectangle(5, 10, 20, 30);
System.out.println(Rectangle.getWidth());   // WRONG
System.out.println(box.getWidth());   // This is OK
```

■ Key Words

You should understand the terms below. The AP CS Exam questions may include references to these terms. The citation in parentheses next to each term identifies the page number where it is defined and/or discussed in *Java Concepts*, 4th ed., and *Big Java*, 2nd ed.

accessor (42)	import (47)	package (47)
assignment operator (36)	integer (43)	parameter (40)
class (38)	method (37)	primitive type (43)
constructor (46)	mutator (46)	private implementation (39)
double (43)	new (45)	public interface (39)
explicit parameter (40)	object (37)	return value (40)
floating-point number (43)	object reference (52)	type (34)
identifier (35)	overloading (53)	variable (34)
implicit parameter (40)		

■ Connecting the Detailed Topic Outline to the Text

The citations in parentheses identify where information in the outline can be located in *Java Concepts*, 4th ed., and *Big Java*, 2nd ed.

- Types and Variables (34–36)
- The Assignment Operator (36–37)
- Objects, Classes, and Methods (42–44)
- Method Parameters and Return Values (40–43)
- Number Types (43–44)
- Constructing Objects (44–46)
- Accessor and Mutator Methods (46–47)
- Implementing a Test Program (47–49)
- Object References (52–54)

■ Practice Questions

Multiple Choice

1. Which of the following statements about *classes* is true?

    a. Classes are examples of objects.
    b. Classes are factories or blueprints for objects.
    c. Every class belongs to an object.
    d. The public interface of a class is hidden from the user.
    e. The `new` operator is used to construct a new class.

2. Constructors are always invoked using

    a. a `println` statement
    b. a `return` statement
    c. the `new` operator
    d. an `=` sign
    e. overloading

3. An object location is stored in

    a. an object variable
    b. a class
    c. a parameter
    d. a `String`
    e. another object

4. If two methods have the same name and different explicit parameters, the method name is

    a. overloaded
    b. encapsulated
    c. implemented
    d. an implicit reference
    e. illegal

5. Which of the following statements about objects and classes is **not** true?

    a. Object locations are stored in object variables.
    b. All object variables must be initialized before you use them.
    c. An object reference describes the location of an object.
    d. Multiple object variables can contain references to the same object.
    e. Every class has a particular type that identifies what kind of information it can hold.

6. The implicit parameter to a method call is

    a. the object on which the method is invoked.
    b. the object returned as the result of the method being executed.
    c. the public interface of the method.
    d. the class in which the method is defined.
    e. the constructor of the method.

7. The PrintStream class defines the println method as

   ```
   public void println(String output)
   ```

   Which of the following statements about this definition is **true**?

   a. The return type of the println method is String.
   b. The implicit parameter of the println method is void.
   c. There is no value returned by the println method.
   d. output is the name of the object on which the println method is invoked.
   e. The return value of the println method is of type String.

8. Which of the following results in the integer variable n having the value 54?

   I. n = new int(54);

   II. int n;
       n = 54;

   III. int n = 54;

   a. I only
   b. II only
   c. III only
   d. II and III only
   e. I, II, and III

9. Consider the following methods of the Rectangle class.

   I. public void translate(int x, int y)
      // Translates this Rectangle the indicated distance, to the right
      // along the x-coordinate axis, and downward along the y-
      // coordinate axis.

   II. public void setRect(double x, double y, double width,
            double height)
      // Sets the bounds of this Rectangle to the specified x, y, width,
      // and height.

   III. public void grow(int h, int v)
      // Resizes the Rectangle so that it is h units larger on both the
      // left and right sides, and v units larger at both the top and
      // bottom.

   Which of these methods are modifiers (mutators)?

   a. I only
   b. II only
   c. III only
   d. I and III only
   e. I, II, and III

10. Consider the following methods of the `Rectangle` class.

    I. ```
        public void setSize(int width, int height)
        // Sets the size of this Rectangle to the specified width and
        // height.
        ```

    II. ```
        public double getY()
        // Returns the y-coordinate of the bounding Rectangle.
        ```

    III. ```
         public double getHeight()
         // Returns the height of the bounding Rectangle as a double.
         ```

    Which of these methods are accessors?

    a.  I only
    b.  II only
    c.  III only
    d.  II and III only
    e.  I, II, and III
         ```

CHAPTER 4

(Covers *Java Concepts* Chapter 3)

An Introduction to Objects and Classes

■ Topic Summary

4.1   Black Boxes

Section 3.1 of your text describes the difference between *using* a device and actually building (or fixing) the internal workings of that device. The term *black box* refers to inner workings. The black box hides these internal workings from those using the device. The process of hiding the implementation details is called *encapsulation*. Encapsulation is very important to us in real life situations. We do not have to know how to build or fix internal circuitry in order to use an electronic device such as a radio. In fact, many electronic devices warn against opening the box that contains this circuitry with a statement such as "This device should be serviced only by a certified professional. If you open this panel, you will void your warranty." A radio is designed in a way that it is easy for you to use. Someone, other than yourself, came up with the right black box so that your radio is easy to use. You see the radio controls. You do not see the inner workings. The *right concept* for a device is discovered through abstraction. Abstraction is taking away inessential features, until only the essence of the concept remains. For example, "radio" is an abstraction. "Car" is an abstraction. We are not looking at or thinking about the details of this device. Abstraction permits us to focus on the essential functionality of a class without being distracted by complex implementation details.

The focus of the AP CS curriculum is an object-oriented approach to programming. In Chapter 2 of your text and Chapter 3 of this guide, you learned to use objects such as `String` objects and the object `System.out`. Although we will continue to *use* objects, we will also design and implement our own classes to allow our objects to carry out behaviors we define. Think of your design process as creating a black box where the operations are visible (the radio controls) and the data and implementation are hidden (the inner circuitry).

4.2   Designing the Public Interface of a Class

Section 3.2 of your text describes the design of a `BankAccount` class. The three behaviors defined for a `BankAccount` object allow users to deposit money, withdraw money, and get the current balance of the account. Behaviors defined for a bank account define the methods for the `BankAccount` class. A `BankAccount` object has a state (a current balance). The state of a `BankAccount` object can be changed by a deposit or a withdrawal. Therefore, the methods `deposit` and `withdraw` are mutator methods or modifiers. These methods do not return a value and so they have a `void` return type. The `getBalance` method does not change the state of our `BankAccount` object and is therefore an accessor method. The method `getBalance` will return the current balance of the `BankAccount` object so it will have a `double` return type (because we usually use floating-point numbers to represent money). The `return` statement is a special statement that instructs the method to terminate and return a value to the statement that called the method. Example 4.1 below is an overview of the `BankAccount` class.

Example 4.1
_____

```
// Class definition
public class BankAccount
{
    // Constructor
    public BankAccount()
    {
        // Code here
    }

    // Constructor
    public BankAccount(double initialBalance)
    {
        // Code here
    }

    // Accessor
    public double getBalance()
    {
        // Code here
    }

    // Modifier
    public void deposit(double amount)
    {
        // Code here
    }
```

```
// Modifier
public void withdraw(double amount)
{
    // Code here
}

// Private instance fields here
}
```

The `BankAccount` class definition above has the following format.

```
accessSpecifier class ClassName
{
        Constructors: There are two constructors in our BankAccount class
        Methods: There are three methods in our BankAccount class
        Instance fields: The private data (instance) fields will be discussed later
}
```

The public constructors and methods of a class form the *public interface* of the class. The access specifier `public` indicates that the users of our `BankAccount` class can create and manipulate `BankAccount` objects through the public constructors and the public `deposit`, `withdraw`, and `getBalance` methods. Example 4.2 below demonstrates this manipulation.

Example 4.2

```
BankAccount momsChecking = new BankAccount(10);
momsChecking.deposit(510);
System.out.println(momsChecking.getBalance());
momsChecking.withdraw(100);
System.out.println(momsChecking.getBalance());
```

A `BankAccount` object is created with an initial balance of $10. A deposit of $510 is made. The current balance (520) is printed. $100.00 is withdrawn and the new balance (420) is printed.

4.3   Commenting the Public Interface

When you define classes, you should include documentation of your methods and constructors. Section 3.3 and Productivity Hint 3.1 of your text explain how to use the `javadoc` utility and implement `javadoc` comments. In the examples presented in this guide, we use `javadoc` comments. Because `javadoc` comments are not part of the AP CS subset, however, the practice questions will not use `javadoc` comments. The AP CS Java subset uses `/* */`, and `//` comments.

4.4   Instance Fields

An object of a class has its own set of instance fields (instance variables or attributes) that define its state (data). These instance fields are usually hidden from the programmer who uses the class (the client program). As mentioned in Section 3.1 on your text, the process of hiding details (the private information or data) and providing ways to access the information (public methods) is called *encapsulation*. We will be designing a black box where the operations are visible and the data and implementation are hidden. *Information hiding* refers to the idea that the client, or user, of a class does not need to know about the inner workings of the class in order to use it. To remain true to the meaning of object-oriented programming, our data (or instance fields) should be declared `private`. Access to this data should be allowed only through the methods defined in the class. Declaring instance fields as `private` does not permit access from methods outside the class. In the AP Java subset, all instance fields are declared as `private`. Example 4.2 accesses the balance of the `BankAccount` object `momsChecking` through the public method `getBalance`.

```
System.out.println(momsChecking.getBalance());
```

The implicit parameter in the call to `getBalance` in the above statement is the `BankAccount` object `momsChecking`. The private instance field is defined in the `BankAccount` class and each object of a class has its own set of instance fields. An object stores its data in these instance fields. A field refers to a storage location inside a block of memory. An instance of a class is an object of the class. There may be many instances of a class (e.g., many `BankAccount` objects). Thus, an instance field is a storage location that is present in each object of the class. Figure 5 in Chapter 3 of your text shows two `BankAccount` objects, each with its own instance field, `balance`.

Example 4.3 below shows an incomplete definition of a `Student` class. The attributes (data) are declared as `private`. The `public` method `getId` returns the value of the private instance variable `id`.

Example 4.3

```
public class Student
{
    // More code here

    public String getId()
    {
        return id;
    }

    // More code here

    private String firstName;
    private String lastName;
    private String id;
    // More code here
}
```

A client program (or test class) containing the statements

```
Student artStudent = new Student("John", "Smith", "111111");
Student mathStudent = new Student("Ann", "Dunn", "222222");
```

creates (or constructs) the two student objects below.

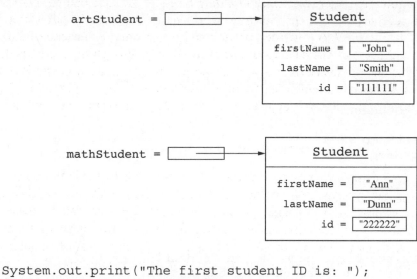

```
System.out.print("The first student ID is: ");
System.out.println(artStudent.getId());
System.out.print("The next student ID is: ");
System.out.println(mathStudent.getId());
```

would print

The first student ID is: 111111.
The next student ID is: 222222.

The expression artStudent.getId() calls the getId method of the artStudent object. The id of artStudent is returned to the client program or calling method. The expression mathStudent.getId() calls the getId method of the mathStudent object. The id of mathStudent is returned to the calling method.

4.5   Implementing Constructors and Methods

Example 4.4 contains the complete implementation of our Student class.

Example 4.4
_____

```
/**
    A Student has a first name, a last name, and an ID number.
    When a student grade is entered, it is added to sumOfGrades and
    the numberOfGrades is incremented by 1.
*/
public class Student
{
    /**
        Constructs a Student with the given information.
        @param first the student's first name
        @param last the student's last name
        @param idNumber the student's identification number
    */
    public Student(String first, String last, String idNumber)
    {
        firstName = first;
        lastName = last;
        id = idNumber;
```

```java
        sumOfGrades = 0.0;
        numberOfGrades = 0;
    }

    /**
        Constructs a Student with default values.
    */
    public Student()
    {
        firstName = "";
        lastName = "";
        id = "";
        sumOfGrades = 0.0;
        numberOfGrades = 0;
    }

    /**
        Gets the first name of the Student.
        @return the first name of the Student
    */
    public String getFirstName()
    {
        return firstName;
    }

    /**
        Gets the last name of the Student.
        @return the last name of the Student
    */
    public String getLastName()
    {
        return lastName;
    }

    /**
        Gets the ID number of the Student.
        @return the id of the Student
    */
    public String getId()
    {
        return id;
    }

    /**
        Modifies sumOfGrades and numberOfGrades to include new
        grade.
        @param grade new grade to add to student record
    */
    public void addGrade(double grade)
    {
        sumOfGrades = sumOfGrades + grade;
        numberOfGrades = numberOfGrades + 1;
    }
```

```
/**
    Gets the GPA of the Student.
    Assumes that the number of grades is greater than 0.
    @return the grade point average of the Student
*/
public double getGpa()
{
    return sumOfGrades / numberOfGrades;
}

private String firstName;
private String lastName;
private String id;
private double sumOfGrades;
private int numberOfGrades;
}
```

The Student class in Example 4.4 contains five private instance variables. When implementing the Student class, we need to think about what attributes a student has. To begin, a student has a first and last name, and an ID number. We include methods that will retrieve this information for the client program (test class). The methods that return the first name, last name, and ID number have String return types because these instance variables are of type String. The student also accumulates test grades throughout the term. We include a method addGrade that allows the user to add a grade for a student. This method increments numberOfGrades and adds the grade to the sumOfGrades. The method addGrade has a void return type because no value will be returned. We then have a method getGpa that returns the average of the student grades (an easy calculation—if we assume that each grade has equal weight!).

4.5.1   Implementing Constructors

We include two constructors in the Student class. Constructors contain instructions to initialize the instance fields of objects. Our Student object has five private instance fields that will be assigned values in the Student constructor. A constructor has the same name as the class and does not have a return type. The syntax for a constructor is:

accessSpecifier ClassName (parameterType parameterName, ...)
{
    constructor implementation
}

The *accessSpecifier* of the constructor is public. In Example 4.4, the first Student constructor has three String parameters. The values of these parameters are used to initialize the appropriate private instance fields firstName, lastName, and id. The instance fields sumOfGrades and numberOfGrades will change in the lifetime of the object and are not part of the information passed to the constructor. We initialize them to 0. We will see how these values change a little later.

The second constructor has no parameters. A constructor with no parameters is called a default constructor.

```
emptyStudent = new Student();
```

This type of constructor initializes the private instance fields with default values where " " denotes an empty string, as shown below.

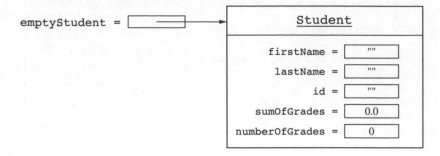

When the same name is used for more than one method or constructor, we say the name is *overloaded*. Constructors are commonly overloaded. Methods can also be overloaded provided that their signatures are different. The signature of a method is determined from the number, types, and order of its parameters. The return type of the method does not matter and is not included when referring to the method signature.

4.5.2 Implementing Methods

The methods `getFirstName`, `getLastName`, and `getId` are accessor methods. They require no parameters to do their tasks. Each of these accessor methods has a `String` return type because the information returned to the calling method is a `String`. The `getGpa` method has a `double` return type. `getGpa` calculates and returns the average of the student's grades. The `addGrade` method changes the value of the private instance fields, `sumOfGrades` and `numberOfGrades`, of a `Student` object. This method is a modifier (or mutator).

```
public void addGrade(double grade)
{
    sumOfGrades = sumOfGrades + grade;    // Adds grade to
                                          // sumOfGrades
    numberOfGrades = numberOfGrades + 1;    // Increments
                                            // numberOfGrades by 1
}
```

Consider the following sequence of statements and resulting student diagrams.

Example 4.3

```
Student goodStudent = new Student("Jamie", "Brown", "222333");
```

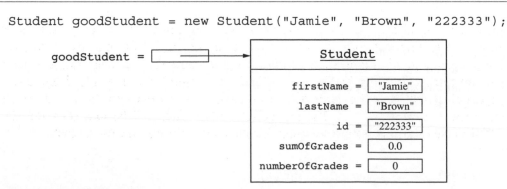

The constructor initializes the private instance fields.

```
goodStudent.addGrade(100);
```

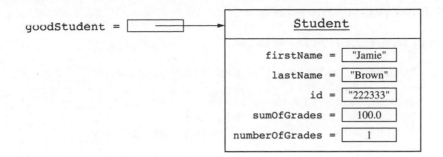

A grade of 100 is added to `sumOfGrades`. `numberOfGrades` is incremented from 0 to 1.

```
goodStudent.addGrade(96);
```

A grade of 96 is added to `sumOfGrades`. `numberOfGrades` is incremented from 1 to 2.

```
System.out.println(goodStudent.getGpa());
```

The method `getGpa` returns 98.0 (196.0 / 2) to the `println` method of the `System.out` object. *98* is printed to the screen.

4.6   Testing a Class

In order to test your class, you can use an interactive development environment such as BlueJ or you can write a simple test class. This is discussed in Section 3.6 of your text. If you choose to write a test class, a good organizational technique is to name the test class with the name of the class you are testing followed by the word "Test" or "Tester". For example, a test class for the `Rectangle` class will have the name `RectangleTest`. A test class for the `Student` class will have the name `StudentTester`. The `StudentTester` class will be in a separate file named `StudentTester.java`. Example 4.5 might be a test class for our `Student` class.

Example 4.5

```
public class StudentTester
{
    public static void main(String[] args)
    {
        Student goodStudent = new Student("Jamie", "Brown",
            "222333");
        goodStudent.addGrade(100);
        goodStudent.addGrade(96);
        System.out.println(goodStudent.getGpa());
    }
}
```

4.6.1 Designing and Implementing a Class

Designing and Implementing a Class is highlighted in *How To 3.1* in your text. You should read this section carefully. The AP CS A and AB Exams may ask you to design and implement a class given a certain problem description. You should follow the steps below.

- Decide what you are asked to do with an object of that class.
- Write the public interface for the class.
  - Decide on methods, return types, and parameters.
  - Decide on what information you need to construct an object and if it is appropriate to have more than one constructor.
- Document the public interface.
- Decide on the private instance fields.
- Implement the constructors and methods.
- Test your class.

Due to the time restriction, the AP Exam usually will not require that you document your classes. However, you should always document your classes when not in an exam situation.

4.7 Categories of Variables

The Student class demonstrates the use of two types of variables: instance fields (firstName, lastName, id, sumOfGrades, numberOfGrades) and parameter variables (grade). The implementation of the BankAccount class in Section 3.5 of your text is another example of a simple class. The BankAccount class demonstrates the use of three types of variables: instance fields (balance), local variables (newBalance), and parameter variables (initialBalance and amount). Instance fields and parameter and local variables have two major differences:

- Life span: Instance fields belong to an object and live as long as some client method refers to the object. Parameter variables and local variables belong to a method. They die (go out of scope) when the method is over.
- Initialization: You must initialize all local variables. If you do not initialize local variables, the compiler complains. Parameter variables are initialized with the values that are supplied in the method call. All instance fields should be initialized but if they are not, those instance fields that are numbers are initialized to 0 and those instance fields that are object references are initialized to a special null value. The AP subsets do not include the rules for the default initialization of numbers to 0, references to null, and boolean variables to false. We will discuss boolean variables in Chapter 6 of this guide.

4.8   Implicit and Explicit Method Parameters

In Example 4.4, the `addGrade` method changes the value of the private instance fields, `sumOfGrades` and `numberOfGrades`, of a `Student` object. Each `Student` object has its own instance fields. Calls to `addGrade` could be

```
artStudent.addGrade(90);
artStudent.addGrade(96);
```

or

```
csStudent.addGrade(85.5);
```

The object whose `sumOfGrades` and `numberOfGrades` will be set is determined by the method call. The statement

```
sumOfGrades = sumOfGrades + grade;
```

will add `grade` to the current object's `sumOfGrades`. The *implicit parameter* of a method is the object on which the method is invoked. The `this` reference denotes this implicit parameter.

```
sumOfGrades = sumOfGrades + grade;
```

is equivalent to

```
this.sumOfGrades = this.sumOfGrades + grade;
```

When an instance field is used in the implementation of a method, the compiler automatically applies the `this` parameter. Every object method has one implicit parameter. The parameter `grade` in `addGrade` is an *explicit parameter*, because it is explicitly named in the method definition.

■ Topics That Are Useful But Not Tested

- If you are not using an integrated development environment, you can invoke the editor, the compiler, the linker, and the program to test manually by using command line editing. This is explained in *Productivity Hint 3.2*.
- The `javadoc` utility produces HTML files from the documentation in your code. Most of the comments included in your text use `javadoc` comments. This utility is explained in *Productivity Hint 3.1*. Your IDE may provide a tool that will produce the HTML files from your `javadoc` comments.
- You can call one constructor from another constructor of the same class using a short-hand notation. This is explained in *Advanced Topic 3.1* of your text.

■ Things to Remember When Taking the AP Exam

- Initialize all objects before you access them.
- Instance fields are initialized with default values if you do not initialize them but it is a good habit to explicitly initialize all instance fields within the constructor. The AP Exam will not test default initialization rules.

- The `return` statement in a method returns the specified value and exits the method immediately. The type of the value you are returning must match the return type of the method.
- When calling an object method from a test class (client program), you must supply an object reference on which to invoke the method.

```
artStudent.getId();   // This is OK.
getId();   // WRONG! You need to supply an object reference.
```

- Do not name parameter variables of methods with the same variable name as your instance fields. A parameter variable with the same name as an instance variable leads to complications when referencing the instance variable in the method. One technique for choosing variable names for your instance fields is to begin the instance field name with `my`. For example `myFirstName` or `myGpa` could be instance fields in the `Student` class. This is a convention that is used in the College Board Marine Biology Simulation Case Study.
- Remember to include a `return` statement if your method is to return a value.
- Do not attempt to access `private` data or methods from outside the class. If you need to use the value of an instance field, look for an accessor method that returns the value of the instance field. If there isn't one, then there probably is no need for you to access that private value outside the class.

■ Key Words

You should understand the terms below. The AP CS Exam questions may include references to these terms. The citation in parentheses next to each term identifies the page number where it is defined and/or discussed in *Java Concepts*, 4th ed., and *Big Java*, 2nd ed.

abstraction (67)	implicit parameter (91)	private (78)
access specifier (70)	initialization (90)	public (79)
black box (66)	instance fields (77)	public interface (72)
constructor (71)	local variables (88)	return (81)
encapsulation (67)	method body (71)	return value (81)
explicit parameter (91)	object-oriented (67)	this (91)
implement (68)	parameter variables (88)	type (77)

■ Connecting the Detailed Topic Outline to the Text

The citations in parentheses identify where information in the outline can be located in *Java Concepts*, 4th ed., and *Big Java,* 2nd ed.

- Black Boxes (66–69)
- Designing the Pubic Interface of a Class (69–74)
- Commenting the Public Interface (74–77)
- Instance Fields (77–79)
- Implementing Constructors and Methods (79–82)
  - ■ Implementing Constructors (79–80)
  - ■ Implementing Methods (80–82)

■ Practice Questions

Multiple Choice

1. Which of the following statements about the public interface of a class is **true**?

    a. The public interface of a class includes the implementation for the constructors but not for the methods.
    b. The public interface of a class includes the implementation for the constructors and the public methods.
    c. The public interface of a class includes a set of methods, with specific types for the parameters and specification for the constructors.
    d. The public interface of a class includes a set of methods, with specific types for the parameters, specification for the constructors, and declarations of the instance fields.
    e. Writing the public interface should be the last step in program design.

2. Suppose the Car class has the following instance field declarations.

    ```
    private double mileage;    // Mileage on odometer
    private double mpg;        // Miles per gallon
    private double tankSize;   // Size of gas tank in gallons
    ```

    What is true about the initialization of the instance fields? **(not tested on the AP Exam)**

    a. The instance fields must be initialized in the constructor. If they are not, there will be a compile-time error.
    b. The instance fields must be initialized in the constructor. If they are not, the program will compile but there will be a run-time error when the Car object constructor is called.
    c. The instance fields should be initialized in the constructor. If they are not, they will automatically be initialized to null.
    d. The instance fields should be initialized in the constructor. If they are not, they will automatically be initialized to 0.
    e. The instance fields should be initialized to null by passing values to the constructor as parameters.

3. The implicit parameter of a method in a class is denoted by

    a. a double
    b. a String
    c. null
    d. this
    e. the empty string

4. Consider the following three method headers.

    I.   `double findAnswer(String a, int b)`
    II. `int findAnswer(String a, int b)`
    III. `double findAnswer(int b, String a)`

    Which of the following statements is **true** about their method signatures?

    a. I and II have the same method signature and this signature is different from the method signature of III.
    b. II and III have the same method signature and this signature is different from the method signature of I.
    c. I and III have the same method signature and this signature is different from the method signature of II.
    d. I, II, and III all have the same method signature.
    e. I, II, and III all have different method signatures.

Questions 5 and 6 refer to the `BankAccount` class whose incomplete definition is shown below.

```java
// A bank account has a balance that can be changed by
// deposits and withdrawals.
public class BankAccount
{
    // Constructs a bank account with a given balance.
    public BankAccount(double initialBalance)
    {
        balance = initialBalance;
    }

    // Deposits money into the bank account.
    public void deposit(double amount)
    {
        double newBalance = balance + amount;
        balance = newBalance;
    }

    // Gets the current balance of the bank account.
    public double getBalance()
    {
        return balance;
    }

    private double balance;
}
```

5. Suppose the following statements were executed.

```java
BankAccount b1 = new BankAccount(500);
BankAccount b2 = new BankAccount(500);

b1.deposit(b2.getBalance());
b2.deposit(b1.getBalance());
```

What are the balances of b1 and b2 after the code is executed?

a.   b1 has balance = 500, b2 has balance = 500.
b.   b1 has balance = 1000, b2 has balance = 500.
c.   b1 has balance = 500, b2 has balance = 1000.
d.   b1 has balance = 1000, b2 has balance = 1000.
e.   b1 has balance = 1000, b2 has balance = 1500.

6.   Suppose the following statements were executed.

```
BankAccount b1 = new BankAccount(500);
BankAccount b2 = b1;

b1.deposit(b2.getBalance());
b2.deposit(b1.getBalance());
```

What are the balances of b1 and b2 after the code is executed?

a.   b1 has balance = 500, b2 has balance = 500.
b.   b1 has balance = 1000, b2 has balance = 500.
c.   b1 has balance = 500, b2 has balance = 1000.
d.   b1 has balance = 1000, b2 has balance = 2000.
e.   b1 has balance = 2000, b2 has balance = 2000.

7.   Which of the following statements about categories of variables is **true**?

I.   Local variables are initialized within a method body.
II.   Instance variables are initialized in the constructor of the class.
III.   Parameter variables are initialized with the values that are supplied in the method call.

a.   II only
b.   I and II only
c.   I and III only
d.   II and III only
e.   I, II, and III.

8.   Which of the following statements about categories of variables is **true**?

I.   Local variables belong to the method and are in existence for the lifetime of the object to which the method belongs.
II.   Instance variables belong to the object and are in existence as long as there is some reference to the object.
III.   Parameter variables are in existence for the lifetime of the method to which they belong.

a.   II only
b.   I and II only
c.   I and III only
d.   II and III only
e.   I, II, and III.

Questions 9 and 10 refer to the `Student` class whose incomplete definition is below.

```
/*
    A Student has a first name, a last name, and an ID number.
    When a student grade is entered, it is added to sumOfGrades and
    the numberOfGrades is incremented by 1.
*/
public class Student
{
    public Student(String first, String last, String idNumber)
    {
        firstName = first;
        lastName = last;
        id = idNumber;
        sumOfGrades = 0.0;
        numberOfGrades = 0;
    }

    // Constructs a Student with default values.
    public Student()
    {
        firstName = "";
        lastName = "";
        id = "";
        sumOfGrades = 0.0;
        numberOfGrades = 0;
    }

    // Returns student's first name.
    public String getFirstName() { }

    // Returns student's last name.
    public String getLastName()  { }

    // Returns student's id.
    public String getId() { }

    // Modifies sumOfGrades and numberOfGrades to include new
    // grade.
    public void addGrade(double grade)
    {
        sumOfGrades = sumOfGrades + grade;
        numberOfGrades = numberOfGrades + 1;
    }

    // Returns student's average grade.
    public double getGpa()
    {
        return sumOfGrades / numberOfGrades;
    }

    private String firstName;
    private String lastName;
    private String id;
    private double sumOfGrades;
```

```
        private int numberOfGrades;
    }
```

Suppose the following statements were executed.

```
        Student one = new Student("Jamie", "Morris", "111");
        Student two = new Student("Jan", "Smith", "222");

        one.addGrade(56);
        one.addGrade(34);
        two.addGrade(one.getGpa());
        two.addGrade(99);
        one.addGrade(two.getGpa());
        System.out.println(one.getGpa());
        System.out.println(two.getGpa());
```

9. What is the value of the instance fields `numberOfGrades` and `sumOfGrades` for the `Student` object `one` after the code is executed?

    a. `numberOfGrades` = 3, `sumOfGrades` = 162
    b. `numberOfGrades` = 3, `sumOfGrades` = 189
    c. `numberOfGrades` = 5, `sumOfGrades` = 279
    d. `numberOfGrades` = 5, `sumOfGrades` = 189
    e. `numberOfGrades` = 3, `sumOfGrades` = 279

10. What is printed to the screen when this code is executed?

    a. *81*
        72
    b. *54*
        72
    c. *81*
        94.5
    d. *93*
        94.5
    e. *54*
        94.5

Free Response Questions

1. An `Employee` object has a first name (a `String`), a last name (a `String`), and a salary (a `double`). An incomplete class definition is given below.

```
    public class Employee
    {
        // Constructs default Employee.
        public Employee()
        {
            myFirstName = "";
            myLastName = "";
            salary = 45000;
        }

        // Other constructor(s) here
```

```
        // Returns employee's salary.
        public double getSalary()
        {
            return salary;
        }

        // Employee salary increased by byPercent percent.
        public void raiseSalary(double byPercent)
        {
            // Code goes here
        }

        private String myFirstName;
        private String myLastName;
        private double salary;
}
```

a. Write a constructor for the `Employee` class that has three parameters: `firstName` (a `String`), `lastName` (a `String`), and `moneyEarned` (a `double`). The private instance variables should be initialized to the values of the parameters.

b. Write a method `raiseSalary` for the `Employee` class. The method `raiseSalary` will raise the employee's salary by a given percentage passed as a parameter to the method. For example:

```
Employee worker1 = new Employee("John", "Smith", 50000);
    // John Smith has salary = $50,000.

worker1.raiseSalary(20);
    // John Smith now has salary = $60,000.
```

Use the method header below to write `raiseSalary`.

```
public void raiseSalary(double byPercent)
```

c. Write a method `calculateBonusAmount` for the `Employee` class. The method `calculateBonusAmount` will calculate and return the amount of money to be given to an employee as a holiday bonus. This amount is based on the salary of the employee and the given percent passed as a parameter to the method. For example:

```
Employee worker1 = new Employee("John", "Smith", 50000);
    // John Smith has salary = $50,000.

System.out.println(worker1.calculateBonusAmount(3));
    // 1500 will be printed
```

Use the method header below to write `calculateBonusAmount`.

```
public double calculateBonusAmount(double byPercent)
```

2. A `Book` class is to be implemented with the following properties. A `Book` object has a title (a `String`), an author (a `String`), and a price (a `double`). An incomplete definition for the `Book` class is shown below.

```
public class Book
{
    // Constructor goes here
```

```
    // Returns price of book.
    public double getPrice()
    {
        return price;
    }

    // Decreases book price.
    public void giveDiscount(double byPercent)
    {
        // Code goes here

    }

    private String title;
    private String author;
    private double price;
}
```

a. Write a constructor for the Book class that has three parameters: a title (a String), an author (a String), and a price (a double).

b. Write the method giveDiscount that modifies the price of the book by decreasing the price of the book by a given percentage. For example:

```
Book myFavoriteBook = new Book("The Cat in the Hat Comes Back",
        "Dr. Seuss", 10.00);
myFavoriteBook.giveDiscount(15);    // price = 8.5
System.out.println("The new price of the book is "
        + myFavoriteBook.getPrice());
        // Output would be The new price of the book is 8.5.
```

Use the method header below to write giveDiscount.

```
public void giveDiscount(double byPercent)
```

CHAPTER 5

Fundamental Data Types

■ Topic Summary

5.1   Number Types

In Java, every value is either a primitive or a reference to an object. We have used the primitive types `double` and `int` in the programs we have written so far. Both `double` and `int` are somewhat restrictive in that they cannot represent very large integer or floating-point numbers. Table 1 in Section 4.1 of your text gives details on the exact ranges of these types. You do not need to memorize the exact upper and lower limits for `int` and `double` numbers but you do need to know that there are restrictions. The `double` type also has a precision problem. Rounding errors occur when an exact conversion between numbers is not possible. Computers represent numbers in the binary number system. Because, in a computer, there is no exact representation of a fraction such as 1/10, roundoff errors may occur when we least expect them. Although you will probably not have to worry about this in writing answers to the free-response questions on the AP Exam, you do need to understand that these precision errors may exist. This is discussed in Section 4.1 and in *Advanced Topic 4.2* of your text.

Let's look at converting one type to another. Consider another version of our `StudentTester` program from Chapter 4 of this guide.

Example 5.1

```
Student goodStudent = new Student("Jamie", "Brown", "222333");
goodStudent.addGrade(100);
goodStudent.addGrade(95);
System.out.println(goodStudent.getGpa());
```

The above `println` statement would print the value 97.5. Suppose our grading system allowed for only integer valued GPAs to be given to the student. We have a few choices. The first of these choices is to ignore the fractional part of this GPA is which case the student will receive 97 instead of the earned 97.5. You may not like this solution. However if we look at a different problem description that involves the same situation, you may change your mind. Suppose you wanted to buy something from a vendor who refused to accept coins. If your total owed involved any cents (e.g., $4.95), and the vendor simple charged you the dollar amount ($4), would you like that? In Java, you can convert (cast) a value to a different type.

```
int newGpa = (int) goodStudent.getGpa();
```

will cast our `double` value to an `int`. The variable `newGpa` will have the value of 97 in our example above. Of course, the other two solutions would be to round *up* to the next higher integer or to round to the nearest integer (closest integer value). These options will be discussed later.

5.1.1   *Numbers in Other Bases*

Roundoff errors occur when binary digits are lost in the internal representation of a floating-point number. Binary Numbers are explained in *Advanced Topic 4.2* of your text. You should be able to represent numbers in different bases. Three common bases are binary (base 2), octal (base 8), and hexadecimal (base 16).

Here is a method for converting the decimal number 100 to a binary number (base 2):

100/2 = 50 remainder 0
50/2 = 25 remainder 0
25/2 = 12 remainder 1
12/2 = 6 remainder 0
6/2 = 3 remainder 0
3/2 = 1 remainder 1
1/2 = 0 remainder 1

If you read the remainders from bottom to top you have the binary representation of the decimal number. 1100100 is the binary representation of the decimal number 100. Binary numbers contain only the digits 0 and 1.

To convert the fractional part of a number to binary, we multiply the fractional part by 2 until we get 0 or until the pattern repeats. Consider the decimal number 0.625.

.625 * 2 = 1.25 → integer part of product = 1
.25 * 2 = 0.5 → integer part of product = 0
.5 * 2 = 1.0 → integer part of product = 1

Read the integer parts going down. .625 is approximately equal to .101 in binary.

Consider the decimal number 0.375.

$.375 * 2 = 0.75 \rightarrow$ integer part of product = 0
$.75 * 2 = 1.5 \rightarrow$ integer part of product = 1
$.5 * 2 = 1.0 \rightarrow$ integer part of product = 1

Read the integer parts going down. .375 is approximately equal to .011 in binary. To convert 100.625 to binary, you convert the integer part and the fractional part separately. The decimal number 100.625 would convert to the binary number 1100100.101.

Advanced Topic 4.2 demonstrates converting the fractional number .35 to binary. This example shows a repeating pattern.

Similarly, to convert the decimal number 100 to an octal number (base 8):

100/8 = 12 remainder 4
12/8 = 1 remainder 4
1/8 = 0 remainder 1

If you read the remainders from bottom to top you have the octal representation of the decimal number. 144_8 is the octal representation of the decimal number 100. Octal numbers contain only the digits 0, 1, 2, 3, 4, 5, 6, and 7.

To convert the decimal number 100 to a hexadecimal number (base 16):

100/16 = 6 remainder 4
6/16 = 0 remainder 6

If you read the remainders from bottom to top you have the hexadecimal representation of the decimal number. 64_{16} is the hexadecimal representation of the decimal number 100. Hexadecimal numbers contain the digits 0–9 plus A, B, C, D, E, and F where A has the value of 10, B has the value 11, C = 12, D = 13, E = 14, and F = 15.

To convert the decimal number 27 to a hexadecimal number (base 16):

27/16 = 1 remainder 11
1/16 = 0 remainder 1

$1B_{16}$ is the hexadecimal representation of the decimal number 27.

You can reverse the algorithm to convert back to base 10. To convert the binary number 1100100 to a decimal (base 10) number, multiply each digit by the corresponding power of 2:

$$(0)(2^0) + (0)(2^1) + (1)(2^2) + (0)(2^3) + (0)(2^4) + (1)(2^5) + (1)(2^6) = 100 \text{ base } 10.$$

To convert the octal number 144_8 to a decimal, multiply by the power of 8:

$$(4)(8^0) + (4)(8^1) + (1)(8^2) = 100 \text{ base } 10.$$

To convert the hexadecimal number 64_{16} to a decimal, multiply by the power of 16:

$$(4)(16^0) + (6)(16^1) = 100 \text{ base } 10.$$

5.2   Constants

Sometimes it is convenient to use *constants* in our programs. A constant is used when the value of a variable remains the same throughout the life of the variable. Some examples might include:

```
MAXSEATS     // The maximum number of seats on an airplane
TAX_RATE     // Sales tax rate
NICKEL_VALUE   // The value of a nickel
```

In Java, we declare constants as `final` variables. Once a `final` variable has been given a value, that variable's value cannot be changed. Constants are usually given variable names that are all uppercase letters. `final` variables declared within a method can be used only within that method. Method `getTotal` below demonstrates the use of constants.

Example 5.2

```
public double getTotal()
{
    final double NICKEL_VALUE = 0.05;
    final double DIME_VALUE = 0.1;
    final double QUARTER_VALUE = 0.25;
    return nickels * NICKEL_VALUE
            + dimes * DIME_VALUE + quarters * QUARTER_VALUE;
}
```

`NICKEL_VALUE`, `DIME_VALUE`, and `QUARTER_VALUE` are only accessible from within the method `getTotal`.

It may be more useful to have these constants accessible throughout the class definition, in which case the `final` variables should be declared as `static` and either `public` or `private`. You declare a constant as `static` if you do not need a copy of the constant for each object. If your constant will be called only by methods within your class, then you should declare it as `private`. If you wish to allow client programs or other classes access to your constants, then you would declare them as `public`.

Example 5.3

```
public class PiggyBank
{
    public double getTotal()
    {
        return nickels * NICKEL_VALUE
                + dimes * DIME_VALUE + quarters * QUARTER_VALUE;
    }

    // Other methods and declarations

    private static final double NICKEL_VALUE = 0.05;
    private static final double DIME_VALUE = 0.1;
    private static final double QUARTER_VALUE = 0.25;
}
```

Section 4.2 in your text includes a more complete example of using constants in the `CashRegister` class.

5.3   Assignment, Increment, and Decrement

The assignment operator sets the variable on the left-hand side of the = operator to the value of the expression on the right-hand side of the = operator. Java also permits the combining of basic arithmetic operators with assignment by providing us with special assignment operators. For example, the arithmetic operation + can be combined with assignment to give us the += operator. The statement

   total += count; is equivalent to total = total + count;

and will add the value of count to the value of total and assign this sum to total. The other combined arithmetic/assignment operators are -=, *=, /=, and %=.

In addition, Java provides an *increment* operator (++) and a *decrement* operator (--). The statement

   count++; has the same effect as count = count + 1;

and

   count--; has the same effect as count = count - 1;

Example 5.4
_____

```
1    int numberOfCoins = 10;    // numberOfCoins = 10
2    int moreCoins = 12;    // moreCoins = 12
3    numberOfCoins = numberOfCoins + 1;    // numberOfCoins = 11
4    numberOfCoins++;    // numberOfCoins = 12
5    numberOfCoins += moreCoins;    // numberOfCoins = 24
6    numberOfCoins--;    // numberOfCoins = 23
```

Lines 1 and 2 assign integer values to int variables.
Line 3 increments the int variable numberOfCoins by 1 and assigns this new value to
   numberOfCoins.
Line 4 increments numberOfCoins by 1.
Line 5 adds the value of moreCoins to the value of numberOfCoins and assigns this new value
   to numberOfCoins.
Line 6 decrements the value of numberOfCoins by 1.

_____

Java is a strongly typed language. We must take care that the type of the value on the right-hand side of the = sign is compatible with the type of the variable on the left-hand side of the = sign. We cannot make the following assignment because Student and int are not compatible types.

```
Student goodStudent = new Student();
goodStudent = 10;    // WRONG
```

An int can be assigned to a double.

```
int numberOfCoins = 7;
double taxRate = numberOfCoins;
System.out.println(taxRate);    // Prints 7.0
```

A double cannot be assigned to an int.

```
double taxRate = 7;    // This is OK.
int numberOfCoins = taxRate;    // WRONG; This is a compile-time
        // error (failure to recognize the loss of precision).
```

Number variables hold values. Assigning a number variable to another number variable assigns its value.

```
int aNum = 5;
int anotherNum = aNum;
```

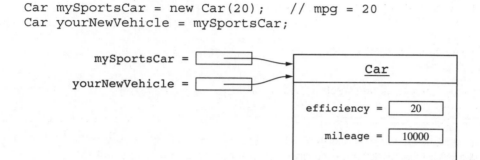

```
        aNum = [    5    ]

  anotherNum = [    5    ]
```

Object variables hold references. Assigning an object reference to another object reference creates another reference to the same object.

```
Car mySportsCar = new Car(20);    // mpg = 20
Car yourNewVehicle = mySportsCar;
```

Changing information for `mySportsCar` will be reflected in `yourNewVehicle`. Both variables refer to the same object. Whether or not `yourNewVehicle` gets 20 miles to the gallon, since `yourNewVehicle` references the same object as `mySportsCar`, that's what you'll get! And when you *drive* `yourNewVehicle`, `mySportsCar`'s mileage goes up! This may not necessarily be your intended result.

5.4   Arithmetic Operations and Mathematical Functions

Most applications require us to write expressions that contain arithmetic operations. Computers will do exactly what we tell them to do, so take care in writing complicated algebraic expressions. Use parentheses just as you do in algebra. The order of operations shown in Table 5.1 lists operators with the highest priority at the top. If two operations on the same level are contained in one expression, these operations are evaluated from left to right, just as they would be in an algebraic expression. Sometimes splitting a complicated expression into smaller parts and combining these parts to obtain the final result enhances readability and decreases errors.

Table 5.1

Operator Precedence

Operator Order of Precedence					
++	--				
*	/				
+	-				
=	*=	/=	%=	+=	-=

If both numbers are integers, then the result of division is always an integer, with the remainder discarded. For example, the result of 7 / 3 is 2. The remainder of 1 is discarded. If you are interested in the remainder, use the modulus operator. The result of 7 % 3 is 1 because the remainder when 7 is divided by 3 is 1. You must be careful when dividing and using the modulus operator in arithmetic expressions, especially if you are combining doubles and integers.

Table 5.2
Arithmetic Expressions

Expression	Operand 1	Operand 2	Result	Result Type
4 + 5	int	int	9	int
14 / 5	int	int	2	int
4 / 5	int	int	0	int
14 / 5.0	int	double	2.8	double
14.0 / 5	double	int	2.8	double
14 % 5	int	int	4	int
4 % 5	int	int	4	int

Java provides a library of math functions that can help us with solutions to complicated applications. The AP CS subsets include only those math functions listed in Table 5.3.

Table 5.3
class java.lang.Math

Method	Method Summary
static int abs(int x)	Returns the absolute value of the integer x.
static double abs(double x)	Returns the absolute value of the double x.
static double pow(double base, double exponent)	Returns the value of base raised to the power exponent.
static double sqrt(double x)	Returns the correctly rounded positive square root of a double number x.

5.5   Calling Static Methods

The functions from java.lang.Math are static functions. You can see this by the word static before the return type in the method header.

```
static double sqrt(double x)
```

This indicates that the method does not operate on an object. To invoke the square root function, we write

```
Math.sqrt(x)
```

Because of the Java convention of naming variables, methods, and classes, we can tell that the call above is a static method. Math begins with a capital letter which designates this as a class and not an object. *Quality Tip 4.2* and Sections 4.2 and 4.5 of your text discuss the convention of naming variables, classes, and methods.

5.5.1   *More on Type Conversion*

We have mentioned that Java is a strongly typed language. This means that the compiler will complain if we try to assign incompatible types.

```
int a = 4;
double b = 2.1;
int c = a + b;    // Compiler complains about loss of precision.
```

If we intentionally want to discard the fractional part of this result, we need to *cast* the result to an int before the assignment can be made.

```
int a = 4;
double b = 2.1;
int c = (int) (a + b);    // Compiler no longer complains.
```

You do need to realize that this results in a loss of precision. The behavior resulting from casting to an int is sometimes referred to as "truncation towards 0" behavior, because the rounding truncates (cuts off) the fractional part of the double number, the result being an integer that is closer to zero than the original double number.

Table 5.4

Truncation Towards 0 Behavior

Expression	Result
int num = (int) (3.4);	3
int num = (int) (3.7);	3
int num = (int) (-3.4);	-3
int num = (int) (-3.7);	-3

You can use this behavior to round floating-point numbers to integer values. The expression

```
(int) (x + 0.5)
```

rounds a positive floating-point number to the nearest integer and the expression

```
(int) (x - 0.5)
```

rounds a negative floating-point number to the nearest integer.

Table 5.5

Rounding Numbers

Statements	Rounding Result
double x = 4.2 int xRounded = (int) (x + 0.5)	4
double x = 4.8 int xRounded = (int) (x + 0.5)	5
double x = -4.2 int xRounded = (int) (x - 0.5)	-4
double x = -4.7 int xRounded = (int) (x - 0.5)	-5

Of course, `java.lang.Math` does provide a method `round`. The `double` parameter is rounded to an integer by adding 1/2, taking the integer that is less than or equal to this result, and casting the result to type `long`. Care has to be taken when using this `Math.round` method with negative numbers. `Math.round(-4.5)` returns -4. The Java `round` method will not be tested on the AP Exams.

5.6   Strings

Strings are one of the most commonly used data types. A `String` is a sequence of characters enclosed within double quotes. A `String` is an object. We have already discussed `String` concatenation. The + operator concatenates two strings. If one expression to the left or right of the + is a `String`, then the other is automatically converted to a `String` and the two parts are concatenated. For example,

```
String s = "The number of ";
s += "Dalmatians is: ";   // Two strings concatenated
```

`s` is now the string: *The number of Dalmatians is:*

```
s += 101;   // 101 is automatically converted
System.out.println(s);
```

The number of Dalmatians is: 101 is printed.

Although the `String` class has many methods, you are responsible for those listed in Table 5.6.

Table 5.6
`class java.lang.String implements java.lang.Comparable`

Method	*Method Summary*
`int compareTo(Object other)`	Compares two strings lexicographically. Returns value < 0 if this `String` is less than `other`. Returns value = 0 if this `String` is equal to `other`. Returns value > 0 if this `String` is greater than `other`.
`boolean equals(Object other)`	Compares this `String` to specified object. The result is `true` if and only if `other` is not `null` and is a `String` object that represents the same sequence of characters as this object.
`int length()`	Returns the length of the `String`.
`String substring(int from, int to)`	Returns a new string that is a substring of this one beginning at `from` and ending at `to` - 1.
`String substring(int from)`	Returns a new string that is a substring of this one beginning at `from` and ending at `length` - 1.
`int indexOf(String str)`	If `str` occurs as a substring within this object, then the index of the first character of the first such substring is returned; if it does not occur as a substring, `-1` is returned.

Example 5.5 demonstrates these `String` methods.

Example 5.5

```
1      public class StringTester
2      {
3         public static void main(String[] args)
4         {
5            String greeting = "Hello";
6            String bookName = "Java Concepts";
7            System.out.println(greeting);
8            System.out.println(bookName);
9
10           String subBook = bookName.substring(5, 12);
11           System.out.println(subBook);
12
13           System.out.println(greeting.length());
14           System.out.println(greeting.substring(3));
15
16           int position = bookName.indexOf("Java");
17           System.out.println(position);
18
19           greeting = greeting + " there!";
20           System.out.println(greeting);
21        }
22     }
```

Lines 5 and 6 create String objects and assign values to these String objects.

Line 7 prints *Hello*

Line 8 prints *Java Concepts*

Line 10 creates a new String containing the characters in positions 5 to 11 inclusive. The first character in a string is in position 0.

Line 11 prints *Concept*

Line 13 prints *5*

Line 14 prints *lo* This prints the substring from position 3 to the end of the string.

Line 16 assigns to the integer variable position the index of the first occurrence of *Java* in the String *Java Concepts*

Line 17 prints *0*

Line 19 creates a new String with the value obtained from concatenating *Hello* with *there!* Strings are immutable objects. This means that a String object is never changed. A new String object is created when an assignment such as the one in line 19 is executed.

Line 20 prints *Hello there!*

The String methods compareTo and equals will be discussed in Chapter 6.

5.6.1   *Escape Sequences*

Some characters have a special meaning in Java and cannot be directly included as a character in a string. Two such characters are the backslash (\ ) and the double quotes ("). The backslash is used as an escape character and the double quotes character either begins or ends a string literal. Java provides escape sequences that enable us to include these characters as characters in a string. Another escape sequence that is often used to help in formatting output denotes a newline or linefeed character (\n).

Example 5.6

```
System.out.println("C:\\My Documents\\Hello.java");
System.out.println("He said: \"Hello!\"");
System.out.println("One\nTwo\nThree");
```

will print

> *C:\My Documents\Hello.java*
> *He said: "Hello!"*
> *One*
> *Two*
> *Three*

■ Expanded Coverage of Material That Is Not Found in the Text

The `String` method `indexOf` is part of the AP CS language subset.

```
int indexOf(String s)
```

If `s` occurs as a substring within this object, then the index of the first character of the first such substring is returned; if it does not occur as a substring, `-1` is returned.

```
String greeting = "Hello";
System.out.println(greeting.indexOf("e"));    // Prints 1
System.out.println(greeting.indexOf("x"));    // Prints -1
```

■ Topics That Are Useful But Not Tested

- `java.lang.Math` has many useful functions that will not be tested on the AP CS Exam. These functions are listed in Table 2 in Section 4.4 of your text.
- The `toUpperCase` and `toLowerCase` methods of the `String` class discussed in Section 2.3 of your text can be very useful.
- If a `String` contains the digits of a number, you can use the `Integer.parseInt` or `Double.parseDouble` method to obtain the number value. This is discussed in Sections 4.1 and 4.6 of your text.
- Strings are composed of individual characters. Characters are values of the `char` type. The `char` type is discussed in *Advanced Topic 4.5* of your text. The `charAt` method can prove to be quite useful when working with strings.
- Sometimes it is convenient to have values input by the person using the program. *Advanced Topic 4.7* discusses reading input using the `JOptionPane.showInputDialog` method. On the AP CS Exam, if input by the user is required, you will see something similar to:

```
double x = call to a method that reads a floating-point number;
```

or

```
double x = IO.readDouble();    // Read user input
```

■ Java 5 Issues

- It is often important to output information in a specific format. You may wish to have a certain number of decimal places printed. You can achieve proper formatting with the `printf` method of the `PrintStream` class. This is explained in *Advanced Topic 4.6* of your text. Since formatting output is not tested on the AP Exam, `printf` will not be tested.
- Java 5 provides the `Scanner` class to read user input. Although input is not tested on the AP Exam, the `Scanner` class is easy to use and gives us an option for reading input in our programs without the dialog box `JOptionPane` provides. The `Scanner` class is discussed in Section 4.7 of your text.

■ Things to Remember When Taking the AP Exam

- Remember to declare all variables before you use them.
- Initialize variables that need to be initialized.
- Use descriptive variable names. This is discussed in *Quality Tip 4.2*.
- Do not use *magic* numbers in your code. Magic numbers are constants that appear in your code with no explanation. They are explained in *Quality Tip 4.1* of your text.
- Use parentheses as you would in algebra. If in doubt about the need for parentheses in an expression, use them.
- Remember that integer divided by integer equals integer. Sometimes casting to a `double` is required to obtain a correct result.
- Remember that the first character of a `String` is in position 0.
- The `indexOf` method of the `String` class returns `-1` if the string being searched for is not found.
- The last character of a `String` `s` is in position `s.length() - 1`.
- When you assign one object variable to another object variable, both object variables reference the same object.

■ Key Words

You should understand the terms below. The AP CS Exam questions may include references to these terms. The citation in parentheses next to each term identifies the page number where it is defined and/or discussed in *Java Concepts*, 4th ed., and *Big Java*, 2nd ed.

assignment (116)	`final` (111)	modulus operator `%` (119)
binary numbers (107)	increment operator (116)	rounding error (105)
cast (106)	magic numbers (115)	static method (123)
concatenation (128)	`Math.sqrt` (120)	`String` (128)
constant (110)	`Math.pow` (120)	substring (129)
decrement operator (116)	`Math.abs` (120)	

■ Connecting the Detailed Topic Outline to the Text

The citations in parentheses identify where information in the outline can be located in *Java Concepts*, 4th ed., and *Big Java*, 2nd ed.

- Number Types (104–110)
  - Numbers in Other Bases (107)
- Constants (110–115)
- Assignment, Increment, and Decrement (116–18)
- Arithmetic Operations and Mathematical Functions (118–123)
- Calling Static Methods (123–124)
- Strings (128–132)
  - Escape Sequences (131)

■ Practice Questions

Multiple Choice

1. Consider the following declarations.

   ```
   int a = some integer value
   int b = some integer value
   int c = some integer value
   ```

   Which of the following statements will correctly calculate the average of a, b, and c?

   a. `int average = (a + b + c) / 3`
   b. `double average = a + b + c / 3`
   c. `double average = (a + b + c) / 3.0`
   d. `double average = (double) ((a + b + c) / 3)`
   e. `double average = (a + b + c) / 3`

2. The expression

   ```
   5 + 6 * 3 % 2 - 1
   ```

   evaluates to

   a. 0
   b. 1
   c. 4
   d. 10
   e. 13

3. Given the following declarations:

   ```
   int m = 18;
   int n = 4;
   ```

   What is the value of the following expression?

   ```
   m / n + m % n
   ```

a. 0
b. 2
c. 6
d. 6.5
e. 10.5

Questions 4 and 5 refer to the following segment of code.

```
String bookName = "Computing Concepts with Java Essentials";
String newWord = bookName.substring(10,18)
        + bookName.substring(6,8) + bookName.substring(0,9);
```

4. After the code is executed, what is the `String` that `newWord` references?

a. " ConcepttiComputin"
b. "Concepts ingComputing "
c. "Concepts in Computing"
d. "ConceptsinComputing"
e. An error message is generated

5. The statement

```
System.out.println(bookName.indexOf("cat"));
```

prints

a. *-1*
b. *0*
c. *null*
d. *1*
e. An error message is generated

Questions 6–9 refer to the following incomplete definition of the `PiggyBank` class.

```
public class PiggyBank
{
    // Constructor-initializes nickels, dimes, and quarters to 0.
    public PiggyBank() {. . .}

    // Adds nickels to the bank.
    public void addNickels(int count) {. . .}

    // Adds dimes to the bank.
    public void addDimes(int count) {. . .}

    // Adds quarters to the bank.
    public void addQuarters(int count) {. . .}

    // Returns total value of all the coins in the bank.
    public double getTotal(){. . .}

    // Takes count dimes from the bank.
    public void subtractDimes(int count)
    {
        // Code goes here
    }
```

```
            private static final double NICKEL_VALUE = 0.05;
            private static final double DIME_VALUE = 0.1;
            private static final double QUARTER_VALUE = 0.25;
            private int nickels;   // Number of nickels in piggy bank
            private int dimes;    // Number of dimes in piggy bank
            private int quarters;    // Number of quarters in piggy bank
        }
```

6. The code for method subtractDimes should be

   a. dimes = dimes - DIME_VALUE * count;
   b. dimes = dimes - count;
   c. double amount = dimes - count;
      return amount;
   d. int amount = dimes - 1;
      return amount;
   e. int amount = dimes - DIME_VALUE * count;
      return amount;

7. A client program is to print the total value of the coins in the PiggyBank object myBank. Which of the following code segments will complete the intended task?

   I. double totalMoney = myBank.getTotal();
       System.out.println(totalMoney);

   II. double totalMoney = nickels * NICKEL_VALUE + dimes
              * DIME_VALUE + quarters * QUARTER_VALUE;
       System.out.println(totalMoney);

   III. double totalMoney = nickels * 0.05 + dimes * 0.10
              + quarters   * 0.25;
       System.out.println(totalMoney);

   a. I only
   b. II only
   c. III only
   d. I and III only
   e. II and III only

8. After the following code is executed, what are the values of c and d?

   ```
   PiggyBank p = new PiggyBank();
   PiggyBank q = p;
   p.addNickels(5);
   q.addNickels(3);
   double c = p.getTotal();
   double d = q.getTotal();
   ```

   a. c = 5   d = 3
   b. c = 0.25   d = 0.15
   c. c = 0.25   d = 0.25
   d. c = 0.15   d = 0.15
   e. c = 0.4   d = 0.4

9. Consider the following code segment.

```
1  int numberOfCoins = 5;
2  double taxRate = 4;
3  double number = 3.0;
4  PiggyBank yourBank;
5  PiggyBank myMoney = new PiggyBank();
6  taxRate = numberOfCoins;
7  numberOfCoins = number;
```

Which of the following statements is **true**?

a. A compile-time error occurs in line 2 because 4 is an `int` and not a `double`.
b. A compile-time error occurs in line 4 because an object is not being created with `new`.
c. An error occurs in line 6 because `numberOfCoins` and `taxRate` are not compatible types.
d. An error occurs in line 7 because a `double` cannot be assigned to an `int`.
e. The program will compile without errors.

10. Which of the following statements about objects and classes is **true**?

a. A `final` variable in a class must be declared as `private`.
b. Multiple object references cannot contain references to the same object.
c. A client program can create only one object of a class.
d. A `static` method is a method that operates on an object that has been instantiated.
e. Every object belongs to a class.

Free Response Questions

1. Consider the `Car` class, whose incomplete definition is shown below.

```
public class Car
{
    // Constructs a car with given values.
    public Car(double milesPerGal, double miles,
            double gasTankHolds, double gasTankHas)
    {
        mpg = milesPerGal;    // Miles per gallon
        mileage = miles;    // Total mileage of car
        tankCapacity = gasTankHolds;    // Amount of gas tank holds
        gasInTank = gasTankHas;    // Amount of gas in the gas tank
    }

    /*
        Updates mileage and gasInTank to reflect numMiles being
        driven. Assumes there is enough gas in tank to make trip.
    */
    public void drive(double numMiles)
    {
        // Code goes here
    }

    // Returns amount of gas consumed by car in numMiles miles.
    public double findGasUsed(double numMiles)
    {
        // Code goes here
```

```
      }

      // Returns the total mileage on car.
      public double getMileage()
      {
         return mileage;
      }

      // Returns the amount of gas in tank.
      public double getGasInTank()
      {
         return gasInTank;
      }

      private double mpg;
      private double mileage;
      private double tankCapacity;
      private double gasInTank;
   }
```

a. Write the method `findGasUsed`. This method should calculate and return the amount of gas used in driving `numMiles` miles. Assume that you have enough gas to make the requested trip!

Call to `findGasUsed`	*mpg*	*Value returned*
`findGasUsed(100)`	20	5.0
`findGasUsed(25.2)`	25	1.008
`findGasUsed(10)`	25	0.4

Use the method header below.

```
      public double findGasUsed(double numMiles)
```

b. Write the method `drive`. The method `drive` is given the number of miles the car has traveled as a parameter. Certain `private` instance variables need to be updated as a result of this action. You may include a call to `findGasUsed` from part a. Assume that this function works as specified regardless of what you wrote for part a. Use the method header below to write your method `drive`.

```
      public void drive(double numMiles)
```

2. A `Purse`, whose definition is shown below, is used to keep track of a number of coins.

```
      // A purse computes the total value of a collection of coins.
      public class Purse
      {
         public Purse()     // Constructor
         {
            nickels = 0;
            dimes = 0;
            quarters = 0;
         }
```

```java
/*
   Add nickels to the purse.
   count is the number of nickels to add
*/
public void addNickels(int count)
{
   nickels += count;
}


/*
   Add dimes to the purse.
   count is the number of dimes to add
*/
public void addDimes(int count)
{
   dimes += count;
}


/*
   Add quarters to the purse.
   count is the number of quarters to add
*/
public void addQuarters(int count)
{
   quarters += count;
}


// Get the total value of the coins in the purse.
// Returns the sum of all coin values
public double getTotal()
{
   return nickels * NICKEL_VALUE + dimes * DIME_VALUE
         + quarters * QUARTER_VALUE;
}


/*
   Returns the total value of the coins in the purse in
   pennies.
*/
public int totalInPennies()
{
   // Code goes here
}


// Returns the number of whole dollars in the purse.
public int getDollars()
{
   // Code goes here
}


/*
   Returns the number of cents in the purse. If the total
   amount in the purse is $7.56, getCents will return 56.
*/
public int getCents()
{
   // Code goes here
```

```
        }

        private static final double NICKEL_VALUE = 0.05;
        private static final double DIME_VALUE = 0.1;
        private static final double QUARTER_VALUE = 0.25;
        private static final int PENNIES_PER_DOLLAR = 100;

        private int nickels;    // Number of nickels in the purse
        private int dimes;      // Number of dimes in the purse
        private int quarters;   // Number of quarters in the purse
}
```

a. Write the method `totalInPennies` that returns the total value of the coins in the purse in pennies. In writing your solution, you may not include calls to `getCents` or `getDollars`. You may include calls to other methods defined in this class.

Total value of coins in Purse	Value returned
2.14	214
0.30	30
2.00	200

Use the method header below.

```
public int totalInPennies()
```

b. Write the method `getDollars` that returns the number of whole dollars in the `Purse` as an integer. In writing your solution, you may include calls to `totalInPennies` from part a. Assume `totalInPennies` works as intended. Examples of calls to `getDollars` appear below.

Total value of coins in Purse	Value returned
2.14	2
0.30	0
2.00	2

Use the method header below.

```
public int getDollars()
```

c. Write the method `getCents` that returns the number of cents in the `Purse` as an integer. In writing your solution, you may include calls to other methods defined in this class. Examples of calls to `getCents` appear below.

Total value of coins in Purse	Value returned
2.14	14
0.30	30
2.00	0

Use the method header below.

```
public int getCents()
```

CHAPTER 6

(Covers *Java Concepts* Chapter 6)

Decisions

■ Topic Summary

6.1   The `if` Statement

The `if` statement is used to control the flow of a program based on a condition. Examples 6.1, 6.2, and 6.3 are the general forms used most often in AP CS.

Example 6.1

```
if (condition)
    statement1;
```

If *condition* evaluates to `true`, *statement1* is executed; otherwise it is not.

Example 6.2

```
if (condition)
    statement1;
else
    statement2;
```

If *condition* evaluates to `true`, *statement1* is executed; otherwise *statement2* is executed.

Example 6.3

```
if (condition1)
    statement1;
else if (condition2)
    statement2;
else
    statement3;
```

If *condition1* evaluates to `true`, *statement1* is executed; otherwise *condition2* is checked. If *condition2* evaluates to `true`, *statement2* is executed; otherwise *statement3* is executed. Example 6.3 could be extended to include more conditions.

Each *statement* in Examples 6.1, 6.2, and 6.3 can be replaced by a block statement as described in Section 6.1 of your text.

```
if (condition)
{
    statement1;
}
else
{
    statement2;
    statement3;
}
```

It is a good idea to always use a block statement format with `if` statements. This makes your code less confusing—especially if you have nested `if` statements (one `if` statement inside another). This blocking also allows for easy insertion of statements in the event that your code is revised. This blocking is necessary if more than one statement is to be executed within the `if` branch or the `else` branch. *Productivity Hint 6.1* and *Quality Tip 6.1* in your text discuss the use of proper indentation and formatting of braces in your code.

6.2   Comparing Values

6.2.1   *Relational Operators*
An `if` statement performs a test. Many of these tests compare values with relational operators. There are six relational operators:

Table 6.1
Relational Operators

Relational Operator	Meaning	Relational Operator	Meaning
>	Greater than	<=	Less than or equal to
>=	Greater than or equal to	==	Equal to
<	Less than	!=	Not equal to

6.2.2   Comparing Floating-Point Numbers

Relational operators involving integer expressions work as you would expect but you should be very careful when comparing doubles. We talked about limited precision and roundoff errors in Chapter 5. Because of these roundoff errors, doubles should never be compared with `==`. Section 6.2.2 in your text discusses this in detail.

6.2.3   Comparing Strings

We also should not use `==` to compare strings. Strings are objects. If you compare two `String` variables with the `==` operator, you are testing whether they reference the same object. The Java `String` class provides methods to compare strings. These methods are `equals` and `compareTo` and are summarized in Table 6.2.

Table 6.2

`class java.lang.String implements java.lang.Comparable`

Method	Method Summary
`int compareTo(Object other)`	Compares two strings lexicographically. Returns value < 0 if this string is less than `other`. Returns value = 0 if this string is equal to `other`. Returns value > 0 if this string is greater than `other`.
`boolean equals(Object other)`	Compares this string to object `other`. The result is `true` if and only if `other` is not `null` and is a `String` object that represents the same sequence of characters as this object.

Strings are really sequences of characters. Each character has a unique representation that is based on the Unicode encoding scheme. The ordering of characters is such that uppercase characters come before lowercase characters (`'D'` comes before `'a'`). When two strings are compared, corresponding letters are compared until one of the strings ends or the corresponding letters differ (`"cat"` comes before `"catch"`; `"cane"` comes before `"cat"`). Strings are compared *lexicographically* (according to their Unicode values).

Example 6.4

```
String s = "Dog";
if (s.compareTo("cat") < 0)
   System.out.println("Dog comes before cat.");
else if (s.compareTo("cat") < 0)
   System.out.println("cat comes before Dog.");
else
   System.out.println("Dog equals cat.");
```

Example 6.4 prints *Dog comes before cat.* because `'D'` comes before `'c'` in the Unicode encoding scheme. *Advanced Topic 4.5* and *Random Fact 4.2* in your text discuss Unicode. *Appendix B* in your text contains the coding for the U.S. English and Western European characters. Section 6.2.3 in your text presents other examples.

Example 6.5 demonstrates the use of the `String` method `compareTo`. The task of this code segment is to examine three strings and determine and print the value of the string that lexicographically comes first.

Example 6.5

```
1    String string1 = "cat";
2    String string2 = "dog";
3    String string3 = "animal";

4    String firstInOrder = string1;
5    if (string2.compareTo(firstInOrder) < 0)
6        firstInOrder = string2;

7    if (string3.compareTo(firstInOrder) < 0)
8        firstInOrder = string3;

9    System.out.println(firstInOrder);
```

Lines 1–3 create `String` objects and assign values to these `String` objects.

Line 4 `firstInOrder` references `"cat"`.

Line 5 compares `"dog"` with `"cat"`. The expression `(string2.compareTo(firstInOrder) < 0)` evaluates to `false` because `"dog"` is not lexicographically before (<) `"cat"`.

Line 6 is not executed.

Line 7 compares `"animal"` with `"cat"`. The expression `(string3.compareTo(firstInOrder) < 0)` evaluates to `true` because `"animal"` is lexicographically before (<) `"cat"`.

Line 8 `firstInOrder` now references `"animal"`.

Line 9 prints *animal*.

Example 6.6 demonstrates the `String` method `equals` and the differences between `equals` and `==` when applied to strings.

Example 6.6

```
1    String string3 = "animal";
2    String string4 = "animal house";
3    if (string3 == string4.substring(0, 6))    // Evaluates to false
4        System.out.println("EQUAL");
5    else
6        System.out.println("NOT EQUAL");

7    if (string3.equals(string4.substring(0, 6)))  // Evaluates to true
8        System.out.println("EQUAL");
9    else
10       System.out.println("NOT EQUAL");
```

The expression in line 3 evaluates to `false` because `string3` and `string4.substring(0,6)` are not referencing the same `String` object. Line 7 evaluates to `true` because both `String` variables are referring to the same literal string `"animal"`.

Because Java treats strings differently than other objects, the result can be somewhat confusing. *Common Error 6.1* in your text explains this in detail. It is very important to remember that the == operator should not be used with strings or with other objects to test whether two objects have the same contents.

6.2.4   Comparing Objects

If you use == when comparing objects, you are asking whether two object variables reference the same object. If your intention is to check whether the objects are equal in value, you need to call an equals method. This method is provided for Java String objects. With your own classes, you will need to write the equals method. It is not automatically provided for you. The equals method can be defined using any criterion that is appropriate for the class. It is always a good idea to check the class methods to be sure equals is included for any class whose objects you want to compare. Chapter 13 of your text covers equals in more detail. The implementation of equals is not tested in the AP Exams.

It is important to remember that when concatenating two strings, a new String object is created. For example,

```
String stringA = "Super";
String stringB = "man";
```

creates references to String objects.

stringA = ["Super"]

stringB = ["man"]

The code segment

```
String stringC = stringA
stringA = stringA + stringB
```

creates a new String object and stringA now references that new object.

stringC = ["Super"]

stringB = ["man"]

stringA = ["Superman"]

6.2.5   Testing for null

Consider the declaration

```
Car myCar;
```

After this statement is executed, no object is allocated. This declaration does not create an object. The variable myCar is uninitialized. The declaration simply states that the variable myCar may reference a Car object. If you attempt to execute the statement

```
System.out.println(myCar.getMileage());
```

the compiler will complain that myCar has not been initialized.

However, sometimes you want to indicate that an object variable *does not* reference an actual object. Then you use the null reference:

```
Car myCar = null;    // I don't have a car right now.
```

The `null` reference refers to no object.

If your program is organized in such a way that you sometimes initialize a variable with `null`, then you need to include a test before applying a method to such a variable:

```
if (myCar != null) mileage = myCar.getMileage();
```

A run-time error occurs when an attempt is made to invoke a method on a `null` reference. In this case, a `NullPointerException` will be thrown. Exceptions will be covered in more detail in Chapter 13 of this guide and Chapter 15 in your text.

The declaration

```
String name;
```

indicates that the variable `name` may hold a reference to a `String` object. At this point `name` is uninitialized.

```
String name = "";
```

initializes `name` with a reference to an *empty* string—a string of length 0 that has no characters. However,

```
String name = null;
```

initializes `name` with `null`. It doesn't refer to any string at all!

You use the `==` operator (not `equals`) to test whether an object reference is a `null` reference.

Example 6.7

```
String a;    // a not initialized
String b = null;   // b initialized to null
String c = "";    // c initialized to the empty string
System.out.println(a);    // Compile-time error
System.out.println(b);    // Prints null
System.out.println(c);    // Prints nothing
System.out.println(a.length());    // Compile-time error
System.out.println(b.length());    // Run-time error: throws
                                    // NullPointerException
System.out.println(c.length());    // Prints 0
```

Note that *instance fields* are always initialized with some value. If you don't specifically initialize an instance field whose type is a class, then it is initialized with `null`. This is a common cause of programming errors. Consider this example,

```
public class Person
{
    . . .
    private String name;
}
```

If the `Person` constructor does not set the `name` field to a specific string, then it is initialized with `null`. Calling a method on the `name` field, such as `name.length()`, causes a `Null-PointerException`. You should always initialize instance fields in the constructor of the class.

6.2.6 *Dangling* `else`

Because you can nest `if` statements (put one `if` statement inside another), the placement of braces becomes very important. Proper indentation will help you (and others) read your program more easily, but indentation does not control the flow of your program.

Example 6.8

```
int x = 9;
if (x < 4)
   if (x < 7)
       System.out.println("Hello there!");
else
   System.out.println("Have a great day!");
System.out.println("See you soon!");
```

Example 6.8 prints *See you soon!* because the `else` is paired with the *nearest* if. The indentation in Example 6.8 is very confusing and misleading. The example is rewritten with proper indentation in Example 6.9.

Example 6.9

```
int x = 9;
if (x < 4)
   if (x < 7)
       System.out.println("Hello there!");
   else
       System.out.println("Have a great day!");
System.out.println("See you soon!");
```

If the intention of Example 6.8 was to print:

> *Have a great day!*
> *See you soon!*

then braces must be used to clarify the pairing of the `else`. Example 6.10 illustrates this.

Example 6.10

```
int x = 9;
if (x < 4)
{
   if (x < 7)
       System.out.println("Hello there!");
}
else
   System.out.println("Have a great day!");
System.out.println("See you soon!");
```

It is always a good idea to design test cases before you begin to write your code. In this way you can think through your algorithm and plan for all possible conditions that need to be tested. *Quality Tip 6.3* in your text discusses test cases and writing a test plan in more detail.

6.3   Multiple Alternatives

Many times we wish to solve problems that involve complex decisions. If our algorithm involves multiple alternatives, the arrangement of the conditions may determine the correctness of our result. Example 6.3 in this guide provides the basic format for multiple alternatives which we will demonstrate in Example 6.11 below.

Consider the task of printing the letter grade equivalent for a given integer valued grade. You wish to use the following grade conversions.

Numerical Grade	Letter Grade
90-100	A
80-89	B
70-79	C
60-69	D
below 60	F

Example 6.11 performs the task as intended.

Example 6.11

```
if (grade < 60)
   System.out.println('F');
else if (grade < 70)
   System.out.println('D');
else if (grade < 80)
   System.out.println('C');
else if (grade < 90)
   System.out.println('B');
else
   System.out.println('A');
```

If grade has the value 62, the output will be *D*. The conditions are *exclusive*. The conditions are checked until the appropriate one is determined. After this occurs, the other conditions are not checked.

Example 6.12 eliminates the elses in Example 6.11.

Example 6.12

```
if (grade < 60)
   System.out.println('F');
if (grade < 70)
   System.out.println('D');
if (grade < 80)
   System.out.println('C');
if (grade < 90)
   System.out.println('B');
else
   System.out.println('A');
```

This example has a very different result. If grade is 62, the output printed will be:

D
C
B

This is not what was intended! The conditions in this example are not exclusive. A grade value of 62 is less than 70 and also less than 80 and also less than 90!

There can also be different results when ordering the conditions differently. You should always trace your code to ensure that you are solving the problem as intended. Section 6.3 in your text gives other examples dealing with multiple alternatives.

6.4   Using Boolean Expressions

Java has another primitive type, boolean. A Boolean variable has a value of true or false. These values do not convert into numbers. They are not objects. You can perform complicated tests by combining Boolean expressions using the logical operators.

Table 6.3
Logical Operators

Logical Operator	Meaning
!	not
&&	and
||	or

When working with Boolean expressions, it is sometimes helpful to review a truth table.

Table 6.4
Truth Table for Logical Operators

A	B	A && B	A || B	!A
true	true	true	true	false
true	false	false	true	false
false	true	false	true	true
false	false	false	false	true

If a legal grade is defined as a grade between 0 and 100 inclusive, an expression that checks whether a grade is legal (from 0 to 100 inclusive) would be:

```
        if (0 <= grade && grade <= 100)
not
        if (0 <= grade <= 100)   // WRONG
```

The expression that checks whether a grade is NOT a legal grade is:

```
        if (!(0 <= grade && grade <= 100))
or
        if (0 > grade || grade > 100)
```

Negating a Boolean expression can be very confusing. Many errors in programming and on the AP CS Exam are due to incorrect Boolean expressions. De Morgan's Law can be used to simplify complicated Boolean expressions. You can safely expect that the AP Exam will include questions that test your understanding of complex Boolean expressions!

```
!(A && B) is the same as (!A || !B)
!(A || B) is the same as (!A && !B)
```

De Morgan's Law is discussed in *Advanced Topic 6.5* in your text.

A method that simply returns a Boolean value based on a condition can easily be simplified. For example, the method `isLegalGrade` below,

```
public boolean isLegalGrade(int grade)
{
    if  (grade >= 0 && grade <=100)
       return true;
    else
       return false;
}
```

can be simplified to

```
public boolean isLegalGrade(int grade)
{
    return (grade >= 0 && grade <=100)
}
```

Note that the value of the Boolean expression evaluates to `true` or `false`. This value is then returned.

6.4.1   Short Circuit Evaluation

The `&&` operator is used to combine two Boolean expressions. If the first expression evaluates to `false`, the second expression is not evaluated. If the first expression evaluates to `true`, then the second expression is evaluated. If it is `true`, the entire expression evaluates to `true`; otherwise it evaluates to `false`. This is called *short circuit evaluation*. For example, suppose the statement

```
if ((n != 0) && (a / n < minSoFar))
```

is executed when n has the value 0. Since the first Boolean expression evaluates to `false`, the second Boolean expression will not be evaluated so there will be no division-by-zero error. If the first expression evaluates to `true` (n != 0), then the entire Boolean expression will be evaluated.

Short circuit evaluation is discussed in *Advanced Topic 6.4 (Lazy Evaluation of Boolean Operators)* in your text.

6.4.2   Using Boolean Variables

A Boolean variable can be used in a test.

```
if (found) is equivalent to if (found == true)
```

The first method is simpler and easier to read. This is explained in Section 6.4.4 of your text. With the inclusion of relational operators, we have an expanded table of operator precedence.

Table 6.5
Expanded Operator Order of Precedence

Operator Order of Precedence				
++	--			
*	/	%		
+	-			
<	<=	>	>=	
==	!=			
&&				
||				
=	*=	/=	%=	+=	-=

■ Topics That Are Useful But Not Tested

- A sequence of statements that has several alternatives can sometimes be written using a `switch` statement instead of multiple `if` statements. This is explained in *Advanced Topic 6.2* of your text.
- The `String` method `equalsIgnoreCase` may be useful when comparing user input. This method is discussed in Section 6.2.3 of your text.

■ Java 5 Issues

- Java 5 introduces enumerated types. An enumerated type has a finite set of values. For example,

```
public enum Suit { CLUBS, DIAMONDS, HEARTS, SPADES }
Suit s = Suit.CLUBS;
if (s == Suit.CLUBS)
    System.out.println(s);
```

defines and uses an enumerated type that may be very useful if you are writing a program that simulates playing cards. It is unlikely that the AP Exams will test on enumerated types. For more information on enumerated types, see *Advanced Topic 6.3* in your text.

■ Things to Remember When Taking the AP Exam

- In Java we check if x is between two values by writing `if (0 < x && x < 100)`. Do not write `if (0 < x < 100)`.
- Do not use `==` with strings. Use the `String` method `equals` to check whether two `String` variables have the same value.
- Do not use `==` with objects if you want to test whether two objects have the same contents. Use the object's `equals` method for this.
- Remember that the `null` reference is not the same as an empty `String`.

- Remember that a local variable that holds `null` is not the same as an uninitialized local variable.
- When comparing strings lexicographically, use the `String` method `compareTo`. Do not use < or > with strings.
- Be careful of a dangling `else` when nesting `if` statements. Remember that the `else` is paired with the *nearest* `if`.
- Do not compare doubles with the `==` operator. Use a method similar to that explained in Section 6.2.2 in your text.
- Do not confuse `==` with `=`. The `==` operator checks equality. The `=` is used for assignment.
- Know De Morgan's Law. It may help you in writing complex Boolean expressions.
- Indent the body of `if/else` statements. Proper indentation makes your program easier to read.
- Remember that indentation does not control the flow of the program. Use braces to create a block statement to improve legibility and when necessary for flow.
- Be careful not to accidentally place a semicolon after the Boolean expression in an `if` statement.

```
if (grade < 0 || grade > 100);   // WRONG
    System.out.println("Illegal grade entry");
```

will always print *Illegal grade entry*. The interpretation of the above statement is: "If the grade is less than 0 or the grade is greater than 100, do nothing." In all cases *Illegal grade entry* will be printed. On the AP Exam, you are usually not penalized for missing semicolons. However, extra semicolons can cause logic errors and change the intention of the code, which would be penalized.

■ Key Words

You should understand the terms below. The AP CS Exam questions may include references to these terms. The citations in parentheses next to each term identify the page numbers where it is defined and/or discussed in *Java Concepts,* 4th ed., and *Big Java,* 2nd ed.

and (215)	De Morgan's Law (218)	logical operator (215)
block statement (193)	`equals` (197)	nesting (194, 206)
Boolean (214)	expressions (213)	`null` (200)
Boolean operators (215)	`if` (190)	or (215)
`boolean` type (213)	`if/else` (192)	relational operators (196)
condition (190)	indentation (194)	short circuit evaluation (217)
dangling `else` (210)	lexicographic (198)	side effects (201)

■ Connecting the Detailed Topic Outline to the Text

The citations in parentheses identify where information in the outline can be located in *Java Concepts,* 4th ed., and *Big Java,* 2nd ed.

- The if Statement (190–195)
- Comparing Values (196–201)
  - Relational Operators (196)
  - Comparing Floating-Point Numbers (196–197)
  - Comparing Strings (197–199)
  - Comparing Objects (199–200)
  - Testing for null (200)
  - Dangling else (210)
- Multiple Alternatives (201–203)
- Using Boolean Expressions (213–219)
  - Short Circuit Evaluation (217)
  - Using Boolean Variables (218–219)

■ Practice Questions

Multiple Choice

1. Consider the following code segment.

```
x = 6;
y = 19;
z = 2;
if (x > y)
    if (z > x)
        z++;
else
    z -= 5;
y += x;
```

After this code is executed, the values of x, y, and z are:

a. x = 6, y = 25, z = -3
b. x = 6, y = 19, z = 2
c. x = 6, y = 25, z = 3
d. x = 6, y = 25, z = 2
e. x = 6, y = 19, z = 3

2. Assume the following declarations have been made.

```
String fName = "Robert";
String lName = "Roberts";
```

Which of the following code segments returns **true**?

```
I.   return (fName == lName.substring(0, fName.length()));
II.  return (fName.equals(lName.substring(0, fName.length())));
III. return (fName.equals(lName.substring(0, lName.length())));
```

a. I only
b. II only
c. III only
d. I and II only
e. II and III only

3. Consider the following code segment.

```
int x = some positive integer value
double a = x;
double c = Math.pow(Math.sqrt(a), 2);
return (a == c);
```

Which of the following statements about the code segment is **true**?

a. A compile-time error occurs because x is not a double.
b. A compile-time error occurs because a method call cannot be a parameter to a method.
c. A run-time error occurs.
d. `true` is returned.
e. `true` or `false` may be returned, depending on roundoff errors.

4. Consider the following segment of code.

```
String word = "compute";
int len = word.length();
int num = 3;
String foo = word.substring(len % num, num);
String hoo = word.substring(num + 1);
if (foo.compareTo(hoo) < 0)
{
   hoo += foo;
}
else
{
   foo += hoo;
}
```

After this code is executed, what are the values of `foo` and `hoo`?

a. foo = "om", hoo = "uteom"
b. foo = "ute", hoo = "omute"
c. foo = "ute", hoo = "uteom"
d. foo = "m", hoo = "utem"
e. foo = "ute", hoo = "mute"

5. In a simplified game of craps you roll 2 dice. If you get a 7 or an 11 on the *first* roll, you win; otherwise the game continues. Given the following declarations,

```
int diceSum;
int numRolls;
```

where `diceSum` holds the sum of the two dice rolled and `numRolls` holds the number of times the dice were rolled, which of the following code segments tests for a *win* and prints *WIN* to the screen if the condition to win, as defined above, is satisfied? Assume `diceSum` and `numRolls` are assigned their values before this code is executed.

I.
```
if (numRolls == 1 && diceSum == 7 || diceSum == 11)
    System.out.println("WIN");
else
    // Game continues
```

II.
```
if (numRolls == 1 && (diceSum == 7 || diceSum == 11))
    System.out.println("WIN");
else
    // Game continues
```

III.
```
if (numRolls != 1 || (diceSum != 7 && diceSum != 11))
    // Game continues
else
    System.out.println("WIN");
```

a. I only
b. II only
c. III only
d. II and III only
e. I and III only

6. Consider the following code segment.

```
int sum = 200;
int n = 0;
if ((n != 0) && (sum / n > 90))
    return sum += sum;
else
    return sum;
```

What is the result when this code is executed?

a. A run-time error occurs when evaluating `sum / n`.
b. A compile-time error occurs when evaluating `sum / n`.
c. `0` is returned.
d. `200` is returned.
e. `400` is returned.

7. Consider the following code segment.

```
String string1 = "Hello";
String string2 = "World";
string2 = string1;
string1 += "There!";
```

After the code is executed, what are the values of `string1` and `string2`?

a. `string1 = "Hello"`, `string2 = "World"`
b. `string1 = "HelloWorld"`, `string2 = "World"`
c. `string1 = "HelloThere!"`, `string2 = "HelloThere!"`
d. `string1 = "HelloThere!"`, `string2 = "World"`
e. `string1 = "HelloThere!"`, `string2 = "Hello"`

Questions 8 and 9 refer to the `Point` class partially defined below.

```java
public class Point
{
    // Constructor
    Point(int x1, int y1)
    {
        x = x1;
        y = y1;
    }

    // Sets new Point coordinates.
    public void setPoint(int num1, int num2)
    {
        x = num1;
        y = num2;
    }

    // Returns x-coordinate of Point.
    public int getX()
    {
        return x;
    }

    // Returns y-coordinate of Point.
    public int getY()
    {
        return y;
    }

    /*
        Returns true if the x-coordinate of this point has the same
        value as its y-coordinate. Returns false otherwise.
    */
    public boolean hasSameXandY()
    {
        // Code goes here
    }

    private int x;    // x-coordinate of point
    private int y;    // y-coordinate of point
}
```

8. A client program needs to check to see whether two `Points` have the same *x*- and *y*-coordinates. Which of the following code segments will test that equality?

I. `if (p1.x == p2.x && p1.y == p2.y)`
   `statement;`

II. `if (p1.equals(p2))`
   `statement;`

III. `if (p1.getX() == p2.getX() && p1.getY() == p2.getY())`
   `statement;`

a. I only
b. II only
c. III only
d. I and II only
e. II and III only

9. Which of the following code segments could replace the body of the `Point` method `hasSameXandY` so that the method returns `true` if the point's *x*-coordinate is the same value as its *y*-coordinate and returns `false` otherwise.

I.
```
if (x == y)
    return true;
else
    return false;
```

II.
```
if ((getX()).equals(getY()))
    return true;
else
    return false;
```

III.
```
if (getX() == getY())
    return true;
else
    return false;
```

a. I only
b. II only
c. III only
d. I and II only
e. I and III only

10. The Boolean expression `!(!A && !B)` is equivalent to

a. `(!A && !B)`
b. `(!A || !B)`
c. `(A || B)`
d. `!(A || B)`
e. `(!A || B)`

Free Response Questions

1. Consider the `Car` class, whose incomplete definition is shown below.

```
public class Car
{
    // Constructor
    public Car(double miles, double milesOnCar,
        double gasTankHolds, double gasTankHas)
    {
        mpg = miles;   // Miles per gallon car gets
        mileage = milesOnCar;   // Total mileage on car
        tankCapacity = gasTankHolds;   // Amount tank holds
        gasInTank = gasTankHas;   // Gas now in tank
    }
```

```
// Returns the gas needed to drive miles (based on mpg).
public double gasNeeded(double numMiles)
{
    // Code goes here
}

// Returns true if the car has enough gas in the tank to drive
// numMiles miles, otherwise returns false.
public boolean enoughGas(double numMiles)
{
    // Code goes here
}

// Updates mileage and gasInTank
// to reflect numMiles being driven.
public void drive(double numMiles)
{
    // Code goes here
}

// If tank is less than half full, fills tank and updates
// gasInTank. Otherwise does nothing.
public void getGas()
{
    // Code goes here
}

// Returns the current mileage on the car.
public double getMileage() {. . .}

// Returns the amount of gas in the gas tank.
public double getGasInTank(){. . .}

private double mpg;
private double mileage;
private double tankCapacity;
private double gasInTank;
}
```

Your solution should not reimplement the functionality provided by methods given in the problem definition, or by the methods written in the previous parts of the problem.

a. Write method `gasNeeded` that will return a `double` indicating the number of gallons of gas needed to make a trip that is `numMiles` long where `numMiles` is the explicit parameter of `gasNeeded`. Use the method header below to write `gasNeeded`.

```
public double gasNeeded(double numMiles)
```

b. Write a method `enoughGas` that is passed a double parameter `numMiles`. The method `enoughGas` will return `true` is there is enough gas in the tank to drive `numMiles` miles. If there is not enough gas in the tank, `enoughGas` will return `false`. Use the method header below to write `enoughGas`.

```
public boolean enoughGas(double numMiles)
```

c. Write the method `getGas` that will fill the gas tank of the car if it is less than half full. If the car has half of a tank of gas or more, `getGas` does nothing. Use the method header below to write `getGas`.

```
public void getGas()
```

d. Write the method `drive` whose parameter is the intended number of miles the car is to travel. However, the gas tank in the car contains a finite amount of gas. If the car has enough gas to travel the specified number of miles, the appropriate private instance variables should be updated. If the car does not have enough gas to make the requested trip, the car should travel until it runs out of gas. The appropriate private variables should be updated.

For example, suppose that a client program constructs a `Car` with the following statement.

```
Car myMini = new Car(25, 600, 20, 20);
```

Examples of calls to `drive` are listed in the table below.

Before call to drive			After call to drive	
gasInTank	mileage	Call to drive	gasInTank	mileage
20	600	myMini.drive(100)	16	700
20	600	myMini.drive(0)	20	600
20	600	myMini.drive(1000)	0	1100

Use the following method header to write your method.

```
public void drive(double numMiles)
```

2. Consider the `Point` class partially defined below.

```java
public class Point
{
    // Constructor
    Point(int x1, int y1)
    {
        x = x1;
        y = y1;
    }

    // Sets new Point coordinates.
    public void setPoint(int num1, int num2)
    {
        x = num1;
        y = num2;
    }

    // Returns x-coordinate of Point.
    public int getX()
    {
        return x;
    }
```

```
// Returns y-coordinate of Point.
public int getY()
{
    return y;
}

// Returns the distance this point is from the point (0,0).
public double getDistanceFromOrigin()
{
    // Code goes here
}

    private int x;    // x-coordinate of point
    private int y;    // y-coordinate of point
}
```

Your solution should not reimplement the functionality provided by methods given in the problem definition, or by the methods written in the previous parts of the problem. Recall that the distance AB between two points A(x_1, y_1) and B(x_2, y_2) is calculated as

$$AB = \sqrt{(x_2 - x_1)^2 + (y_2 - y_1)^2}$$

a. Write the method `getDistanceFromOrigin` that will return the distance between the `Point` and the origin (0,0). Use the following header.

    ```
    public double getDistanceFromOrigin()
    ```

b. A *client* program is to include a method `findFarPoint` that accepts three points as parameters and returns the `Point` that is the farthest away from the origin (0,0). Write your method using the header below.

    ```
    public static Point findFarPoint(Point p1, Point p2, Point p3)
    ```

Assume that `getDistanceFromOrigin` works as intended regardless of what you wrote for part a. Your solution should not reimplement the functionality provided by methods given in the problem definition, or by methods written in part a of this problem.

Assume that no two points are the same distance from the point (0,0).

CHAPTER

(Covers *Java Concepts* Chapter 7)

Iteration

TOPIC OUTLINE

■ Topic Summary

7.1 while Loops

Many applications require us to execute statements (or blocks of statements) multiple times. For example, averaging grades for all of the students in a particular course, printing a calendar of twelve months, processing a payroll for many employees, and any number of other applications involve doing the same task more than once. One way to implement this type of algorithm is to use a while loop. The general form of a while loop is

```
while (condition)
{
    statement;
}
```

Example 7.1 uses a while loop to sum the positive integers less than 10.

Example 7.1

```
int sum = 0;
int x = 1;   // Initializes loop control variable x.
while (x < 10)   // Checks end condition.
{
    sum += x;
    x++;   // Loop control variable updated.
}
// At the termination of the loop, x has value 10.
```

The three important pieces of a loop are initializing the variable(s) that are involved in the condition, testing for the end condition, and advancing the value of the variables involved in the condition so that progress is made toward the termination of the loop. If you don't change the variable value within the loop, you create an endless loop.

Example 7.2

```
int sum = 0;
int i = 1;
while (i < 10)    // Infinite loop
{
    sum += i;    // WRONG! i is not incremented.
}
```

Example 7.2 will add i to sum repeatedly but, because the value of i starts at 1 and never changes, i is always less than 10. The end condition of the loop is never satisfied. This is called an *infinite loop*. *Common Error 7.1* discusses infinite loop errors. When writing a while loop, be sure that the body of the loop makes progress towards the termination of the loop! Consider Example 7.3 below. Try different positive integer values for a and b. Does the body of the loop make progress toward termination? Can you figure out what the value of a represents after the loop terminates?

Example 7.3

```
int a = some positive integer;
int b = some positive integer;

while (a != b)
{
    if (a < b)
        b = b - a;
    else
        a = a - b;
}
```

As long as both a and b are positive integers, the loop terminates when a = b. The value of a (and b) after the termination of the loop is their greatest common divisor (the largest integer that divides evenly into both a and b).

It is common to have off-by-one errors when writing loops. Example 7.4 counts the number of times an "a" occurs in the word "mathematics." This program segment accomplishes this task but there are several places where an *off-by-one* error can occur. We will loop through each letter of "mathematics". Each time an "a" is encountered, a counter will be incremented.

Example 7.4

```
1    String word = "mathematics";
2    int count = 0;
3    String lookFor = "a";
4
5    int j = 0;   // Initialize to 0
6    while (j < word.length())    // Note: < not <=
7    {
8        String temp = word.substring(j, j + 1);
```

```
 9          if (lookFor.indexOf(temp) != -1)
10          {
11              count++;
12          }
13          j++;   // Increment outside if
14      }
```

Possible Off-by-One Errors

- The loop variable starts at 0, not 1, because the index of the first letter in a String is 0. (Line 5)
- The loop test is < word.length() not <= word.length() because the last letter in a String has index length() - 1. (Line 6)
- The variable used as the counter is initialized to 0, not 1 (Line 2)

Off-by-one errors are discussed in *Common Error 7.2* in your text.

7.2   for Loops

Another method for iterative control is a for loop. If you know exactly how many times a block is to be executed, a for loop is often the best choice. The general form of a for loop is

```
for (initialization; test; update)
{
    statement;
}
```

Examples 7.5 and 7.6 add the integers 1 to 10 inclusive. The order in which the integers are added is different but the result is the same.

Example 7.5

```
sum = 0;
for (int i = 1; i <= 10; i++)
{
    sum += i;
}
// At the termination of this loop, i has value 11.
```

Example 7.6

```
sum = 0;
for (int i = 10; i >= 1; i--)
{
    sum += i;
}
// At the termination of this loop, i has value 0.
```

The loop control variable, i, is initialized and the loop test is evaluated. The loop continues while the test is true. The variable i is updated (incremented or decremented) by 1 each time the loop executes. Example 7.7 gives the equivalent while loop for Example 7.6.

Example 7.7

```
sum = 0;
int i = 10;
while (i >= 1)
{
    sum += i;
    i--;
}
```

The initialization, the test, and the update in the `for` header should be related (see Example 7.8). The code to update the loop control variable should occur in the `for` header only, not in the body of the loop (see Example 7.9).

Example 7.8

```
int j = 1;
int k = 8;
for (int i = 0; j <= 10; k = k + 2)    // BAD STYLE!
        // Variables are not related.
{
    j += 2;
    i = i + 1;
    System.out.println(i + " " + j + " " + k);
}
```

Example 7.9

```
for (int i = 0; i <= 10; i++)
{
    sum += i;
    i = i + 1;    // WRONG! Update should occur only in for header.
}
```

It is common to see the loop control variable declared in the header as it is initialized.

```
for (int i = 0; i < 10; i++)
{
    statement;
}
```

A variable declared in this manner cannot be accessed outside the loop. We say that the *scope* of the variable extends to the end of the loop. This is explained in *Advanced Topic 7.2* in your text.

Let us again consider our program of counting the number of times "a" occurs in the word "mathematics." We will again loop through each letter of "mathematics" and each time an "a" is encountered, we will increment a counter.

Example 7.10

```
1   String word = "mathematics";
2   int count = 0;
3   String lookFor = "a";
4
5   for (int i = 0; i < word.length(); i++)
6   {
7       if (word.substring(i, i + 1).equals(lookFor))
```

```
 8           {
 9               count++;
10           }
11      }
```

The possible off-by-one errors still can occur in the same ways.

- The loop variable starts at 0, not 1, because the index of the first letter in a `String` is 0. (Line 5)
- The loop test is `<` `word.length()` not `<=` `word.length()` because the last letter in a `String` has index `length() - 1` (Line 5)
- The variable used as the counter is initialized to 0, not 1 (Line 2)

Think through your intended task and take care when deciding on the initialization, update, and end conditions in your loops.

A `for` loop should be used when a statement, or group of statements, is to be executed a *known* number of times. *Quality Tip 7.1* in your text discusses this. Use a `for` loop for its intended purpose only. *How To 7.1* in your text discusses the appropriate uses for the different types of loops and walks you through the process of implementing a loop.

7.3 Nested Loops

Loops can be nested (one loop inside another loop). One application of a nested loop is printing a table with rows and columns.

Example 7.11

```
final int MAXROW = 5;
final int MAXCOL = 4;
for (int row = 1; row <= MAXROW; row++)
{
    for (int col = 1; col <= MAXCOL; col++)
    {
        System.out.print("*");
    }
    System.out.println();
}
```

This program prints:

```
****
****
****
****
****
```

7.4 Processing Sentinel Values

Occasionally you may wish to process data input until a certain condition is met. Suppose we want to find and print the average grade for an exam given in an AP CS class. Example 7.12 is a possible solution to the problem.

Example 7.12

```
int numGrades = 0;
int total = 0;
System.out.print("Enter number of students.");
int num = get input from user
for (int i = 1; i <= num; i++)
{
    int grade = get input from user
    total += grade;
    numGrades++;
}
if (numGrades != 0)
    System.out.println((double) total / numGrades);
else
    System.out.println("No grades entered.");
```

Although the solution above is perfectly acceptable, it requires the user to input the number of times the loop is to be executed. Example 7.13 demonstrates one possible solution to the same problem that does not require this information.

Example 7.13

```
int numGrades = 0;
int total = 0;

System.out.println("Enter student grade. Enter -1 to Quit.");
int grade = get input from user

while (grade != -1)
{
    total += grade;
    numGrades++;
    System.out.println("Enter student grade. Enter -1 to Quit.");
    grade = get input from user
}
if (numGrades != 0)
    System.out.println((double) total / numGrades);
else
    System.out.println("No grades entered.");
```

The special value that signals the end of the input (–1 in this case) is called a *sentinel* value. This sentinel value must be a value that could not possibly be legal input. We also get the first value from the user before we enter the loop. There are many chances to err with this code. You must be careful when you increment numGrades and when you add the grade to total. You do not want to include the sentinel value as part of your input.

Example 7.14 uses a sentinel value and sets a Boolean variable to indicate the termination of a loop. Example 7.14 is easier to understand than Example 7.13 and doesn't have quite as many chances for errors in incrementing variables. We still have the sentinel value to worry about. This value *must* be a value that is not possible for legal input.

Example 7.14

```
System.out.println("Enter student grades. Enter -1 to Quit.");
int total = 0;
int numGrades = 0;
boolean done = false;
while (!done)
{
    int grade = in.nextInt();
    if (grade == -1)
    {
        done = true;
    }
    else
    {
        total += grade;
        numGrades++;
    }
}
if (numGrades != 0)
    System.out.println((double) total / numGrades);
else
    System.out.println("No grades entered.");
```

Section 7.4 in your text defines a method of using a `String` value for input. The `String` input is then converted to a `double`. Although the conversion methods used are not included in the AP subsets, this method eliminates the need for choosing appropriate numeric sentinel values.

7.5   Random Numbers and Simulations

Random number generators are useful in programs that simulate events. The Java library's `Random` class implements a *random number generator*. This random number generator can produce random integers and random floating-point (double) numbers.

The AP testable subset includes the `java.util.Random` methods listed in Table 7.1.

Table 7.1
class `java.util.Random`

Method	*Method Summary*
`int nextInt(n)`	Returns a random integer in the range from `0` to `n - 1` inclusive.
`double nextDouble()`	Returns a random floating-point number between 0 (inclusive) and 1 (exclusive).

Example 7.15 demonstrates basic calls to the methods of the `Random` class.

Example 7.15

```
Random generator = new Random();
    // Constructs the number generator.

int randInt = generator.nextInt(10);
    // Generates a random integer from 0-9 inclusive.

double randDouble = generator.nextDouble();
    // Generates a random double from 0(inclusive) to 1(exclusive).
```

When writing programs that include random numbers, keep in mind that two `Random` objects created within the same millisecond will have the same sequence of random numbers. For example, if the following declarations are executed in the same millisecond,

```
Random generator1 = new Random();
Random generator2 = new Random();
```

`generator1` and `generator2` will generate the same sequence of random numbers.

A better idea is to share a single random number generator in the entire program. We rarely want to generate identical sequences of random numbers!

Example 7.16 uses the `Random` class to simulate rolling two 6-sided dice until doubles are rolled (the same number appears on both dice). The variable `count` counts the number of rolls it takes to roll doubles.

Example 7.16

```
Random die = new Random();
int count = 1;
while (die.nextInt(6) != die.nextInt(6))
{
    count++;
}
// Count is the number of rolls it takes to roll doubles.
System.out.println("Doubles were rolled on roll #" + count);
```

7.5.1   Loop Invariants (AB only)

A loop invariant is a statement that is true before a loop executes, at the start of each iteration of the loop, and after the loop terminates. Loop invariants can be used to help explain algorithms that are not completely obvious. They are also statements that can be used for proving the correctness of loops. Correctness proofs, though not part of the AP CS subset, are discussed in *Random Fact 7.2* in your text.

Example 7.17

This segment of code is intended to count the number of letters in `word` that are vowels (a, e, i, o, or u).

```
String vowel = "aeiou";
String word = some String;
int count = 0;
```

```
// Loop invariant:
// count = number of vowels in word.substring(0, i)
for (int i = 0; i < word.length(); i++)
{
    if (vowel.indexOf(word.substring(i, i + 1) >= 0)
        count++;
}
```

The `for` loop visits each letter of `word`. If the letter is a vowel, `indexOf` returns a value between 0 and 4 and `count` is incremented. After each execution of the loop, `count` is the number of vowels in the substring looked at so far. The loop invariant is true before the loop executes, after each iteration of the loop, and after the loop terminates. After the loop terminates, `count` is the number of vowels (a, e, i, o, u) in `word`.

A more detailed example of a loop invariant is discussed in *Advanced Topic 7.5* in your text.

■ Topics That Are Useful But Not Tested

- It is sometimes useful to traverse the characters in a string using the `charAt` method of the `String` class. This method uses the primitive type `char` which is not tested on the AP CS Exams. An example of its use is demonstrated in *How To 7.1* in your text.
- Sometimes you may want to execute the body of a loop at least once and perform the loop test at the end of the loop. A `do` loop serves this purpose and is explained in *Advanced Topic 7.1* in your text.
- Several examples in your text get input from the user using the `Scanner` class (Java 5) and print information to the screen using the method `System.out.printf` (Java 5). Both of these Java 5 additions can make testing methods and classes easy.

■ Things to Remember When Taking the AP Exam

- When implementing a `while` loop be sure to initialize the variable(s) that are involved in the condition, test for the end condition, and advance the value of the variables involved in the condition so that progress is made toward the termination of the loop.
- Be careful not to put a semicolon after a `for` loop header or a `while` statement.

    ```
    for (i = 1; i < 10; i++);    // WRONG!
    while (i < 10);    // WRONG!
    ```

- Be sure to use braces where needed for the body of a loop. If in doubt, use the braces.
- Check the initialization and the test condition in your loops. It is common to have an off-by-one error when writing loops.
- Be careful when implementing tables with nested loops. The outer loop controls the rows of the table and the inner loop controls the columns.
- **(AB only)** Know the definition of a loop invariant. You may be asked to choose the correct loop invariant on a multiple-choice question.

■ Key Words

You should understand the terms below. The AP CS Exam questions may include references to these terms. The citations in parentheses next to each term identify the page numbers where it is defined and/or discussed in *Java Concepts*, 4th ed., and *Big Java*, 2nd ed.

`for` loops (241)	nested loops (248)	simulation (260)
infinite loops (236)	random number	variable scope (247)
loop invariants (265)	generator (260)	`while` (232)
(AB only)	random numbers (260)	

■ Connecting the Detailed Topic Outline to the Text

The citations in parentheses identify where information in the outline can be located in *Java Concepts*, 4th ed., and *Big Java*, 2nd ed.

- `while` Loops (232–240)
- `for` Loops (241–248)
- Nested Loops (248–250)
- Processing Sentinel Values (251–259)
- Random Numbers and Simulations (260–265)
  - Loop Invariants **(AB only)** (265–267)

■ Practice Questions

Multiple Choice

1. Consider the following segment of code.

```
String word = "mathematics";
String vowels = "aeiou";
String tempWord = "";
String newWord = "";

for (int i = 0; i < word.length(); i++)
{
   tempWord = word.substring(i, i + 1);
   if (vowels.indexOf(tempWord) >= 0)
   {
      newWord += tempWord;
   }
}
```

After the loop is terminated, what is the value of `newWord`?

  a. `"mathematics"`
  b. `"mthmtcs"`
  c. `"aeai"`
  d. `"aei"`
  e. the empty string

2. Consider the `Die` class as defined below.

```
public class Die
{
    // Constructs an s-sided die.
    public Die(int s) {. . .}

    // Simulates a throw of the die, returning a random integer
    // from 1 to s (the number of sides) inclusive.
    public int cast() {. . .}

    // Private stuff goes here
}
```

The following declaration is made.

```
Die d1 = new Die(6);
```

Which segment of code returns the number of rolls it takes to roll double 1s (both rolls of the die result in the value 1)?

I.
```
count = 1;
int d1 = die.cast();
int d2 = die.cast();
while (!(d1 == 1 && d2 == 1))
{
    count++;
    d1 = die.cast();
    d2 = die.cast();
}
return count;    // Double 1s rolled on roll #count.
```

II.
```
count = 1;
int d1 = die.cast();
int d2 = die.cast();
while (true)
{
    if (d1 == 1 && d2 == 1)
    {
        return count;    // Double 1s rolled on roll #count.
    }
    count++;
    d1 = die.cast();
    d2 = die.cast();
}
```

III.
```
count = 1;
int d1 = die.cast();
int d2 = die.cast();
while (d1 != 1 || d2 != 1)
{
    count++;
    d1 = die.cast();
    d2 = die.cast();
}
return count;    // Double 1s rolled on roll #count.
```

   a. I
   b. II
   c. III
   d. I and III only
   e. I, II, and III

3. Consider the following code segment.

```
for (int i = 0; i < 5; i++)
{
    for (int j = 0; j < 5; j++)
        System.out.print(i * j % 5);
    System.out.println();
}
```

What is the output produced?

   a. *01234*
      12340
      23401
      34012
      40123

   b. *12345*
      12345
      12345
      12345
      12345

   c. *00000*
      01234
      23401
      34012
      40123

   d. *00000*
      01234
      02413
      03142
      04321

   e. *00000*
      00000
      00011
      00112
      00123

4. The following triangle design is to be printed.

   4
   33
   222
   1111

Which of the following code segments correctly prints this design?

```
I.  for (int i = 4; i >= 1; i--)
    {
        for (int j = 4 - i + 1; j >= 1; j--)
            System.out.print(i);
        System.out.println();
    }

II. for (int i = 1; i <= 4; i++)
    {
        for (int j = 1; j <= i; j++)
            System.out.print(4 - i + 1);
        System.out.println();
    }

III. for (int i = 1; i <= 4; i++)
     {
        for (int j = 4; j >= 4 - i + 1; j--)
            System.out.print(4 - i + 1);
        System.out.println();
     }
```

a. I only
b. II only
c. III only
d. I and II only
e. I, II, and III

5. Consider the following code segment.

```
int n = some integer value;
int a = 0;
while (n > 0)
{
    a += n % 10;
    n /= 10;
}
System.out.println("answer is :" + a);
```

Which of the following statements best describes the result of executing this code?

a. *0* is printed.
b. The number of digits in n is printed.
c. The sum of the digits in n is printed.
d. The original value of n is printed.
e. An endless loop results.

6. Consider the code segment below.

```
String word = "computer";
String tempWord = "";
for (int i = word.length() - 1; i >= 0; i--)
{
    tempWord = word.substring(i, i + 1) + tempWord;
}
System.out.println(tempWord);
```

What will be printed when the code is executed?

a.   *computer*
b.   *retupmoc*
c.   *erteutpumpomco*
d.   Nothing will be printed. `tempWord` is an empty `String`.
e.   An error message.

7.   Consider the following code segment in which `IO.readInt()` is a call to a method that reads an integer.

```
String tempSequence = "";
int x = IO.readInt();
int y = IO.readInt();
while (y >= x)
{
    tempSequence += x;
    x = y;
    y = IO.readInt();
}
tempSequence += x;
System.out.println(tempSequence);
```

What is the output if the series of integers being input is: 1 1 2 3 5 4 7 8?

a.   *1 1 2 3*
b.   *1 2 3 5*
c.   *1 1 2 3 5*
d.   *1 2 3 5 4 7 8*
e.   *1 1 2 3 5 4 7 8*

8.   Consider the following code segment where `IO.readWord()` is a call to a method that reads a `String`.

```
String word = IO.readWord();
for (int i = 0; i < word.length() - 1; i++)
{
    if (word.substring(i, i + 1).equals(word.substring(
        i + 1, i + 2)))
    {
        return true;
    }
}
return false;
```

Which of the following describes its results?

a.   Returns `true` if any letter in `word` is repeated, `false` otherwise.
b.   Returns `true` if the first and second letters are the same, `false` otherwise.
c.   Returns `true` if any two consecutive letters are the same, `false` otherwise.
d.   Always returns `true`.
e.   Always returns `false`.

9. Given the following declarations:

```
String vowel = "aeiou";
String word = some String value;
int count = 0;
```

Which of the following segments of code accurately counts the number of letters in `word` that are vowels (a, e, i, o, or u)?

I.
```
for (int j = 0; j < vowel.length(); j++)
{
    String temp = vowel.substring(j, j + 1);
    if (word.indexOf(temp) != -1)
    {
        count++;
    }
}
```

II.
```
for (int j = 0; j < word.length(); j++)
{
    String temp = word.substring(j, j + 1);
    if (vowel.indexOf(temp) != -1)
    {
        count++;
    }
}
```

III.
```
for (int i = 0; i < word.length(); i++)
{
    for (int k = 0; k < vowel.length(); k++)
    {
        if (word.substring(i, i + 1).equals(vowel.substring(
            k, k + 1)))
        {
            count++;
        }
    }
}
```

a. I only
b. II only
c. III only
d. I and III only
e. II and III only

10. Consider the following code segment. **(AB only)**

```
int p = 1;
int i = 1;
int n = some positive integer value;
// Loop invariant
while (i <= n)
{
    p = p * i;
    i++;
}
```

Which of the following statements is a correct loop invariant?

a. $i < n$
b. $0 < i < n$
c. $p = i!$
d. $p = (i - 1)!$
e. $p = n^i$

11. Consider the following code segment.

```
for (int i = 0; i < 5; i++)
    for (int j = i; j < 5; j++)
        System.out.print("*");
```

How many stars will be printed?

a. 5
b. 10
c. 15
d. 20
e. 25

12. Consider the following code segment.

```
int count = 0;
for (int x = 0; x < 3; x++)
    for (int y = x; y < 3; y++)
        for (int z = y; z < 3; z++)
            count++;
```

What is the value of count after the code segment is executed?

a. 81
b. 27
c. 10
d. 9
e. 6

13. Each segment of code below correctly calculates the sum of the integers from 1 to n inclusive and stores this value in the integer variable sum.

```
I.  int sum = 0;
    for (int i = 1; i <= n; i++)
        sum += i;
```

```
II. int sum = 0;
    int i = n;
    while (i > 0)
    {
        sum += i;
        i--;
    }
```

```
III. int sum = (n + 1) * n / 2;
```

Informally, execution efficiency can be viewed as the number of operations performed in a segment of code. For large values of n, which of the following statements is true about the execution efficiency of the above code segments?

a. I is more efficient than II and III because it sums the numbers in increasing numeric order.
b. II is more efficient than I and III because it sums the numbers beginning with the largest value.
c. III is more efficient than I and II because there are fewer operations.
d. I and II are more efficient than III because they are easier to understand.
e. I, II, and III always operate with the same execution efficiency.

Questions 14 and 15 refer to the following code segment.

```
int val = some integer value;
int x = 0;

while (val > 0)
{
    val = val / 2;
    x++;
}
```

14. If *n* refers to the original integer value, *val*, which of the following statements is always true after the loop is terminated?

a. $2^{x-1} = n$
b. $2^x \geq n$
c. $2^x \leq n$
d. $2 \cdot x = n$
e. $2 \cdot n = x$

15. If *val* has the value of 32 before the loop is executed, how many times is the statement

```
x++;
```

executed?

a. 2
b. 5
c. 6
d. 8
e. 16

Free Response Questions

1. Consider the Investment class, whose incomplete definition is shown below.

```
public class Investment
{
    // Constructs an Investment object from a starting balance and
    // interest rate.
    public Investment(double aBalance, double aRate)
    {
```

```
        balance = aBalance;
        rate = aRate;
        years = 0;
    }

    // Interest is calculated and added to balance at the end of
    // each year for y years.
    public void waitForYears(int y)
    {
        // Code goes here
    }

    // Returns the current investment balance.
    public double getBalance() {. . .}

    // Returns the number of years this investment has accumulated
    // interest.
    public int getYears() {. . .}

    // Balance is compounded n times annually for y years.
    public void compoundTheInterest(int y, int n)

    // Other methods here

    private double balance;
    private double rate;
    private int years;
}
```

a. Write the method `waitForYears` for the `Investment` class that will calculate the amount of interest earned in a given number of years. Interest is accumulated and the balance is updated at the end of each year. The table below contains sample data values and appropriate updates.

Starting Balance	Interest Rate	Years (y)	Ending Balance
100.00	5%	10	162.89
500.00	4%	20	1095.56
1000.00	5%	10	1628.89

Implement the method `waitForYears` using the following header.

```
public void waitForYears(int y)
```

b. Write the method `compoundTheInterest` for the `Investment` class that will calculate the amount of interest earned in y years compounded n times per year at an annual interest rate of r%. The method `compoundTheInterest` will update the balance appropriately. For example, if your original balance is $100.00 and you invest your money in a bank with an annual interest rate of 5% compounded quarterly (4 times a year) and you leave your money in the bank for 1 year, the interest and the ongoing balance is calculated as described below.

If your original balance is $100.00, then

After the first quarter, your balance is $100 + (100)(.05/4) = \$101.25$.
After the second quarter, your balance is $101.25 + (101.25)(.05/4) = \$102.52$.
After the third quarter, your balance is $102.52 + (102.52)(.05/4) = \$103.80$
After the fourth quarter, your balance is $103.80 + (103.80)(.05/4) = \$105.09$

Your balance at the end of the year is $105.09.

The private instance variable, `balance`, should be updated appropriately. The table below contains sample data values and appropriate updates.

Starting Balance	Interest Rate	Years (y)	Times Per Year (n)	Ending Balance
100.00	5%	10	12	164.70
500.00	4%	20	4	1108.36
1000.00	5%	10	4	1643.62

Use the method header below to write `compoundTheInterest`.

```
public void compoundTheInterest(int y, int n)
```

2. A modified game of roulette is played as follows. A player has a purse that contains coins. The player bets one coin (chosen randomly from the purse) on a number on the roulette wheel. This modified roulette wheel is shown below.

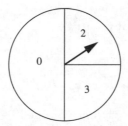

The spinner spins. If the spinner lands on "0", the player gets nothing back. If the spinner lands on "2", the player gets the wagered coin back and an additional coin of equal value. If the spinner lands on "3", the player gets 3 coins of the same value as the coin that was bet.

In this particular version of roulette, you either win big or you lose big because the spinning continues until you double the money in your purse or you have no coins left in your purse! The classes used are:

- The `Spinner` class, used to "spin" the roulette wheel
- The `Coin` class, which defines a coin
- The `Purse` class that holds the coins
- The `Game` class that simulates the roulette game

Incomplete definitions of these classes are below.

```
// The Spinner class is used to simulate the spin.
public class Spinner
{
    // Constructs a spinner with s choices.
    public Spinner(int s) {. . .}
```

```
// Returns an integer from 0 to the number of choices - 1
// inclusive.
public int spin() {. . .}

    // Private stuff here
}
```

```
public class Coin
{
    // Constructs a coin.
    // aValue the monetary value of the coin
    // aName the name of the coin
    public Coin(double aValue, String aName) {. . .}

    // Returns the coin value.
    public double getValue() {. . .}

    // Returns the coin name.
    public String getName() {. . .}

    // Other methods and private stuff here
}
```

```
public class Purse
{
    // Constructs an empty purse.
    public Purse() {. . .}

    // Adds a coin to the purse.
    public void add(Coin aCoin) {. . .}

    // Removes a coin from the purse.
    public Coin removeCoin() {. . .}

    // Returns the total value of the coins in the purse.
    public double getTotal() {. . .}

    // Returns the number of coins in the purse.
    public int coinCount() {. . .}

    // Other methods and private stuff goes here
}
```

```
public class Game
{
    // Game constructor
    // Creates the roulette wheel by constructing the
    // appropriate Spinner.
    public Game()
    {
        // Code goes here
    }
```

```
// Simulates a spin returning a 0, 2, or 3 as defined by the
// roulette wheel pictured in the problem.
public int spinTheWheel()
{
    // Code goes here
}


// Simulates the game of roulette as follows:
// Until the purse total is twice its original value
// or there are no coins left in the purse,
// removes a coin from the purse, and updates the
// number of coins in purse according to the winnings.

// Returns the total value in the purse.
public double playRoulette(Purse myPurse)
{
    // Code goes here
}

    private Spinner myWheel;
}
```

a. Write the `Game` constructor. This constructor should construct a `Spinner` that will be able to appropriately simulate the wheel shown in the problem description above. Notice that all outcomes on the wheel do not have equal probabilities. The constructor for this class simply creates a wheel with a certain number of equally likely outcomes. The probability of the outcomes and the result of a spin are not handled in the constructor.

b. Write the `Game` method `spinTheWheel` that will call `spin` to generate a random number and then return the appropriate number on the roulette wheel. Notice that all outcomes on the wheel do not have equal probabilities. Use the header below when writing `spinTheWheel`.

```
public int spinTheWheel()
```

c. Write the `Game` method `playRoulette` that will simulate the game of Roulette as follows. The following steps of the game continue until the player doubles the original amount of money in the purse or has no coins left in the purse.
   • bet (remove a coin from the purse)
   • spin the roulette wheel
   • accumulate appropriate winnings by adding coins to the purse (updates the number of coins in the purse).

The method `playRoulette` will return the total value in the purse. Write `play-Roulette` using the method header below.

```
public double playRoulette(Purse myPurse)
```

CUMULATIVE REVIEW 1

Chapters 2–7

This review will check your knowledge of material in Chapters 2–7. You should consider this a mini-practice for the AP Exam. Look over the material in these chapters and read over the section *Things to Remember When Taking the AP Exam* below. Have available the Quick Reference Guide or the Exam Reference Materials for the AP Exam that you will be taking. Because you will have reference materials available to you during the exam, you should become familiar with them now. You can download the reference materials for the Computer Science A exam at:

    http://www.collegeboard.com/prod_downloads/student/testing/ap/compsci_a_ref.pdf

and for the Computer Science AB exam at:

    http://www.collegeboard.com/prod_downloads/student/testing/ap/compsci_ab_ref.pdf

■ Things to Remember When Taking the AP Exam

General Guidelines
- Write clear, correct code in answering all free-response questions.
- Do not spend time writing comments in your free-response answers unless your solution needs to be explained or you are specifically instructed to include comments.

Variable Declaration and Initialization
- Declare all variables before you use them.
- Initialize all objects and variables before you use them.
- Do not try to reset an object by calling a constructor. You cannot invoke a constructor on an existing object.

Naming Variables, Parameters, Methods
- When deciding on a variable name, choose a name that describes the purpose of the variable.
- Do not name the variable with the same word as the class name.
- Do not give parameter variables of methods the same names as your instance fields.
- Follow the Java conventions when naming variables, classes, and methods.
- Java is case sensitive. Avoid using names that differ only by case.

Invoking Methods and Returning Values
- When calling methods from a test class (client program), include the implicit parameter in the call.
- Do not use a class name when an object name should be used.

- The `return` statement in a method returns the specified value and exits the method immediately. The type of the value you are returning must match the return type of the method.
- Include a `return` statement if your method is to return a value.

Access

- Do not attempt to access `private` data or methods from outside the class.
- Do not use *magic* numbers in your code. Magic numbers are constants that appear in your code with no explanation. Use defined constants instead.
- In mathematical and logical expressions, use parentheses as you would in algebra.
- Remember that integer divided by integer equals integer. Sometimes casting one of the operands to a `double` is required to obtain a correct result.
- Remember that the first character of a `String` is in position 0.
- The `indexOf` method of the `String` class returns `-1` if the string being searched for is not found.
- The last character of a `String` s is in position `s.length() - 1`.
- When you assign one object variable to another object variable, both object variables reference the same object.
- In Java we check if x is between two values by writing `if (0 < x && x < 100)`. Do not write `if (0 < x < 100)`.
- Do not use `==` with strings. Use the `String` method `equals` to check whether two `String` variables have the same value.
- Do not use `==` with objects if you want to test whether two objects have the same contents. Use the object's `equals` method for this.
- Remember that the `null` reference is not the same as an empty `String`.
- Remember that a local variable that holds `null` is not the same as an uninitialized local variable.
- When comparing strings lexicographically, use the `String` method `compareTo`. Do not use `<` or `>` with strings.
- Be careful of a dangling `else` when nesting `if` statements. Remember that the `else` is paired with the *nearest* `if`.
- Do not compare `doubles` with the `==` operator.
- Do not confuse `==` with `=`. The `==` operator checks equality. The `=` is used for assignment.
- Know De Morgan's Law. It may help you in writing complex Boolean expressions.
- Indent the body of `if`/`else` statements. Proper indentation makes your program easier to read.
- Remember that indentation does not control the flow of the program. Use braces to create a block statement when necessary for flow, and also to improve legibility.
- Be careful not to accidentally place a semicolon after the Boolean expression in an `if` statement or after a `for` loop header or a `while` statement.

```
if (grade < 0 || grade > 100);  // WRONG
for (i = 1; i < 10; i++);   // WRONG!
while (i < 10);   // WRONG!
```

- Be sure to initialize variables used in the loop condition before the loop begins and to adjust their values appropriately inside the loop.
- Use braces where needed for the body of a loop. If in doubt, use the braces.
- Check the initialization and the test condition in your loops. It is common to have an off-by-one error when writing loops.
- Be careful when implementing tables with nested loops. The outer loop usually controls the rows of the table and the inner loop controls the columns.
- **(AB only)** Know the definition of a loop invariant. You may be asked to choose the correct loop invariant in a multiple-choice question.
- When writing code for a free-response question, be sure to hand trace your code to ensure it works for the examples given, as well as several of your own test cases.

■ Practice Questions

Multiple Choice

1. What output is produced by the following code segment?

    ```
    System.out.println("\"One\"");
    System.out.print(2 + "Two");
    System.out.println(" \"Three\"" + 3);
    ```

    a. *"One"*
        2Two "Three"3

    b. *One*
        2Two
        Three3

    c. *"One"*
        2"Two" "Three"3

    d. *"One"*
        2"Two"
        "Three"3

    e. Nothing is printed. There is a syntax error.

2. Consider the following output.

    ```
    *
    **
    ***
    ```

    Which of the following code segments prints the design above?

    I.   ```
         System.out.println("*");
         System.out.println("**");
         System.out.println("***");
         ```

    II.  ```
         System.out.print("*\n");
         System.out.print("**\n");
         System.out.print("***\n");
         ```

    III. ```
         System.out.println("*\n**\n***\n");
         ```

    a.  I only
    b.  II only
    c.  III only
    d.  I and III only
    e.  I, II, and III

3.  Which of the following is **not** a legal string?

    a.  `"//"`
    b.  `"\n\""`
    c.  `"\"\\"`
    d.  `"\n\n"`
    e.  `"\⬛\"`
         ```

4. Which of the following does **not** describe a syntax error?

    a. a misspelled variable name
    b. a missing semicolon
    c. an if statement without parentheses around the Boolean condition
    d. a class definition that has a class name beginning with a lower-case letter
    e. a missing closing brace

5. An object stores its state in

    a. reference variables
    b. instance fields
    c. double variables
    d. a constructor
    e. a String

6. Consider the BankAccount class whose incomplete definition is shown below.

```
// A bank account has a balance that can be changed by
// deposits and withdrawals.
public class BankAccount
{
   // Constructs a bank account with a given balance.
   public BankAccount(double initialBalance)
   {
      balance = initialBalance;
   }

   // Deposits money into the bank account.
   public void deposit(double amount)
   {
      double newBalance = balance + amount;
      balance = newBalance;
   }

   // Gets the current balance of the bank account.
   public double getBalance()
   {
      return balance;
   }

   private double balance;
}
```

Suppose the following statements were executed.

```
BankAccount b1 = new BankAccount(1000);
BankAccount b2 = new BankAccount(500);

b1.deposit(b2.getBalance());
b2.deposit(b1.getBalance());
b1.deposit(b2.getBalance());
```

What are the balances of b1 and b2 after the code is executed?

a. b1 has balance = 1000, b2 has balance = 500.
b. b1 has balance = 3500, b2 has balance = 500.
c. b1 has balance = 3500, b2 has balance = 2000.
d. b1 has balance = 1000, b2 has balance = 1000.
e. b1 has balance = 500, b2 has balance = 1000.

7. What is the result when the following segment of code is executed?

```
for (int i = 0; i < 4; i++)
{
    for (int k = 0; k < i; k++)
    {
        System.out.print(" ");
    }

    for (int j = 4; j > i; j--)
    {
        System.out.print("$");
    }
    System.out.println();
}
```

a. $$$$
    $$$
    $$
    $

b. $$$$
     $$$
      $$
       $

c. $
    $$
    $$$
    $$$$

d. $
       $$
      $$$
     $$$$

e. $ $ $ $
     $ $ $
      $ $
       $

8. Consider the following code segment.

```
int count = 0;
for (int i = 1; i < 5; i++)
    for (int j = i; j > 0; j--)
        count++;
```

After this code segment is executed, the value of count is

a. 0
b. 1
c. 5
d. 10
e. 15

Questions 9 and 10 refer to the following information.

The Internal Revenue Service withholding tax schedule for single people earning no more than $68,800 for the 2003 tax year can be found in the following incomplete table.[1]

If TAXABLE INCOME Is Greater Than or Equal to	But Not Over	The TAX Is This Amount	Plus This %	Of the Excess Over
$0	$7,000	$0.00	10%	$0
$7,000	$28,400	$700.00	15%	$7,000
$28,400	$68,800	$3,910.00	25%	$28,400

The class Taxes, whose incomplete definition is below, is designed to calculate and return the amount of withholding tax as defined by the table above.

```
public class Taxes
{
    /*
        Assumes money >= 0.
        Returns money rounded to the nearest hundredth.
    */
    public static double roundedAmount(double money)
    {
        // Code goes here
    }

    /*
        Assumes income >= 0.
        Returns withholding tax based on tax table.
    */
    public static double calculateTaxAmount(double income)
    {
        // Code goes here
    }

    /*
        Assumes income >= 68800.
        Returns correct withholding tax for income.
    */
    private static double more(double income) {. . .}
}
```

Assume that the method more returns the tax withheld for amounts equal or exceeding $68,800.

9.   Which of the following code segments should replace the body of method calculateTaxAmount?

```
I.   if (income >= 0 && income < 7000)
         return 0.10 * income;
     if (7000 <= income && income < 28400)
         return 700 + 0.15 * (income - 7000);
     if (28400 <= income && income < 68800)
         return  3910 + 0.25 * (income - 28400);
     else
         return more(income);
```

---

[1] http://www.irs.gov/formspubs/article/0,,id=109877,00.html

```
II. double tax;
    if (income >= 0 && income < 7000)
        tax = 0.10 * income;
    if (7000 <= income && income < 28400)
        tax = 700 + 0.15 * (income - 7000);
    if (28400 <= income && income < 68800)
        tax = 3910 + 0.25 * (income - 28400);
    else
        tax = more(income);
    return tax;

III. double tax;
    if (income >= 0 && income < 7000)
        tax = 0.10 * income;
    else if (7000 <= income && income < 28400)
        tax = 700 + 0.15 * (income - 7000);
    else if (28400 <= income && income < 68800)
        tax = 3910 + 0.25 * (income - 28400);
    else
        tax = more(income);
    return tax;
```

a. I only
b. II only
c. III only
d. I and III only
e. I, II, and III

10. The method `roundedAmount` will return a `double` that is the result of rounding its `double` parameter to the nearest hundredth. For example,

Method Call	Returns
roundedAmount(7345.045)	7345.05
roundedAmount(7345.053)	7345.05
roundedAmount(7345.00)	7345.00

Which of the following code segments should replace the method body of `roundedAmount` so that the method works as intended and returns a `double` representing money rounded to the nearest hundredth?

```
a. return (int) money * 100
b. return ((int) (money * 100 + .5)) / 100;
c. return ((int) (money * 100 - .5)) / 100;
d. return ((int) (money * 100 + .5)) / 100.0;
e. return ((int) (money * 100 - .5)) / 100.0;
```

11. The first-class mail rate for letters is based on weight and is calculated to be $0.37 for the first ounce and $0.23 for each additional ounce. A partial ounce counts as an ounce. The method `postageDue` should return the cost of mailing a first-class letter given its weight in ounces as its one `double` parameter. Which of the definitions below functions as intended?

```
I.  public static double postageDue(double ounces)
    {
        int tempOunces = (int) ounces;
        double leftOver = ounces - tempOunces;
        if (leftOver > 0)
            tempOunces++;
        return 0.37 + (tempOunces - 1) * 0.23;
    }
```

```
II. public static double postageDue(double ounces)
    {
        int temp = 0;
        double numounces = ounces;
        while (numounces >= 0)
        {
            temp++;
            numounces--;
        }
        return (temp - 1) * 0.23 + 0.37;
    }

III. public static double postageDue(double ounces)
     {
         double temp = ounces - 1;
         return 0.37 + (int) temp * 0.23;
     }
```

a. I only
b. II only
c. III only
d. I and II only
e. I, II, and III

Questions 12–14 refer to the following code segment which simulates an experiment based on the assumption that 10% of the population is left-handed.

```
Random generator = new Random();
double prob = 1.0 / 10.0;   // probability of being left-handed
int count;
int num = 0;
for (int g = 0; g < 500; g++)
{
    count = 0;
    for (int p = 0; p < 20; p++)
    {
        double rand = generator.nextDouble();
        if (rand < prob)
        {
            count++;
        }
    }
    if (count > 2)
    {
        num++;
    }
}
```

12. In the code segment above, how many times is a random number generated?

a. 1
b. 20
c. 21
d. 500
e. 10,000

13. Which description below best describes the value of count after the segment is executed?

    a. count is the approximate number of left-handed people in a population of 10,000 people.
    b. count is the approximate number of left-handed people in a population of 500 people.
    c. count is the approximate number of left-handed people in a population of 20 people.
    d. count is the approximate number of right-handed people in a population of 1000 people.
    e. count is the approximate number of right-handed people in a population of 20 people.

14. Which description below best describes the value of num after the segment is executed?

    a. num is the number of left-handed people in a population of 10,000 people.
    b. num is the number of left-handed people in a population of 20 people.
    c. num is the number of groups of 20 people that had less than 10% left-handed population.
    d. num is the number of groups of 20 people that had more than 10% left-handed population.
    e. num is the number of right-handed people in a population of 10,000 people.

15. After the code segment below is executed, what is the value of t?

```
String s = "computer";
String t = "";
int len = s.length();
for (int x = 0; x < len / 2 ; x++)
{
    t += (s.substring(len - x - 1,len - x));
}
```

    a. "computer"
    b. "retupmoc"
    c. "comp"
    d. "retu"
    e. "pmoc"

16. Consider the following code segment.

```
String s = "mathematics";
String vowels = "aeiou";
int number = 0;
for (int i = 0; i < s.length(); i++)
{
    number += s.indexOf(vowels.substring(0));
}
```

    What is the value of number after the execution of the above code?

    a. 19
    b. 11
    c. 4
    d. −1
    e. −11

17. Consider the following method mysteryRoll that deals with rolling 6-sided dice.

```
public static boolean mysteryRoll()
{
    Random generator = new Random();
    int rand = generator.nextInt(6) + 1;

    for (int i = 0; i < 4; i++)
    {
        int temp = generator.nextInt(6) + 1;
        if (temp != rand)
        {
            return false;
```

```
        }
    }
    return true;
}
```

Which of the following is the best description of the value returned by `mysteryRoll`?

a. Returns `true` if any two rolls of four dice have the same value, `false` otherwise.
b. Returns `true` if the first two rolls of five dice have the same value, `false` otherwise.
c. Returns `true` if all four rolls of four dice have the same value, `false` otherwise.
d. Returns `true` if all five rolls of five dice have the same value, `false` otherwise.
e. Always returns `true`.

18. Consider the following code segment.

```
Random generator = new Random();
int num = 0;
for (int count = 0; count < 6; count++)
{
    int roll = generator.nextInt(2);
    if (roll == 1)
        num++;
}
```

Which of the following is the best description of the value of `num` after the code segment is executed?

a. The number of ones rolled in the tossing of six 6-sided dice.
b. The number of sixes rolled in the tossing of two 6-sided dice.
c. The number of heads rolled in the tossing of two coins.
d. The number of heads rolled in the tossing of six coins.
e. The number of times a coin is tossed.

Questions 19 and 20 refer to the `FunNumber` class whose incomplete definition is below. The `FunNumber` class is intended to provide various methods that return information about the `FunNumber`.

```
// Creates and manipulates a number, which is fun!
public class FunNumber
{
    // Constructs a FunNumber representation of the integer n. Assumes n > 0
    public FunNumber(int n) {. . .}

    /*
        Constructs a FunNumber representation of the String n.
        n is a string representation of an integer.
        Assumes n > 0
    */
    public FunNumber(String n) {. . .}

    // Returns the sum of the integers less than or equal to this
    // FunNumber.
    // Method sumInts goes here
    // Other methods not shown

    private int myNum;
}
```

19. Which of the following statements correctly instantiates a `FunNumber`?

I.   `FunNumber funny = new FunNumber();`
II. `FunNumber funny = new FunNumber(123);`
III. `FunNumber funny = new FunNumber("123");`

a.   II only
b.   III only
c.   I and II only
d.   II and III only
e.   I, II, and III

20. The method `sumInts` is intended to return the sum of the integers less than or equal to the number represented by this `FunNumber`. For example,

```
FunNumber funny = new FunNumber(5);
System.out.println(funny.sumInts());
```

would print *15* because $1 + 2 + 3 + 4 + 5 = 15$.

Which of the following implementations for `sumInts` would return the intended result?

I.   ```
public String sumInts()
{
    String sum = "";
    for (int c = 0; c < myNum; c++)
    {
        sum += c;
    }
    return sum;
}
```

II.  ```
public int sumInts()
{
    int sum = 0;
    for (int c = 1; c <= myNum; c++)
    {
        sum += c;
    }
    return sum;
}
```

III. ```
public int sumInts()
{
    int len = myNum.length();
    int sum = 0;
    for (int c = 0; c < len; c++)
    {
        sum += myNum.substring(c, c + 1);
    }
    return sum;
}
```

a.   I only
b.   II only
c.   III only
d.   I and II only
e.   I, II, and III

## Free Response Questions

1.   The `FunNumber` class returns interesting (or fun) information about the integer representation of itself. The `FunNumber` object can return the number of digits it has, the sum of its digits, whether or not it's a prime number, and whether or not it's a perfect number. An incomplete definition of the `FunNumber` class appears below.
```

```
    // Creates and manipulates a number, which is fun!
    public class FunNumber
    {
        // Constructs a FunNumber representation of the integer n. Assumes n > 0
        public FunNumber(int n) {. . .}

        /*
           Constructs a FunNumber representation of the String n.
           n is a string representation of an integer
           Assumes n > 0
        */
        public FunNumber(String n) {. . .}

        // Returns the number of digits in this FunNumber.
        public int numDigits()
        {
            // Code goes here
        }

        // Returns the sum of the digits in this FunNumber.
        public int sumDigits()
        {
            // Code goes here
        }

        // Returns true if this FunNumber is perfect, false otherwise.
        public boolean isPerfect()
        {
            // Code goes here
        }

        // Returns the FunNumber that is the reverse of this FunNumber.
        public FunNumber reverseNum()
        {
            // Code goes here
        }

        // Returns the string representation of this FunNumber.
        public String toString() {. . .}

        private int myNum;
    }
```

a. Write the `FunNumber` method `numDigits` that returns the number of digits in this `FunNumber`. For example,

```
    FunNumber funny = new FunNumber(12);
    System.out.println(funny.numDigits());
```

would print *2* because there are two digits in 12.

Use the method header below.

```
    public int numDigits()
```

b. Write the `FunNumber` method `sumDigits` that returns the sum of digits in this `FunNumber`. For example,

```
    FunNumber funny = new FunNumber(123);
    System.out.println(funny.sumDigits());
```

would print *6* because 1 + 2 + 3 = 6.

Use the method header below.

```
    public int sumDigits()
```

c. Write the `FunNumber` method `isPerfect` that returns true if this `FunNumber` is perfect, false otherwise. A number is perfect if the sum of all of its proper factors (factors that are less than the number itself) equals the number. The numbers 6, 28, and 496 are perfect numbers because their proper factors sum to equal the number itself.

$$6 = 1 + 2 + 3$$
$$28 = 1 + 2 + 4 + 7 + 14$$
$$496 = 1 + 2 + 4 + 8 + 16 + 31 + 62 + 124 + 248$$

Use the method header below.

```
public boolean isPerfect()
```

d. Write the `FunNumber` method `reverseNum` that returns a `FunNumber` that is the reverse of this `FunNumber`.

```
FunNumber funny = new FunNumber(123);
System.out.println(funny.reverseNum());   // Would print 321.
```

Use the method header below.

```
public FunNumber reverseNum()
```

2. There are many card games that are played with a deck of 52 playing cards. In this deck of 52 cards, there are 13 cards with denominations 2, 3, 4, 5, 6, 7, 8, 9, 10, Jack, Queen, King, Ace in each of four suits (Clubs, Diamonds, Hearts, and Spades). The incomplete `Card` class is below.

```
public class Card
{
    /*
        denom is a one-character card String for the denomination,
        i.e. "2","J","A"
        suit is a one character String designating the suit "S", "H",
        "D", or "C"
        Constructs a card with given suit and denomination.
        myValue is a numerical value determined for each card.
    */
    public Card(String denom, String suit)
    {
        mySuit = suit;
        myDenom = denom;
        myValue = getValue();
    }

    /*
        Returns the card suit determined by the instance field mySuit.
        Returns "Hearts" for H, "Spades" for S, "Clubs" for C,
        or "Diamonds" for D
    */
    public String getSuit()
    {
        // Code goes here
    }

    /*
        Returns the denomination of the card, 2,3,4,5,6,7,8,9,10,
        Jack, Queen, King, or Ace.
    */
    public String getDenomination()
    {
        // Code goes here
    }
```

```
        /*
           Returns the value of the card. The value is the card number
           if the card is between 2 and 10 inclusive, 11 for "J",
           12 for "Q", 13 for "K", 14 for "A".
        */
        public int getValue()
        {
            // Code goes here
        }

        /*
           Returns the String representation of the card,
           i.e. "Ace of Spades" OR "4 of Hearts".
        */
        public String toString()
        {
            // Code goes here
        }

        private String mySuit;
        private String myDenom;
        private int myValue;
    }
```

a. Write the `Card` method `getSuit` that returns the card suit determined by the instance field `mySuit`. The method `getSuit` returns `"Hearts"` for H, `"Spades"` for S, `"Clubs"` for C, or `"Diamonds"` for D. Use the method header below.

```
public String getSuit()
```

b. Write the `Card` method `getDenomination` that returns the denomination of the card: 2, 3, 4, 5, 6, 7, 8, 9, 10, Jack, Queen, King, or Ace as a `String`.

Use the method header below.

```
public String getDenomination()
```

c. Write the `Card` method `getValue` that returns the value of the card. The value returned will be the card number if the card is between 2 and 10 inclusive, 11 for `"J"`, 12 for `"Q"`, 13 for `"K"`, or 14 for `"A"`. Use the method header below.

```
public int getValue()
```

d. Write the `Card` method `toString` that returns the `String` representation of this card. i.e. `"King of Spades"`, `"5 of Diamonds"`. Use the method header below. In writing your solution, you may include calls to methods written in other parts of this problem. Assume these methods work as intended.

```
public String toString()
```

3. In a card game, a player is dealt cards. We call a player's dealt cards a *hand*. In our simplified card game, a `SimpleHand` class will hold two `Card` objects. The incomplete definition of the `SimpleHand` class is below.

```
public class SimpleHand
{
    // Constructs a hand of two cards.
    public SimpleHand(Card c1, Card c2)
    {
        card1 = c1;
        card2 = c2;
    }
```

```
    /*
        Returns true if both cards in the hand are the same
        denomination, false otherwise.
    */
    public boolean isPair()
    {
        // Code goes here
    }

    /*
        Returns true if both cards in the hand are the same suit,
        false otherwise.
    */
    public boolean sameSuit()
    {
        // Code goes here
    }

    /*
        Returns true if both cards in the hand are the same color,
        false otherwise.
    */
    public boolean sameColor()
    {
        // Code goes here
    }

    /*
        Returns total value of the two cards. If the card is a
        numbered card 2-10, the value of the card is that number.
        The value of an Ace is 11 and the value of a Jack,
        Queen, or King is 10.
    */
    public int getTotal()
    {
        // Code goes here
    }

    private Card card1;
    private Card card2;
}
```

a. Write the `SimpleHand` method `isPair` that returns `true` if both cards in the hand are the same denomination, `false` otherwise. For example, `isPair` would return `true` if the hand consisted of two fours or two queens and would return `false` if the hand contained a four and a king. Use the method header below.

```
public boolean isPair()
```

b. Write the `SimpleHand` method `sameSuit` that returns `true` if both cards in the hand are the same suit, `false` otherwise. For example, `sameSuit` would return `true` if the hand consisted of two Clubs or two Hearts and would return `false` if the hand contained a Spade and a Club. Use the method header below.

```
public boolean sameSuit()
```

c. Write the `SimpleHand` method `sameColor` that returns `true` is both cards in the hand are the same color, `false` otherwise. Hearts and Diamonds are red and Clubs and Spades are Black. For example, `sameColor` would return `true` if the hand consisted of two Clubs or a Heart and a Diamond and would return `false` if the hand contained a Spade and a Heart. Use the method header below.

```
public boolean sameColor()
```

d.   Write the `SimpleHand` method `getTotal` that returns the total value of the two cards in the hand. For this game, if the card is a numbered card 2-10, the value of the card is that number. The value of an Ace is 11 and the value of a Jack, Queen, or King is 10. Usc the method header below.

```
public int getTotal()
```

CHAPTER **8**

(Covers *Java Concepts* Chapter 8)

Arrays and Array Lists

■ Topic Summary

8.1 Arrays

It is very common for applications to require us to store a large amount of data and process that data in any number of ways. Up to now, we have dealt only with data that we were able to store in a single field as a primitive data type or as a reference to an object. We will now look at a way to store large amounts of data in a single collection that can be referred to with a single variable.

An *array* is a fixed-length sequence of values of the same type. One-dimensional arrays store linear sequences of primitive types or references to objects. When we use arrays to store data we can easily and quickly access a single element in the sequence. We can explicitly overwrite an element at a specified position in the sequence, thus changing its value. We can easily and quickly inspect the element at a specified location in the sequence.

When an array variable is declared, it must be given a length before adding elements to it.

Example 8.1

```
private static final int MAX_ELEMENTS = 10;
int[] array1 = new int[MAX_ELEMENTS];
    // array1 is an array of 10; int values initialized to 0
for (int i = 0; i < MAX_ELEMENTS; i++)
{
   array1[i] = i;   // array1 = { 0 1 2 3 4 5 6 7 8 9 }
}
System.out.println("Printing array1");
for (int i = 0; i < array1.length; i++)
   // length is attribute of array1
   // Notice that this is NOT a method call
{
   System.out.print(array1[i] + " ");   // 0 1 2 3 4 5 6 7 8 9
}
```

Arrays can also be instantiated using initializer lists. Example 8.2 below and *Advanced Topic 8.1* in your text give an example of initializer lists.

Example 8.2

```
int[] array2 = { 10, 20, 30, 40, 50, 60, 70, 80 };
    // Initializer list
System.out.println("Printing array2");
for (int i = 0; i < array2.length; i++)   // array2's length is 8
{
   System.out.print(array2[i] + " ");   // 10 20 30 40 50 60 70 80
}
```

When you declare an array of a certain size, its length is fixed. What happens if you run out of room before you are done filling it? If this happens, you could create another array that is twice as large as the first, copy all of the elements from the first array to the second, and assign the reference of the first array to the second. Example 8.3 demonstrates this technique.

Example 8.3

```
int currentLength = array1.length;
int[] copyOfarray1 = new int[2 * currentLength];
   // copyOfarray1 is twice as big as array1

for (int i = 0; i < currentLength; i++)
{
   copyOfarray1[i] = array1[i];
      // Primitive types copied (ints) and the rest of the
      // elements of copyOfarray1 are initialized to 0.
}

System.out.println("Printing copyOfarray1");
for (int i = 0; i < copyOfarray1.length; i++)
{
   System.out.print(copyOfarray1[i] + " ");
      // 0 1 2 3 4 5 6 7 8 9 0 0 0 0 0 0 0 0 0 0
```

```
        }
        array1 = copyOfarray1;      // length = 20
                                    // current number of values = 10
                                    // currentLength is 10
```

As you can see in Example 8.3, the number of elements you actually put into the new array may be different from the new array's `length`. Working with arrays will often require that you keep track of the number of filled elements with another variable. After the code in Example 8.3 is executed, `array1` has room for more elements (`int`s in this case). The next `int` value would be assigned to `array1[10]` because this is the first available location. The variable `currentLength` keeps track of the current number of filled elements and therefore the position to which the next element will be added. When an element is added to the new array, `currentLength` should be incremented. *Advanced Topic 8.4* in your text discusses partially-filled arrays.

Also remember to be careful when copying elements from one array to another. If your array contains *objects*, you are dealing with references. Example 8.4 below makes a *shallow* copy of the array `coins`. This means that *references* are copied, not actual objects.

Example 8.4

```
1     final int MAX_ELEMENTS = 3;
2     Coin[] coins = new Coin[MAX_ELEMENTS];
3     coins[0] = new Coin(0.05, "nickel");
4     coins[1] = new Coin(0.10, "dime");
5     coins[2] = new Coin(0.01, "penny");

6     // Copies references to coin objects into money.
7     Coin[] money = new Coin[MAX_ELEMENTS];
8     for (int i = 0; i < coins.length; i++)
9     {
10        money[i] = coins[i];
11    }
```

Line 2 declares an array `coins` that will hold references to three `Coin`s.
Lines 3–5 construct `Coin` objects and assign an array reference to each `Coin` object.
Line 8–11 loop through the `coins` array.
Line 10 assigns references.

After execution of code:

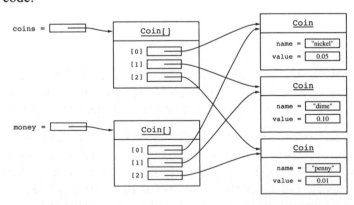

A change to the object referenced by coins [1] would also result in a change to the information referenced by money [1]. If it is your intention to actually have a copy of the array then take care to create a new object for each object that you want to copy. Example 8.5 performs a *deep* copy. This means that the actual objects are copied.

Example 8.5

```
1    final int MAX_ELEMENTS = 3;
2    Coin[] coins = new Coin[MAX_ELEMENTS];
3    coins[0] = new Coin(0.05, "nickel");
4    coins[1] = new Coin(0.10, "dime");
5    coins[2] = new Coin(0.01, "penny");
6
7    // Copies coins into money.
8    Coin[] money = new Coin[MAX_ELEMENTS];
9    for (int i = 0; i < coins.length; i++)
10   {
11      Coin temp = new Coin(coins[i].getName(), coins[i].getValue());
12      money[i] = temp;
13   }
```

Line 2 declares an array coins that will hold three Coins.
Lines 3–5 construct Coin objects and assign an array reference to each Coin object.
Line 9–13 loop through the coins array.
Line 11 constructs a new Coin object that is a copy of the corresponding Coin object in coins.
Line 12 stores a reference to this new Coin in the corresponding position in the money array.

After execution of code:

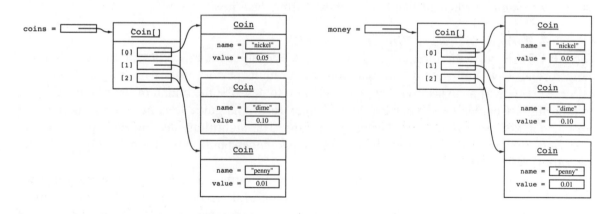

8.1.1   A Word about Efficiency

In inserting and removing elements from an array, we must manipulate the array elements. To insert an element at the end of the array (as the last element), we must make sure the array has room. If there is enough room, we simply add the element in the first available position.

If we want to insert an element into an array in position 0, we must first make sure we have room. We do not want to replace the element in position 0, so all of the elements in the array need to be shifted before the element is added to position 0. You need to think about the order in which the shifting occurs. For example, if you want to insert newValue into arrayName in position 0, the following code segment will NOT perform the intended task!

```
    // numElements is the number of filled elements in arrayName
    if (numElements < arrayName.length())   // Is there room?
    {
        for (int i = 1; i <= numElements; i++)
        {
            arrayName[i] = arrayName[i - 1];   // WRONG
        }
        arrayName[0] = newValue;
        numElements++;
    }
```

The `for` loop above will overwrite all of the elements of the array with whatever is in the original `arrayName[0]`. That is NOT the intended result! The code segment below will accomplish the intended task if the array has room.

```
    // numElements is the number of filled elements in arrayName.
    if (numElements < arrayName.length())   // Is there room?
    {
        for (int i = numElements; i > 0; i--)
        {
            arrayName[i] = arrayName[i - 1];   // CORRECT
        }
        arrayName[0] = newValue;
        numElements++;
    }
```

When removing the last element of an array, no shifting of elements is necessary. However, removing an element in position 0 requires all of the elements in the array to be shifted! The number of filled elements, tracked by another variable (`numElements` in the above examples), will be decremented when an element is removed from the array.

8.1.2 A Formal Analysis of Efficiency (AB only)

The AP CS AB curriculum requires you to be able to analyze the efficiency of an algorithm in a more formal way. You should understand how algorithms perform as a data set gets larger and larger. This type of analysis uses *"big-Oh"* notation to describe the bound of the running time of an algorithm. Chapter 19 of your text and Chapter 16 of this guide look at several examples of big-Oh notation with more complicated algorithms. The algorithms dealing with inserting and removing elements of an array are relatively simple to understand, so the formal analysis of these algorithms is included here.

- When adding an element to the end of the array, no shifts are necessary. Assuming that we know the array index of the first available position in the array, we can insert this element and update the value of the variable holding the number of filled array elements if appropriate. This is done in constant time. The big-Oh analysis of this running time is $O(1)$.

- When removing the last element of an array, no shifting of elements is necessary. Assuming that we know the index of the last filled position, we simply subtract 1 from the value of the variable that keeps track of the number of elements we have in the array. Again, this is done in constant time. The analysis of the running time is $O(1)$.

- When inserting an element in position 0, we must shift all of the elements in the array to the right one. Only after that is done should we insert the new value in position 0 and update the value of the variable holding the number of filled elements in the array. If there are n elements in our array, this requires approximately n operations. The analysis of the running time is therefore $O(n)$.

- When removing an element from position 0, we must shift all of the elements in the array to the left one and update the value of the variable holding the number of filled elements in the array. If there are *n* elements in our array, this requires approximately *n* operations. The analysis of the running time is $O(n)$.

8.2   Array Lists

An array list is a sequence of objects that grows and shrinks as needed. Unlike the array, the array list does not have to be given a size when it is instantiated. This Java construct provides us with a means to easily deal with large amounts of data. The `ArrayList` class is part of the `java.util` package of the Java standard class library. There are many advantages to using array lists to store data, including

- Each element in the sequence can be accessed separately.
- We can explicitly overwrite an object at a specified location in the sequence, thus changing its value.
- We can inspect the object at a specified location in the sequence.
- We can add an object to a specified location in the sequence.
- We can add an object to the end of the sequence.
- We can remove an object from a specified location in the sequence.

Although the `ArrayList` class has many methods, only those listed in Table 8.1 are included in the AP Java subset to be tested on the AP CS Exam. Example 8.6 demonstrates `ArrayList` methods.

Table 8.1
class `java.util.ArrayList`

Method	Method Summary
`boolean add(Object x)`	Adds x to the end of the list and adjusts the size of the array list.
`void add(int index, Object x)`	Inserts x at position `index`, sliding elements at position `index` and higher to the right (adds 1 to their indices), and adjusts size.
`Object get(int index)`	Returns the element at `index`.
`Object remove(int index)`	Removes the element at position `index`, sliding elements at position `index + 1` and higher to the left (subtracts 1 from their indices), and adjusts size.
`Object set(int index, Object x)`	Replaces the element at `index` with x and returns the element formerly at the specified position.
`int size()`	Returns the number of elements in this list.
`Iterator iterator()` (AB only)	Returns an iterator over the elements in this list in proper sequence.

It is important to remember that an array list contains references to *objects*. With Java 5, we specify the type of object our array list will reference. This is referred to as a *parameterized* (or typed) array list or the *generic* `ArrayList` class. The examples in your text use Java 5's generic `ArrayList` class. If a prior version of Java is used, our array lists are *untyped*. They are simply array lists that contain `Objects`. Because of this, when we access elements from the untyped array list, many times we must *cast* the element to its appropriate type before we can invoke the object's methods. In this guide, as in your text, we will use primarily the generic `ArrayList` class but will include examples and review questions using the untyped array list as well. When Java 5 is used, the example or question will indicate this. For the AP Exam, you may write answers to free-response questions using either unless specified otherwise.

We will examine array list methods by looking at a simple example. As you read through the following array list example, think about the order in which the array list is being built.

Example 8.6

```
1    import java.util.ArrayList;
2
3    public class ArrayListTester
4    {
5       public static void main(String[] args)
6       {
7          ArrayList students = new ArrayList();
8             // Java 5 declaration would be
9             // ArrayList<String> students = new ArrayList<String>();
10
11         students.add("Mary");
12         students.add("James");
13         students.add("Kevin");
14
15         students.add(1, "Tanya");
16
17         String temp = (String) students.get(3);
18             // Java 5 assignment would be
19             // String temp = students.get(3);
20
21         System.out.println(temp);
22         students.remove(2);
23
24         students.set(1, "John");
25         System.out.println(students.size());
26      }
27   }
```

Line 1 imports the `ArrayList` class contained in the `java.util` package.

Line 7 constructs an `ArrayList`. This `ArrayList` is empty.

Line 9 is a comment containing the Java 5 equivalent to line 7.

Lines 11, 12, and 13 add `String` objects to the `ArrayList`, each at the end of the list. At this point, `students` contains [Mary, James, Kevin].

Line 15 inserts "Tanya" into position 1 of `students`.

- The first position in an `ArrayList` has index 0. At this point, `students` contains [Mary, Tanya, James, Kevin].

Line 17 accesses the object in position 3 and assigns this to the `String` variable `temp`.

- `temp` is a `String` so you must *cast* the `ArrayList` Object to a `String`.

Line 19 is a comment containing the Java 5 equivalent of line 17.

Line 21 prints *Kevin*.

Line 22 removes "James" from `students`. At this point, `students` contains [Mary, Tanya, Kevin].

Line 24 overwrites the object in position 1 thus changing "Tanya" to "John". At this point, `students` contains [Mary, John, Kevin].
Line 25 prints *3*.

Although Example 8.6 deals with `String` objects, array lists can contain references to any type of objects. Section 8.2 of your text uses `BankAccount` objects to demonstrate these same methods with the generic `ArrayList` class.

8.2.1   *Another Word about Efficiency*

To add a student into a specific position in the array list requires one call to the `ArrayList` method `add`. From Example 8.6,

```
students.add(1, "Tanya"); // Adds Tanya to position 1 of students.
```

or, more generally

```
students.add(p, name);    // Adds name to position p of students.
```

The "hidden" implementation of this operation requires much more work than is visible to us with that one simple call! When the `add` method is called with two parameters, the elements in the `ArrayList` starting at position p (specified by first parameter) are each shifted "up" one position so that the new object can be inserted in the requested position. Of course, the "hidden" implementation takes care of making room for our addition and shifting the elements (adjusting the indices) correctly.

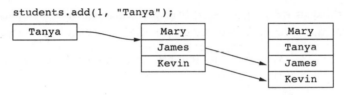

The `remove` method of the `ArrayList` class also requires more work than is evident to us. In Example 8.1, the call

```
students.remove(2);    // Removes Object in position 2 of students.
```

or, more generally

```
students.remove(p);    // Removes Object in position p of students.
```

removes the object is position p and shifts elements with indices greater than p "down" one.

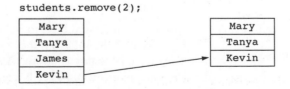

The "hidden" implementation again takes care of adjusting the `ArrayList` size and shifting the elements (adjusting the indices) correctly so we now must be careful not to index the out-of-bounds element by calling `students.get(3)`!

The `size`, `get`, and `set` methods operate in constant time. This means that the efficiency is not dependent on the size of the array list. These operations are very efficient. The `add` operation's hidden implementation shifts elements. If we add an element to the end of the array list, no shifts are necessary. If we add an element to an array list in position 0, all of the elements in the array list need to be shifted. With the `remove` operation, removing the last element requires no shifting of elements. Removing an element in position 0 requires all of the elements in the array list to be shifted.

8.2.2   *A Formal Analysis of Efficiency (AB only)*
The formal analysis for inserting and removing an element in an array list is the same as for the array.
- Inserting an element at the beginning of an array list is $O(n)$.
- Inserting an element at the end of an array list is $O(1)$.
- Removing an element from the beginning of an array list is $O(n)$.
- Removing an element from the end of an array list is $O(1)$.

Although we only include one statement to accomplish each of the tasks above, the hidden implementation may require much more work.

8.3   Wrappers and Auto-boxing

One of the advantages of using array lists is that an array list grows dynamically. The size of the array list is not fixed. But array lists must contain references to objects. Numbers are not objects. In order to store doubles or integers in array lists you must use *wrapper* classes. These wrapper classes wrap numbers into objects. You can then store references to these objects in array lists.

The methods of the `Integer` wrapper class that are tested on the AP CS Exam are listed in Table 8.2.

Table 8.2
class java.lang.Integer implements java.lang.Comparable

Method	*Method Summary*
`Integer(int value)`	Constructs an object that represents the specified `int` value.
`int intValue()`	Returns the value of this `Integer` as an `int`.
`boolean equals(Object other)`	Compares this object to `other`. The result is `true` if and only if the argument is not `null` and is an `Integer` object that contains the same `int` value as this object.
`String toString()`	Returns a `String` object representing this `Integer`'s value.
`int compareTo(Object other)`	Compares this `Integer` object to `other`. If the object is an `Integer`, returns the value 0 if the argument is an `Integer` numerically equal to this `Integer`; a value less than 0 if `other` is an `Integer` numerically greater than this `Integer`; and a value greater than 0 if `other` is an `Integer` numerically less than this `Integer`. If the object is not an `Integer`, it throws a `ClassCastException` (because `Integer` objects are only comparable to other `Integer` objects).

8.4   The Enhanced `for` Loop

With Java 5, conversion between primitive types and their corresponding wrapper classes is automatic. With older versions of Java, this is not true and you must invoke the appropriate method calls to *"unbox"* the wrapper class object. The following two code segments demonstrate the difference between Java 5 and older versions of Java.

Versions before Java 5:

```
Integer n = new Integer(123);
int num = n.intValue();
```

Java 5:

```
Integer n = new Integer(123);
int num = n;    // Auto-unboxing provided in Java 5
```

These conversion details are explained in Section 8.3 in your text.

You should be familiar with the simple array list algorithms that are discussed in Section 8.5 of your text. These algorithms include searching for a specific item in an array list, counting occurrences of some value in the list, and finding the minimum value or maximum value in the list. In many of these algorithms, an array list is traversed. We can do this with a simple `for` loop.

Example 8.7

```
for (int i = 0; i < students.size(); i++)
{
   String temp = (String) students.get(i);
   // Process temp
   // Remember that an untyped ArrayList contains Objects and
   // casting the Object may be necessary.
   // A generic ArrayList requires no casting.
}
```

Java 5 introduces the enhanced `for` loop. This is a shortcut method used to visit each element in the array or array list. Example 8.8 demonstrates the enhanced `for` loop.

Example 8.8 (Java 5)

```
ArrayList<Student> mathClass = new ArrayList<Student>();
. . . // ArrayList filled here

for (Student s : mathClass)
{
   System.out.println(s.getId());
}
```

The enhanced `for` loop is discussed in Section 8.4 of your text.

8.5   Simple Array Algorithms

Suppose we wish to write a program that generates some random number of random integers. These integers will be stored in an array list. The contents of the array list will be printed to the screen and the largest number in the array list will be found and printed to the screen. Let's look at a few methods that might help us accomplish these tasks. Examples 8.9 and 8.10 use an untyped `ArrayList`.

Example 8.9   Filling the List

```java
public static ArrayList generateRandomIntegers(ArrayList nums)
{
    final int UPLIMIT = some positive integer value;
    final int TOPNUM = some positive integer value;
    Random generator = new Random();
    int rnum;
        // Generates the number of numbers that nums will have.
        // 0 <= numberOfNums < UPLIMIT
    int numberOfNums = generator.nextInt(UPLIMIT);
    for (int i = 0; i < numberOfNums; i++)
    {
        rnum = generator.nextInt(TOPNUM);    // A random int,
                                             // 0 <= rnum < TOPNUM
        nums.add(new Integer(rnum));    // Wrapped in Integer
    }
    return nums;
}
```

Example 8.10   Printing the List

```java
public static void printArrayList(ArrayList nums)
{
    for (int i = 0; i < nums.size(); i++)
    {
        System.out.print(nums.get(i) + " ");
    }
    System.out.println();
}
```

Notice that `nums.get(i)` returns an `Object`. When included in the `System.out.print` statement, the `toString` method of the `Object` (in this case an `Integer`) returned by `get` is called. This results in the intended output of the integers. We will discuss this call to the `toString` method in more detail in Chapters 11 and 12.

Example 8.11 prints the contents of a typed `ArrayList` of `Integers` using the enhanced `for` loop ("for each" loop).

Example 8.11   Printing the List (Java 5)

```java
public static void printArrayList(ArrayList<Integer> nums)
{
    for (int i : nums)    // Each element in nums is visited.
    {
        System.out.print(i + " ");    // The toString method of each
                                      // element in nums is invoked.
    }
```

```
            System.out.println();
    }
```

The next example demonstrates finding the largest number in a generic `ArrayList`. This example uses the enhanced `for` loop as well as the Java 5 *auto-boxing/unboxing* feature. This feature automatically *unboxes* the wrapper class object to a primitive type. Auto-boxing is explained in Section 8.3 of your text.

Example 8.12   Finding the Largest Number in the List (Java 5)

```
    public static int findLargest(ArrayList<Integer> nums)
    {
        int large = nums.get(0);    // Initializes large to
                                    // first element (unboxes)
        for (Integer i : nums)
        {
            if (i > large)    // Compares each element to large
            {
                large = i;    // Assigns value to large if larger
                              // value found (unboxes)
            }
        }
        return large;    // Returns the int value of large
    }
```

Example 8.13 performs the same task without the Java 5 features.

Example 8.13   Finding the Largest Number in the List

```
    public static int findLargest(ArrayList nums)
    {
        Integer large = (Integer) nums.get(0);    // Initializes large
                                                  // to first element
        for (int i = 0; i < nums.size(); i++)
        {
            Integer tempLarge = (Integer) nums.get(i);
            if (tempLarge.compareTo(large) > 0)    // Compares each
                                                   // element to large
            {
                large = tempLarge;    // Reassigns to large if larger
                                      // value found
            }
        }
        return large.intValue();    // Returns the int value of large
    }
```

An alternate method for finding the largest value in an array list can be found in Section 8.5.3 in your text. You should understand that storing wrapped numbers is inefficient. If possible, arrays should be used to store primitive types.

You are also responsible for the `Double` wrapper class. The `Double` wrapper class is very similar to the `Integer` wrapper class. The methods tested on the AP CS Exam are listed in Table 8.3.

Table 8.3

class java.lang.Double implements java.lang.Comparable

Method	Method Summary
Double(double value)	Constructs an object that represents the specified double value.
double doubleValue()	Returns the value of this Double as a double.
boolean equals(Object other)	Compares this object to other. The result is true if and only if the argument is not null and is a Double object that contains the same double value as this object.
String toString()	Returns a String object representing this Double's value.
int compareTo(Object other)	Compares this Double object to other. If the object is a Double, returns the value 0 if the argument is a Double numerically equal to this Double; a value less than 0 if other is a Double numerically greater than this Double; and a value greater than 0 if other is a Double numerically less than this Double. If the object is not a Double, it throws a ClassCastException (because Double objects are only comparable to other Double objects).

8.6   Two-Dimensional Arrays *(AB only)*

Occasionally we want to store data in the form of a table consisting of rows and columns. Examples include airline or movie theater seating, survey results, or even a tic-tac-toe game (really, any board game). To construct such a table variable (*matrix*) we need to specify the number of rows and columns that we have.

```
final int ROWS = 3;
final int COLUMNS = 4;
int[][] table = new int[ROWS][COLUMNS];
```

This declaration results in a table with 12 ints.

table[0][0]	table[0][1]	table[0][2]	table[0][3]
table[1][0]	table[1][1]	table[1][2]	table[1][3]
table[2][0]	table[2][1]	table[2][2]	table[2][3]

table.length = 3 is the number of rows.
table[0].length = 4 is the number of columns.

You can also use initializer lists to instantiate two-dimensional arrays.

```
int[][] table2 = {{1, 2, 3, 4}, {5, 6, 7, 8}, {9, 10, 11, 12}};
```

would result in the following 2-dimensional array being created.

1	2	3	4
5	6	7	8
9	10	11	12

Many of the problems involving two-dimensional arrays deal with visiting all of the elements in the table. We usually do this with nested loops, where the outer loop traverses the rows and the inner loop traverses the columns. Example 8.14 prints the contents of `table2` in the order shown in the table above.

Example 8.14

```
1    int[][] table2 = {{1, 2, 3, 4}, {5, 6, 7, 8}, {9, 10, 11, 12}};
2    for (int row = 0; row < table2.length; row++)
3    {
4       for (int col = 0; col < table2[0].length; col++)
5       {
6          System.out.print(table2[row][col] + "\t");
7                // \t tabs between columns
8       }
9       System.out.println();   // Advance to next line for next row.
10   }
```

Line 1 instantiates `table2` using initializer lists.

Line 2 loops through the rows of `table2`. Note that `table2.length` is the number of rows in `table2`.

Line 4 loops through the columns of `table2`. Note that `table2[0].length` is the number of columns.

Although Java allows for two-dimensional arrays where each row has a different number of columns (ragged arrays), this will not be tested on the AP CS Exam.

■ Expanded Coverage of Material That is Not Found in the Text

ArrayList Iterators (AB only)

The AB Exam may also include questions on traversing an `ArrayList` using an `Iterator`. The Java `ArrayList` class implements the `Iterator` interface. An `ArrayList` iterator works very much like the `ListIterator` described for linked lists in Chapter 20 of your text. The methods of the `Iterator` interface that will be tested on the AP CS AB Exam are listed in Table 8.4.

Table 8.4

`interface java.util.Iterator`

Method	Method Summary
`boolean hasNext()`	Returns `true` if the iteration has more elements.
`Object next()`	Returns the next element in the iteration.
`void remove()`	Removes the last element returned by `next`.

Consider the `for` loop we used to access our untyped `ArrayList` entries in Example 8.7.

```
for (int i = 0; i < students.size(); i++)
{
    String temp = (String) students.get(i);
    // Process temp
}
```

This `for` loop can be replaced by the code in Example 8.15 that implements the use of an `Iterator`.

Example 8.15

```
Iterator it = students.iterator();
while (it.hasNext())
{
   String temp = (String) it.next();
   // Process temp
}
```

or

```
for (Iterator it = students.iterator(); it.hasNext();)
{
   String temp = (String) it.next();
   // Process temp
}
```

Example 8.16 demonstrates the movement of an `Iterator` in an `ArrayList`. It uses iterators to demonstrate the same operations that Example 8.6 demonstrated. The initial position of the `Iterator` is before the first element of the `ArrayList`. The `next` method advances the `Iterator`. The `remove` method removes and returns the element that was last referenced by the `next` method. Be careful not to call `remove` more than once after a call to `next` because the first `remove` removes the object that was last referenced by the `next` method. The second `remove` will try to remove an item that's no longer there!

Example 8.16 (Java 5)

```
import java.util.ArrayList;
import java.util.Iterator;    // Need to import class here.

public class IteratorTester
{
   public static void main(String[] args)
   {
      ArrayList<String> students = new ArrayList<String>();

      students.add("Mary");
      students.add("James");
      students.add("Kevin");
      students.add("Tanya");    // Mary, James, Kevin, Tanya (MJKT)

      // The symbol '#' indicates position of iterator
      Iterator<String> it = students.iterator();    // #MJKT

      it.next();    // M#JKT
      it.next();    // MJ#KT
      it.remove();    // M#KT
      // Another it.remove statement here would throw an
      // IllegalStateException.
      it = students.iterator();    // Resets iterator: #MKT
      while (it.hasNext())
      {
         System.out.println(it.next());    // Mary, Kevin, Tanya
      }
   }
}
```

The iterator class is also a generic type. An `Iterator<String>` iterates through an `ArrayList` of strings; an `Iterator<Student>` visits the elements in an `ArrayList<Student>`. If you do not indicate a type for the `Iterator`, the `next` method will return an `Object`. This may require you to cast to an appropriate type as in Example 8.15 above.

■ Topics That Are Useful But Not Tested

- Copying arrays can be done using the static `System.arraycopy` method. This is explained in Section 8.7 of your text.

■ Java 5 Issues

- The generic `ArrayList` class allows us to specify the type of objects the array list will reference. Most of the examples and questions in this guide and the examples in your text use the generic `ArrayList` class. Beginning with the 2007 AP CS exam, questions may include the generic `ArrayList` notation.
- When using iterators with the generic `ArrayList` class, you should use a typed iterator. Example 8.16 demonstrates this concept. If you do not use a typed iterator, the array list element referred to by `next` and `remove` are of type `Object` and will probably need to be cast to the appropriate type.
- Auto-boxing and unboxing is a process that automatically converts between primitive types and their corresponding wrapper types. This eliminates some of the overhead with using wrapper classes. Auto-boxing is explained in Section 8.3 of your text.
- The enhanced `for` loop is a shortcut for a loop that traverses through an array or an arraylist. The enhanced `for` loop will likely be included in the AP CS subset defined for the 2007 exam. The syntax for this loop is explained in Section 8.4 of your text.

■ Things to Remember When Taking the AP Exam

- Remember that the first element of both an array list and an array has index 0.
- The single most common loop error that occurs when dealing with arrays is an out-of-bounds error while the list is being traversed. The tests

```
    while (index <= arrayName.length)    // WRONG
and
    while (index <= arrayListName.size())    // WRONG
```

both try to access an out-of-bounds element. The test should be `<`, not `<=`. Remember that the last element in an array has index `arrayName.length - 1` and the last element in an `ArrayList` has index `arrayListName.size() - 1`. Think carefully about loop bounds when accessing array and `ArrayList` elements.
- Remember that an untyped `ArrayList` stores references to objects. When accessing these objects to process, you will have to cast the object to the appropriate type. When using the Java 5 generic `ArrayList` class, casting is unnecessary.

- Do not confuse `.length` with `.size()`. Remember that `arrayName.length` is an instance variable that holds the length of an array (not necessarily the number of filled elements in the array) and `arrayListName.size()` is a method that returns the number of elements in an `ArrayList`.
- To access the sixth element of an array we write `arrayName[5]`. To access the sixth element of an `ArrayList`, we write `arrayListName.get(5)`.
- Using `equals` with array lists compares references, not contents. `equals` returns `true` if two `ArrayList` references are the same, `false` otherwise.
- When you use `equals` with arrays, you are also comparing references. `array1.equals(array2)` is asking if `array1` and `array2` reference the same array.
- **(AB only)** When visiting elements in a two-dimensional array, do not confuse rows and columns. This is a common mistake on the AP Exam.
- When shifting elements in an array, be careful not to overwrite values of other array elements. It is rare that this is an intended task! Think about the order in which the elements are being shifted.
- Iterators are included in the AB subset only. However, many problems are simplified if an array list is traversed using an iterator rather than looping through the array list with an index. If you are a student in AP CS A, you may want to cover iterators.

■ Key Words

You should understand the terms below. The AP CS Exam questions may include references to these terms. The citations in parentheses next to each term identify the page numbers where it is defined and/or discussed in *Java Concepts*, 4th ed., and *Big Java,* 2nd ed.

array (280)	cast (289)	object (289)
array initialization (284)	counting (293)	parameterized (289)
array length (282)	`Double` (290)	size (289)
`ArrayList` (284)	index (281)	two-dimensional array (298)
auto-boxing (290)	`Integer` (290)	wrapper class (290)
bounds error (283)		

■ Connecting the Detailed Topic Outline to the Text

The citations in parentheses identify where information in the outline can be located in *Java Concepts*, 4th ed., and *Big Java,* 2nd ed.

- Arrays (280–284)
- Array Lists (284–289)
- Wrappers and Auto-boxing (290–291)
- The Enhanced `for` Loop (292–293)
- Simple Array Algorithms (293–297)
- Two-Dimensional Arrays (298–302)
- Copying Arrays (303–306)

■ Practice Questions

Multiple Choice

1. Consider the following declaration.

    ```
    int[] A = new int[10];
    ```

    Which of the following choices describes the state of array A after this statement is executed?

    a.   The elements A[1]...A[10] are not yet initialized and contain unknown int values.
    b.   The elements A[1]...A[10] are initialized to 0.
    c.   The elements A[0]...A[9] are not yet initialized and contain unknown int values.
    d.   The elements A[0]...A[9] are initialized to 0.
    e.   The elements A[0]...A[10] are initialized to 0.

Questions 2 and 3 refer to the Coin class whose incomplete definition is below.

```
public class Coin
{
    // Constructor
    public Coin(double aValue, String aName) {. . .}

    // Returns coin value.
    public double getValue() {. . .}

    // Returns coin name.
    public String getName() {. . .}

    /*
        Returns true if this and other have same values,
        false otherwise.
    */
    public boolean equals(Object other)

    private double value;
    private String name;
}
```

2. Assume that the variable money has been initialized as follows.

    ```
    ArrayList money = new ArrayList();
    ```

    and that 10 Coins were added to money.

    Which of the following statements or pair of statements would print the name of the sixth Coin in money?

    a.   ```
         String temp = (String) money[5].getName()
         System.out.println(temp);
         ```

    b.   ```
         System.out.println(money[5].getName());
         ```

    c.   ```
         Coin temp = Coin(money.get(5));
         System.out.println(temp);
         ```
         ```

    d.
```
Coin temp = (Coin) money.get(5);
System.out.println(temp.getName());
```

    e.
```
System.out.println(money.get(5).getName())
```

3. (Java 5) Assume that the variable money has been initialized as follows.

```
ArrayList<Coin> money = new ArrayList<Coin>();
```

and that several Coins were added to money. The following segment of code is intended to find the total value of the Coins in money.

```
 1  public double getTotal()
 2  {
 3      double total = 0;
 4      int i = 0;
 5      while (i < money.size())
 6      {
 7          Coin tempCoin = money.get(i);
 8          total += tempCoin.getValue();
 9          i++;
10      }
11      return total;
12  }
```

Which of the following statements about this method is **true**?

    a. There will be a compile-time error because the cast is missing in line 7.

    b. There will be an indexOutOfBoundsException thrown during runtime because line 7 will try to access an element not in bounds of money.

    c. The method will compile and run but the total returned will be incorrect.

    d. There will be a run-time error when money contains no Coins, otherwise the method works as intended.

    e. This method will execute as intended.

4. Consider the method doTask defined below.

```
public static int doTask(int[] a)
{
    int index = 0;
    int soFar = 1;
    int count = 1;
    for (int k = 1; k < a.length; k++)
    {
        if (a[k] == a[k - 1])
        {
            count++;
            if (count > soFar)
            {
                soFar = count;
                index = k;
            }
        }
        else
        {
            count = 1;
        }
```

```
        }
        return a[index];
    }
```

When the following code segment is executed,

```
    int[] arr = {1, 2, 3, 3, 3, 3, 4, 2, 2, 2, 2, 2, 2, 2, 5, 6, 6, 6,
            6, 6, 6, 4, 7, 8};
    System.out.println(doTask(arr));
```

what is printed to the screen?

a. *1*
b. *2*
c. *6*
d. *7*
e. *24*

5. Assume that the following declarations have been made.

```
    int[] A = {1, 2, 3, 4, 5, 6, 7, 8};
    int[] B = {4, 5, 6, 7, 8};
```

Also assume that the method `printContents` is defined with the following header and works as specified in the comment.

```
    // Prints the contents of array arr to the screen.
    public static void printContents(int[] arr)
```

If the following segment of code is executed, what will be printed to the screen?

```
    B = A;
    B[3] = 0;
    printContents(A);
    printContents(B);
```

a. *1 2 3 4 5 6 7 8*
   4 5 6 0 8

b. *1 2 3 0 5 6 7 8*
   1 2 3 0 5 6 7 8

c. *4 5 6 0 8*
   4 5 6 0 8

d. *1 2 3 0 5 6 7 8*
   4 5 6 7 8

e. *1 2 3 4 5 6 7 8*
   4 5 6 7 8

6. Which of the following statements about arrays and array lists is **not** true?

a. A method can change the length of an array that is passed as a parameter.
b. A method can change the length of an `ArrayList` that is passed as a parameter.
c. A method can reverse the order of elements in its array parameter.
d. A method can reverse the order of elements in its `ArrayList` parameter.
e. A method can remove all of the elements in an `ArrayList`.

7. Consider the following method `doTask`.

    ```java
    public static boolean doTask(int[] arr)
    {
        boolean found = true;
        for (int i = 0; i < arr.length; i++)
        {
            found = found && (arr[i] % 2 == 1);
        }
        return found;
    }
    ```

    Which of the following statements is **true** about method `doTask`?

    a. Method `doTask` returns `true` if all elements in its array parameter `arr` are even, `false` otherwise.
    b. Method `doTask` returns `true` if all elements in its array parameter `arr` are odd, `false` otherwise.
    c. Method `doTask` returns `true` if all elements in its array parameter `arr` are positive, `false` otherwise.
    d. Method `doTask` returns `true` if all elements in its array parameter `arr` are equal to 1, `false` otherwise.
    e. Method `doTask` will always return `true`.

8. (Java 5) Consider the following method definitions intended to find the smallest integer value in its `ArrayList` parameter. You may assume that the array list contains at least one value.

    I.
    ```java
    public static int findSmallest(ArrayList<Integer> nums)
    {
        Integer small = nums.get(0);
        for (int i = 1; i < nums.size(); i++)
        {
            Integer tempSmall = nums.get(i);
            if (tempSmall.compareTo(small) < 0)
            {
                small = tempSmall;
            }
        }
        return small.intValue();
    }
    ```

    II.
    ```java
    public static int findSmallest(ArrayList<Integer> nums)
    {
        Integer small = nums.get(0);
        for (int i = 1; i < nums.size(); i++)
        {
            Integer tempSmall = nums.get(i);
            if (tempSmall.intValue() < small.intValue())
            {
                small = tempSmall;
            }
        }
        return small.intValue();
    }
    ```

```
III. public static int findSmallest(ArrayList<Integer> nums)
     {
         int small = (nums.get(0)).intValue();
         for (int i = 1; i < nums.size(); i++)
         {
             int tempSmall = (nums.get(i)).intValue();
             if (tempSmall < small)
             {
                 small = tempSmall;
             }
         }
         return small;
     }
```

Which of the method definitions above will work as intended?

a. I only
b. II only
c. I and II only
d. II and III only
e. I, II, and III

9. (Java 5) Consider the following method definitions intended to determine whether the two `ArrayList` parameters of `Student` are equal (have the same number of elements in the same order). Assume the `equals` method for `Student` works as intended.

```
I.  public static boolean isTheSame(ArrayList<Student> A,
            ArrayList<Student> B)
    {
        if (A.size() != B.size())
            return false;
        return (A == B);
    }
```

```
II. public static boolean isTheSame(ArrayList<Student> A,
            ArrayList<Student> B)
    {
        if (A.size() != B.size())
            return false;
        for (int i = 0; i < A.size(); i++)
        {
            if (!(A.get(i)).equals(B.get(i)))
            {
                return false;
            }
        }
        return true;
    }
```

```
III. public static boolean isTheSame(ArrayList<Student> A,
            ArrayList<Student> B)
     {
         if (A.size() != B.size())
             return false;
         return (A.equals(B));
     }
```

Which of the method definitions above will work as intended?

a. I only
b. II only
c. I and II only
d. II and III only
e. I, II, and III

10. Consider the following operations on an array. Insertions and deletions are done so that the original order of the array elements is not changed.

I. Inserting an element at position 0 of an array.
II. Inserting an element at the end of an array.
III. Removing an element from the beginning of an array.
IV. Removing an element from the end of an array.

Which of the following statements about the efficiency of these operations is **true**?

a. If the array is large, I and II are more efficient than III and IV.
b. If the array is large, I and III are more efficient than II and IV.
c. If the array is large, III and IV are more efficient than I and II.
d. If the array is large, II and IV are more efficient than I and III.
e. All methods have the same efficiency. No method requires more work than any other.

11. Consider the following operations with an `ArrayList`.

I. Inserting an element at position 0 of an `ArrayList`.
II. Inserting an element at the end of an `ArrayList`.
III. Removing an element from the beginning of an `ArrayList`.
IV. Removing an element from the end of an `ArrayList`.

Which of the following statements about the efficiency of these operations is **true**?

a. If the `ArrayList` is large, I and II are more efficient than III and IV.
b. If the `ArrayList` is large, I and III are more efficient than II and IV.
c. If the `ArrayList` is large, III and IV are more efficient than I and II.
d. If the `ArrayList` is large, II and IV are more efficient than I and III.
e. All methods have the same efficiency. No method requires more work than any other.

12. An experiment consists of tossing ten 6-sided dice and counting the number of 1's that appear on one toss of ten dice. There are 11 possibilities (0–10).

This experiment is to be repeated 500 times. The results of the 500 experiments are to be printed in a frequency table for occurrences of 1's tossed. The table will show the number of the 500 experiments that resulted in 0 ones, the number that resulted in 1 one, the number that resulted in 2 ones, and so on.

Which of the following data structures is the best choice to hold the necessary information?

a. An array of length 6.
b. An array of length 11.
c. An array of length 500.
d. An `ArrayList` of size 100.
e. An `ArrayList` of size 500.

(Java 5) **(AB only)** Questions 13 and 14 refer to the `Person` class and the array list `people` below.

```
public class Person
{
    // Constructor
    public Person(String aName, int howOld)
    {
        name = aName;
        age = howOld;
    }
    // Returns name of person.
    public String getName() {. . .}

    // Returns age of person.
    public int getAge() {. . .}

    // Other methods here

    private int age;
    private String name;
}
ArrayList<Person> people = new ArrayList<Person>();
```

13. Which of the code segments below will correctly print the names of the `Person` objects in `people`?

    I. ```
        for (Iterator<Person> it = people.iterator(); it.hasNext();)
        {
            Person temp = it.next();
            System.out.println(temp.getName());
        }
        ```

    II. ```
        for (Iterator<Person> it = people.get(0); it.hasNext();)
        {
            Person temp = it.next();
            System.out.println(temp.getName());
        }
        ```

    III. ```
        Iterator<Person> it = people.iterator();
        while (it.hasNext())
        {
            Person temp = it.next();
            System.out.println(temp.getName());
        }
        ```

    a.  I only
    b.  II only
    c.  III only
    d.  I and III only
    e.  I, II, and III

14. The following segment of code is executed.

    ```
    people.add(new Person("Anna", 23));
    people.add(new Person("Thomas", 17));
    people.add(new Person("Lara", 19));
    people.add(new Person("David", 34));
    ```
    ```

```
people.add(new Person("Karen", 22));

Iterator<Person> it = people.iterator();
it.next();
it.next();
Person temp = it.next();
it.remove();
temp = it.next();
System.out.println(temp.getName());
```

What will be printed to the screen?

a. *Anna*
b. *Thomas*
c. *Lara*
d. *David*
e. *Karen*

15. **(AB only)** Consider the following code segment that is intended to fill and print a 2-dimensional array.

```
int x = 3; int y = 4; int z = 2;
int [] [] tbl = new int [x] [y];

for (int r = 0; r < x; r++)
{
   for (int c = 0; c < y; c++)
   {
      if (r != c)
         tbl [r] [c] = y;
      else
         tbl [r] [c] = z;
   }
}
for (int r = 0; r < x; r++)
{
   for (int c = 0; c < y; c++)
   {
      System.out.print (tbl [r] [c]);
   }
   System.out.println ();
}
```

Which of the following is the 2-dimensional array that is printed?

a. *422*
   242
   224

b. *2444*
   4244
   4424
   2222

c. *2444*
   4244
   4424

d. *4222*
   2422
   2242

e. *3222*
   2322
   2232

Free Response Questions

1. A `FooList` is a class that defines a list of strings and a string length. All strings in a `FooList` have the same length. There is no preset number of strings that a `FooList` can hold. For example,

   The `FooList` list1 may contain the strings aa, bb, cc, and dd (all strings of length 2).

   The `FooList` list2 may contain the strings cat, dog, pig, fox, bat, and eel (all strings of length 3).

   An incomplete implementation of the `FooList` class appears below.

```
public class FooList
{
    /*
        Constructor implementation initializes
        fooLength (the length of the strings in FooList's list) and
        possibleFoos (FooList's list of strings).
    */
    // Constructor code goes here

    /*
        Returns true if the string, key, is found in
        the FooList's list of strings, false otherwise.
    */
    public boolean found(String key)
    {
        // Code goes here
    }

    /*
        Adds the string, entry, to FooList's list implementation if
        it is the correct length and not already in the list. If the
        string is already in the list or if the string is not the
        correct length, it is not added.
    */
    public void addFoo(String entry)
    {
        // Code goes here
    }

    /*
        Removes and returns a random string entry from FooList's
        list of strings.
    */
    public String removeRandomFoo()
    {
```

```
        //  Code goes here
    }

    /*
        Returns the string in position i of FooList's list
        implementation. The first string is in position 0.
    */
    public String getFoo(int i) {. . .}

    // Returns length of a foo.
    public int getFooLength() {. . .}

    // Fills FooList's list with strings input by the user.
    public void fillFooList() {. . .}

    /*
        Since we really only need one random number generator for the
        class, this is a static instance field. This is explained in
        detail in Chapter 9.
    */
    private static Random generator = new Random();
    private int fooLength;

    // Java 5
    private ArrayList<String> possibleFoos;

    // Use the following declaration for Java versions prior to Java 5
    // private ArrayList possibleFoos;
}
```

a. You are to implement the `FooList` constructor. This constructor will have one parameter that will indicate the length of each string in `FooList`'s list. The constructor will initialize `fooLength` with this value and will initialize `FooList`'s list of strings, `possibleFoos`, to have 0 entries.

b. You are to implement the `FooList` method `found`. The method `found` returns `true` if its `String` parameter `key` is found in the list of strings, `false` otherwise. Use the header below when writing `found`.

```
public boolean found(String key)
```

c. You are to implement the method `addFoo` as specified in the method comment shown above. Use the following header in writing `addFoo`. You may call method `found` that is specified in part b of this problem. Assume that `found` works as intended regardless of what you wrote for part b.

```
public void addFoo(String entry)
```

d. You are to implement the method `removeRandomFoo` that will remove and return a random string entry from `FooList`'s list of strings. Use the following header in writing `removeRandomFoo`.

```
public String removeRandomFoo()
```

2. Concentration is a game in which tiles are placed face-down in rows on a "concentration board". Each tile contains an image. For each tile, there is exactly one other tile with the same image. The player is to pick a tile, see which image it has, and try to find its match from

the remaining face-down tiles. If the player fails to turn over its match, both tiles are turned face-down and the player attempts to pick a matching pair again. The game is over when all tiles on the board are turned face-up.

In this implementation of a simplified version of concentration,
- Images will be strings chosen from a FooList. Assume that all FooList methods specified in Question 1 work as intended regardless of what you wrote.
- The concentration board will contain an even number of Tiles.
- The Board will be implemented as a one-dimensional array of Tiles.

For example, if the size of the concentration board is requested to be 4, the board will have 16 Tiles. The one-dimensional array, gameboard, can be viewed as a 4-by-4 concentration board as follows:

```
gameboard[0]     gameboard[1]     gameboard[2]     gameboard[3]
gameboard[4]     gameboard[5]     gameboard[6]     gameboard[7]
gameboard[8]     gameboard[9]     gameboard[10]    gameboard[11]
gameboard[12]    gameboard[13]    gameboard[14]    gameboard[15]
```

An incomplete implementation of the Tile class and an incomplete implementation of the Board class appear below.

```java
public class Tile
{
    // Constructs a Tile whose faceUp shows word.
    public Tile(String word)
    {
        image = word;
        faceUp = false;
    }

    /*
        Returns image on face of Tile if Tile is face-up. Returns
        the empty string if tile is not face-up.
    */
    public String showFace() {. . .}

    // Returns true if Tile is face-up, false otherwise.
    public boolean isFaceUp() {. . .}

    /*
        Returns true if the image on other is the same as this
        image.
    */
    public boolean equals(Object other) {. . .}

    // Postcondition: Tile is turned face-up.
    public void turnFaceUp() {. . .}

    // Postcondition: Tile is turned face-down.
    public void turnFaceDown() {. . .}

    private String image;
    private boolean faceUp;
}
```

```
public class Board
{
    /*
        Constructs n by n concentration board of Tiles whose values
        are chosen from the already filled FooList list.
        Precondition: n is the length of a side of the board,
        n is an even positive integer
        FooList contains at least n * n / 2 strings.
    */
    public Board(int n, FooList list)
    {
        gameBoard = new Tile[n * n];     // Concentration board
        size = gameBoard.length;    // Board size
        numberOfTilesFaceUp = 0;    // Number of Tiles face-up
        rowLength = n;    // Number of Tiles in a row
        possibleTileValues = list;    // Possible tile images
        fillBoard();    // Calls method to fill board with Tiles
    }

    /*
        Randomly fills this concentration board with tiles. The
        number of distinct tiles used on the board is size / 2.
        Any one tile image appears exactly twice.
        Precondition: number of positions on board is even,
        possibleTileValues contains at least size / 2 elements.
    */
    private void fillBoard()
    {
        // Code goes here
    }

    /*
        Assume that Tile in position p is face-down.
        After execution, Tile in position p is face-up.
    */
    public void lookAtTile(int p)
    {
        // Code goes here
    }

    /*
        Checks whether the Tiles in pos1 and pos2 have the same
        image. If they do, the Tiles are turned face-up. If not, the
        Tiles are turned face-down.
        Precondition: gameBoard[pos1] is face-up,
        gameBoard[pos2] is face-up.
    */
    public void checkMatch(int pos1, int pos2)
    {
        // Code goes here
    }

    /*
        Board is printed for the player. If the Tile is turned face-
        up, the image is printed. If the Tile is turned face-down,
        the Tile position is printed.
    */
```

```
public void printBoard()
{
    //  Code goes here
}

// Returns Tile in position pos.
public Tile pickTile(int pos) {. . .}

// Returns right-justified number with p places as a string.
public String format(int number, int p) {. . .}

// Returns right-justified word with p places.
public String format(String word, int p) {. . .}

/*
    Returns true if all Tiles are turned face-up, false
    otherwise.
*/
public boolean allTilesUp() {. . .}

private Tile[] gameBoard;    // Concentration board of Tiles
private int size;    // Number of Tiles on board
private int rowLength;    // Number of Tiles printed in a row
int numberOfTilesFaceUp;    // Number of Tiles face-up
private FooList possibleTileValues;    // Possible Tile images

/*
    Only one random number generator is needed for the class,
    so this is a static instance field.
*/
private static Random generator = new Random();
}
```

a. Write the implementation for the Board method fillBoard. The method fillBoard will randomly fill the concentration Board with Tiles whose images are randomly chosen from strings contained in the FooList possibleTileValues. A tile image that appears on the board appears exactly twice on the board. Use the header below to write fillBoard.

```
private void fillBoard()
```

b. Write the implementation for the Board method lookAtTile. This method will call the appropriate method of the Tile class to turn the Tile face-up. Assume that the method you wrote for part a and the other methods whose headers and comments are given in the problem specification work as intended. Use the header below to write lookAtTile.

```
public void lookAtTile(int p)
```

c. Write the implementation for the Board's method checkMatch. This method will check whether the tiles in its two integer parameter positions on gameBoard have the same image. If they do, the tiles will remain face-up. If they have different images, the tiles will be turned face-down. Assume that the methods you wrote for parts a and b and the other methods whose headers and comments were given in the problem specification work as intended. Use the header below to write checkMatch.

```
public void checkMatch(int pos1, int pos2)
```

d. Complete the implementation for `printBoard` so that the concentration board is printed as described in the comment above and illustrated below. You should call the `Board` method `format` to right-justify the printing of the `Tile` image or the printing of the `Tile` position. For example, if `MAXPLACES = 5`,

```
System.out.print(format("go", MAXPLACES));
    // Will print ["   go"]

i = 4;
System.out.print(format(i, MAXPLACES));
    // Will print ["    4"]
```

Complete the implementation of `printBoard` that appears below.

```
public void printBoard()
{
    final int PADDING = 3;    // Spacing of tiles
    int spacing = possibleTileValues.getFooLength() + PADDING;
    for (int i = 0; i < size; i++)
    {
        // Code goes here
    }
}
```

An example of `printBoard` for a 4 by 4 concentration board that is partially solved is shown below after 4 matches have been found. The `FooList` passed as a parameter to the `Board` constructor contains strings of length 3.

fox	fox	dog	dog
cow	5	6	7
cow	cat	10	11
12	13	14	cat

3. **(AB only)** Suppose that the implementation of the concentration board constructed a two-dimensional array as an alternative to the one-dimensional array used in Question 2.

Board constructor

```
/*
    Constructs n by n Concentration Board.
    n is an even positive integer
*/
public Board(int n, FooList list)
{
    gameBoard = new Tile[n][n];    // Concentration board

    size = n * n;    // Number of Tiles on Board
    numberOfTilesFaceUp = 0;    // Number of Tiles face up
    rowLength = n;    // Number of Tiles in a row

    possibleTileValues = list;    // Possible Tile values
    fillBoard();    // Calls method to fill board with Tiles
}
```

Private instance fields

```
private Tile[][] gameBoard;    // Concentration board of Tiles
private int size;    // Number of Tiles on board
private int rowLength;    // Number of Tiles printed in a row
int numberOfTilesFaceUp;    // Number of Tiles face-up
private FooList possibleTileValues;    // Possible Tile values
```

a. Implement the Board method fillBoard using this two-dimensional array implementation. Use the header below to write fillBoard.

```
private void fillBoard()
```

b. Implement the Board method printBoard using this two-dimensional array implementation. Use the header below to write printBoard.

```
public void printBoard()
```

CHAPTER 9

(Covers *Java Concepts* Chapter 9)

Designing Classes

TOPIC OUTLINE

■ Topic Summary

9.1 Choosing Classes

Object-oriented programming is a major focus of AP Computer Science. The center of this programming paradigm in Java is a class. Both the AP CS A and AB Exams may test your ability to design and implement a class. The AP CS AB Exam may also test your ability to decompose a problem into classes and to define the relationships and responsibilities of those classes. A class should represent a single concept from the problem description. Some examples of classes that we have studied so far include `Rectangle`, `Student`, `BankAccount`, and `Car`. The properties of these classes were relatively easy to understand. The names of these classes are nouns that clearly identify the class. When you choose a class to implement, it should represent a single concept and should be named with a noun that easily identifies the class.

One particular category of classes is called an *actor* class. This type of class does work for you, as the `Random` class did. We also have *utility* classes, such as `Math`, that have no objects. These types of classes are explained in Section 9.1 of your text. The AP subsets do not require you to classify classes as actor or utility classes.

154

9.2   Cohesion and Coupling

A class should represent one concept. All of the class responsibilities (interface features) should be closely related to the concept that the class represents. If they are, we say the class is *cohesive* or has a high degree of cohesion. Sometimes a class needs other classes so that it can do its job. A `Purse` class needs the `Coin` class because a purse contains coins. A roulette `Game` class needs the `Spinner` class to create and spin the roulette wheel. If many classes in a program depend on each other, we say that there is a high degree of *coupling*. It is a good programming practice to have high cohesion and low coupling. If a high degree of coupling exists, then modifying one class may affect many other classes. Figure 2 in Section 9.2 of your text illustrates high and low class coupling. When designing a class, you should be able to list the class's responsibilities and collaborators (the classes that it uses or depends on). Doing so will help you see the amount of cohesion and coupling in your class design.

Let's look at an example of class responsibilities and collaborators.

Consider a state lottery game. Each evening the lottery is televised and we observe the following. There is a *container* that holds the numbered *balls* such that no two balls have the same number. There is a *popper* that "pops" a random ball. It is this popped ball's number that is one of the lottery number choices.

Classes:
- `Container` has a collection of `Balls`. If asked for a `Ball`, the `Container` will remove a `Ball` at random from the set of `Balls` it contains and return it.
  - Responsibilities
    - hold `Objects` (`Balls`);
    - remove and return an `Object` (`Ball`);
  - Collaborators (other classes the `Container` needs or uses)
    - `Ball`
    - `Random`
- `Ball` has a number on it. It can return its number to whoever wants to know it.
  - Responsibilities
    - return its number
  - Collaborators (other classes the `Ball` needs or uses)
    - none
- `Popper` will ask the `Container` for a `Ball` and display the number on the `Ball`.
  - Responsibilities
    - ask `Container` for `Ball`.
    - ask `Ball` for its number.
    - display number on `Ball`.
  - Collaborators (other classes the `Popper` needs or uses)
    - `Ball`
    - `Container`
- `Random` (Java library class)
  - Responsibilities
    - return a random number
  - Collaborators
    - none

We see that there is some degree of coupling in this example because classes collaborate with other classes. We also see that the `Ball`'s cohesion allows it to be used in other games: billiards (add a color to the "ball"), croquet, Scrabble (add a letter to the "ball" and view it as a "tile"), and any game that has a game "piece" with a number on it.

9.3   Accessors, Mutators, and Immutable Classes

A class defines the behavior of its objects by supplying methods. These methods either change the state of the object or they do not. Methods that change the state of an object are called *mutator* methods or *modifiers* and usually have a `void` return type. Examples of modifiers include `deposit` and `withdraw` in the `BankAccount` class. Both of these methods change the state of the `BankAccount` object by modifying its `balance`. The methods `drive` and `fillTank` in the `Car` class change the state of a `Car` object by modifying its `mileage` and `gasInTank`. Accessor methods do not change the state of the object. The method `getBalance` returns the balance of a `BankAccount` object without changing the state of the object. The method `getMileage` returns the total mileage of a `Car` object without changing the state of the object.

A class with no modifiers is an immutable class. The `String` class is immutable. After a string has been constructed, its contents cannot change. The methods of the `String` class do not change the state of the `String` object.

```
String s1 = "Hello";
String s2 = s1;
String s3 = "World";

s1 += s3;    // s1 is now HelloWorld. A new string was created.
             // s2 is still Hello.
             // s3 is World.
```

As you recall from Chapter 6 in this guide, string concatenation does not actually *add to* a string. A new string is created.

9.3.1   Parameter Passing

In Java, a method can never change the values of its parameters. A method with a parameter whose value is an object reference can change the state of the object referred to, but cannot replace the parameter reference with another. Example 9.1 demonstrates these very important concepts.

Example 9.1
_____

```
public class Point
{
   Point(int x1, int y1)
   {
      x = x1;
      y = y1;
   }

   public void setPoint(int xCoordinate, int yCoordinate)
   {
      x = xCoordinate;
      y = yCoordinate;
```

```
        }

        public int getX()
        {
            return x;
        }

        public int getY()
        {
            return y;
        }

        public String toString()
        {
            String s = "(" + x + "," + y + ")";
            return s;
        }

        private int x;
        private int y;
    }
```

```
public class ParamsTester
{
    public static void main(String[] args)
    {
        // Trying to change primitive parameters
        int a = 10;
        int b = 11;
        System.out.println("Before call to change:");
        System.out.println("a = " + a + " b = " + b);
                // a = 10 b = 11
        change(a, b);
        System.out.println("After call to change:");
        System.out.println("a = " + a + " b = " + b);
                // a = 10 b = 11
        System.out.println();

        // Trying to change object references
        Point p1 = new Point(1, 2);
        Point p2 = new Point(3, 4);
        System.out.println("Before call to changePoints:");
        System.out.println("p1 = " + p1);    // p1 = (1, 2)
        System.out.println("p2 = " + p2);    // p2 = (3, 4)
        changePoints(p1, p2);
        System.out.println("After call to changePoints:");
        System.out.println("p1 = " + p1);    // p1 = (1, 2)
        System.out.println("p2 = " + p2);    // p2 = (3, 4)
        System.out.println();

        // Changing the state of an object
        System.out.println("Before call to changeState:");
        System.out.println("p1 = " + p1);    // p1 = (1, 2)
        System.out.println("p2 = " + p2);    // p2 = (3, 4)
        changeState(p1, p2);
        System.out.println("After call to changeState:");
```

```
        System.out.println("p1 = " + p1);    // p1 = (3, 4)
        System.out.println("p2 = " + p2);    // p2 = (3, 4)
        System.out.println();
    }

    public static void change(int x, int y)
    {
        x = 123;
        y = 789;
    }

    public static void changePoints(Point first, Point second)
    {
        Point anotherPoint = new Point(9, 9);
        first = anotherPoint;
        second = first;
    }

    public static void changeState(Point first, Point second)
    {
        first.setPoint(second.getX(), second.getY());
    }
}
```

Output of ParamsTester

Before call to change:
a = 10 b = 11
After call to change:
a = 10 b = 11

Before call to changePoints:
p1 = (1, 2)
p2 = (3, 4)
After call to changePoints:
p1 = (1, 2)
p2 = (3, 4)

Before call to changeState:
p1 = (1, 2)
p2 = (3, 4)
After call to changeState:
p1 = (3, 4)
p2 = (3, 4)

Example 9.1 shows that all argument values are copied into the parameter variables when a method starts. You may see this described as "primitive parameters are passed by value". With objects, the object *reference* is passed by value, not the object. *Common Error 9.1* in your text discusses primitive type parameters. *Advanced Topic 9.1* in your text discusses "call by value" in more detail.

9.4   Side Effects

Every method should be designed to do one task. A side effect of a method is any externally observable behavior outside the object on which the method is invoked. Your text explains different types of side effects dealing with the `BankAccount` class and the possible consequences of these side effects. You should minimize side effects. Do not add `System.out.println` statements to indicate that a method has been completed. The `System.out.println` statement is extraneous code that manipulates the `System.out` object. Unwanted side effects such as this will result in a deduction of points on the free-response portion of the AP CS Exam. *Quality Tip 9.2* in your text discusses side effects and classifies method behavior.

9.5   Preconditions and Postconditions

Preconditions and postconditions are statements that document the intended behavior of the method. They should appear in the method documentation. A *precondition* is a statement that describes the requirements that must be met in order for the method to complete its intended task correctly. If the precondition is not met, no promise about the method's behavior is made. It is the responsibility of the calling method to satisfy the precondition. If the precondition is not satisfied, how should the method behave? One way of handling a violation of the precondition is to throw an *exception* to indicate that the method was called inappropriately. Exceptions are introduced in Section 9.5 of your text and discussed more thoroughly in Chapter 15. We will look at exceptions in more detail in Chapter 13 of this guide.

A *postcondition* is a promise that the value returned by the method is computed correctly or that the object is in a certain state. A postcondition's promise is valid only if the precondition is satisfied. Example 9.2 contains information about a `Product` class. The class contains the name and the number of available products with this name. The method `buyProduct` shows a pre- and postcondition and throws an appropriate exception when the precondition is not met.

Example 9.2

```
/**
    Product contains information about products in a store.
    Class invariant: getNumAvailable() >= 0
*/
public class Product
{
    /**
        Constructs a product with given name and number available.
        Precondition: nm is the name of a product, number >= 0
    */
    public Product(String nm, int number)
    {
        numAvailable = number;
        name = nm;
    }

    /**
        Postcondition: returns number of product available.
        @return number of product available
    */
```

```
public int getNumAvailable()
{
    return numAvailable;
}

/**
    Precondition: numWanted <= numAvailable
    Postcondition: numAvailable is updated accounting for the
    number of items bought
*/
public void buyProduct(int numWanted)
{
    if (numWanted > numAvailable)
        throw new IllegalArgumentException();
    numAvailable -= numWanted;
}

//  Other methods here

private int numAvailable;
private String name;
//  Other private stuff
}
```

Note that the comment

```
Postcondition: returns number of product available.
@return number of product available
```

is redundant. Since `javadoc` comments are not required in AP CS, you may see the postcondition explicitly written as in the first line of the comment above. If using `javadoc` comments, this postcondition can be stated as the `@return` comment.

If you supply a method that only works correctly under certain conditions, be sure to use preconditions to document this fact. If you supply a method that is guaranteed to have a certain effect, use postconditions to document this fact. When you are using other classes in your programs, be sure to read the pre- and postconditions carefully. Remember that the calling method is responsible for satisfying the preconditions.

Reading and understanding pre- and postconditions is important. Many times an algorithm for solving a free-response question is given in the documentation.

An *assertion* is a logical condition in a program that is believed to be true. When the statement

```
numAvailable -= numWanted; // Assertion: numAvailable >= numWanted
```

is executed, the number of available products, `numAvailable`, is greater than or equal to the number of products desired, `numWanted`.

9.5.1   Class Invariants (AB Only)

In addition to pre- and postconditions, a *class invariant* was also included in Example 9.2. A class invariant is a statement that is true about an object after every constructor and that is preserved by every modifier provided that the preconditions were met. Class invariants are discussed in *Advanced Topic 9.2* in your text.

9.6   Static Methods

Up to now, the methods we have included in our classes have been *instance* methods. These methods belong to the object and operate on the object that is instantiated. A *static* method belongs to the *class*, not to an object, and is sometimes referred to as a *class* method. A static method has no implicit parameter. Static methods should be invoked through a class, not an object (i.e., `Class.methodName()`, not `obj.methodName()`) and cannot refer to instance fields or call instance methods. In the `Car` class shown in Example 9.3, the class variable `numCarsMade` keeps a count of the number of `Car` objects that have been instantiated. Each time a `Car` object is created, `numCarsMade` is incremented by 1. The class method `getNumCarsMade` returns that number to the calling method.

9.7   Static Fields

The class variable, `numCarsMade`, is a static field of the `Car` class. The initialization of `numCarsMade` is done only once, when the `Car` constructor is called the first time. The statement

```
System.out.println(Car.getNumCarsMade());
```

will print the value of `numCarsMade` which is the number of `Car` objects constructed.

Example 9.3

```java
public class Car
{
   /**
      Default constructor initializes instance variables.
   */
   public Car()
   {
      // Private instance variables initialized here
      numCarsMade++;   // Number of cars manufactured so far
   }

   // Other public methods here

   /**
      @return number of cars manufactured so far
   */
   public static int getNumCarsMade()
   {
      return numCarsMade;
   }

   // Counts cars instantiated
   private static int numCarsMade = 0;
         // Initializes static field
}
```

Static fields should be declared as `private` to ensure that methods of other classes do not change their values. Static *constants* can be declared as public or private. If your constant will be called only by methods within your class, then you should declare it as `private`. If you wish to allow the client programs or other classes access to your constants, then you would declare them as `public`. Static constants are initialized when they are declared. Static constants are discussed in Chapter 4 and in Section 9.7 in your text.

9.8 Scope

The word *scope* is used to describe the part of a program in which a variable is accessible. We have already discussed instance variables, local variables of methods, parameter variables, and variables declared in the initialization of `for` loops. The issue of variable scope is an important reason to choose variable names wisely. It is bad programming technique to give instance variables the same names as the parameter or local variables. If you do, the scope issues become complicated. The constructor in Example 9.4 illustrates an error involving instance fields that is commonly made by students.

Example 9.4

```java
public class Student
{
    /**
        Constructs a Student with the given information.
        @param first is the student's first name
        @param last is the student's last name
        @param idNumber is the student identification number
    */
    public Student(String first, String last, String idNumber)
    {
        String firstName = first;    // WRONG. A local variable is
                                     // being initialized, NOT the
                                     // the instance field!

        lastName = last;
        id = idNumber;
        sumOfGrades = 0.0;
        numberOfGrades = 0;
    }

    // Other code here

    private String firstName;
    private String lastName;
    private String id;
    private double sumOfGrades;
    private int numberOfGrades;
}
```

The statements

```
Student csStudent = new Student("Jay", "Delmonti", "333");
System.out.println(csStudent.getFirstName() + " " +
    csStudent.getLastName());
```

would result in

null Delmonti

being printed. The programmer of this class constructor *accidentally* created a local variable
`firstName` with the same name as the instance field. The type `String` should be eliminated in
the constructor body. The private instance field types are given when they are declared.

9.8.1   *Scope of Local Variables*
The scope of a local variable extends from the point of its declaration to the end of the block that
encloses it. If a variable is declared in the loop initialization, it is accessible only within the loop.
If a variable is declared at the start of a method, it is accessible in that method. Parameter
variables in a method header are accessible only within that method. If you try to give two local
variables with overlapping scopes the same name, the compiler will complain. You can have
local variables with the same name if their scopes do not overlap. Example 9.5 illustrates these
concepts.

Example 9.5

```
1     Student csStudent = new Student("Jay", "Delmonico", "333");
2
3     ArrayList<Student> apClass = new ArrayList<Student>();    // Java 5
4     for (int i = 0; i < 5; i++)
5     {
6         String tempId = "11" + i;
7         Student csStudent = new Student("name1", "name2", tempId);
8         apClass.add(csStudent);
9     }
10    System.out.println(i);
11    for (int i = 0; i < 5; i++)
12    {
13        System.out.println((apClass.get(i)).getId());
14             // No casting needed here.
15    }
```

Line 1 declares and initializes variable `csStudent`.
Line 7 will cause the compiler to complain because there is an attempt to declare and initialize a
    variable with the same name that would overlap the scope of the first `csStudent` variable.
Line 10 would cause the compiler to complain because the scope of `i` is restricted to the loop.
Line 11 uses the name `i` as the loop control variable name again. This is OK because the scope of
    the two variables named `i` do not overlap.
This example also demonstrates the use of Java 5 generics. No casting is necessary in line 13.

To avoid confusion with scope, use different names for different variables and never change the
values of parameter variables.

9.8.2   Scope of Class Members

Within an instance method of a class, you can access all other methods and all fields of that class by their simple names (without an object name prefix). If you are using a method outside the object, you must qualify it by prefixing the method name with the object name (for an instance method) or by the class name (for a class method). Whenever you see an instance method call without an implicit parameter (object name prefix), the method is called on the `this` parameter. Several examples of referencing variables with different scopes are given in Sections 9.8.2 and 9.8.3 of your text. *Common Error 9.2* discusses the pitfalls of declaring a local variable with the same name as an instance field.

9.8.3   Initializing Variables

The methods for initializing variables depend on the type of variable. The initialization of different variable types is summarized below:

- Local variables belong to an individual method. A local variable can be accessed only from within that method and must be initialized before you use it. Failure to initialize will cause the compiler to complain.
- Parameter variables also belong to an individual method. Parameter variables are initialized with the values that are supplied by the calling method.
- Instance fields belong to an object and can be used by all methods of its class. Instance fields should be initialized in the constructor of the class. If instance fields are not initialized explicitly, default values are assigned. Numbers are initialized to 0, objects to `null`, and `boolean` values to `false`. Even though these default values are assigned to instance fields, it is good programming practice to initialize instance variables in the constructors. The AP CS Exam will expect you to implement constructors that initialize all instance variables.
- Static fields are initialized when the class is loaded. This should be done by an explicit initializer. However, if no initialization is done explicitly, default values are assigned. Numbers are initialized to 0, objects to `null`, and `boolean` values to `false`.
- Static constants are initialized with a value.

The AP Exam will not test default initializations. You should initialize instance variables in constructors and you should include explicit initializers for static fields.

9.9   Packages

A package is a set of related classes. Several common packages that we use in Java are listed in Table 1 of Section 9.9 in your text. If you are using classes that belong to any of these packages (except `java.lang`), you must `import` the package. The `import` directive allows you to refer to the class of the package without fully qualifying the class name with the package prefix each time you use it.

```
import java.awt.Rectangle
// Other stuff here

Rectangle = new Rectangle(5, 10, 15, 20);
```

is much easier to read and understand than

```
java.awt.Rectangle = new java.awt.Rectangle(5, 10, 15, 20);
```

You are expected to have a basic understanding of packages and a reading knowledge of `import` statements. *Common Error 9.3* discusses Java naming conventions that can help you avoid confusion when looking at names with many connecting dots!

You will not be required to create packages on the AP Exam.

■ Topics That Are Useful But Not Tested

- You can sometimes avoid duplication of code when writing multiple constructors for a class by calling one constructor from another. An example of this is given in *Advanced Topic 9.4* of your text.
- Overlapping scope (Section 9.8.3) and shadowing (*Common Error 9.2*) will not be tested but reading these sections in your text will give you a more thorough understanding of variable scope.
- More information on creating packages and choosing package names is given in Section 9.9 of your text. This section also explains how classes are located by the compiler.
- Section 9.5 in your text discusses Java's `assert` statement. This feature helps us check assertions in our program. You are required to understand the meaning of *assertion* but you will not be tested on the `assert` statement.

■ Things to Remember When Taking the AP Exam

- Do not put extraneous `System.out.println` statements in free-response answers to indicate that the method is done or to print the answer before returning its value. This is a side effect and will result in a deduction of points on free-response questions.
  - Do not print error messages inside of methods unless specifically instructed to do so. This is a side effect and will result in a deduction of points on free-response questions.
- On the AP Exam, you do not need to check that the precondition of the method is satisfied unless explicitly told to do so. A method should not be called unless its precondition is satisfied.
  - Remember that you cannot modify parameters of a primitive type. A Java method can never modify numbers that are passed to it. Do not try to replace an object reference parameter with another reference. You can change the state of an object reference parameter but you cannot replace the object reference with another.
  - Remember that you cannot change the contents of parameter variables within methods by reassigning values to them or by getting new values for them from input. Do not use parameter variables as temporary variables. This is discussed in *Quality Tip 9.3* of your text.
- Carefully read the pre- and postconditions given in problems, especially in the free-response questions. Many times an algorithm for solving the problem is given in the problem documentation. Read the documentation carefully!
- Unless specifically asked to write pre- and postconditions on the AP Exam, do not spend time doing this.

■ Key Words

You should understand the terms below. The AP CS Exam questions may include references to these terms. The citations in parentheses next to each term identify the page numbers where it is defined and/or discussed in *Java Concepts*, 4th ed., and *Big Java,* 2nd ed.

assertion (336)	`import` (312)	scope (346)
assessor method (329)	mutator method (329)	side effect (330)
class invariant (339)	package (351)	static method (340)
cohesion (326)	postcondition (336)	static field (342)
coupling (327)	precondition (335)	utility class (325)
immutable (329)		

■ Connecting the Detailed Topic Outline to the Text

The citations in parentheses identify where information in the outline can be located in *Java Concepts*, 4th ed., and *Big Java,* 2nd ed.

- Choosing Classes (324–325)
- Cohesion and Coupling (326–328)
- Accessors, Mutators, and Immutable Classes (329)
- Side Effects (329–330)
- Preconditions and Postconditions (335–338)
  - Class Invariants **(AB only)** (339)
- Static Methods (340–341)
- Static Fields (342–344)
- Scope (346–349)
  - Scope of Local Variables (346)
  - Scope of Class Members (347)
  - Initializing Variables (345)
- Packages (351–355)

■ Practice Questions

Multiple Choice

1. A class is being designed to represent an athlete. Which of the following public methods would **not** be a good choice for a cohesive public interface for this class?

   a. `getName()`
   b. `getSport()`
   c. `getFavoriteSong()`
   d. `setPointsPerGame()`
   e. `getTotalGamesPlayed()`

2. Which of the following statements is **true** about designing programs involving multiple classes?

    a. It is a good practice to have high degree of cohesion and a high degree of coupling.
    b. It is a good practice to have low degree of cohesion and a low degree of coupling.
    c. It is a good practice to have high degree of cohesion and a low degree of coupling.
    d. It is a good practice to have low degree of cohesion and a high degree of coupling.
    e. It is a good practice to have neither class cohesion or coupling with a program involving multiple classes.

3. An immutable class in Java is

    a. a class that has no private methods.
    b. a class that has no accessor methods.
    c. a class that has no instance fields.
    d. a class that has no modifier methods.
    e. a class that has only modifier methods.

4. Consider the problem of modeling a `Point` class. A `Point` object represents a point in the rectangular coordinate system. A `Point` object has an *x*-coordinate and a *y*-coordinate. Which of the following methods would **not** be a good choice for a cohesive public interface for this class?

    a. `getX();`
    b. `setY();`
    c. `distancefromOrigin();`
    d. `distanceFrom(Point a);`
    e. `perimeter(Point a, Point b, Point c);`

5. **(AB)** A `CashDrawer` class contains a method `giveChange` that accepts two parameters: `cost` and `tendered`, where `cost` is a `double` representing the price of an item and `tendered` is a `double` representing the amount tendered by the purchaser. The method has the following header, precondition, and postcondition:

    ```
    // Precondition: Money tendered >= cost and cost > 0
    // Postcondition: Returns the amount of change
    public double giveChange(double tendered, double cost)
    ```

    To ensure that the precondition is met, which of the following code segments is the best choice for the method body?

    ```
    a. if (tendered < cost || cost <= 0)
       {
           System.out.println("WRONG! Your values to this
                   function are not correct!");
           return 0;
       }
       else return (tendered - cost)
    ```

b.
```
if (tendered < cost || cost <= 0)
{
    System.out.println("WRONG! Your values to this
            function are not correct!");
    return 0;
}
else return (cost - tendered)
```

c.
```
if (tendered < cost || cost <= 0)
{
    cost = tendered;
}
else return 0;
```

d.
```
if (tendered < cost || cost <= 0)
{
    throw new IllegalArgumentException();
}
else return (tendered - cost);
```

e.
```
if (tendered < cost || cost <= 0)
{
    throw new IllegalArgumentException();
}
else
{
    tendered = tendered - cost;
}
```

(Note: Using `javadoc` comments, the postcondition in Question 5 would be replaced by the `@return` comment. Since the AP subset does not include `javadoc` comments, the type of postcondition shown may appear on the AP Exam.)

6. Which statement below is **true** about preconditions?

   a. It is the method's responsibility to check that its precondition is satisfied.
   b. A precondition describes what is returned by the method.
   c. A precondition describes the parameters and their restrictions in order for the method to function as intended.
   d. A precondition describes how a method is implemented.
   e. If a precondition is not satisfied, the compiler will automatically throw an exception.

Questions 7 and 8 refer to the `Student` class whose incomplete definition is below.

```
public class Student
{
    public Student()
    {
        firstName = "";
        lastName = "";
        id = "";
        gpa = 0.0;
    }
```

```
public Student(String first, String last,
    String idNumber, double gradePointAvg)
{
    firstName = first;
    lastName = last;
    id = idNumber;
    gpa = gradePointAvg;
}

public double getGpa()
{
    return gpa;
}

public void setGpa(double newGpa)
{
    gpa = newGpa;
}

private String firstName;
private String lastName;
private String id;
private double gpa;
}
```

7. Consider a client program of the Student class that includes the following methods.

```
public static void change1(Student stdt1, Student stdt2)
{
    stdt1 = stdt2;
}

public static void change2(Student stdt1, Student stdt2)
{
    stdt1.setGpa(stdt2.getGpa());
}
```

After the code segment below is executed,

```
Student student1 = new Student();
Student student2 = new Student("Joe", "Smith", "111", 3.86);
Student student3 = new Student("Marie", "Jones", "222", 3.52);
change1(student1, student2);
change2(student3, student1);
```

what are the gpas of student1, student2, and student3?

a. student1.gpa = 0.0, student2.gpa = 3.86, student3.gpa = 0.0
b. student1.gpa = 0.0, student2.gpa = 3.86, student3.gpa = 3.52
c. student1.gpa = 3.86, student2.gpa = 3.86, student3.gpa = 3.86
d. student1.gpa = 3.52, student2.gpa = 3.52, student3.gpa = 3.52
e. student1.gpa = 3.52, student2.gpa = 3.86, student3.gpa = 3.52

8. For the `Student` class defined above, which of the following statements is **true** regarding constructors, accessor methods, and mutator methods?

    a. The `Student` class has 1 constructor and 3 accessor methods.
    b. The `Student` class has 1 constructor and 3 mutator methods.
    c. The `Student` class has 2 constructors and 2 accessor methods.
    d. The `Student` class has 2 constructors and 2 mutator methods.
    e. The `Student` class has 2 constructors, 1 accessor method, and 1 mutator method.

9. Consider the following program description: A user inserts coins into a vending machine to purchase candy. Which is the best choice of classes to be implemented for this program?

    I.   A `VendingMachine` class that defines private instance variables to hold coin values and product items.
    II. A `VendingMachine` class that defines private instance variables to hold product information and uses coins from a `Coin` class.
    III. A `VendingMachine` class that uses coins from a `Coin` class and products from a `Product` class.

    a. Method I is the best choice because there is a high degree of cohesion with this method.
    b. Method II is the best choice because products are a part of the vending machine's structure but coins are not.
    c. Method III is the best choice because the different vending machines can be implemented using different products and the products and coins can be used in other applications.
    d. None of the above methods. The coins and products should be part of a utility class because they are used by the `VendingMachine` class and they will not be instantiated.
    e. All methods are equally good.

10. Consider the following code segment.

    ```java
    public class TriangleTester
    {
        public static void main(String[] args)
        {
            printTriangle(5);
            // scopeCheck1
        }

        public static void printTriangle(int maxStars)
        {
            int count = 0;
            for (int r = 1; r <= maxStars; r++)
            {
                for (int c = 1; c <= r; c++)
                {
                    System.out.print("*");
                    count++;
                    // scopeCheck2
                }
                System.out.println();
            }
            // scopeCheck3
        }
    }
    ```

Which of the following statements is **true** about variable scope?

a. At **scopeCheck1**, variables maxStars, r, c, and count are accessible.
b. At **scopeCheck1**, only variables r, c, and count are accessible.
c. At **scopeCheck2**, variables maxStars, r, c, and count are accessible.
d. At **scopeCheck2**, only variables maxStars, c and count are accessible.
e. At **scopeCheck3**, variables maxStars, r, c, and count are accessible.

Free Response Questions

1. Consider the problem of modeling book information for a small book store. A book has these attributes:
    *   The book title
    *   The author's name
    *   An identification number that is unique to each book title. The identification numbers are positive integers assigned in increasing numerical order as the Book objects are created.
    *   The price of the book (a floating-point number).

    When a new Book object is created, it must be assigned an identification number that will be the next consecutive identification number available. The new book is created with a title, an author's name, and a price. The only operations valid for a Book object are:
    *   Retrieve the identification number for the book.
    *   Retrieve the author's name.
    *   Set the price of the book (in the event that the price of the book is to be changed). The price of the book will always be a positive number.
    *   Retrieve the price of the book.

    The class described above will be called Book.

    a. Write the public interface for the Book class as it would appear in a Book.java file. In writing this, you should write the headers for the constructor and the public methods. You must:
        *   Choose appropriate variable and method names.
        *   Provide the preconditions and postconditions where necessary.
        *   Provide appropriate data representation for the specifications above.
        *   Be consistent with information-hiding principles.

        DO NOT WRITE THE IMPLEMENTATIONS OF THE METHODS.

        Use the following class declaration to write your interface.

        ```
        public class Book
        {
            //  Your interface goes here
        }
        ```

    b. Write the declarations for the private instance fields and private class fields that will be needed in the Book class.

    c. Implement the Book class constructor. (**AB Students**: If appropriate, include exception handling to ensure that the precondition is satisfied.)

d. Describe two alternative actions that the programmer of a method can take if a precondition of the method is not satisfied. Give an advantage and/or disadvantage for each alternative.

2. Get Lean Fitness (GLF) is a company dedicated to improving the fitness level of its clients. GLF has several weight reduction plans. Each plan is an instance of a class `WeightCalculator`. That class has the following public interface.

```
public class WeightCalculator
{
    //  Constructor(s) here

    /*
        Precondition: gender is sex of person,
        howTall is height of person
        Postcondition: Returns the ideal weight for a person
        with height howTall
    */
    public int getIdealWeight(String gender, int howTall) {. . .}

    /*
        Precondition: gender is sex of person,
        howTall is height of person
        Postcondition: Returns recommended calorie intake for a
        person with the given height and gender
    */
    public int getCalorieIntake(String gender, int howTall) {. . .}

    //  Private implementation here
}
```

The company keeps a record on each client. This client record includes the person's name, height, initial weight, and gender (all attributes of the client). The client record also includes the client's suggested daily calorie intake.

Consider the problem of modeling the client information for Get Lean Fitness in a class called `Client`.

*   When a new `Client` object is created, it is created with the name, gender, height, and weight of the client.

The operations available on a `Client` object are:
*   Retrieve the client's name.
*   Retrieve the client's gender.
*   Retrieve the client's height.
*   Retrieve the client's weight.
*   Set the client's recommended calorie intake per day.
*   Retrieve the client's recommended calorie intake per day.

a. Write the public interface for the `Client` class (except for the `setRecommendedCalories` method) as it would appear in the `Client.java` file. The `setRecommendedCalories` method will be described in part c. In writing the interface, you should write the headers for the constructor and the public methods.

You should:
- Choose appropriate variable and method names.
- Provide the preconditions and postconditions where necessary.
- Provide appropriate data representation for the specifications above.
- Be consistent with information-hiding principles.

DO NOT WRITE THE IMPLEMENTATIONS OF THE METHODS.

Use the following class declaration to write your interface.

```
public class Client
{
    //  Your interface goes here
}
```

b. Write the declarations for the private instance fields that will be needed in the `Client` class.

c. A client's ideal weight is based on gender and height and is found by giving the required information to the appropriate method of a `WeightCalculator`. Implement the `Client` method that sets the suggested number of calories to be consumed per day. An instance of the `WeightCalculator` is a parameter of the client's `setRecommendedCalories` method. The algorithm used to determine daily calorie intake is as follows.
- If the client's weight is less than or equal to the client's ideal weight, the calorie intake per day is the value that is returned by the `WeightCalculator`'s `getCalorieIntake` method.
- If the client's weight is more than the client's ideal weight, the calorie intake per day is the value that is returned by the `WeightCalculator`'s `getCalorieIntake` method minus the constant 500.

Use the following method header.

```
public void setRecommendedCalories(WeightCalculator plan)
```

CHAPTER 10

(Covers *Java Concepts* Chapter 10)

Testing and Debugging

■ Topic Summary

10.1   Unit Tests

Most computer programs have errors when they are first written. We have discussed compile-time errors, run-time errors, and logic errors, and the *Common Error* sections that appear throughout your text discuss some of the more common programming errors and how to avoid them. Your goal should be to minimize the likelihood and impact of errors. Even though you take precautions and attempt to program defensively, sometimes your programs will not function exactly as expected. When this happens, you will need to use debugging strategies to locate the errors.

The most important testing technique is the *unit test*. This is the process of compiling and testing a class in isolation. In the BlueJ environment, an object can be created, its attributes can be inspected, and each of its methods can be tested individually by choosing them from a list of methods for that object. In other environments, it is an easy task to write a test class (test harness) that supplies values to the individual methods for testing.

10.2   Providing Test Input

Values for testing individual methods can be supplied by user input, by file input, by random generation of values, or by variable assignment.

Generating the appropriate test data is an important debugging skill. You should test your programs using legitimate (or typical) test cases, boundary test cases, and negative test cases. Legitimate test cases are the values you would expect the user to supply. Boundary test cases are

174

values that lie on the boundary of acceptable input. You should test a value on the boundary, one that is one unit below the boundary and one that is one unit above the boundary to ensure that you are not off-by-one with your calculations. Negative test cases (or degenerate values) are values that the program should reject. Test these values and decide on a method of handling illegal input. Section 10.2 and *Advanced Topic 10.1* of your text include examples of each type of input.

You want to make sure that each part of your program is executed at least once by one of your test cases. This ensures that all branches in all conditional statements are executed during your tests.

After all individual classes have been thoroughly tested, you should begin the process of integration testing, in which the classes are put together in a program and tested.

After a program is completed, it is a good idea to keep the test cases in the event that modifications are made to the program. You can then retest your new version with the old test cases to see if the functionality is the same. One way to easily keep test case data is to create a text file from which the data is read by using text file input. This is discussed in Chapter 16 of your text. Reading from text files is not tested on the AP CS Exam.

10.3 Test Case Evaluation

After you have selected test data and decided on the input method, you need to determine whether the output produced by the program is correct. One way to verify the output is to calculate the values by hand. Other methods for checking output are discussed in Section 10.3 of your text.

10.4 Program Traces

A program trace is a procedure in which output messages are added to a program to show its path of execution. For a proper trace, messages should be added at each method entry and exit point. More messages can be added to give additional information. Of course, your program will be more difficult to read because of the additional message statements and the output may be confusing; these statements should be removed when testing is complete. That means, if you revise the program at a later time, the procedure of adding and deleting message statements has to be repeated.

It is possible to create a `Debug` class to generate trace messages that you can turn on and off at your discretion. In this way, you can determine if and when you want to print your debugging messages, and you do not have to constantly add and delete these extra statements. This `Debug` class would be a utility class whose methods are `static`. There would be no need to create instances of this class. The College Board case study uses this technique to provide debugging statements throughout the Java Marine Biology Simulation case study.

You can also hand-trace the program. To do so, develop a set of test data. Calculate the correct results by hand so that you know what results to expect. Then simply use the test data and simulate a computer. Trace the execution of the program to see what the program will do. In order to be successful with this, you must keep track of variables (both primitive and reference) and their states.

10.5   The Debugger

The debugging method that is most popular among professional programmers is the use of a debugger. Most modern development environments contain a special program called a debugger that allows you to follow the execution of a program in order to locate errors. Adding breakpoints to your programs, inspecting variables, and stepping through the program execution are a few tools included in most debuggers. The debugger and a debugging session are discussed in Sections 10.6 and 10.7 of your text. The use of a debugger is not tested on the AP Exam. For less complicated programs, the use of testing techniques is sufficient and is easier than mastering the use of a debugger.

How To 10.1 lists strategies that you can use to recognize program errors and their causes.

■ Topics That Are Useful But Not Tested

- Regression testing, black-box testing, and white-box testing are classifications given to particular testing procedures. Although we have discussed these methods, we did not refer to them by any particular classification. These testing methods are described in Section 10.4 in your text. The AP CS Exam will not require you to know this vocabulary, but the concept of testing programs is included in the AP CS Topic Outline.
- The use of `assert` as a way to monitor pre- and postconditions is discussed in Section 9.5 in your text.
- JUnit is an excellent tool for designing and organizing test cases and is discussed in *Advanced Topic 10.2* in your text.
- Section 10.7 in your text describes a sample debugging session. Following this session might help you familiarize yourself with the debugger available in your integrated development environment.
- The `java.util.Logger` class is useful for analyzing the behavior of a program and is explained in Section 10.5 in your text.

■ Things to Remember When Taking the AP Exam

- Understand the differences among compile-time errors, run-time errors, and logic errors.
- If asked to choose test data for a situation, remember to include legitimate, boundary, and degenerate test cases.
- When you develop code, carefully hand trace your code to eliminate many errors.

■ Key Words

You should understand the terms below. The AP CS Exam questions may include references to these terms. The citations in parentheses next to each term identify the page numbers where it is defined and/or discussed in *Java Concepts*, 4th ed., and *Big Java,* 2nd ed.

assertion (336)	negative test cases (378)	typical test cases (378)
boundary test cases (378)	program trace (387)	unit test (372)
debugger (389)	test harness (372)	

■ Connecting the Detailed Topic Outline to the Text

The citations in parentheses identify where information in the outline can be located in *Java Concepts*, 4th ed., and *Big Java,* 2nd ed.

- Unit Tests (372–376)
- Providing Test Input (376–379)
- Test Case Evaluation (380–383)

- Program Traces (387)
- Using a Debugger (389–397)

■ Practice Questions

Multiple Choice

1. Which of the following statements about debugging is **true**?

    a. All classes that are needed for the program should be written. Integration of these classes should be tested first. If there is a problem, the debugging procedure should be initiated.
    b. Each class should be written and tested separately before integrating the classes in a program.
    c. Message output statements should be included at the entry and exit points of all methods when they are initially written. This will make the program easier to read.
    d. To accurately trace a program, input statements should be included at the entry and exit points of all methods when you initially write them.
    e. Adding pre- and postconditions to methods will allow the inspection of variable values during program execution.

2. Which of the following errors is **not** classified as a compile-time error?

    a. Division by 0
    b. Missing semicolon
    c. Misspelled variable name
    d. Uninitialized local variable
    e. Mismatched parentheses

3. Assume that a class provides the following instance methods for easily reading integers from a file. The object variable `input` represents the file and the file is open and ready for reading.

    ```
    // Returns true if the end-of-file was read on the previous read,
    // false otherwise.
    public boolean eof()

    // Returns the next integer in file
    public int readInt()
    ```

    Consider the following code segment that is intended to find the average of the integer values read from `input`.

    ```
    int n, count = 0, sum = 0;
    while (!input.eof())   // testing for end-of-file
    {
       n = input.readInt();   // read integer from file
       if (!input.eof())
    ```

```
        {
            sum += n;
            count++;
        }
    }
    double avg = sum / count;
    System.out.println("The average is: " + avg);
```

I. A logic error may occur because the variable n is not initialized.
II. A run-time error will occur if the file is empty.
III. A logic error may occur because the average returned is not always the correct value.

Which statement(s) above correctly describe the errors in this code segment?

a. I only
b. II only
c. III only
d. II and III only
e. I, II, and III

Questions 4–6 refer to the following problem.

The method weeklyPay is to return the amount of pay an employee will receive for one week's work. The parameters for weeklyPay are the hours worked during the week and the hourly pay. The weekly pay is based on the following standards. If the employee worked 40 hours or less during the week, he receives his regular hourly rate times the number of hours he worked. For every hour over 40 hours, the employee receives time and a half (1.5 times his regular hourly pay). The following information and method header is given.

```
final int MAX_HOURS_IN_WEEK = 168;    // 7 * 24
/*
    Precondition: 0 <= hoursWorked and
    hoursWorked <= MAX_HOURS_IN_WEEK, 0 < hourlyPay
*/
public static double weeklyPay(double hoursWorked,
        double hourlyPay)
```

4. Which is the best set of test values for the variable hoursWorked?

a. 0, 40, 168
b. 5, 10, 20, 30, 40, 170
c. −1, 0, 1, 39, 40, 41, 167, 168, 169
d. −10, 20, 30, 40, 50, 200
e. −20, −10, 10, 20, 30, 40, 100, 200

5. Which of the following method calls would test illegal input?

I. weeklyPay(0, 0)
II. weeklyPay(168, 169)
III. weeklyPay(0, 200)

a. I only
b. II only
c. III only
d. I and II only
e. I and III only

6. Which of the method calls would be good choices to test boundary conditions or branches of conditionals in the `weeklyPay` method?

    I.   `weeklyPay(0, 10)`
    II. `weeklyPay(168, 20)`
    III. `weeklyPay(40, 40)`

    a. I only
    b. II only
    c. III only
    d. I and II only
    e. I, II, and III

7. Values for testing a method can come from all of the following **except**

    a. user input
    b. file input
    c. generating random numbers
    d. non-initialized local variables
    e. variable assignment

8. Which of the following statements is **not** true about program testing?

    a. Once a method has passed all of the test cases, the cases should be discarded because they are of no more use.
    b. A method of checking the accuracy of a program is to test a set of input values and then compute the results by hand using the same input values.
    c. A method of testing revisions in a program is to test against past failures.
    d. A method of checking the accuracy of a program is to use values for which you know the answers.
    e. A method of testing a program is to use test cases that ensure that each statement of your program has been executed at least once.

9. Which of the following is **true** about unit testing?

    a. A unit test simultaneously checks all classes that are included in a program.
    b. A unit test simultaneously checks a set of cooperating classes in a program.
    c. A unit test simultaneously checks all of the methods of one class.
    d. A unit test checks a single method or set of cooperating methods in a class.
    e. A unit test checks a single statement in a method.

10. Which of the following is the best description of a *debugger*?

    a. A debugger is a person hired to find the mistakes in your program.
    b. A debugger is the output from your program's test data.
    c. A debugger is a hardware component available to automatically analyze and correct run-time errors.
    d. A debugger is a program you use to execute another program and analyze its run-time behavior.
    e. A debugger is a hardware component available to automatically analyze and correct compile-time errors.

Free Response Questions

1. Consider the `BankAccount` class incompletely defined below.

```java
public class BankAccount
{
    // Constructs a bank account with a given balance.
    public BankAccount(double initialBalance)
    {
        balance = initialBalance;
    }

    // Returns the current balance.
    public double getBalance()
    {
        return balance;
    }

    // Precondition goes here
    public void withdraw(double amount)
    {
        // Code goes here
    }

    private double balance;
}
```

The public method `withdraw` has one parameter of type `double`. The method `withdraw` will modify the private instance variable `balance` by removing the specified amount of money (passed as a parameter to the method) from the account. The header for the method `withdraw` is below.

```java
public void withdraw(double amount)
```

a. Write the precondition for `withdraw`.

b. Write the public method `withdraw`. (**AB students** may throw an exception if the precondition is not met.)

c. Assume that a `BankAccount` object was constructed with the following statement.

```java
BankAccount myAccount = new BankAccount(500);
```

Describe the test data that you would use to test your `withdraw` method and list these test values.

Interfaces and Polymorphism

■ Topic Summary

11.1 Using Interfaces for Code Reuse

A Java interface declares methods that classes are expected to implement. It encapsulates a set of associated behaviors that can be used by dissimilar classes. Interfaces contain no instance fields and cannot be instantiated (you cannot construct an object of an interface type). A class implements an interface by providing the implementation for all of the methods in the interface. An interface can be implemented by many classes and a class can implement multiple interfaces. To implement an interface, a class must express its intention to implement it by means of its header, and then must provide implementations of all of the methods dictated by the interface. Consider the following trivial but illustrative example. A `Flier` is one that flies.

Figure 11.1

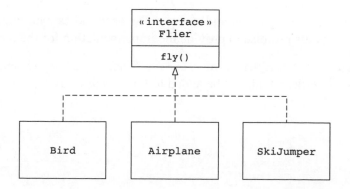

Figure 11.1 is a UML diagram. Although UML diagrams will not be tested on the AP CS Exam, you will see them throughout your text as they are commonly used to illustrate relationships among classes.

It is clear that the three classes `Bird`, `Airplane`, and `SkiJumper` are three dissimilar classes. Each of these classes defines the method `fly` in a very different way. The interface for this trivial descriptive example would be

```
public interface Flier
{
    void fly();
}
```

Notice that the `public` visibility modifier is not included for the `fly` method. The methods declared in an interface are public by default. The classes that implement this interface might include the following code implementation for the `fly` method.

Example 11.1

```
public class Bird implements Flier
{
    public void fly()
    {
        System.out.println("Using my wings to fly");
    }
}
```

```
public class Airplane implements Flier
{
    public void fly()
    {
        System.out.println("Using my jet engines to fly");
    }
}
```

```
public class SkiJumper implements Flier
{
    public void fly()
    {
        System.out.println("Using skis to take me into the air");
    }
}
```

The class headers of `Bird`, `Airplane`, and `SkiJumper` each indicate an intention to implement the `Flier` interface and thus promise to provide the implementation for the method `fly`.

Example 11.2 creates an `ArrayList` of `Fliers`. Since `SkiJumper` and `Airplane` both implement the `Flier` interface, both can be added to this `ArrayList`.

Example 11.2 (Java 5)

```
ArrayList<Flier> airborne = new ArrayList<Flier>();
airborne.add(new SkiJumper("Jumper", "One"));
airborne.add(new SkiJumper("Jumper", "Two"));
airborne.add(new Airplane());
```

Now, let's be more specific about our `SkiJumper`. An athlete is one that competes. A `SkiJumper` is an `Athlete`. An athlete trains for hours to perfect performance in a particular sport. Most of us would agree that neither a `Bird` nor an `Airplane` is an `Athlete`. Therefore, if `Athlete` were an interface, a `SkiJumper` might implement `Athlete` as well as `Flier`.

Figure 11.2

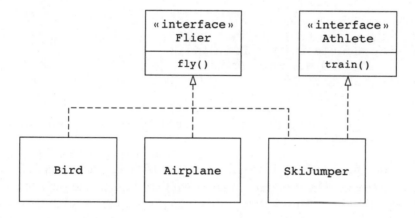

Example 11.3

```
public interface Athlete
{
    void train(double hours);
}
```

```
public class SkiJumper implements Flier, Athlete
{
    // Constructor
    public SkiJumper(String firstName, String lastName)
    {
        myFirstName = firstName;
        myLastName = lastName;
        myNumberOfJumps = 0;
        myHoursTraining = 0;
    }

    public void fly()
    {
        System.out.println("Using skis to take " + myFirstName + " "
                + myLastName + " into the air.");
        myNumberOfJumps++;
    }
```

```
    public void train(double hours)
    {
       System.out.println("I am on the slopes " + hours
             + " hours today.");
       myHoursTraining += hours;
    }

    public double getHoursTrained()
    {
       return myHoursTraining;
    }

    public int getJumps()
    {
       return myNumberOfJumps;
    }

    private String myFirstName;
    private String myLastName;
    private double myHoursTraining;
    private int myNumberOfJumps;
}
```

Now that you have an intuitive understanding of an interface and how it works, look at two examples that might be a bit more useful.

Section 11.1 in your text defines the `Measurable` interface. The `Measurable` interface is implemented by `Coin` and `BankAccount`, two dissimilar classes. The only method declared in this interface is `getMeasure`. This method simply returns a `double`. In the text example, either a coin's value or a bank account's balance is returned. The `DataSet` class in Section 11.1 in your text becomes usable in different circumstances by implementing a method `add` whose parameter implements the `Measurable` interface. The variable `x` refers to a class object that implements `Measurable`.

```
public void add(Measurable x)
```

This method will add `Coin` values or `BankAccount` balances (or any other object instantiated by a class that implements `Measurable`) and will keep track of the largest `Coin` value or `BankAccount` balance in the private instance field `maximum`.

Example 11.4

```
public class DataSet
{
   // More code here

   public void add(Measurable x)
   {
      sum = sum + x.getMeasure();
      if (count == 0 || maximum.getMeasure() < x.getMeasure())
         maximum = x;
      count++;
   }
```

```
11          public Measurable getMaximum()
12          {
13              return maximum;
14          }

15          //  Other variables here
16          private Measurable maximum;
17          private int count;
18          private double sum;
19      }
```

Line 4: The parameter x is of any type that implements the Measurable interface. If the declaration were

```
DataSet bankData = new DataSet();
```

the call to this method might be

```
bankData.add(new BankAccount(100));
```

If the declaration were

```
DataSet coinData = new DataSet();
```

the call to this method might be

```
coinData.add(new Coin(0.25, "quarter"));
```

Line 6: Adds values as defined in the getMeasure method of the individual class. If x were instantiated from the BankAccount class, we would be adding balances. If x were instantiated from the Coin class, we would be adding Coin values.

Lines 7–8: Checks for a new largest object based on the comparison of double values and resets present value of maximum if necessary. Notice that maximum is of a type that implements the Measurable interface. For the BankAccount class, maximum will store a BankAccount object. For the Coin class, maximum will store a Coin object.

Line 13: getMaximum will return the object with the largest measure.

Line 16: The private instance field is of type Measurable. This field can refer to any class that implements the Measurable interface.

Nothing prevents mixing Coin objects, BankAccount objects, or any other type of objects in this DataSet. However, this would not be a very good program design!

Our third example of an interface is one that we have already used with the String class.

```
class java.lang.String implements java.lang.Comparable
```

The Comparable interface has one method declared, compareTo. The String class implements this method so that it can compare two strings lexicographically.

Table 11.1

`class java.lang.String implements java.lang.Comparable`

Method	Method Summary
`int compareTo(Object other)`	Compares two strings lexicographically. Returns value < 0 if this `String` is less than `other`. Returns value = 0 if this `String` is equal to `other`. Returns value > 0 if this `String` is greater than `other`.

Table 11.2

`interface java.lang.Comparable`

Method	Method Summary
`int compareTo(Object other)`	Returns a value < 0 if `this` is less than `other`. Returns a value = 0 if `this` is equal to `other`. Returns a value > 0 if `this` is greater than `other`.

When a class implements an interface, the class makes a contract to provide the implementation for the methods of the interface as they are declared in the interface. Therefore, the method definition in the class must have the same exact parameter types as it does in the interface. Note that the type of the `compareTo` method's parameter is `Object`.

We might want a `Student` class to allow for the ordering of students, perhaps by the student GPA, or the student ID number. If a `Student` class implemented `Comparable`, we would add our preferred definition of `compareTo` to the `Student` class implementation. The `Comparable` interface can be implemented by the `Coin` class, the `Car` class, and any class that may want to provide an ordering for objects instantiated from the class. `Coin` objects may be compared based on their value. `Car` objects may be compared based on their mileage or their price.

Since the parameter type of the method is `Object`, in order to effectively define `compareTo` for our class, we will need to cast `Object` to the correct class type. This is explained in more detail in the next section and is illustrated in the `compareTo` implementations of the `Car` class and the `Coin` class below.

A `Car` class might implement `compareTo` in the following way.

```
public int compareTo(Object obj)
{
    Car temp = (Car) obj;
    if (mileage < temp.mileage)
        return -1;
    if (mileage > temp.mileage)
        return 1;
    return 0;
}
```

The `Coin` class defined below,

```
public class Coin
{
    public Coin(double aValue, String aName) {...}

    public double getValue() {...}
```

```
        public String getName() {...}

        private double value;
        private String name;
}
```

would implement compareTo in the following way:

```
        public int compareTo(Object obj)
        {
            Coin tempMoney = (Coin) obj;
            if (value < tempMoney.value)
                return -1;
            else if (value > tempMoney.value)
                return 1;
            else
                return 0;
        }
```

need accessors   bad style

The methods in an interface are *abstract*. That is, they are not implemented in the interface. Since all methods in an interface are public by default, the access modifier *public* doesn't need to be included in the method headers in the interface. When a class defines a method of an interface that it implements, the method must be declared as public.

An interface should not grow. Many classes implement an interface. If the interface is modified, all classes that implement the interface will be affected.

11.1.1   *Constants in Interfaces*

An interface can also declare constants. Since all variables declared in an interface are public static final, those keywords can be omitted when defining the constants. *Advanced Topic 11.1* in your text and Example 11.5 below demonstrates this.

Example 11.5

```
        public interface Flier
        {
            int MAX_ALTITUDE = 10000;
            void fly();
        }
```

```
        public class SkiJumper implements Flier
        {
            public void fly()
            {
                System.out.println("Using skis to take me into the air");
                System.out.println("Will not go higher than "
                    + Flier.MAX_ALTITUDE + " feet.");
            }
        }
```

Notice that the constant is called by specifying the interface name before the constant name (Flier.MAX_ALTITUDE).

11.2   Converting Between Class and Interface Types

In Example 11.4, the call to the method add could be

```
bankData.add(new BankAccount(100));
```
or
```
coinData.add(new Coin(0.25, "quarter"));
```

Any object whose class implements Measurable can be passed as a parameter to add. In this case, since a Coin is Measurable, it can be passed to a parameter that is of type Measurable. This type conversion from the class to the interface is legal. Section 11.2 of your text explains this example in detail.

When converting from an interface type to a class type, you must cast to the appropriate class type. The example that is explained in your text casts Measurable to Coin.

```
Measurable max = coinData.getMaximum();
String name = ((Coin) max).getName();   // Notice parentheses!
```

Parentheses are necessary because of the order of precedence of the operators in this statement. In Java, the access class feature (.) has higher precedence than the (cast). Without parentheses we would have

```
(Coin) max.getName()
```

where max is of type Measurable and getName is not defined for Measurable. Without the parentheses, a compile-time error will result. It is a common error to forget these needed parentheses! Table 11.3 contains a summary of operator precedence.

Table 11.3

Operator Order of	Description	Associativity
.	Access class feature	Left to Right
[]	Array subscript	Left to Right
()	Method call	Left to Right
++ --	Increment, decrement	Right to Left
!	Boolean not	Right to Left
+ (unary) - (unary)	Unary operators	Right to Left
(*TypeName*)	Cast	Right to Left
new	Object allocation	Right to Left
* / %	Arithmetic operators	Left to Right
+ -	Arithmetic operators	Left to Right
< <= > >=	Relational operators	Left to Right
== !=	Equals, not equals	Left to Right
&&	And	Left to Right
||	Or	Left to Right
= *= /= %= += -=	Assignment with	Right to Left

We demonstrated casting when converting from an interface type to a class type in the implementations of compareTo for the Car and Coin classes.

11.3 Polymorphism

Polymorphism means having many shapes or many forms. When the interface name is used to declare an object reference variable, the variable can refer to any object that is instantiated from a class that implements the interface. In the declaration

```
Flier skyReacher;    // skyReacher is an object variable.
                     // The interface CANNOT be instantiated.
```

skyReacher can refer to objects of different types if those types implement the Flier interface.

```
        skyReacher = new Airplane();
or
        skyReacher = new Bird();
or
        skyReacher = new SkiJumper("Joe", "Smith");
```

The actual type of the object skyReacher is determined at run-time.

Consider the statement

```
        skyReacher.fly();
```

The actual type of the object determines the method to be called. This principle is called *polymorphism*. The program has to run before the object to which skyReacher refers is determined. The virtual machine selects the appropriate method, not the compiler. This is referred to as late, or *dynamic*, binding.

Example 11.5

```
        Flier skyReacher;
        skyReacher = new SkiJumper("Joe", "Smith");
        skyReacher.fly();
```

This segment of code will bind skyReacher to a SkiJumper object and the method call to fly will print *Using skis to take Joe Smith into the air*.

Early binding takes place at compile time. This type of binding occurs with method overloading. Your text explains this difference in Section 11.3.

■ Topics That Are Useful But Not Tested

- Using interfaces for callbacks describes a method for improving code reusability and is explained in Section 11.4 of your text.
- An inner class is a class that is declared inside another class. They are commonly used for tactical classes that are not visible elsewhere in the program. Inner classes are explained in Section 11.5 of your text.
- UML diagrams are useful for illustrating class relationships and dependencies. The UML notation for showing dependency and interface realization is explained in Section 11.1 of your text.
- Timer events are useful for programming animations and are explained in Section 11.6 of your text.

■ Things to Remember When Taking the AP Exam

- Early binding (overloading) of methods occurs if the *compiler* selects a method from several possible candidates before the program is run. Late binding (polymorphism) occurs if the method selection takes place when the program runs. This is an important distinction.
- All methods in an interface are public. The methods in the interface are not declared as public because they are public by default. When implementing the methods of the interface in a class, remember to include the keyword `public`.
- An interface does not have any instance variables.
- An interface does not implement any methods.
- You can convert from a class type to an interface type without casting if the class implements the interface, but you need a cast to convert from an interface type to a class type.
- For both the A and the AB Exams, you should be able to read the definitions of interfaces and be able to design your own interfaces.
- An interface does not have constructors and cannot be instantiated, but you can assign an object created from a class that implements the interface. For example,
  - `Flier f = new Flier();   // WRONG!`
  - `Flier f = new Airplane();   // OK`

■ Key Words

You should understand the terms below. The AP CS Exam questions may include references to these terms. The citations in parentheses next to each term identify the page numbers where it is defined and/or discussed in *Java Concepts*, 4th ed., and *Big Java*, 2nd ed.

abstract (412)	early binding (419)	late (dynamic) binding (419)
cast (417)	implements (412)	polymorphism (419)
constants (416)	interface (410)	

■ Connecting the Detailed Topic Outline to the Text

The citations in parentheses identify where information in the outline can be located in *Java Concepts*, 4th ed., and *Big Java*, 2nd ed.

- Using Interfaces for Code Reuse (410–416)
  - Constants in Interfaces (416)
- Converting Between Class and Interface Type (416–418)
- Polymorphism (418–419)

■ Practice Questions

Multiple Choice

1. Which of the following choices might serve as an interface for the other choices listed?

    a. `Piano`
    b. `Drum`
    c. `Guitar`
    d. `Instrument`
    e. `FrenchHorn`

Questions 2–5 refer to the `Flier` and `Athlete` interfaces and the `Airplane` and `SkiJumper` classes whose incomplete definitions are given below.

```java
public interface Flier
{
    void fly();
}
```

```java
public interface Athlete
{
    void train(double hours);
}
```

```java
public class Airplane implements Flier
{
    public void fly()
    {
        System.out.println("Using my jet engines to fly");
    }
}
```

```java
public class SkiJumper implements Flier, Athlete
{
    // Constructor
    public SkiJumper(String firstName, String lastName)
    {
        myFirstName = firstName;
        myLastName = lastName;
        myNumberOfJumps = 0;
        myHoursTraining = 0;
    }

    public void fly()
    {
        System.out.println("Using skis to take " + myFirstName + " "
                + myLastName + " into the air.");
        myNumberOfJumps++;
    }
```

```
public void train(double hours)
{
    System.out.println("I am on the slopes for " + hours
            + "hours per day.");
    myHoursTraining += hours;
}

public double getHoursTrained()
{
    return myHoursTraining;
}

public int getJumps()
{
    return myNumberOfJumps;
}

private String myFirstName;
private String myLastName;
private double myHoursTraining;
private int myNumberOfJumps;
}
```

2. Which of the following code segments causes a compile-time error?

a. `Airplane boeing707 = new Airplane();`
b. `Flier boeing707 = new Flier();`
c. `Flier boeing707 = new Airplane();`
d. `Airplane boeing707 = new Airplane();`
   `Flier airTraveler = boeing707;`
e. `Airplane boeing707 = new Airplane();`
   `Flier airTraveler;`
   `airTraveler = (Airplane) boeing707;`

3. Consider the following code segment.

```
1    Airplane skyRider = new Airplane();
2    Flier skyRider2 = skyRider;
3    Athlete skyRider3 = (Athlete) skyRider2;
4    Airplane skyRider4 = (Airplane) skyRider2;
5    Flier skyRider5 = skyRider4;
```

Which statement above will cause a run-time error and throw an exception?

a. Statement 1
b. Statement 2
c. Statement 3
d. Statement 4
e. Statement 5

Questions 4 and 5 refer to the following declarations.

```
Airplane c = new Airplane();
Flier f = new Airplane();
Athlete a = new SkiJumper("Ann", "Smith");
SkiJumper s = new SkiJumper("John", "Doe");
```

4. Which of the following statements is **not** legal?

    a. `c.fly();`
    b. `f.fly();`
    c. `a.train(3);`
    d. `s.train(3);`
    e. `a.fly();`

5. Which of the following statements needs a cast?

    I. `f = c;`
    II. `a = s;`
    III. `s = a;`

    a. I only
    b. II only
    c. III only
    d. I and II only
    e. I and III only

6. Suppose a class `C` implements an interface `I` by implementing all of the methods of `I` and no further methods. Then which of the following *must* be **true**?

    a. All instance variables of `C` are public.
    b. All methods of `C` are abstract.
    c. All methods of `C` are public.
    d. All constants of `C` are public.
    e. All instance variables of `C` are private.

7. Which of the following statements is **true** about casting?

    a. You must cast to convert from an interface type to a class type.
    b. You must cast to convert from a class type to an interface type.
    c. You cannot cast to convert an interface type to a class type.
    d. You cannot cast from a class type to an interface type.
    e. Both a and b above are true.

8. Which of the following statements is **true** about dynamic binding?

    a. Dynamic binding occurs during compile time.
    b. Dynamic binding occurs when the appropriate overloaded method is selected.
    c. Dynamic binding is another name for early binding.
    d. In dynamic binding, the virtual machine selects the appropriate method.
    e. Dynamic binding occurs only when an interface declares `public static final` constants.

9. Which of the following statements about interfaces is **not** true?

    a. An interface can specify constants that can be used by all classes that implement the interface.
    b. An interface can specify variables that can be used by all classes that implement the interface.
    c. An interface can specify methods that must be defined by all classes that implement the interface.

    d.   An interface name cannot be instantiated.

    e.   The interface contains declarations but not implementations.

10. Suppose `foo` is an object of class `C`, and `C` implements the interface type `I`. Which of the following statements *must* be **true**?

    a.   `foo` was constructed with the constructor of `I`.

    b.   `C` assigns values to all constants declared in the interface `I`.

    c.   `C` supplies an implementation for all methods of the interface `I`.

    d.   `foo` must be declared as

```
I foo = new C();
```

    e.   All methods of `I` are declared as `private`.

Free Response Questions

1. The `SkiJumper` class is to implement the `Comparable` interface. The present definition of `SkiJumper` is defined below.

```java
public class SkiJumper implements Flier, Athlete
{
    // Constructs a default ski jumper.
    public SkiJumper(String firstName, String lastName)
    {
        myFirstName = firstName;
        myLastName = lastName;
        myNumberOfJumps = 0;
        myHoursTraining = 0;
    }

    // Simulates a ski jumper flying.
    public void fly()
    {
        System.out.println("Using skis to take " + myFirstName
            + " " + myLastName + " into the air.");
        myNumberOfJumps++;
    }

    /*
        Adds hours to total training time.
        hours is the number of hours to add
    */
    public void train(double hours)
    {
        System.out.println("I am on the slopes " + hours
            + " hours today.");
        myHoursTraining += hours;
    }

    // Returns hours of training.
    public double getHoursTrained()
    {
        return myHoursTraining;
    }
```

```
        // Returns total jumps made.
        public int getJumps()
        {
            return myNumberOfJumps;
        }

        private String myFirstName;
        private String myLastName;
        private double myHoursTraining;
        private int myNumberOfJumps;
}
```

a. Adjust the class header so that the `Comparable` interface is implemented by `SkiJumper`.

b. Implement the necessary methods so that the `Comparable` interface is implemented by the `SkiJumper` class. `SkiJumper` objects are compared by the number of jumps completed.

2. Modify the `Purse` class defined below to implement the `Comparable` interface. Purses are compared by the total value of money contained in the purse.

```
        public class Purse implements Comparable
        {
            // Constructs an empty purse.
            public Purse()
            {
                nickels = 0;
                dimes = 0;
                quarters = 0;
            }

            /*
                Adds nickels to the purse.
                count is the number of nickels to add
            */
            public void addNickels(int count)
            {
                nickels += count;
            }

            /*
                Adds dimes to the purse.
                count is the number of dimes to add
            */
            public void addDimes(int count)
            {
                dimes += count;
            }

            /*
                Adds quarters to the purse.
                count is the number of quarters to add
            */
            public void addQuarters(int count)
            {
                quarters += count;
```

```
      }

      /*
         Gets the total value of the coins in the purse.
         Returns the sum of all coin values.
      */
      public double getTotal()
      {
         return nickels * NICKEL_VALUE
               + dimes * DIME_VALUE + quarters * QUARTER_VALUE;
      }

      private static final double NICKEL_VALUE = 0.05;
      private static final double DIME_VALUE = 0.1;
      private static final double QUARTER_VALUE = 0.25;

      private int nickels;
      private int dimes;
      private int quarters;
   }
```

3. Consider the partial hierarchy of orchestra instruments given below.

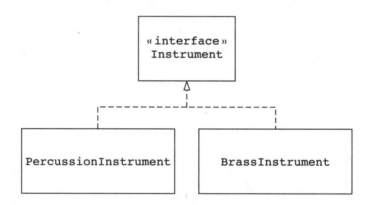

The following functionality is defined for all orchestra instruments.
*   An instrument has one piece of information, an orchestra seat assignment, which is passed as a String to its one-parameter constructor. This seat assignment can be publicly accessed and can be changed after the instrument is created.
*   All instruments *tune* but they tune in very different ways. Percussion instruments may adjust the tension of the drumhead while brass instruments may tune a middle G first.

Because a PercussionInstrument is a kind of Instrument and a BrassInstrument is a kind of Instrument, BrassInstrument and PercussionInstrument implement the Instrument interface.

a. Write the Instrument interface that abstracts this functionality.

b. Write the complete class definition for BrassInstrument. In writing your class, you should
    *   choose appropriate method and variable names.
    *   provide the functionality specified above.

Comments are not required, but may be used as desired to clarify what you write.

CHAPTER 12

(Covers *Java Concepts* Chapter 13)

Inheritance

■ Topic Summary

12.1   Introduction to Inheritance

Inheritance is used to extend classes that already exist. By extending existing classes, you can create new, more specific classes *and* take advantage of code that is already written. Chapter 13 of your text revisits the `BankAccount` class to illustrate the key concepts of inheritance. We will revisit our `SkiJumper` class and redefine `Athlete` to illustrate these same concepts and to provide you with another example. In this example, `Athlete` will now be a class, not an interface. All methods in the `Athlete` interface are now implemented in the `Athlete` class.

We will make some basic assumptions:
• All athletes have a name and a sport in which they participate.
• An athlete keeps track of the number of hours of training done.
• All athletes train for the sport in which they participate.
• An athlete participates in only one sport.
• Athletes participating in different sports may train in different ways.

Figure 12.1

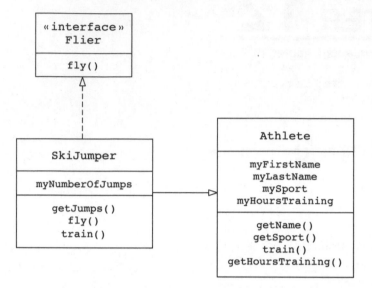

Figure 12.1 shows our SkiJumper class *implementing* the Flier interface and *extending* the Athlete class. SkiJumper is a *subclass* of Athlete. Athlete is a *superclass* of SkiJumper. SkiJumper *inherits* the instance fields myFirstName, myLastName, mySport, and myHoursTraining and defines an additional instance field, myNumberOfJumps that is specific to SkiJumper and not particularly applicable to other athletes. SkiJumper will implement the methods fly (as promised when implementing the Flier interface) and getJumps. SkiJumper will also *override* the method train by implementing the train method in a particular way that differs from the training routine of other athletes. Inheriting from Athlete differs from implementing Flier. Flier is an interface and cannot be instantiated. Flier does not have state or behavior. Athlete is a class. Athlete defines state and behavior and can be instantiated. Example 12.1 adds code to our visual interpretation.

Example 12.1

```
/**
    Describes any class whose objects can fly.
*/
public interface Flier
{
    void fly();
}
```

```
/**
    Defines an athlete.
*/
public class Athlete
{
    /**
        Constructs an athlete; myHoursTraining is initialized to 0.
        @param firstName first name of athlete
        @param lastName last name of athlete
        @param sportPlayed sport in which athlete participates
```

```java
    */
    public Athlete(String firstName, String lastName,
            String sportPlayed)
    {
        myFirstName = firstName;
        myLastName = lastName;
        mySport = sportPlayed;
        myHoursTraining = 0;
    }


    /**
        Updates myHoursTraining.
        @param hours number of hours athlete trained
    */
    public void train(double hours)
    {
        System.out.println("Athlete training for "
                + hours + " hours.");
        myHoursTraining += hours;
    }


    /**
        Gets athlete name.
        @return name of athlete
    */
    public String getName()
    {
        return (myFirstName + " " + myLastName);
    }


    /**
        Gets sport of athlete.
        @return sport participated in
    */
    public String getSport()
    {
        return mySport;
    }


    /**
        Gets hours trained by athlete.
        @return myHoursTraining
    */
    public double getHoursTraining()
    {
        return myHoursTraining;
    }

    private String myFirstName;
    private String myLastName;
    private String mySport;
    private double myHoursTraining;
}
```

```
public class SkiJumper extends Athlete implements Flier
{
    /**
        Constructs a SkiJumper object.
        Sport is ski jumping.
        Number of jumps is initialized to 0.
        @param first the first name
        @param last the last name
    */
    public SkiJumper(String first, String last)
    {
        super(first, last, "Ski Jumping"); // Call to super must be
                                           // first executable
                                           // statement in
                                           // constructor.
        myNumberOfJumps = 0;
    }

    /**
        Increments myNumberOfJumps, simulates flying.
    */
    public void fly()
    {
        System.out.println("Using skis to take " + getName()
            + " into the air.");
        myNumberOfJumps++;
    }

    /**
        Simulates training.
        @param hours hours of training
    */
    public void train(double hours)
    {
        System.out.println("I am on the slopes " + hours
            + " hours today.");
        super.train(hours);
    }

    /**
        Gets the current number of jumps of the SkiJumper.
        @return current myNumberOfJumps
    */
    public int getJumps()
    {
        return myNumberOfJumps;
    }

    private int myNumberOfJumps;
}
```

The SkiJumper class extends Athlete and implements Flier. A class can extend only one
superclass but can implement many interfaces.

12.2 Inheritance Hierarchies

When the hierarchy in Section 12.1 was designed, the features and behaviors common to all athletes were collected in the `Athlete` superclass. All athletes have a first name, a last name, and a sport. It is therefore useful to include public methods that can return the name and sport of the athlete. All athletes train and it may be useful to return the number of hours of training for any athlete. Figure 12.2 adds a `Runner` to our hierarchy and Example 12.2 implements the `Runner`. A `Runner` races. A `Runner` keeps track of the number of races run and the number of miles raced. A `Runner` does not fly.

Figure 12.2

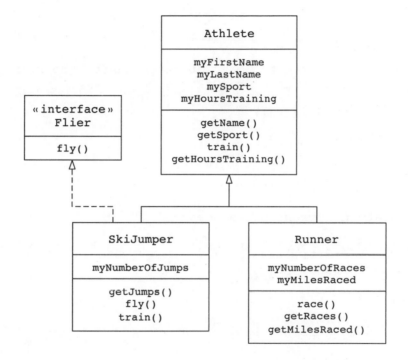

Example 12.2

```
public class Runner extends Athlete
{
    /**
        Constructs a Runner with a specified name.
        Sport is running.
        Number of races is initialized to 0.
        Miles raced is initialized to 0.
        @param first the first name
        @param last the last name
    */
    public Runner(String first, String last)
    {
        super(first, last, "Running");   // Call to super must be
                                         // first executable
                                         // statement in
                                         // constructor.
```

```
        myNumberOfRaces = 0;
        myMilesRaced = 0;
    }

    /**
        Increments number of races and updates miles raced.
        Simulates running a race.
    */
    public void race(double raceLength)
    {
        System.out.println(getName() + " is racing in a "
            + raceLength + " mile race.");
        myNumberOfRaces++;
        myMilesRaced += raceLength;
    }

    /**
        Gets the current number of races run by the runner.
        @return current numberOfRaces
    */
    public int getRaces()
    {
        return myNumberOfRaces;
    }

    /**
        Gets the current miles raced by the runner.
        @return current milesRaced
    */
    public double getMilesRaced()
    {
        return myMilesRaced;
    }

    private int myNumberOfRaces;
    private double myMilesRaced;
}
```

Notice that the `Runner` does not override `train`. The runner trains as a generic athlete trains but, in addition to hours of training, a `Runner` keeps track of hours racing and number of races run. The behavior and state of a `Runner` differ from those of the `SkiJumper`.

12.3 Inheriting Instance Fields and Methods

The methods `getName`, `getSport`, and `getHoursTraining` are inherited by the `SkiJumper` and the `Runner`.

The subclass `SkiJumper` of the `Athlete` class specifies the additional `getJumps` method and the `Runner` specifies the additional methods `race`, `getRaces`, and `getMilesRaced`.

The instance fields `myFirstName`, `myLastName`, `mySport`, and `myHoursTraining` are inherited by `SkiJumper` and `Runner`. The subclass `SkiJumper` of the `Athlete` class specifies the additional instance field `myNumberOfJumps` and the `Runner` specifies the additional instance fields `myNumberOfRaces` and `myMilesRaced`.

Although the subclass inherits the private instance fields of the superclass, the subclass has no access to the private fields of the superclass. *Private* means that only the class in which the instance field or method is defined has direct access. A class can allow access to private instance fields by providing public (or protected) mutator methods that modify the values of the instance fields. In our examples, we update the private instance field myHoursTraining of the superclass when the Runner trains and when the SkiJumper trains. This is done by invoking the public method train of the superclass thus preserving encapsulation. Each subclass does this in a different way.

- The Runner subclass does not have a train method defined. The train method that is invoked by Runner is the train method inherited from Athlete. Athlete's train method updates Athlete's own private instance variable myHoursTraining that is inherited by the Runner.

- The SkiJumper subclass implements a method train with the same signature as the method train of its superclass, Athlete. The SkiJumper's train method overrides the Athlete's train method. In order to update the inherited private instance field myHoursTraining, the SkiJumper's train method invokes the superclass train method with the call super.train(...). The super keyword is used to call a method of the superclass that is overridden by a subclass.

We will discuss protected access in Section 12.7.

Subclasses should not attempt to override instance fields. Subclasses can inherit instance fields and define new instance fields but should not attempt to override existing instance fields. The consequences of attempting to overriding instance fields are explained in Section 13.3 and *Common Error 13.2* in your text.

12.4   Subclass Construction

The constructor for Athlete has three String parameters, a first name, a last name, and a sport. The Athlete constructor initializes the appropriate instance fields with the values of these parameters and initializes myHoursTraining to 0.

When the Runner or SkiJumper constructor is called, two String parameters are passed, the first and last names of the athlete. For example,

```
Runner racer1 = new Runner("Joe", "Thomas");
SkiJumper jumper = new SkiJumper("Jane", "Smith");
```

The Runner constructor invokes the Athlete constructor passing these two parameters and the String "Running" (the sport name) to the superclass constructor.

```
public Runner(String first, String last)
{
    super(first, last, "Running");    // Call to super must be
                                       // first executable
                                       // statement in constructor
    myNumberOfRaces = 0;
    myMilesRaced = 0;
}
```

The SkiJumper constructor invokes the Athlete constructor passing these two parameters and the String "Ski Jumping" (the sport name) to the superclass constructor.

```
public SkiJumper(String first, String last)
{
    super(first, last, "Ski Jumping");
    myNumberOfJumps = 0;
}
```

The call to the superclass constructor ensures that all inherited instance fields are properly initialized. When the superclass constructor is called from the subclass, it must be the first statement in the subclass constructor. If the subclass constructor does not include the call to the superclass constructor, the default constructor for the superclass will automatically be called. However, if there is no default constructor (as with `Athlete`), an error will be reported.

The instance fields that are not inherited are initialized in the subclass constructor. Any attempt to change the inherited instance fields, which are private, will result in an error. You should avoid creating instance fields in a subclass with the same names as the instance fields in the superclass.

12.5   Converting Between Subclass and Superclass Types

If we wanted to have the ability to compare ski jumpers based on the number of jumps completed, the `SkiJumper` class would implement the `Comparable` interface and supply the `compareTo` method.

```
public class SkiJumper extends Athlete implements Flier,
    Comparable
```

and implement the `compareTo` method.

```
public int compareTo(Object other)
{
    SkiJumper temp = (SkiJumper) other;
    if (getJumps < temp.getJumps()) return -1;
    if (getJumps() > temp.getJumps()) return 1;
    return 0;
}
```

Figure 12.3

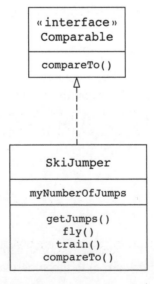

Since we want to compare the number of jumps of two `SkiJumpers`, we cast the `Object` parameter to a `SkiJumper`.

Suppose the following declarations were made.

```
SkiJumper jumper1 = new SkiJumper("John", "Miller");
SkiJumper jumper2 = new SkiJumper("Jane", "Dole");
Athlete jumper3 = new SkiJumper("Mark", "Morris");
Runner racer1 = new Runner("Mary", "Smith");
```

The following calls to `compareTo` are legal.

```
if (jumper1.compareTo(jumper2) > 0)
    // Code here
if (jumper2.compareTo(jumper1) > 0)
    // Code here
if (jumper1.compareTo(jumper3) > 0)
    // Code here
```

However, the statement

```
if (jumper3.compareTo(jumper1) > 0)    // WRONG!
    // Code here
```

will not compile. The variable `jumper3` is an `Athlete` and `compareTo` is not defined in the `Athlete` class.

The statement

```
if (jumper1.compareTo(racer1) > 0)
    // Code here
```

will compile but will throw a `ClassCastException` at runtime because the `compareTo` method of the `SkiJumper` class tries to cast a `Runner` to a `SkiJumper` in the first statement.

The statements

```
jumper3.fly();
racer1.fly();
```

will cause compile-time errors because `fly` is not defined for `Athlete` or for `Runner`.

The statement

```
jumper3.train(2);
```

is a legal statement because `train` is defined for `Athlete`. The `train` method of the `SkiJumper` class is invoked. Method calls are always determined by the type of the actual object (`SkiJumper`), not the type of the object reference (`Athlete`). This is an example of late (dynamic) binding.

The assignment

```
jumper3 = jumper1;    // OK because SkiJumper is a subclass of
                      //   Athlete
```

is legal. An object reference of a subclass can be assigned to an object of its superclass without casting.

The assignment

```
jumper1 = (SkiJumper) jumper3    // OK, cast necessary
```

is legal. An object reference of a superclass can be assigned to an object reference of its subclass with proper casting.

Example 12.3 is a sample client program to test these concepts.

Example 12.3
___

```java
public class InheritanceTester
{
    public static void main(String[] args)
    {
        SkiJumper jumper1 = new SkiJumper("John", "Miller");
        SkiJumper jumper2 = new SkiJumper("Jane", "Dole");
        Athlete jumper3 = new SkiJumper("Mark", "Morris");

        jumper1.fly();
        jumper1.fly();
        jumper2.fly();
        jumper2.fly();
        jumper2.fly();

        if (jumper1.compareTo(jumper2) > 0)
        {
            System.out.println(jumper1.getName() + " is better than "
                  + jumper2.getName() + ".");
        }
        else if (jumper1.compareTo(jumper2) < 0)
        {
            System.out.println(jumper2.getName() + " is better than "
                  + jumper1.getName() + ".");
        }
        else
        {
            System.out.println("The jumpers have completed an equal
                  number of jumps!");
        }
        jumper3.train(2);
    }
}
```

The results of program execution are:

> *Using skis to take John Miller into the air.*
> *Using skis to take John Miller into the air.*
> *Using skis to take Jane Dole into the air.*
> *Using skis to take Jane Dole into the air.*
> *Using skis to take Jane Dole into the air.*
> *Jane Dole is better than John Miller.*
> *I am on the slopes 2.0 hours today.*
> *Athlete training for 2.0 hours.*

The statement

```
jumper3.train(2);
```

first invokes the `train` method of `SkiJumper` class which prints "*I am on the slopes 2.0 hours today.*" After that statement is printed, a call to `super.train(2)` is made. This call invokes the `train` method of the superclass, `Athlete`. It is the `Athlete train` method that causes "*Athlete training for 2.0 hours.*" to be printed.

12.6 Abstract Classes

An abstract method is a method whose implementation is not specified. An abstract class is a class that contains one or more abstract methods. Abstract classes cannot be instantiated. Abstract classes can be used if you want to force programmers to define a method. Let's redefine our `Athlete` class one more time to demonstrate an `abstract` class. In the following example, `Athlete` is an abstract class, which means it cannot be instantiated.

Example 12.4

```
public abstract class Athlete
{
   public Athlete(String firstName, String lastName,
        String sportPlayed)
   {
      myFirstName = firstName;
      myLastName = lastName;
      mySport = sportPlayed;
      myHoursTraining = 0;
   }

   // Other methods defined here

   public abstract String getEquipment();
   // More code here
   // Private instance fields here
}
```

Example 12.4 mandates that any subclass of `Athlete` must implement the method `getEquipment`. If the subclass does not define this `abstract` method, the subclass cannot be instantiated and must be declared as `abstract` itself. `Runner` might define `getEquipment` in the following way.

```
public String getEquipment()
{
   return "Running shoes";
}
```

An abstract class differs from an interface because an abstract class can have instance variables and concrete (implemented) methods that are inherited by subclasses. Although you cannot instantiate an abstract class, you can still have an object reference whose type is an abstract class. For example, the following assignment is legal.

```
Athlete jumper3 = new SkiJumper("Mark", "Morris");   // This is OK.
```

12.7 Access Control

Java has four levels of access to fields, methods, and classes.
- public
- private
- protected
- package

The AP CS Java subset does not include `protected` and package visibilities. The Java Marine Biology Simulation case study uses `protected` access control. Any questions about `protected` access control on the AP Exam will be limited to the case study questions.

The `protected` level of visibility allows for access by all subclasses and all classes in the same package. This method of access control is explained in *Advanced Topic 13.3* of your text. In our `Athlete` example, if we declared `myHoursTraining` as `protected`, then the `Runner` and the `SkiJumper` would be able to access and update this instance field of `Athlete` directly. In our example, the `Athlete`'s `train` method is called to update this variable because it is private. It is a good habit to declare all instance fields as private. If you want subclasses to be able to modify inherited instance fields, provide `protected` mutator methods that do this. If you want the world to have the ability to modify the values of the instance fields, provide `public` mutator methods to do this.

12.8 `Object`: The Cosmic Superclass

In Java, all classes inherit from the `Object` class. The methods of the `Object` class included in the AP CS subset are listed in Table 12.1.

Table 12.1
class java.lang.Object

Method	Method Summary
String toString()	Returns `String` representation of the object.
boolean equals(Object other)	Indicates whether the object `other` is "equal to" this one.

12.8.1 Inheritance and the `toString` Method

The `toString` method is automatically called by `System.out.println`. If our `InheritanceTester` client program invokes the statement

```
System.out.println(jumper1);
```

`Object`'s `toString` method is called and a cryptic message about `SkiJumper` is printed to the screen. However, we may wish to print a meaningful message about `SkiJumper` that includes values of the instance variables. This will allow us to inspect the object for possible errors in our program. In order to do this, `SkiJumper` must override the `Object` `toString` method.

```
public String toString()
{
    return "SkiJumper number of jumps = " + myNumberOfJumps;
}
```

The statement

```
System.out.println(jumper1);
```

will now print *SkiJumper number of jumps = 2.*

It may be more useful to provide a `toString` method that prints the values of all instance fields. This becomes a very good way to test your programs. A `toString` method for `Athlete` might be:

```
public String toString()
{
    return ("class Athlete: \nname = " + myFirstName + " "
        + myLastName + "\nsport = " + mySport
        + "\nhours training = " + myHoursTraining);
}
```

and the more inclusive `toString` method for `SkiJumper` would be:

```
public String toString()
{
    String s = super.toString();
    return (s + "\nclass SkiJumper:\nnumber of jumps = "
        + myNumberOfJumps);
}
```

The statement

```
System.out.println(jumper2);
```

would print

```
class Athlete:
name = Jane Dole
sport = Ski Jumping
hours training = 0.0
class SkiJumper:
number of jumps = 3
```

You can include whatever meaningful information you need when you override `Object`'s `toString` method. It is a good programming habit to supply a `toString` method in the classes that you write. Example 12.5 visits our `Athlete`, `SkiJumper`, and `Runner` classes one more time. Each of these classes overrides `Object`'s `toString` method.

Example 12.5

```
public abstract class Athlete
{
    public Athlete(String firstName, String lastName,
        String sportPlayed)
    {
        // Instance fields initialized here
    }
```

```
        public String toString ()
        {
            return("class Athlete: \nname = " + myFirstName + " "
                    + myLastName + "\nsport = " + mySport
                    + "\nhours training = " + myHoursTraining);
        }
        // Other methods here
        // Private declarations here
    }
```

```
    public class SkiJumper extends Athlete implements Flier
    {
        public SkiJumper(String firstName, String lastName)
        {
            super(firstName, lastName, "Ski Jumping");
            // Instance fields initialized here
        }

        public String toString()
        {
            String s = super.toString();
            return (s + "\nclass SkiJumper:\nnumber of jumps = "
                    + myNumberOfJumps);
        }

        // Other methods here
        // Private instance fields here
    }
```

```
    public class Runner extends Athlete
    {
        public Runner(String firstName, String lastName)
        {
            super(firstName, lastName, "Running");
            // Instance fields initialized here
        }
        public String toString()
        {
            String s = super.toString();
            return (s + "\n" + getName() + " is a runner.");
        }

        // Other methods here
        // Private instance fields here
    }
```

Example 12.6 demonstrates adding `Athletes` to an `ArrayList` and then printing the contents of the `ArrayList` by calling `System.out.println` for each element of the `ArrayList`. The `println` method of the `PrintStream` class invokes the `toString` method of each object it is requested to print. Example 12.6 is implemented using the generic `ArrayList` and enhanced `for` loop.

Example 12.6 (Java 5)

```
ArrayList<Athlete> teamMembers = new ArrayList<Athlete>();
teamMembers.add(new SkiJumper("SkiJumper", "One"));
teamMembers.add(new SkiJumper("SkiJumper", "Two"));
teamMembers.add(new Runner("Runner", "One"));
teamMembers.add(new Runner("Runner", "Two"));
for (Athlete i : teamMembers)
{
    System.out.println(i);
}
```

Example 12.6 prints:

class Athlete:
name = SkiJumper One
sport = Ski Jumping
hours training = 0.0
class SkiJumper:
number of jumps = 0
class Athlete:
name = SkiJumper Two
sport = Ski Jumping
hours training = 0.0
class SkiJumper:
number of jumps = 0
class Athlete:
name = Runner One
sport = Running
hours training = 0.0
Runner One is a runner.
class Athlete:
name = Runner Two
sport = Running
hours training = 0.0
Runner Two is a runner.

12.8.2 Inheritance and the `equals` Method

If you wish to test whether two objects have equal states (have the same contents), you need to override `Object`'s equals method. An `equals` method for `Athlete` would be:

```
public boolean equals(Object other)
{
    Athlete temp = (Athlete) other;
    return ((myFirstName.equals(temp.myFirstName))
            && (myLastName.equals(temp.myLastName))
            && (mySport.equals(temp.mySport))
            && (myHoursTraining == temp.myHoursTraining));
}
```

The parameter `other` needs to be cast to `Athlete`. Since three of the instance fields are objects (`Strings`), they need to be compared using the `String` equals method. The `myHoursTraining` instance field is a number. Numbers are compared using the `==` operator. Objects are compared using `equals`.

If a class implements `Comparable` and has defined `compareTo`, the best implementation for that class's `equals` method would be:

```
public boolean equals(Object other)
{
    return compareTo(other) == 0;
}
```

or

```
public boolean equals(Object other)
{
    return this.compareTo(other) == 0;
}
```

This ensures that comparison of two objects of the same class is consistent (`equals` and `compareTo` compare the same way).

Although the implementation of the `equals` method is not part of the AP CS testable Java subset, you do need to understand the difference between object equality (`equals`) and identity (`==`).

■ Expanded Coverage of Material That Is Not Found in the Text

- The inheritance relationship between a subclass and its superclass is an *IS-A* relationship. The subclass is more specific than the superclass. For example,
  - A `SkiJumper` IS A `Athlete`
  - A `Runner` IS A `Athlete`

Not all athletes are runners. Not all athletes are ski jumpers. A good check for subclass selection is to apply this IS-A phrase. Ask yourself if your IS-A statement is true. Chapter 17 of your text covers IS-A relationships in more detail. When determining if an assignment statement is legal, read from right to left with IS-A. If `SkiJumper` implements `Athlete` and the following instantiation is made,

  - `SkiJumper s = new SkiJumper("John", "Bates");`
  - `Athlete a = new SkiJumper("Mary", "Williams");`
  - `a = s;`   OK because a `SkiJumper` IS-A `Athlete`.
  - `s = a;`   WRONG because an `Athlete` is NOT always a `SkiJumper`.

- An object can be composed of other objects. For example, an `Athlete` has a first name, a last name, and a sport. All three of these instance fields are `String` objects. This situation is an example of a *HAS-A* relationship. *HAS-A* relationships are used when a class is composed of other types of objects. This is often referred to as composition. For example,
  - A `SkiJumper` HAS-A name (`String`).
  - A `DeckOfPlayingCards` HAS-A `Card`.
  - An `Airplane` HAS-A `Engine`.

Chapter 17 of your text covers HAS-A relationships in more detail.

■ Topics That Are Useful But Not Tested

- The `instanceof` operator tests whether an object belongs to a particular type. This is explained in Section 13.5 of your text.
- `protected` features can be accessed by all subclasses and all classes in the same package. `protected` access is explained in *Advanced Topic 13.3* of your text.
- The `getClass().getName()` call can be used to print the class name in a `toString` method. This is explained in *Advanced Topic 13.4* of your text.
- The `getClass` method can also be used to test if two objects belong to the same class. This is explained in *Advanced Topic 13.5* of your text.

■ Things to Remember When Taking the AP Exam

- A subclass inherits the behavior and state of its superclass.
- Do not give an instance field of a subclass the same name as an instance field of its superclass. This "shadowing of instance fields" is explained in *Common Error 13.2* of your text.
- A subclass has no direct access to the private fields or private methods of its superclass.
- The call to a superclass constructor, if included, must be the first statement in a subclass constructor. Otherwise, the superclass must have a default constructor, and that default constructor will be called.
- An object reference of a subclass can be assigned to an object reference of its superclass.
- An object reference of a superclass can be assigned to an object reference of its subclass with the appropriate casting.
- An abstract class cannot be instantiated.
- The AP CS Java subset specifies that all classes are public and all instance variables are private. The AP CS Java subset does not use `protected` and package (default) visibility but you may see these access modifiers in the case study. If the AP Exam contains any questions relating to `protected` visibility, they will be based on its use in the case study.
- For both the A and AB Exams you should be able to extend existing code using inheritance. For the AP CS A Exam, you should be able to modify subclass implementations. For the AP CS AB Exam, you should be able to design and implement subclasses.
- An abstract class is a class containing one or more abstract methods. For the AP CS A Exam, you should understand the concepts of abstract classes. For the AP CS AB Exam, you should be able to design and implement abstract classes.
- Implementing the `equals` method is not part of the AP CS subset, but you do need to understand the difference between object equality (`equals`) and identity (`==`).

■ Key Words

You should understand the terms below. The AP CS Exam questions may include references to these terms. The citations in parentheses next to each term identify the page numbers where it is defined and/or discussed in *Java Concepts*, 4th ed., and *Big Java*, 2nd ed.

abstract class (490)	inheritance (468)	super (481)
abstract method (490)	Object (495)	subclass (469)
access control (492)	object reference (491)	superclass (469)
code reuse (470)	override (475)	toString (496)
equals (498)	private (477)	
extends (469)	public (477)	

■ Connecting the Detailed Topic Outline to the Text

The citations in parentheses identify where information in the outline can be located in *Java Concepts*, 4th ed., and *Big Java*, 2nd ed.

- An Introduction to Inheritance (468–472)
- Inheritance Hierarchies (473–475)
- Inheriting Instance Fields and Methods (475–480)
- Subclass Construction (481–482)
- Converting Between Subclass and Superclass Types (482–484)
- Polymorphism (485–490)
  - Abstract Classes (490–491)
- Access Control (492–495)
- Object: The Cosmic Superclass (495)
  - Inheritance and the toString Method (496–498)
  - Inheritance and the equals Method (498–501)

■ Practice Questions

Multiple Choice

1. A programmer notices that a method of a subclass has the same signature as a method in its superclass. Which of the following statements best characterizes this situation?

    a. The superclass method is overloaded.
    b. The superclass method shadows the subclass method.
    c. The subclass method overrides the superclass method.
    d. The superclass method overrides the subclass method.
    e. The program will not compile because methods of two classes in the same inheritance hierarchy cannot have the same name.

2. Which of the following statements is **true** about abstract classes?

    a. Instance fields declared in abstract classes are automatically `public`.
    b. Instance fields cannot be declared in abstract classes.
    c. A subclass that extends an abstract class must override instance variables declared in the abstract class.
    d. A subclass that extends an abstract class inherits the instance variables in the abstract class.
    e. The instance fields declared in an abstract class are automatically `static final`.

3. Which of the following statements is **not** true about subclass methods?

    a. A subclass can override methods in a superclass.
    b. A subclass can define new methods that are not in the superclass.
    c. A subclass can inherit methods in a superclass.
    d. A subclass can access private methods in a superclass.
    e. A subclass can access public methods of its superclass.

Questions 4, 5, and 6 refer to the `Employee`, `Manager`, and `Programmer` classes incompletely defined below.

```
public class Employee
{
    // Constructors and other methods here

    public void work()
    {
        System.out.println("Employee working.");
    }

    // Instance fields here
}
```

```
public class Manager extends Employee
{
    // Constructors and other methods here

    public void work()
    {
        System.out.println("Manager working.");
    }

    // Instance fields here
}
```

```
public class Programmer extends Employee
{
    // Constructors and other methods here

    public void work()
    {
        System.out.println("Programmer working.");
```

```
        }

            //  Instance fields here
        }
```

4. Which of the following declarations will cause a compile-time error?

    a. `Employee employA = new Employee();`
    b. `Employee employB = new Manager();`
    c. `Manager employC = new Manager();`
    d. `Manager employD = new Employee();`
    e. `Programmer employE = new Programmer();`

5. Consider the following declarations.

    ```
    Employee employ1 = new Employee();
    Manager employ2 = new Manager();
    Employee employ3 = new Manager();
    ```

Which of the following assignments is legal?

    I.   `employ1 = employ2;`
    II. `employ2 = (Manager) employ3;`
    III. `employ1 = (Manager) employ2;`

    a. I only
    b. II only
    c. III only
    d. I and II only
    e. I, II, and III

6. Consider the following declarations.

    ```
    Employee employ1 = new Employee();
    Manager employ2 = new Manager();
    Employee employ3 = new Manager();
    ```

    What will be printed if the code segment below is executed?

    ```
    employ1 = (Manager) employ2;
    employ1.work();
    employ3.work();
    ```

    a. *Manager working.*
        Manager working.

    b. *Employee working.*
        Employee working.

    c. *Employee working.*
        Manager working.

    d. *Manager working.*
        Employee working.

    e. Nothing is printed. A `ClassCastException` occurs.

7. You implement three classes: `Person`, `Student` and `Instructor`. A `Person` has a name and a year of birth. A `Student` has a major, and an `Instructor` has a salary. Which of the following would be the best design for this situation?

    a. `Person` should be an interface. `Student` and `Instructor` should implement `Person`.
    b. `Person` should be an abstract class that includes declarations for four abstract methods: `getName`, `getYearOfBirth`, `getMajor`, `getSalary`.
    c. `Person` should be an abstract class that includes declarations for two abstract methods: `getName` and `getYearOfBirth`.
    d. `Person` should be a superclass that includes implementations for four methods: `getName`, `getYearOfBirth`, `getMajor`, `getSalary`. `Student` and `Instructor` will be subclasses of `Person`.
    e. `Person` should be a superclass that includes implementations for two methods: `getName`, `getYearOfBirth`. The `Student` class and the `Instructor` class will be subclasses of `Person`.

Questions 8 and 9 refer to the following scenario.

A Barbershop Quartet is a group of four singers: a lead, a tenor, a bass, and a baritone. These four singers harmonize to produce a purely American form of music developed in the 19th century. Consider the incomplete class definitions below.

```java
public class BarberShopQuartet
{
    public BarberShopQuartet()
    {
        Tenor highSinger = new Tenor();
        Baritone bari = new Baritone();
        Lead melody = new Lead();
        Bass lowSinger = new Bass();
        System.out.println("Quartet created.");
    }
}
```

```java
public class Singer
{
    public Singer()
    {
        System.out.println("Singing...");
    }
}
```

```java
public class Tenor extends Singer
{
    public Tenor()
    {
        System.out.println("Singing...the high notes");
    }
}
```

```
public class Baritone extends Singer
{
    public Baritone()
    {
        System.out.println("Singing...harmonizing with the lead");
    }
}
```

```
public class Lead extends Singer
{
    public Lead()
    {
        System.out.println("Singing...the melody and providing the
            emotion");
    }
}
```

```
public class Bass extends Singer
{
    public Bass()
    {
        System.out.println("Singing...the very low notes");
    }
}
```

8. What output would be produced if the following code was executed?

```
BarberShopQuartet fourSingers = new BarberShopQuartet();
System.out.println("This quartet is on stage!");
```

a. *Quartet created.*
    This quartet is on stage!

b. *This quartet is on stage!*

c. *Singing ... the high notes*
    Singing ... harmonizing with the lead
    Singing ... the melody and providing the emotion
    Singing ... the very low notes
    This quartet is on stage!

d. *Singing ... the high notes*
    Singing ... harmonizing with the lead
    Singing ... the melody and providing the emotion
    Singing ... the very low notes
    Quartet created.
    This quartet is on stage!

e. *Singing ...*
    Singing ... the high notes
    Singing ...
    Singing ... harmonizing with the lead
    Singing ...
    Singing ... the melody and providing the emotion
    Singing ...
    Singing ... the very low notes
    Quartet created.
    This quartet is on stage!

9. Which of the following IS-A, HAS-A relationships is **true**?

    a. A `BarberShopQuartet` is-a `Singer`.
    b. A `Tenor` is-a `Singer`.
    c. A `Baritone` has-a `BarberShopQuartet`.
    d. A `Singer` has-a `BarberShopQuartet`.
    e. A `Singer` has-a `Lead`.

10. Which of the following statements about inheritance is **not** true?

    a. A class can be both a subclass and a superclass at the same time.
    b. Every class is a subclass of the `Object` class.
    c. Common features should be located as high in the inheritance hierarchy as possible.
    d. The `toString` and `equals` methods are inherited by all classes.
    e. The type of the reference, not the type of the object, is used to determine which version of an overridden method is invoked.

Free Response Questions

1. Consider the following detailed inheritance hierarchy diagram.

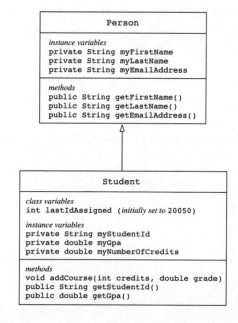

a. The `Person` constructor has two `String` parameters, a first name and a last name. The constructor initializes the e-mail address to the first letter of the first name followed by the first five letters of the last name followed by @jc.com. If the last name has fewer than five letters, the e-mail address will be the first letter of the first name followed by the entire last name followed by @jc.com. Examples:

Name	Email address
Jane Smith	JSmith@jc.com
John Morris	JMorri@jc.com
Mary Key	MKey@jc.com

Implement the `Person` constructor.

b. Override `Object`'s `toString` method for the `Person` class. The `toString` method should return the present state of the object. Assume that the constructor written for the previous part of this problem works as intended.

c. Write the `Student` class header so that the `Student` is a subclass of `Person` and implements the `Comparable` interface.

d. The `Student` constructor will be called with two `String` parameters, the first name and the last name of the student. When the `Student` is constructed, the inherited fields `myFirstName`, `myLastName`, and `myEmailAddress` will be properly initialized, the student's GPA (`myGpa`) and number of credits (`myNumberOfCredits`) will be set to 0. The variable `lastIdAssigned` will be properly incremented each time a `Student` is constructed and the student ID (`myStudentId`) will be set to the next available ID number as tracked by the class variable, `lastIdAssigned`. Implement the `Student` constructor. Assume that the constructor written for part a of this problem works as intended.

e. Override `Object`'s `toString` method for the `Student` class. The `toString` method should return the present state of the object. Assume that all methods and constructors written for the previous parts of this problem work as intended.

f. Students are compared to each other by comparing GPAs. Implement the `compareTo` method for the `Student` class.

2. Refer to the `Athlete` class and the `Runner` class below.

```
public class Athlete
{
    public Athlete(String firstName, String lastName,
        String sportPlayed)
    {
        myFirstName = firstName;
        myLastName = lastName;
        mySport = sportPlayed;
        myHoursTraining = 0;
    }
```

```java
    public void train(double hours)
    {
        System.out.println("Athlete training for " + hours
                + " hours.");
        myHoursTraining += hours;
    }

    public String getName()
    {
        return (myFirstName + " " + myLastName);
    }

    public String getSport()
    {
        return mySport;
    }

    public double getHoursTraining()
    {
        return myHoursTraining;
    }

    private String myFirstName;
    private String myLastName;
    private String mySport;
    private double myHoursTraining;
}
```

```java
public class Runner extends Athlete
{
    public Runner(String firstName, String lastName)
    {
        super(firstName, lastName, "Running");
        myNumberOfRaces = 0;
        myMilesRaced = 0;
    }

    public void race(double raceLength)
    {
        System.out.println(getName() + " is racing in a "
                + raceLength + " mile race.");
        myNumberOfRaces++;
        myMilesRaced += raceLength;
    }

    public int getRaces()
    {
        return myNumberOfRaces;
    }

    public double getMilesRaced()
    {
        return myMilesRaced;
    }
```

```
        private int myNumberOfRaces;
        private double myMilesRaced;
    }
```

A `Marathoner` is a long distance `Runner`. Write the `Marathoner` class according to the following specifications.

The `Marathoner` is a subclass of the `Runner` class. The `Marathoner`'s sport is "Running". However, in order for a race to "count" as a race for the `Marathoner`, the race must be at least 10 miles in length. If it is shorter than 10 miles, the race counts as a training run and the training time credited to `myHoursTraining` is 8 1/2 minutes for each mile run. The variable `myNumberOfRaces` is not incremented, nor is `myMilesRaced` increased if the race is shorter than 10 miles in length. The `Marathoner` class will override the `Runner`'s race method so that these specifications are met.

3. Consider the following list of classes.

```
Person
Course
Teacher
HomeAddress
MathDepartmentChairperson
Student
Object
Employee
ClassRoster
Secretary
Nurse
```

a. List the HAS-A relationships that exist in the list of classes above.

b. Sketch a class hierarchy illustrating the IS-A relationships that exist for the classes above.

CHAPTER 13

(Covers *Java Concepts* Chapter 15)

Exception Handling

TOPIC OUTLINE

■ Topic Summary

13.1 Introduction to Exceptions

You plan a vacation to the Florida Keys to do some SCUBA diving. On the morning of your first day of diving, you arrive at the boat dock, prepared with all the appropriate equipment. Before launching the boat, the skipper listens to the weather report. The skipper finds out that the sea is far too rough, cancels the dive, and gives you a memo confirming cancellation. This is akin to *throwing an exception.* An exceptional situation causes abrupt termination of the normal processing (the SCUBA dive). Note that throwing an exception doesn't tell you how to *recover* from the exceptional situation. An example of recovery would be if the manager, upon seeing the cancellation memo, buys everyone breakfast, or refunds the dive trip costs. In Java, a *catch clause* is responsible for recovering from an exceptional condition.

Java provides an exception mechanism for handling *exceptional,* or abnormal, conditions in your programs. These problematic conditions prevent the continuation of the method execution. Exceptions in Java are represented by objects. These objects store information that includes the type of exception and where the exception was created. In the example, the cancellation memo confirmed this type of information about our SCUBA trip.

As we have seen in many of our programs, when we encounter run-time errors, a message on the screen describes the reason for that error. For example, the statements below are included in a program that compiles without error.

```
int[] numbers = new int[2];
numbers[0] = 54;
numbers[1] = 12;
numbers[2] = 14;
```

When the program is executed, the following message is printed.

Exception in thread "main" java.lang.ArrayIndexOutOfBoundsException
at ArrayTester.main(ArrayTester.java:12)

The segment of code *throws an exception* to indicate an error condition. The Java exception handling mechanism terminates the program with an error message. The information given includes the exception type (`ArrayIndexOutOfBoundsException`) and the location at which the exception was created (line 12 of the `main` method of the `ArrayTester` class in the file `ArrayTester.java`).

You can handle abnormal or problematic situations by including exception handling code in your program. For example, if a person tries to withdraw more money than a bank account has, you may wish to have the program terminated and indicate the reason rather than to alter the balance and cause unpredictable results later. The `throw` statement is used to invoke the exception handling mechanism. To throw an exception, you create an exception object with `new` and then throw it, using the `throw` keyword. The current flow of the method execution is terminated and the exception handler takes over.

13.1.1   Understanding Exceptions

You are responsible for understanding the exceptions that are commonly generated in your Java programs. Table 12.1 lists some common exceptions and their meaning.

Table 13.1

Common Run-time (Unchecked) Exceptions

Exception	Exception Summary
ArithmeticException	Thrown when an illegal arithmetic operation has occurred. For example, an integer "divide by zero" throws an instance of this class.
ArrayIndexOutOfBoundsException	Thrown when there is an attempt to access an array index that is either negative or greater than or equal to the size of the array. This class is a subclass of the IndexOutOfBoundsException class.
ClassCastException	Thrown when there is an attempt to cast an object to a class of which it is not an instance.
IllegalArgumentException	Thrown when a method is passed an illegal or inappropriate argument.
IllegalStateException	Signals that a method has been invoked at an illegal or inappropriate time.
IndexOutOfBoundsException	Thrown when an index is out of range. ArrayIndexOutOfBoundsException and StringIndexOutOfBoundsException are subclasses of this class.
NoSuchElementException	Thrown when an attempt to access a nonexistent element is made.

NullPointerException	Thrown when there is an attempt to use null where an object is required.
NumberFormatException	Thrown when an attempt to convert a string to one of the numeric types is made when the string does not have the appropriate format. This class is a subclass of IllegalArgumentException.
StringIndexOutOfBoundsException	Thrown when an index is either negative or greater than the size of the string. This class is a subclass of the IndexOutOfBoundsException class.

Examples of various exceptions are given below.

ArithmeticException
If the following code were executed,

```
int num = some integer value;
int count = 0;
System.out.println(num / count);   // ArithmeticException
```

An ArithmeticException (division by 0) would occur in the System.out.println statement.

ClassCastException
Manager is a subclass of the Employee class.

```
Employee worker1 = new Employee();
System.out.println((Manager) worker1);   // ClassCastException
```

worker1 is an Employee, not a Manager.

IndexOutOfBoundsException
Consider the following code segment.

```
int[] anArray = new int[10];
anArray[11] = 0;   // ArrayIndexOutOfBoundsException

ArrayList aList = new ArrayList();
aList.add("Ann");
System.out.println(aList.get(1)); // IndexOutOfBoundsException

String s = "aString";
System.out.println(s.substring(0,8));
       // StringIndexOutOfBoundsException
```

The exceptions that are thrown are subclasses of the IndexOutOfBoundsException class.

NoSuchElementException
Consider the following code segment.

```
ArrayList friends = new ArrayList();

Iterator it2;
for (it2 = friends.iterator(); it2.hasNext();)
{
```

```
        String temp2 = (String) it2.next();
        System.out.println(temp2);
    }
    System.out.println(it2.next());   // NoSuchElementException
```

Assuming that the `ArrayList friends` is declared, the `for` loop has the iterator traverse the entire array. In the second `println` statement, the iterator `it2` tries to access an element after the last one has been accessed. Iterators are part of the AP CS AB subset.

NullPointerException

```
    Manager worker1 = null;
    String temp = worker1.getName();   // NullPointerException
```

We cannot access an instance method of a `null` object.

NumberFormatException

```
    int units = Integer.parseInt("1234a");
    System.out.println(units + 1);
```

Although `parseInt` is not required in the AP CS subsets, it can be useful when getting input from the user. It can also lead to `NumberFormatExceptions`. In the above example, `"1234a"` is not a valid number so a `NumberFormatException` occurs. If `"1234a"` were replaced by `"12345"`, *12346* would be printed.

13.2   Throwing Exceptions (AB only)

Throwing exceptions allows you to ensure that certain conditions exist when your programs are executed. Although it is the responsibility of the calling procedure to meet the preconditions of a called method, it can be useful to check that the preconditions of your own methods are met. To do this, you can have your methods throw the appropriate exception if the precondition is not met. For example, the `Runner` class (Example 12.2 in this guide) has a method `race` that requires a `double` parameter. This parameter indicates the length of a race in miles. The length of a race should be a positive number. If the user passes a non-positive value to this method, you may choose to throw an exception.

IllegalArgumentException

```
    public void race(double raceLength)
    {
        if (raceLength <= 0)
        {
            throw new IllegalArgumentException("Race length must be
                greater than 0.");
        }
        System.out.println(getName() + " is racing in a " + raceLength
            + " mile race.");
        myNumberOfRaces++;
        myMilesRaced += raceLength;
    }
```

When the exception is thrown, the method terminates immediately. Execution is transferred to the exception handler. You can pass whatever `String` makes sense for the error condition you are checking or you can call the default constructor by not passing any parameter. Of course, it is more meaningful to pass a `String` parameter that adequately identifies the specific error.

IllegalStateException

An `IllegalStateException` might be thrown if a class invariant is violated. For example, a `BankAccount` is constructed with a non-negative balance. If an attempt is made to construct a `BankAccount` with a negative balance, an `IllegalStateException` could be thrown.

```
public BankAccount(double initialBalance)
{
    if (initialBalance < 0)
    {
        throw new IllegalStateException("Initial balance must be
            non-negative.");
    }
    balance = initialBalance;
}
```

AB students are expected to be able to throw `IllegalStateException` and `NoSuchElement-Exception` in their own methods.

13.3   Checked and Unchecked Exceptions

There are two types of exceptions: checked exceptions and unchecked exceptions. Checked exceptions are compiler-enforced exceptions. This means that when you call a method that throws a *checked* exception, you *must* tell the compiler what you are going to do about the exception if it is thrown. Checked exceptions are due to external circumstances that the programmer cannot prevent. They are subclasses of the `Exception` class but are not subclasses of `RuntimeException`. Figure 1 in Section 15.1 of your text illustrates the inheritance hierarchy for exceptions. Checked exceptions are not part of the AP CS Java subset but they are discussed in Section 15.2 of your text.

Unchecked exceptions are subclasses of `RuntimeException`. In the programming of a method, an unchecked exception is thrown to indicate an exceptional or problematic situation. We have already been exposed to several unchecked exceptions, which are listed in Table 13.1 above. To reiterate, these are errors such as division by 0 which are not checked by the compiler (in fact they can't be), but that you may encounter.

■ Topics That Are Useful But Not Tested

- Checked exceptions are due to external circumstances that the programmer cannot prevent. The compiler checks that your program handles these exceptions. Checked exceptions are explained in Section 15.2 of your text.
- The `throws` specifier is used to indicate that a method may throw a checked exception. The `throws` specifier is discussed in Section 15.2 of your text.
- Designing your own exceptions can help to more accurately describe the exceptional situation. Designing your own exceptions is discussed in Section 15.5 of your text.
- Every exception should be handled somewhere in your program. The exceptions discussed in this chapter cause your program to terminate. The `try` block, `catch` clause, and `finally`

clause describe a more professional way to handle exceptions. These topics are explained in Sections 15.3–15.4 of your text.

■ Things to Remember When Taking the AP Exam

- Know the conditions under which the common exceptions listed in this chapter are thrown.
- AB students should be able to throw the unchecked `IllegalStateException` and `NoSuchElementException` in their own methods.

■ Key Words

You should understand the terms below. The AP CS Exam questions may include references to these terms. The citations in parentheses next to each term identify the page numbers where it is defined and/or discussed in *Java Concepts*, 4th ed., and *Big Java*, 2nd ed.

argument (553)	`RuntimeException` (555)
checked exception (555)	`throws` (557)
exception handler (555)	unchecked exception (555)
`IllegalArgumentException` (553)	

■ Connecting the Detailed Topic Outline to the Text

The citations in parentheses identify where information in the outline can be located in *Java Concepts*, 4th ed., and *Big Java*, 2nd ed.

- Throwing Exceptions **(AB only)** (552–555)
- Checked and Unchecked Exceptions **(AB only)** (555–558)

■ Practice Questions

Multiple Choice

1. Which of the following statements about checked and unchecked exceptions is **true**?

   a. Checked exceptions are subclasses of `RuntimeException`.
   b. Unchecked exceptions are subclasses of `RuntimeException`.
   c. Checked and unchecked exceptions generate compile-time errors.
   d. Unchecked exceptions are checked by the compiler and will not terminate your program.
   e. In order for an unchecked exception to be generated, you must include a `throws` clause in your method.

2. Which of the following exceptions will be generated when the code segment below is executed?

```
int numerator = 10;
int denominator = 0;
int wholePart = numerator / denominator;
```

   a. ArithmeticException

   b. IllegalArgumentException

   c. NumberFormatException

   d. IndexOutOfBoundsException

   e. IllegalStateException

Questions 3 and 4 refer to the Person constructor below. The Person constructor has two String parameters, a first name and a last name. The constructor initializes the e-mail address to the first letter of the first name followed by the first five letters of the last name followed by @jc.com. If the last name has fewer than five letters, the e-mail address will be the first letter of the first name followed by the entire last name followed by @jc.com. Examples:

Name	*E-mail address*
Jane Smith	JSmith@jc.com
John Morris	JMorri@jc.com
Mary Key	MKey@jc.com

```
public Person(String firstName, String lastName)
{
    myFirstName = firstName;
    myLastName = lastName;
    emailAddress = myFirstName.substring(0, 1)
            + myLastName.substring(0, 5)
            + "@jc.com";
}
```

3. Which of the following exceptions may be thrown by this constructor?

   a. ArithmeticException

   b. IllegalArgumentException

   c. NumberFormatException

   d. StringIndexOutOfBoundsException

   e. IllegalStateException

4. Which of the following calls to the Person constructor will cause the exception in Question 3 to be thrown?

   a. Person scm1 = new Person("Marian", "Jones");

   b. Person scm2 = new Person("Joe", "Thomas");

   c. Person scm3 = new Person("Harry", "Tote");

   d. Person scm4 = new Person("J", "Franks");

   e. Person scm5 = new Person("Ellen", "Johnson");

Questions 5 and 6 refer to the `ArrayList friends` as declared below.

```
ArrayList friends = new ArrayList();
friends.add("Mary");
friends.add("James");
friends.add("Kevin");
friends.add(1, "Tanya");
```

5. Consider the method `search` defined below.

```
public static int search(String key, ArrayList a)
{
    int count = 0;
    String temp = (String) (a.get(count));
    while (count < a.size() && !temp.equals(key))
    {
        count++;
        temp = (String) (a.get(count));
    }
    if (count < a.size())
        return count;
    else
        return -1;
}
```

Suppose the following call to `search` was made.

```
int indexFound = search("John", friends);
```

Which of the following statements best describes the result of this call?

a. −1 is returned.
b. 0 is returned.
c. 4 is returned.
d. An `IndexOutOfBoundsException` is thrown.
e. A compile-time error occurs.

6. What is the result of the call

```
String s = (String) friends.get(4);
```

a. `s` is assigned the value `"Kevin"`
b. A compile-time error occurs.
c. A `ClassCastException` is thrown.
d. An `IllegalArgumentException` is thrown.
e. An `IndexOutOfBoundsException` is thrown.

Questions 7–9 refer to the `Employee` class and the `Manager` class incompletely defined below.

```
public class Employee
{
    public Employee()
    {
        myFirstName = null;
        myLastName = null;
        salary = 0;
    }
```

```java
        public Employee(String firstName, String lastName,
            double money)
        {
            myFirstName = firstName;
            myLastName = lastName;
            salary = money;
        }

        public String getName()
        {
            return (myFirstName + " " + myLastName);
        }

        public void work()
        {
            System.out.println("Employee working.");
        }

        private String myFirstName;
        private String myLastName;
        private double salary;
    }
```

```java
    public class Manager extends Employee
    {
        public Manager()
        {
            super();
        }

        public Manager(String firstName, String lastName, double money)
        {
            super(firstName, lastName, money);
        }

        public void work()
        {
            System.out.println("Manager working.");
        }
    }
```

The following code is executed.

```java
    ArrayList workers = new ArrayList();
    workers.add(new Manager());
    workers.add(new Employee());
    workers.add(new Manager("John", "Doe", 20000));
```

7. Which of the following statements results in a ClassCastException being thrown?

   I.   Employee temp = (Manager) workers.get(0);
   II. Employee temp = (Manager) workers.get(1);
   III. Employee temp = (Manager) workers.get(2);
   IV. Employee temp = (Manager) workers.get(3);

    a. I only
    b. II only
    c. III only
    d. IV only
    e. None of the statements above cause a `ClassCastException` to be thrown.

8. Which of the statements below execute without exceptions being thrown?

```
I.   Employee temp = (Manager) workers.get(0);
II.  Employee temp = (Manager) workers.get(1);
III. Employee temp = (Manager) workers.get(2);
IV.  Employee temp = (Manager) workers.get(3);
```

    a. I only
    b. I and II only
    c. I and III only
    d. I, II, III only
    e. I, II, III, and IV

9. The statement

```
String temp = ((Manager) (workers.get(2))).getName();
```

    a. Compiles and executes without error
    b. Reports a compile-time error: Incompatible types.
    c. Causes a `ClassCastException` to be thrown.
    d. Causes a `StringIndexOutOfBoundsException` to be thrown.
    e. Causes an `IllegalStateException` to be thrown.

10. Which of the following exceptions is **not** an unchecked exception?

    a. `IndexOutOfRangeException`
    b. `IOException`
    c. `IllegalArgumentException`
    d. `ArithmeticException`
    e. `NumberFormatException`

Free Response Questions

1. You are to design a `Teacher` class that is a subclass of the `Person` class whose incomplete definition is below.

```java
public class Person
{
   public Person(String firstName, String lastName)
   {
      // Constructor code goes here.
      // Private instance variables are initialized.
   }

   public String getName()
   {
      return myFirstName + " " + myLastName;
```

```
        }

        public String getEmail()
        {
            return emailAddress;
        }

        public String toString()
        {
            return ("name = " + getName() + "\n"
                    + "email address = " + getEmail());
        }

        private String myFirstName;
        private String myLastName;
        private String emailAddress;
    }
```

The `Teacher` class inherits instance variables and methods from `Person`. In addition, a `Teacher` has a private instance field, `salary` (of type `double`) and a public instance method `getRaise`. The method `getRaise` has a `double` parameter and will increment the `Teacher`'s salary by the amount of its parameter. You are to implement the `Teacher` class according to the specifications given. The `Teacher` has one constructor that expects three parameters: a first name (`String`), a last name (`String`), and a salary (`double`).

AB only: You should design your constructor to throw the appropriate exception if the salary passed is not a positive number. In writing `getRaise`, you should throw the appropriate exception if the parameter passed is not a positive number.

2. For a study in probability, we want to simulate the tossing of coins. A `CoinTosser` object tosses a coin a random number of times and reports on its outcomes. The `CoinTosser` constructor constructs a random number generator and generates a random integer between 0 and 20 (inclusive). This generated value determines how many tosses this particular coin tosser will carry out.

It has the following public interface:

```
    public class CoinTosser
    {
        // Constructor
        public CoinTosser()
        {
            // Code goes here
        }

        // Postcondition: returns true if the coin tosser has more
        // coin tosses to report.
        public boolean hasMoreTosses()
        {
            // Code goes here
        }

        // Postcondition: returns "HEAD" or "TAIL"
        public String nextToss()
        {
            // Code goes here
```

```
        }
    . . .     // Private implementation
}
```

a. List the necessary private instance fields and their types.

b. Implement the `CoinTosser` constructor as described in the problem definition above.

c. Implement the `hasMoreTosses` method that returns `true` if there are tosses remaining, `false` otherwise. Use the header below.

```
public boolean hasMoreTosses()
```

d. Write the `nextToss` method that generates a random integer between 0 and 1 (inclusive) and returns one of the two strings "HEADS" or "TAILS". You should **not** construct a new random number generator in this method. Use the header below.

```
public String nextToss()
```

(AB only) The `nextToss` method should throw a `NoSuchElementException` if it is called after the `hasMoreTosses` method has returned false.

CHAPTER 14

(Covers *Java Concepts* Chapter 17)

Object-Oriented Design

TOPIC OUTLINE
14.1 The Software Life Cycle
14.2 Discovering Classes

14.3 Relationships Between Classes

■ Topic Summary

14.1 The Software Life Cycle

The AP CS Topic Outline requires that all AP Computer Science students
- Understand encapsulation.
- Understand the *is-a* and *has-a* inheritance relationships.
- Understand and be able to implement an inheritance class hierarchy according to given specifications.
- Design and implement a class according to given specifications.
- Understand when to use an interface and be able to design an interface.
- Extend a given class with inheritance.

In addition to the above, AP Computer Science AB students should be able to
- Discover and design classes.
- Determine relationships between classes.
- Determine responsibilities of each class.
- Use object-oriented design to build a program from a set of interacting classes.

We have introduced many of these topics separately. This chapter will give you practice pulling the pieces together to design a program involving more than one class.

The five steps in the software life cycle are listed and defined in Table 14.1.

Table 14.1

Process	Process Description
Analysis	The *analysis* phase is the time when you determine what your software system is intended to accomplish.
Design	The *design* phase is when you develop a plan to implement your system.
Implementation	The *implementation* phase is when you write the code according to the specifications made in the design phase.
Testing	During the *testing* phase you verify that the system works as intended.
Deployment	The *deployment* phase is when the intended user of the system installs and uses it.

Sections 17.1 and 17.4 in your text explain this life cycle in detail.

14.2   Discovering Classes

In the design phase, you need to be able to describe a set of classes that can be used to implement the task(s) your software system is intended to accomplish. Look for *nouns*.

- Task: Print an invoice
    Candidate classes: `Invoice, Item, Customer`
- Task: Publish a book
    Candidate classes: `Book, Page, Binding`
- Task: Organize a 5-mile race
    Candidate classes: `Race, Runner, VolunteerWorker`
- Task: Play the lottery
    Candidate classes: `Ball, BallPicker, BallShaker`
- Task: Build a house
    Candidate classes: `Wall, Window, Roof`

Some of these classes may consist of objects defined by other classes. For example, a customer has a name (`String` object), a customer identification number (an `int`), an address (perhaps an object instantiating an `Address` class composed of a street address, a city, and a state).

14.3   Relationships Between Classes

It is sometimes useful to classify relationships between classes. There are several different types of class relationships. The AP CS Topic Outline includes the following two relationships:

- *is-a* relationships
- *has-a* relationships

Using some of the examples already presented, we have:

- A `Bank` *has-a* `Customer`.
- A `Customer` *has-a* `BankAccount`.
- A `SavingsAccount` *is-a* `BankAccount`.

- A `Car` *is-a* `Vehicle`.
- A `Car` *has-a* `Tire`.

- A `Race` *has-a* `Runner`.
- A `Marathoner` *is-a* `Runner`.

- A `Purse` *has-a* `Coin`.

A class is *associated* with another class if the class has an instance field whose type is another class. Your textbook covers another relationship, the *uses-a* relationship or *dependency*. A class *depends* on another class if it *uses* an object of the other class. The original version of `Purse` *uses* a `Coin`. The `Purse` did not have a private instance field of type `Coin`, nor did it have an `ArrayList` that collected `Coin` objects. The distinction between *association* and *dependency* is not part of the AP CS subsets, but understanding this concept can help you in designing your software systems.

Remember, if many classes in a program depend on each other, there is high coupling. In designing system software, one should strive for low coupling and high cohesion.

Once the set of classes has been identified, you need to define the responsibilities (behaviors) of each class. When you look for these behaviors, look for *verbs* in the task description. The verbs will define the candidate methods.
- Task: Print an invoice
    Candidate classes: `Invoice, Item, Customer`
    Example candidate methods:
        `Invoice` has method `computeAmountDue`.
        `Item` has method `getPrice`.
        `Customer` has method `getName`.
- Task: Organize a 5-mile race
    Candidate classes: `Race, Runner, VolunteerWorker`
    Example candidate methods:
        `Race` has methods `addRunner, getNumberOfRunners`.
        `Runner` has methods `getRaceNumber, setFinishTime`.
        `VolunteerWorker` has methods `getName, setJob`.

When designing a class, it is also useful to list the attributes (usually instance fields) that a class might have.
- A `Runner` has a `name`, a `raceNumber`, a `finishTime`.
- A `Race` has a *list* (probably an array list) of `Runners`, a `raceDistance`, a *list* of `VolunteerWorkers`.

When trying to decide which class has what responsibilities, start by listing the tasks that your system needs to accomplish and assign each task to the class that is responsible for carrying out that task. If an action modifies the state (the private instance fields or attributes) of the object, it is the responsibility of the object itself. One way to ensure this is to keep the attributes of the object private.

One popular way to illustrate class relationships is with the use of CRC cards. CRC stands for "classes", "responsibilities", and "collaborators". CRC cards are discussed in Section 17.2 in your text. *How To 17.1* in your text lists the steps in the design process that will help you discover class interactions and responsibilities.

You may also need to provide a data representation for your software design. So far, we have studied arrays and array lists. You will need to choose a data representation consistent with the specifications given in the problem description.

Consider a state lottery game. Each evening the lottery is televised and we observe the following. There is a *container* that holds the numbered *balls* such that no two balls have the same number. There is a *popper* that "pops" a random ball. It is this popped ball's number that is one of the lottery number choices.

Classes:
- `Container` has a collection of `Ball`s. If asked for a `Ball`, the `Container` will remove a `Ball` at random from the set of `Ball`s it contains and return it.
- `Ball` has a number on it. It can return its number to whoever wants to know it.
- `Popper` will ask the `Container` for a `Ball` and display the number on the `Ball`.
- `Random` (Java library class)

The `Container` is a collection of `Ball` objects. A data representation that is consistent with the problem requirements needs to be chosen in order to implement the lottery game. Example 14.1 contains one such data representation in an incomplete implementation of the `Container` class.

Example 14.1

```
public class Container
{
    public Container(int numberOfBalls)
    {
        for (int i = 1; i <= numberOfBalls; i++)
            lotteryBalls.add(new Ball(i));
    }

    // Other methods

    private ArrayList lotteryBalls = new ArrayList();
}
```

The data representation chosen in Example 14.1 is an array list. Array lists contain objects. In this problem, `Ball` objects need to be added to and removed from the `Container`. An array list is a reasonable choice for the following reasons:
- `add` and `remove` methods are defined for the `ArrayList`.
- The `Popper` will ask the `Container` for a ball.
- The `Container` will return a random ball to the `Popper`. The `Popper` will ask the `Ball` for its number and display that number.

■ Topics That Are Useful But Not Tested

- Using CRC (classes-responsibilities-collaborators) cards is an excellent way to discover class responsibilities and class collaborators. CRC cards are described in Section 17.2 in your text.
- UML diagrams can be used to illustrate class relationships. Section 17.3 in your text discusses the use of UML diagrams for illustrating relationships between classes and interfaces.
- The aggregation (*has-a*) relationship and the dependency relationship (*uses*) are discussed in detail in Section 17.2 and *Advanced Topic 17.3* in your text.

- Extreme Programming is a development methodology that strives for simplicity by removing formal structure and focusing on best practices. Extreme programming has become very popular and is discussed in Section 17.1 in your text.

■ Things to Remember When Taking the AP Exam

- Read the free-response questions very carefully. Hints to the answer may appear in the way the question is worded.
- Look for key words: "extends", "is a", "is a kind of". These phrases indicate an inheritance relationship.
- Look for key words: "has a", "has", "is made from", "uses". These phrases indicate an aggregation or dependency relationship.
- Modifying the state of an object is the responsibility of the object itself.

■ Key Words

You should understand the terms below. The AP CS Exam questions may include references to these terms. The citation within parentheses next to each term identifies the page number where it is defined and/or discussed in *Java Concepts*, 4th ed., and *Big Java*, 2nd ed.

analysis (608)	deployment (609)	*is-a* relationship (617)
candidate classes (614)	design (609)	software life cycle (608)
collaborators (615)	*has-a* relationship (617)	testing (609)
CRC cards (615)	implementation (609)	uses (618)
dependency (618)		

■ Connecting the Detailed Topic Outline to the Text

The citations in parentheses identify where information in the outline can be located in *Java Concepts*, 4th ed., and *Big Java*, 2nd ed.

- The Software Life Cycle (608–613)
- Discovering Classes (614–616)
- Relationships Between Classes (617–622)

■ Practice Questions

Multiple Choice

1. Which of the following choices gives the correct order of the software development processes for a complex program?

   a. Analysis, Design, Implementation, Testing, Deployment
   b. Design, Analysis, Implementation, Testing, Deployment
   c. Design, Implementation, Testing, Analysis, Deployment
   d. Design, Implementation, Testing, Deployment, Analysis
   e. Analysis, Design, Implementation, Deployment, Testing

2. Which of the following pairs is **not** an inheritance (*is-a*) relationship?

   a. Violin, Instrument
   b. Car, Vehicle
   c. Tire, Car
   d. Student, Person
   e. Sedan, Car

3. Which of the following is a *has-a* relationship?

   a. Student directory, Student
   b. Student, Person
   c. Truck, Vehicle
   d. Student, Freshman
   e. Fruit, Apple

4. You are to design a program that simulates a vending machine. Your design might include all of the following except

   a. `Product`
   b. `Coin`
   c. `VendingMachine`
   d. `Customer`
   e. `ChangeMachine`

5. In designing a software system, you should:

   I.   Look for nouns in the system description to identify candidate classes.
   II. Look for verbs in the system description to identify class responsibilities.
   III. Describe relationships among the candidate classes.

   a. I only
   b. II only
   c. III only
   d. I and II only
   e. I, II, and III

Questions 6 and 7 refer to the following design problem.

You are to create a software design that simulates a fast food restaurant. You will have food items (hamburgers, hot dogs, chicken sandwiches) and drink items (Coke, Sprite, root beer). The drinks come in various sizes given in ounces (for example: 12, 24, 48). Food items will be assigned a price when they are created but this price can be changed by the employee taking the order if the customer requests "extras" such as bacon, cheese, tomato, etc. The price for drink items will be assigned according to the size of the drink.

6. Which of the following would be the best choice for the design of this system?

   a. The design should include the following classes: `Hamburger`, `HotDog`, `Chicken`, `Coke`, `Sprite`, and `RootBeer`.

   b. The design should include the following classes: `FoodItem` with `Hamburger`, `HotDog`, and `Chicken` extending `FoodItem` and `DrinkItem` with `Coke`, `Sprite`, and `RootBeer` extending `DrinkItem`.

   c. The design should include the following classes: `Item` with `FoodItem` and `DrinkItem` extending `Item`; `Hamburger`, `HotDog`, and `Chicken` extending `FoodItem`; and `DrinkItem` with `Coke`, `Sprite`, and `RootBeer` extending `DrinkItem`.

   d. The design should include the following classes: `FoodItem` and `DrinkItem`. The individual types of food and drink are only descriptions of the food or drink and should not be separate classes.

   e. The design should include the following classes: `Item` with `FoodItem` and `DrinkItem` extending `Item`. The individual types of food and drink are objects that are instances of these classes, not separate classes.

7. The fast food restaurant also offers value meals. A value meal is a drink and a food item purchased at the same time. A 10% discount off the full price of purchasing each separately is applied to the price of a value meal. A deluxe value meal costs $0.50 more than a value meal and includes apple pie for dessert. Which of the following is the best choice for this system design?

   a. `DeluxeValueMeal` should be a subclass of `ValueMeal`.

   b. `ValueMeal` should be a subclass of `DeluxeValueMeal`.

   c. Both `DeluxeValueMeal` and `ValueMeal` should be separate classes that have no inheritance relationship.

   d. `ValueMeal` has an association (*has-a*) relationship with `DeluxeValueMeal`.

   e. `ValueMeal` and `DeluxeValueMeal` both have an instance field of type `Meal` which is a superclass of both `ValueMeal` and `DeluxeValueMeal`.

Questions 8–10 refer to the problem stated below.

Your task is to automate the booking system of a travel agency. Some customers of the travel agency only purchase a single ticket, but others purchase whole trips consisting of multiple airline, boat, or train tickets, hotel stays, and car rentals.

8. Consider these statements about a possible system design:

   I. A class `Ticket` has subclasses `AirlineTicket`, `BoatTicket`, `TrainTicket`.

   II. A class `Trip` *has-a* collection of `Ticket` objects, describing all tickets needed for the trip.

   III. To facilitate travelers who only buy a single ticket, we use inheritance so that a `Ticket` *is-a* `Trip`.

   Which of the choices above describe suitable design decision(s) for the travel agency's booking system?

a. I only
b. II only
c. III only
d. I and II only
e. I, II, and III

9. A good travel agent is expected to check that a customer does not accidentally end up with mismatched reservations, such as a flight from New York to Rome and a hotel reservation in Karachi on the same night. Thus, there is a need to implement the responsibility "check trip" that flags itineraries with mismatched reservations. These flagged itineraries require special attention. Consider these statements about the assignment of this responsibility:

I. The `Ticket` and `HotelReservation` class are jointly responsible for carrying out the "check trip" responsibility.
II. The "check trip" responsibility must lie with the `Trip` class.
III. It is useless to implement this responsibility because some customers might get a rental car and drive to an unknown destination.

Which of the choices above describe suitable design decision(s) for the travel agency's itinerary system?

a. I only
b. II only
c. III only
d. I and II only
e. I, II, and III

10. Consider these statements about the implementation of the `Trip` class:

I. The `Trip` class can use an `ArrayList` of `Ticket` objects to store a variable number of tickets.
II. The `Trip` class should have an instance field of type `CarRental`.
III. The `Trip` class must contain a field of type `String[]` to store hotel names.

Which of the choices above describe suitable implementation decision(s) for the `Trip` class?

a. I only
b. II only
c. III only
d. I and II only
e. I, II, and III

Free Response Questions

1. A used car lot contains cars of various makes and models. The size of a car lot is fixed. The owner of the car lot wants to inventory the cars he has available. For the inventory, he needs the following information about each car:

Make (Toyota, Ford, etc.)
Year (1997, 2001, etc.)
Mileage (120734.6, 23555.2, etc.)
Cost (20000.00, 24500.00, etc.)

When a new car is created, the make, the car year, and the mileage are given. The cars are occasionally taken for test rides. A test ride alters the mileage of the car. The price of the car is set by the owner of the car lot. The car dealer will eventually need to print all of the information about each car in the lot. It will also be necessary for the car dealer to request and print a list of all cars with a specified year and make.

a. Implement the `Car` class. In implementing the class, you should:
- Choose appropriate variable names, parameter names, and method names.
- Properly identify access modifiers (private, public) of each method and instance field.
- Include a `toString` method that will print the information about a car.

Consider the `CarLot` class partially implemented below.

```
public class CarLot
{
    // Constructs an array of cars.
    public CarLot()
    {
        lot = new Car[MAX_CARS];
    }

    // Precondition: numberOfCars < MAX_CARS
    public void addCar(Car aNewCar)
    {
        // Code goes here
    }

    // Prints the information about the cars in the car lot.
    public void printCarsInLot()
    {
        // Code goes here
    }

    /*
        Fills the array list with cars in the car lot that have the
        same year and make as the parameters passed to the method.
    */
    private ArrayList findMatchingCars(int year, String make)
    {
        // Code goes here
    }

    /*
       Prints the year, make, mileage, and price of each car in the
       lot that has the same year and make as the method parameters.
    */
    public void printMatchingCars(int year, String make)
    {
        // Code goes here
    }

    private static final int MAX_CARS = 100;
    private static int numberOfCars = 0;
    private Car[] lot;
}
```

b. Write the `CarLot` method, `addCar`, that will add a `Car` to the car lot in the next available place. (AB students: If there are no more spaces available, throw an appropriate exception.) Use the method header below.

```
public void addCar(Car aNewCar)
```

c. Write the `CarLot` method, `printCarsInLot`, that will print the information about each car in the lot. Use the method header below.

```
public void printCarsInLot()
```

d. Write the `CarLot` method `findMatchingCars`, that will return an `ArrayList` of cars that match the year and make passed as the parameters to the method. Use the method header below.

```
private ArrayList findMatchingCars(int year, String make)
```

e. Write the `CarLot` method, `printMatchingCars`, that will print the year, make, mileage, and price of each car in the lot that matches the year and make passed as parameters to the method. If there are no cars with the requested specifications, an appropriate statement should be printed. Use the method header below.

```
public void printMatchingCars(int year, String make)
```

2. Consider the task of modeling record keeping for a real estate company. The company keeps records on each of its real estate agent employees. Each employee's record contains the following information:
    - The employee first name
    - The employee last name
    - The employee identification number (integer)
    - The total value of real estate property sold by the employee (floating-point number)

When a new employee record is created, it is created with the employee's first name and last name. The next available employee identification number is assigned to the employee and the total real estate property sold is initialized to 0.

The company keeps a list of employees that is constantly updated so that newly hired employees are added to the list and employees that quit or are fired are removed from the list. A newly created real estate company has no employees.

Among the many tasks that need to be completed are:
- Create a new employee record given the first and last name of the employee.
- Add the value of real estate property sold to an employee record given the property value.
- Get commission earned to date for an employee. Commission earned is 6% of the total value of real estate property sold by the employee.
- Create a new real estate company.
- Add an employee to the company list of employees.
- Gets a list of current company employees.
- Remove an employee from the list of employees given the employee identification number.
- Retrieve the employee who sold the highest value of real estate.

a. **(AB only)** Design each class that is needed in the real estate system described above. The class design should include:
- Class name
- Constructor header for each constructor
- Method signatures (include parameters) and return type for each method
- Instance fields
- Static variables

In completing each class design, you should:
- Choose appropriate variable names, parameter names, and method names.
- Properly identify access modifiers (private, public) for each method, instance field, and static variable.

b. Write the class header, declare and initialize any static and instance variables, and write the constructor(s) for the class that creates a new employee record. Follow the specifications given in the problem description.

c. Write the class header, declare and initialize any static and instance variables, and write the constructor(s) for the class that creates a new real estate company. Follow the specifications given in the problem description.

3. The game of Nim is a well-known game with a number of variants. We will consider the following variant, which has an interesting winning strategy. Two players alternately take marbles from a pile. In each move, a player chooses how many marbles to take. The player must take at least one but at most half of the marbles. Then the other player takes a turn. The player who takes the last marble loses.

You will design a program in which the computer plays against a human opponent. Nim specifications include:
- The initial size of the pile will be a random integer generated between two values passed to the constructor of NimGame by the calling method.
- A random integer between 0 and 1 inclusive will be generated to decide whether the computer or the human takes the first turn.
- A random integer between 0 and 1 inclusive will be generated to decide whether the computer plays smart or stupid. A computer knows if it is smart or stupid.
- A player that is not smart simply takes a random legal value (between 1 and $n/2$) from the pile whenever it has a turn, where n is the number of marbles in the pile.
- A smart player takes off enough marbles to make the size of the pile a power of two minus 1 that is, 3, 7, 15, 31, 63, etc.. That is always a legal move, except if the size of the pile is currently one less than a power of two. In that case, the smart player makes a random legal move.
- A human player has a name that is given when asked. A human player is asked how many marbles s/he wishes to take.
- The computer's name is "ROBO COMPUTER".

You will note that a smart player cannot be beaten when it has the first move, unless the pile size happens to be 1 less than a power of 2. Of course, a human player who has the first turn and knows the winning strategy can win against the computer.

In implementing this game, choose the following classes:

```
NimGame
NimPile
Player
HumanPlayer
SmartPlayer
```

The following methods are available to you in a `Utilities` class.

```
getRandNumber
largestPowerOfTwoMinusOneBelow
isPowerOfTwoMinusOne
readInt
readWord
```

The public interface for the `Utilities` class is below.

```java
public class Utilities
{
    /*
        Generates random integer in [low, high].
        Precondition: low is smallest integer generated, high is
        largest integer generated; low < high
        Postcondition: Returns a random integer in [low, high]
    */
    public static int getRandNumber(int low, int high) {. . .}

    /*
        Tests whether n has the form pow(2, k) - 1.
        Precondition: n > 0
        Postcondition: returns true if n is a power of two minus
        one, false otherwise.
    */
    public static boolean isPowerOfTwoMinusOne(int n) {. . .}

    /*
        Precondition: n > 0
        Postcondition: Returns the largest power of two minus one
        below a given number (the largest pow(2, k) - 1 < n).
    */
    public static int largestPowerOfTwoMinusOneBelow(int n) {. . .}

    /*
        Reads an integer from the keyboard.
        Returns integer entered by user
    */
    public static int readInt();

    /*
        Reads a string from the keyboard.
        Returns string entered by user
    */
    public static String readWord();
}
```

The main method that invokes the game of Nim is:

```
public static void main(String[] args)
{
    NimGame nim = new NimGame(10, 100);
        // The pile will have a random number of marbles between
        // 10 and 100 inclusive.
    nim.playNim();
}
```

a. Find and list the *has-a* and *is-a* relationships between the following classes.
    *   NimGame
    *   NimPile
    *   Player
    *   HumanPlayer
    *   SmartPlayer

b. Find the responsibilities of each of the classes in part a, and provide the following for each class.
    *   Class name
    *   Constructor headers for each constructor
    *   Method signatures (including parameters) and return type for each method
    *   Instance fields

c. Implement the methods that you determined in the preceding step.

Note: It is highly improbable that the AP Exam will ask you to implement an entire program such as Nim. Consider part c a "just for fun" activity!

CUMULATIVE REVIEW 2

Chapters 8–14

This review will check your knowledge of material in Chapters 8–14. You should consider this a mini-practice for the AP Exam. Look over the material in these chapters and read over the section *Things to Remember When Taking the AP Exam* below. Have available the Quick Reference Guide or the Exam Reference Materials for the AP Exam that you will be taking. Because you will have reference materials available to you during the exam, you should become familiar with them now.

■ Things to Remember When Taking the AP Exam

General Guidelines
- Do not put extraneous `System.out.println` statements in free-response answers to indicate that the method is done, to print an error message, or to print the answer before returning its value. This is a side effect and will result in a deduction of points.
- Unless specifically asked to write pre- and postconditions on the AP Exam, do not spend time doing this.
- You do not need to check that the precondition of the method is satisfied unless explicitly told to do so. A method should not be called unless its precondition is satisfied.
- Do not try to modify parameters of a method by reassigning values to these variables.
- Carefully read the pre- and postconditions given in problems, especially in the free-response questions. Many times an algorithm for solving the problem is given in the problem documentation. Read the documentation carefully!
- Understand the differences among compile-time errors, run-time errors, and logic errors.
- If asked to choose test data for a situation, remember to include legitimate, boundary, and degenerate test cases.
- Check the code you write for free-response questions by hand tracing your code for the examples given and for your own additional examples.
- Know the conditions under which the common exceptions are thrown.
- AB students should be able to throw the unchecked `IllegalStateException` and `NoSuchElementException` in their own methods.

Arrays and Array Lists
- Remember that the first element of both an array list and an array has index `0`.

- The single most common loop error that occurs when dealing with arrays is an out-of-bounds error while the list is being traversed. The tests

```
    while (index <= arrayName.length)    // WRONG
```
and
```
    while (index <= arrayListName.size()    // WRONG
```

  both try to access an out-of-bounds element. The test should be `<`, not `<=`. Remember that the last element in an array has index `arrayName.length - 1` and the last element in an `ArrayList` has index `arrayListName.size() - 1`. Think carefully about loop bounds when accessing array and `ArrayList` elements.

- Remember that an untyped `ArrayList` stores references to `Objects`. When accessing these objects to process, you will have to cast the object to the appropriate type. When using the Java 5 generic `ArrayList` class, casting is unnecessary.

- Do not confuse `.length` with `.size()`. Remember that `arrayName.length` is an instance variable that holds the length of an array (not necessarily the number of filled elements in the array) and `arrayListName.size()` is a method that returns the number of elements in an `ArrayList`.

- To access the sixth element of an array we write `arrayName[5]`. To access the sixth element of an `ArrayList`, we write `arrayListName.get(5)`.

- Using `equals` with array lists compares references, not contents. `equals` returns `true` if two `ArrayList` references are the same, `false` otherwise.

- When you use `equals` with arrays, you are also comparing references. `array1.equals(array2)` is asking if `array1` and `array2` reference the same array. The result of comparing two arrays with `==` is identical to the result using `equals`.

- **(AB only)** When visiting elements in a two-dimensional array, do not confuse rows and columns.

- When shifting elements in an array, be careful not to overwrite values of other array elements. It is rare that this is an intended task! Think about the order in which the elements are being shifted.

- Iterators are included in the AB subset only. However, many problems are simplified if an iterator is used to traverse the array list instead of a `while` loop or a `for` loop. If you are a student in AP CS A, you may want to learn to use iterators.

Polymorphism and Inheritance

- Early binding (overloading) of methods occurs if the *compiler* selects a method from several possible candidates. Late binding (polymorphism) occurs if the method selection takes place when the program runs. This is an important distinction.

- All methods in an interface are public. The methods in the interface are not declared as public because they are public by default. When implementing the methods of the interface in a class, remember to include the keyword `public`.

- An interface does not have any instance variables.

- An interface does not implement any methods.

- An interface cannot be instantiated.

- You can assign an object reference from a class type to an interface type if the class implements the interface, but you need to cast to assign an object reference from an interface type to a class type.

- For both the A and the AB Exams, you should be able to read the definitions of interfaces. For the AB exam, you should be able to define your own interfaces.

- An interface does not have constructors and cannot be instantiated, but you can assign an object created from a class that implements the interface. For example, recall that `Flier` is an interface and `Airplane` is a class that implements `Flier`, so

  - `Flier f = new Flier();   // WRONG!`
  - `Flier f = new Airplane();   // OK`

- A subclass inherits the behavior and state of its superclass.

- Do not name an instance field of a subclass the same name as an instance field of its superclass.

- Do not give variables a name that differs only in case from the class name (i.e. `Fish fish = new Fish();`).

- A subclass has no direct access to the private fields of its superclass.
- The call to a superclass constructor must be the first statement in the subclass constructor.
- An object of a subclass can be assigned to an object of its superclass.
- An object of a superclass can be assigned to an object of its subclass with the appropriate casting.
- An abstract class cannot be instantiated.
- An abstract class usually has instance variables.
- An abstract class will have methods that are implemented and at least one which is not.
- An abstract class always has at least one class that extends it.
- You can convert from a class type to an abstract class type if the class extends the abstract class, but you need a cast to convert from an abstract class type to a class type.
- The AP CS Java subset specifies that all classes should be designated public and all instance variables should be designated private. The AP CS Java subset does not use `protected` and package (default) visibility but you may see these access modifiers in the case study. If the AP Exam contains any questions relating to `protected` visibility, it will be related to the use in the case study.
- Look for key words: "extends", "is a", "is a kind of". These phrases indicate an inheritance relationship.
- Look for key words: "has a", "has", "is made from", "uses". These phrases indicate a class association.
- Modifying the state of an object is the responsibility of the object itself.

■ Practice Questions

Multiple Choice

1. (Java 5) Consider the following segment of code.

```
ArrayList<String> names = new ArrayList<String>();
names.add("Joe");
names.add("Mary");
names.add("Ann");
names.add("David");
names.add("Harry");
names.add("Rob");
names.add("Lance");

int i = 1;
while (i < names.size())
{
   names.remove(i - 1);
   i += 2;
}
```

What will the `ArrayList names` contain as a result of executing this code?

   a. [Joe, Mary, Ann, David, Harry, Rob, Lance]
   b. [Joe, Ann, Harry, Lance]
   c. [Mary, David, Rob]
   d. [Mary, Ann, Harry, Rob, Lance]
   e. [Mary, Ann, Harry, Rob]

Questions 2 and 3 refer to the following problem description.

Suppose it is known that 10% of the population is left-handed. You are asked to simulate this statistic in a Java program by generating handedness values for 500 random samples of 30 people each. You must record your results in such a way as to be able to answer questions similar to, "In how many of the 500 samples were there exactly 3 left-handed people?" or "In how many of the 500 samples were there more than 5 left-handed people?"

2. Which of the following is the best choice to store your information so that you can efficiently answer the questions posed above?

   a. an array of size 500
   b. an array of size 30
   c. an array list of size 500
   d. an array list of size 30
   e. an array of size 31

3. Given the following declaration,

   ```
   Random randNumGen = new Random();
   ```

   which of the following code segments will correctly allow you to simulate a left-handed person?

   a.
   ```
   double probOfLefty = 1.0 / 10.0;
   if (randNumGen.nextDouble() < probOfLefty) . . .
   ```

   b.
   ```
   double probOfLefty = 1.0 / 10.0;
   if (randNumGen.nextDouble() > probOfLefty) . . .
   ```

   c.
   ```
   double probOfLefty = 1.0 / 30.0;
   if (randNumGen.nextDouble() < probOfLefty) . . .
   ```

   d.
   ```
   double probOfLefty = 10.0 / 30.0;
   if (randNumGen.nextDouble() < probOfLefty) . . .
   ```

   e.
   ```
   double probOfLefty = 1.0 / 10.0;
   if (randNumGen.nextDouble(1, 10) < probOfLefty) . . .
   ```

4. Which of the following statements about arrays is **not** true?

   a. All elements of an array are of the same type.
   b. Array subscripts must be integers.
   c. Arrays cannot contain string references as elements.
   d. Arrays cannot use strings as subscripts.
   e. A method cannot change the size of an array.

5. The method `weeklyPay` is to return the amount of pay an employee will receive for one week's work. The parameters for `weeklyPay` are the hours worked during the week and the hourly pay. The weekly pay is based on the following standards. If the employee worked 40 hours or less during the week, he receives his regular hourly rate times the number of hours he worked. For every hour over 40 hours, the employee receives time and a half (1.5 times his regular hourly pay). The following information and method header is given.

   ```
   final int MAX_HOURS_IN_WEEK = 168;   // 7 * 24
   /*
      Precondition: 0 <= hoursWorked and
      hoursWorked <= MAX_HOURS_IN_WEEK, 0 < hourlyPay
   */
   public static double weeklyPay(double hoursWorked, double hourlyPay)
   ```

   If all preconditions are satisfied, what assertion can you make as a result of the execution of the following statement?

   ```
   myPay = weeklyPay(hours, rate);
   ```

   a. `hours >= 0` and `rate >=0`
   b. `myPay > 0`
   c. `myPay >= 0`
   d. `rate >= 0`
   e. No assertion can be made.

6. Consider the following incomplete implementation of the `BankAccount` class.

```
public class BankAccount
{
    // Constructs a bank account with a given balance.
    // Precondition: initialBalance >= 0
    public BankAccount(double initialBalance)
    {
        balance = initialBalance;
    }

    // Returns the current balance.
    public double getBalance()
    {
        return balance;
    }

    // Deposits amount in account. Updates balance.
    // Precondition: amount >= 0
    public void deposit(double amount)
    {
        balance += amount;
        // Assertion : ???????
    }

    private double balance;
}
```

If all preconditions are satisfied, which of the following statements should replace `???????` as an assertion after the statement

```
balance += amount;
```

in the `deposit` method is executed?

a. `amount < 0`
b. `balance > 0`
c. `amount <= balance`
d. `amount < balance`
e. `amount >= balance`

7. A Java program contains the following declaration and initialization of an array a.

```
int[] a = {1,2,3,4,5,6,7,8,9};
```

It is necessary to provide a method to exchange the values of two array elements. Which of the following method implementations and call to the method will swap the values in two specified positions in the array? For example, if the specified positions were 1 and 2, array a would have the values

```
a = {1,3,2,4,5,6,7,8,9}
```

after the method is executed.

I. Method implementation
```
// Swaps the values in array positions b and c.
public static void swap(int b, int c)
{
    int temp = b;
    b = c;
    c = temp;
}
```
Method Call: `swap(a[1], a[2]);`

II. Method implementation

```
// Swaps the values in array positions b and c.
public static void swap(int[] arr, int b, int c)
{
    int temp = arr[b];
    arr[b] = arr[c];
    arr[c] = temp;
}
Method Call: swap(a, 1, 2);
```

III. Method implementation

```
// Swaps the values in array positions b and c.
public static void swap(int b, int c, int[] arr)
{
    int temp = arr[b];
    arr[b] = arr[c];
    arr[c] = temp;
}
Method Call: swap(a[1], a[2], a);
```

a. I only
b. II only
c. III only
d. II and III only
e. I, II, and III

(Java 5) Questions 8 and 9 refer to the following problem description.

Consider the following incomplete Point class given below.

```
public class Point
{
    // Constructs the point (x1, y1)
    Point(double x1, double y1) {. . .}

    // Returns the x-coordinate of this point.
    public double getX() {. . .}

    // Returns the y-coordinate of this point.
    public double getY() {. . .}

    // Sets the x-coordinate of this point to xValue.
    public void setX(int xValue) { . . .}

    // Sets the y-coordinate of this point to yValue.
    public void setY(int yValue) { . . .}

    // Returns the distance this point is from its Point parameter.
    public double distanceFromPoint(Point p) {. . .}

    // Returns the string representation of this point: (x,y).
    public String toString() {. . .}

    private double x;
    private double y;
}
```

Suppose the ArrayList<Point> manyPoints contains more than two Point objects and all points in manyPoints are unique.

The incomplete code segment below is intended to find the two points that are closest in distance to each other.

```
Point a = manyPoints.get(0);
Point b = manyPoints.get(1);
int numPoints = manyPoints.size();
double minimumDistance = a.distanceFromPoint(b);

for (int i = 0; i < numPoints; i++)
{
    missing code
}
```

8. Which of the following code segments could replace *missing code* so that the segment works as intended?

a.
```
for (int j = i + 1; j < numPoints; j++)
{
    double currentDistance =
            manyPoints.get(i).distanceFromPoint(manyPoints.get(j));
    if (currentDistance < minimumDistance)
    {
        minimumDistance = currentDistance;
        a = manyPoints.get(i);
        b = manyPoints.get(j);
    }
}
```

b.
```
for (int j = i; j <= numPoints; j++)
{
    double currentDistance =
            manyPoints.get(i).distanceFromPoint(manyPoints.get(j));
    if (currentDistance < minimumDistance)
    {
        minimumDistance = currentDistance;
        a = manyPoints.get(i);
        b = manyPoints.get(j);
    }
}
```

c.
```
double currentDistance =
        manyPoints.get(i).distanceFromPoint(manyPoints.get(i + 1));
if (currentDistance < minimumDistance)
{
    minimumDistance = currentDistance;
    a = manyPoints.get(i);
    b = manyPoints.get(i + 1);
}
```

d.
```
int j = numPoints - 1;
while (j > 0)
{
    double currentDistance =
            manyPoints.get(i).distanceFromPoint(manyPoints.get(j));
    if (currentDistance < minimumDistance)
    {
        minimumDistance = currentDistance;
        a = manyPoints.get(i);
        b = manyPoints.get(j);
    }
    j--;
}
```

```
e.  int j = i + 1;
    while (j < numPoints)
    {
       double currentDistance =
             manyPoints.get(i).findDistanceFromPoint(manyPoints.get(j));
       if (currentDistance < minimumDistance)
       {
          minimumDistance = currentDistance;
          a = manyPoints.get(i);
          b = manyPoints.get(j);
       }
       j = i + 1;
    }
}
```

9. **(AB)** The correct algorithm looks at each possible pair of `Point` objects to determine the two points with the minimum distance between them. Mathematically, for n distinct points, this evaluates to $n(n-1)/2$ possible pairs of points. This would imply that the algorithm would have a big-Oh time efficiency of:

   a. $O(1)$
   b. $O(n)$
   c. $O(2n)$
   d. $O(n^2)$
   e. $O(n^3)$

10. Consider the following code segment.

```
ArrayList<String> names = new ArrayList<String>();
names.add("Joe");
names.add("Mary");
names.set(1, "Ann");
names.add(1, "David");
names.add("Harry");
System.out.println(names);
```

What is printed as a result of executing the code segment?

   a. [Joe, Mary, David, Ann, Harry]
   b. [Joe, Mary, Ann, David, Harry]
   c. [Joe, David, Ann, Harry]
   d. [Ann, David, Joe, Mary Harry]
   e. [Joe, Mary, David, Ann, Harry]

11. A pet adoption agency needs a program to store information about the pets available for adoption. For each pet, they want to keep track of breed, age, and whether or not the pet is friendly to other pets. Which of the following is the best design?

   a. Use four unrelated classes: `Pet`, `Breed`, `Age`, `Friend`.
   b. Use one class, `Pet` that has three instance fields: `String breed`, `int age`, and `boolean friendly`.
   c. Use a class `Pet` which has three subclasses: `Breed`, `Age`, and `Friend`.
   d. Use a class `Pet` which has a subclass `Breed` and `Breed` has two instance fields `int age`, and `boolean friendly`.
   e. Use a class `Breed` that has a subclass `Pet` that has two instance fields `int age`, and `boolean friendly`.

Questions 12–15 refer to the `Person`, `Employee`, and `Manager` classes defined below.

`Person` **Class**

```java
public class Person
{
    public Person(String theName, int birth, String sex)
    {
        name = theName;
        dob = birth;
        gender = sex;
    }

    public void work()
    {
        getWorkDetail(this);
    }

    public void getWorkDetail(Employee e)
    {
        System.out.println("This person is an Employee.");
    }

    public void getWorkDetail(Manager m)
    {
        System.out.println("This person is the boss.");
    }

    public void getWorkDetail(Person p)
    {
        System.out.println("This person is not an Employee.");
    }

    public String toString()
    {
        return name + "\nDate of Birth: " + dob  + "\n";
    }

    private String name;
    private int dob;
    private String gender;
}
```

`Employee` **Class**

```java
public class Employee extends Person
{
    public Employee(String theName, int birth, String sex,
            String jobAssignment)
    {
        super(theName, birth, sex);
        department = jobAssignment;
        salary = 30000;
    }

    public Employee(String theName, int birth, String sex)
    {
        super(theName, birth, sex);
        department = "Not Assigned";
        salary = 30000;
    }
```

```java
    public void setSalary(double moneyEarned)
    {
        salary = moneyEarned;
    }

    public double getSalary()
    {
        return salary;
    }

    public void work()
    {
        super.work();
    }

    public void printSalary(Employee e)
    {
        System.out.println("Salary has not changed.");
    }

    public String toString()
    {
        String s = super.toString();
        s += "Department: " + department + "\nSalary = " + getSalary()+ "\n";
        return s;
    }

    String department;
    double salary;
}
```

Manager Class

```java
public class Manager extends Employee
{
    public Manager(String theName, int birth, String sex)
    {
        super(theName, birth, sex, "Manager");
        double oldSalary = getSalary();
        double newSalary = 0.20 * oldSalary + oldSalary;
        setSalary(newSalary);
    }

    public void work()
    {
        super.work();
    }

    public void printSalary(Manager m)
    {
        System.out.println("More money");
    }

    public void printSalary(Employee e)
    {
        System.out.println("Regular pay");
    }
}
```

12. Which of the following declarations is **not** legal?

    a. `Person p1 = new Person("Person1", 1988, "Male");`
    b. `Employee e1 = new Employee("Employee1", 1980, "Female", "Foods");`
    c. `Employee e2 = new Manager("Employee1", 1981, "Female");`
    d. `Person e3 = new Manager("Person2", 1987, "Male");`
    e. `Manager m1 = new Employee("Employee1", 1980, "Female", "Art");`

13. What is printed as a result of executing the following code segment in a client program?

    ```
    Employee e1 = new Manager("Manager1", 1976, "Female");
    System.out.println(e1);
    Person p3 = new Employee("Person3", 1980, "Male", "Operations");
    System.out.println(p3);
    ```

    a. ```
       Manager1
       Date of Birth: 1976
       Department: Not Assigned
       Salary = 36000.0

       Person3
       Date of Birth: 1980
       Department: Operations
       Salary = 30000.0
       ```

    b. ```
       Manager1
       Date of Birth: 1976
       Department: Not Assigned
       Salary = 30000.0

       Person3
       Date of Birth: 1980
       Department: Operations
       Salary = 30000.0
       ```

    c. ```
       Manager1
       Date of Birth: 1976
       Department: Manager
       Salary = 36000.0

       Person3
       Date of Birth: 1980
       Department: Operations
       Salary = 30000.0
       ```

    d. ```
       Manager1
       Date of Birth: 1976
       Department: Not Assigned
       Salary = 30000.0

       Person3
       Date of Birth: 1980
       ```

    e. An error message would be printed because `Manager` does not define a `toString` method.

14. What is printed as a result of the following code segment in a client program?

    ```
    Employee e1 = new Employee("Manager1", 1976, "Female");
    e1.work();
    ```

    a. *This person is an employee.*
    b. *This person is the boss.*
    c. *This person is not an employee.*
    d. Nothing would be printed. A `ClassCastException` would be thrown.
    e. Nothing would be printed. A compile-time error would occur.

15. What is printed as the result of the following code in a client program?

```
Employee e1 = new Employee("Employee1", 1972, "Female");
Employee e2 = new Manager("Employee2", 1976, "Female");
Manager m1 = new Manager("Manager1", 1980, "Male");

e2.printSalary(e2);
e1.printSalary(e1);
m1.printSalary(m1);
e1.printSalary(m1);
```

a. Regular pay
    Salary has not changed
    More money
    Salary has not changed

b. Regular pay
    Regular pay
    More money
    Regular pay

c. Salary has not changed
    Salary has not changed
    More money
    Salary has not changed

d. Regular pay
    Regular pay
    More money
    More money

e. Salary has not changed
    Salary has not changed
    More money
    More money

16. Consider the following declaration and initializations.

```
int[] a = new int[20];
Random generator = new Random();
```

What is the outcome of the following code segment?

```
for (int k = 0; k < 20; k++)
{
   int r = generator.nextInt(100) + 1;
   int j = k;
   while (j >= 0 && r != a[j])
      j--;
   if (j < 0)
      a[k] = r;
   else
      k--;
}
```

a. Array a contains 20 random integers in the range of 1 to 100 inclusive in ascending order.
b. Array a contains 20 random integers in the range of 1 to 100 inclusive in descending order.
c. Array a contains 20 copies of one random integer in the range of 0 to 100 inclusive.
d. Array a contains 20 non-duplicated random integers in the range of 1 to 100 inclusive.
e. Array a contains 20 non-duplicated random integers in the range of 0 to 100 inclusive.

17. **(AB)** Consider the following code segment.

```java
public int mystery(int[] a, int value)
{
    int current = 0;
    // Invariant
    while (current < a.length)
    {
        if (a[current] == value)
            return current;
        else
            current++;
    }
    return -1;
}
```

What is the loop invariant of the `while` loop above?

a. `current <= a.length` and value was not found in `a[0]...a[current]`
b. `current < a.length` and value was not found in `a[0]...a[current - 1]`
c. `current <= a.length` and value was not found in `a[0]...a[current - 1]`
d. value is found in `a[current]` or `value = -1`
e. value was not found in `a` or `value = a[current - 1]`

18. The method `noDuplicates` is intended to return an array of 20 non-duplicated random integers in the range of 1 to 100 inclusive. Which of the algorithms below successfully completes this task?

I.
```java
public static int[] noDuplicates()
{
    int[] a = new int[20];
    int[] b = new int[101];
    Random generator = new Random();
    int n = 100;
    for (int i = 0; i < b.length; i++)
        b[i] = i;
    for (int k = 0; k < 20; k++)
    {
        int r = generator.nextInt(n) + 1;
        a[k] = b[r];
        b[r] = b[n];
        n--;
    }
    return a;
}
```

II.
```java
public static int[] noDuplicates()
{
    int[] a = new int[20];
    int[] b = new int[100];
    Random generator = new Random();
    int n = 100;
    for (int i = 0; i < b.length; i++)
        b[i] = i + 1;
    for (int k = 0; k < 20; k++)
    {
        int r = generator.nextInt(100);
        int temp = b[r];
        b[r] = b[k];
        b[k] = temp;
    }
    for (int i = 0; i < 20; i++)
        a[i] = b[i];
    return a;
}
```

```
III. public static int[] noDuplicates()    // Java 5
     {
         int[] a = new int[20];
         ArrayList<Integer> b = new ArrayList<Integer>(); // Generic
         Random generator = new Random();
         for (int i = 0; i < 100; i++)
             b.add(i + 1); // Auto-boxing
         for (int k = 0; k < 20; k++)
         {
             int r = generator.nextInt(b.size());
             a[k] = b.get(r); // Auto-unboxing
             b.remove(r);
         }
         return a;
     }
```

a. I only
b. II only
c. III only
d. I and III only
e. I, II, and III

Questions 19 and 20 refer to the following interface and classes.

```
interface SampleInterface
{
    void someMethod();
}
```

```
class SampleClassA implements SampleInterface
{
    public void someMethod()
    {
        System.out.println("test in A");
    }
}
```

```
class SampleClassB extends SampleClassA
{
    public void someMethod()
    {
        System.out.println("test in B");
    }
}
```

19. Which of the following declarations are legal?

```
I.   SampleClassA a = new SampleClassB();
II.  SampleInterface s1 = new SampleClassA();
III. SampleInterface s2 = new SampleInterface();
```

a. I only
b. II only
c. III only
d. I and II only
e. I, II, and III

20. Consider the following incompletely defined method in a client program.

```
public static void testInClient(SampleInterface s) {. . .}
```

Which of the following statements is **true** concerning this method?

   a. The method header is illegal because the parameter type cannot be an interface type.
   b. The method header is legal and an object of any class that extends `SampleInterface` can be passed as a parameter to the method.
   c. The method header is legal but only a variable that is declared as `SampleInterface` type can be passed as a parameter to the method.
   d. The method header is legal and an object of any class that implements `SampleInterface` can be passed as a parameter to the method.
   e. The method header is legal but only objects of type `SampleInterface` and subclasses of `SampleInterface` can be passed as a parameter to the method.

Free Response

1. There are many card games that are played with a deck of 52 playing cards. In this deck of 52 cards, there are 13 cards with denominations 2, 3, 4, 5, 6, 7, 8, 9, 10, Jack, Queen, King, and Ace in each of four suits (Clubs, Diamonds, Hearts, and Spades). The incomplete `Card` class is below.

Card **Class**

```java
public class Card implements Comparable
{
    /*
        denom is a String representing the card denomination, i.e., "2",
        "Jack", "Ace"
        suit is "Hearts", "Diamonds", "Clubs", or "Spades"
        Constructs a card with given suit and denomination. Value is the card
        number if the card is between 2 and 10 inclusive, 11 for "J", 12 for
        "Q", 13 for "K", 14 for "A".
    */
    public Card(String denom, String suit)
    {
        mySuit = suit;
        myDenom = denom;
        myValue = getValue();
    }

    // Returns the suit. Hearts for H, Spades for S, Clubs for C,
    // Diamonds for D.
    public String getSuit() {. . .}

    /*
        Returns the String representation of the denomination of the
        card: 2,3,4,5,6,7,8,9,10, Jack, Queen, King, or Ace.
    */
    public String getDenomination(){. . .}

    /*
        Returns the value of the card. The value is the card number
        if the card is between 2 and 10 inclusive, 11 for "J",
        12 for "Q", 13 for "K", 14 for "A".
    */
    public int getValue(){. . .}
```

```
    // Returns the string representation of the card.
    public String toString()
    {
        return getDenomination() + " of " + getSuit();
    }

    public int compareTo(Object other)
    {
        Card c = (Card) other;
        return myValue - c.myValue;
    }

    public boolean equals(Object other)
    {
        return compareTo(other) == 0;
    }

    private String mySuit;
    private String myDenom;
    private int myValue;
}
```

Many card games require that the player is dealt a *hand* of cards. The number of cards in a hand is dependent on the card game being played. The incomplete Hand class is below.

Hand Class

```
public class Hand
{
    // Constructs new hand with capacity for numCards cards.
    public Hand(int numCards)
    {
        // Code goes here
    }

    // If possible, adds a card to this hand.
    public void addCard(Card c)
    {
        // Code goes here
    }

    // Returns true if hand is full (cardsInHand = myHand.length),
    // false otherwise.
    public boolean isHandFull() {. . .}

    // Reorders cards in ascending order.
    public void sortCards()

    // Returns a copy of the array of Cards in myHand.
    public Card[] getHand()
    {
        Card[] cards = new Card[myHand.length];
        for (int i = 0; i < myHand.length; i++)
            cards[i] = new Card(myHand[i].getDenomination(),
                    myHand[i].getSuit());
        return cards;
    }

    // Prints the Cards in Hand to screen.
    public void printHand()
    {
        // Code goes here
    }
```

```
        private Card[] myHand;
        private int cardsInHand;
            // Actual number of cards in myHand at a particular time
    }
```

Poker is a card game requiring a `Hand` of 5 `Cards`. The value of a poker hand is based on the combination of denominations and suits of the individual cards in the hand. These combinations are identified in the incomplete definition of the `PokerHand` class below and are explained in the individual method comments.

PokerHand Class

```
    public class PokerHand extends Hand
    {
        // Constructs an empty poker hand.
        public PokerHand()
        {
            super(MAX_CARDS);
        }

        /*
            Precondition: isHandFull() returns true
            Returns true if all cards in this hand are the same suit,
            otherwise returns false.
        */
        public boolean isFlush()
        {
            // Code goes here
        }

        /*
            Precondition: isHandFull() returns true
            Returns true if the cards in this hand are of consecutive
            values when ordered, otherwise returns false.
        */
        public boolean isStraight()
        {
            // Code goes here
        }

        /*
            Precondition: isHandFull() returns true
            Returns true if the cards in this hand are consecutive values when
            ordered and all cards are the same suit. Otherwise, returns false.
        */
        public boolean isStraightFlush()
        {
            // Code goes here
        }

        /*
            Precondition: isHandFull() returns true
            Returns true if the cards in this hand are consecutive values
            with the largest value being 14 when ordered and all cards are
            the same suit. Otherwise, returns false.
        */
        public boolean isRoyalFlush()
        {
            // Code goes here
        }
```

```
    /*
        Precondition: isHandFull() returns true
        Returns true if the hand consists of three cards of one value
        and 2 cards of another value. Otherwise, returns false.
    */
    public boolean isFullHouse()
    {
        // Code goes here
    }

    private static final int MAX_CARDS = 5;
}
```

In writing solutions to the following problems, assume that methods provided in the classes above work as specified. Also assume that the methods you write in parts previous to the question you are working on work as specified, regardless of what you wrote. Solutions that reimplement functionality provided, rather than invoking the appropriate method, will not receive full credit.

a.   Write the `Hand` constructor that constructs an empty card hand with capacity for `numCards` cards, where `numCards` is the constructor's one `int` parameter. Use the header below.

```
public Hand(int numCards)
```

b.   The `Hand` method `addCard` adds a card to this `Hand` if the hand has fewer than `cardsInHand` cards (the maximum number of cards in the hand). Use the following header in writing `addCard`.

```
public void addCard(Card c)
```

c.   Write the `Hand` method `printHand` that prints the `String` representations of the cards in the hand. Use the following header in writing `printHand`.

```
public void printHand()
```

d.   Write the `PokerHand` method `isFlush` that returns `true` if all cards in hand are the same suit, otherwise returns `false`. For example, `isFlush` would return `true` for the poker hand composed of the five cards 10 of Clubs, 2 of Clubs, 6 of Clubs, 9 of Clubs, and Ace of Clubs. Use the following header in writing `isFlush`.

```
public boolean isFlush()
```

e.   Write the `PokerHand` method `isStraight` that returns `true` if the cards in this hand have consecutive values when ordered, otherwise returns `false`. For example, `isStraight` would return `true` for the poker hand composed of the five cards 10 of Clubs, Jack of Clubs, 8 of Hearts, 7 of Diamonds, and 9 of Spades. Use the following header in writing `isStraight`.

```
public boolean isStraight()
```

f.   Write the `PokerHand` method `isStraightFlush` that returns `true` if the cards in this hand are all the same suit and have consecutive values when ordered, otherwise returns `false`. For example, `isStraightFlush` would return `true` for the poker hand composed of the five cards 3 of Clubs, 5 of Clubs, 6 of Clubs, 4 of Clubs, and 7 of Clubs. Use the following header.

```
public boolean isStraightFlush()
```

g.   Write the `PokerHand` method `isRoyalFlush` that returns `true` if the cards in this hand are all the same suit, have consecutive values when ordered, and the highest card value is 14 (Ace); otherwise returns `false`. For example, `isRoyalFlush` would return `true` for the poker hand composed of the five cards 10 of Clubs, Jack of Clubs, Queen of Clubs, King of Clubs, and Ace of Clubs. Use the following header in writing `isRoyalFlush`.

```
public boolean isRoyalFlush()
```

h.   Write the `PokerHand` method `isFullHouse` that returns `true` if there are 3 cards of one denomination and 2 cards of a second denomination, otherwise returns `false`. For example, `isFullHouse` would return `true` for the poker hand composed of the five cards 10 of Clubs, 3 of Clubs, 10 of Diamonds, 10 of Spades, and 3 of Diamonds. Use the following header.

```
public boolean isFullHouse()
```

2.   The need to use descriptive statistics in many areas has grown enormously in the past 50 or so years. Your task is to complete the utility class `Stats` that includes methods to calculate the most commonly used statistical measurements. The incomplete `Stats` class appears below.

Stats **Class**

```
public class Stats
{
    /*
        Returns an array with the values of sampleData sorted in
        increasing numerical order.
    */
    private static int[] sortValues(int[] sampleData){. . .}

    /*
        Precondition: sampleData.length > 0;
        Returns the average of the values in sampleData.
    */
    public static double mean(int[] sampleData)
    {
        // Code goes here
    }

    /*
        Precondition: sampleData.length > 0;
        Returns the variance of the values in sampleData.
    */
    public static double variance(int[] sampleData)
    {
        // Code goes here
    }

    /*
        Precondition: sampleData.length > 0;
        Returns the standard deviation of the values in sampleData.
    */
    public static double standardDeviation(int[] sampleData)
    {
        // Code goes here
    }

    /*
        Precondition: sampleData.length > 0;
        Returns the mode of the values in sampleData. If there is more than
        one mode, returns the smallest mode value.
    */
    public static int mode(int[] sampleData)
    {
        // Code goes here
    }
```

```
/*
    Precondition: sampleData.length > 0;
    Returns the median of the values in sampleData.
*/
public static double median(int[] sampleData)
{
    // Code goes here
}


/*
    Precondition: sampleData.length > 0; for all j such that
    0 <= j < sampleData.length, sampleData[j] <= 100.
    Prints a stem and leaf plot representing the values in sampleData.
*/
public static void stemAndLeafPlot(int[] sampleData)
{
    // Code goes here
}
}
```

In writing solutions to the following problems, assume that the method `sortValues` provided in the class above works as specified. Also assume that the methods you write in parts previous to the question you are working on work as specified, regardless of what you wrote. Solutions that reimplement functionality provided, rather than invoking the appropriate method, will not receive full credit.

a. Write the `Stats` method `mean` that will return the average of the values in `sampleData`. The mean of n numbers is their sum divided by n. Use the header below in writing `mean`.

```
public static double mean(int[] sampleData)
```

b. One of the most useful statistical measures is the standard deviation. This is a measure of data variation from the mean. To calculate the standard deviation, find the difference between each value in the data set and the mean of the data set. Sum the squares of these differences. Divide this sum by $n - 1$ and take the square root of this number. Therefore, the standard deviation of a set of values, denoted by s, is calculated as

$$s = \sqrt{\frac{\sum \left(X - \overline{X} \right)^2}{n - 1}}$$

and its square, the *variance*, is

$$s^2 = \frac{\sum \left(X - \overline{X} \right)^2}{n - 1}$$

where $\overline{X}$ is the mean of the values in the set of data.

Write the `Stats` method `variance` that will return the variance of the values in `sampleData`. The variance is found by dividing the sum of the squared deviations from the mean by $n - 1$ where n is the number of items in `sampleData`. The formula to calculate the variance is given above. Use the header below in writing `variance`.

```
public static double variance(int[] sampleData)
```

c. Write the `Stats` method `standardDeviation` that will return the standard deviation of the values in `sampleData`. The standard deviation is found using the formula for s above. Use the header below.

```
public static double standardDeviation(int[] sampleData)
```

d. Write the `Stats` method `mode` that will return the *mode* of the values in `sampleData`. The *mode* is the value that occurs with the most frequency in the set of values. If there is more than one mode, the smallest mode value will be returned. Use the header below in writing `mode`.

```
public static int mode(int[] sampleData)
```

e. Write the `Stats` method `median` that will return the median of the values in `sampleData`. If `sampleData` contains *n* items arranged in increasing order, the *median* is defined to be the value of the middle item if *n* is odd and the mean of the two middle items if *n* is even. Use the header below.

```
public static double median(int[] sampleData)
```

f. Write the `Stats` method `stemAndLeafPlot` that will illustrate the values in `sampleData` graphically. A stem-and-leaf plot displays the data by breaking each number into two parts: `number / 10` (informally called the tens digit) and `number % 10` (informally called the units digit), grouping together the values that share the same tens digit. The tens digit is aligned vertically and the units digits is displayed to the right. The value 67 is represented as 6 | 7. Single digit numbers are assumed to have a "tens digit" of 0. The numbers 100 – 109 would be assumed to have a "tens digit" of 10. For example, if

```
sampleData = { 14, 23, 24, 25, 35, 36, 40, 42, 42, 43, 43, 45, 58,
        67, 68, 82, 88, 91, 94, 95}
```

the stem-and-leaf display would be:

```
 0  |
 1  | 4
 2  | 3 4 5
 3  | 5 6
 4  | 0 2 2 3 3 5
 5  | 8
 6  | 7 8
 7  |
 8  | 2 8
 9  | 1 4 5
10  |
```

Use the header below in writing `stemAndLeafPlot`.

```
public static void stemAndLeafPlot(int[] sampleData)
```

3. In order to satisfy national certification requirements, an Emergency Medical Technician (EMT) is required to stay current by completing continuing education courses. Each continuing education course is designated as *required* or *elective* and is worth a designated number of continuing education units (CEUs). An EMT is required to complete at least 48 required credits and at least 48 elective credits within a certain time period.

You are to design and implement classes to represent an Emergency Medical Technician and a Continuing Education Course.

The information about an Emergency Medical Technician includes a name (`String`), a social security number (`String`), and a record of all courses completed by the EMT. It is possible to retrieve all of this information about an EMT. Courses are added to the EMT's record but not deleted.

The course information includes a course name, the number of continuing education credits the course is worth, and a designation indicating whether this course is a required course or not.

An EMT's record is periodically reviewed to see if the EMT has satisfied the requirements of completing a minimum of 48 required credits and a minimum of 48 elective credits.

CHAPTER **15**

(Covers *Java Concepts* Chapter 18)

Recursion

TOPIC OUTLINE

■ Topic Summary

15.1 Thinking Recursively

In Chapter 7 we discussed iterative control structures (the `for` loop and the `while` loop). In this chapter we look at another method of repetition, recursion. A recursive computation solves a problem by calling itself to solve a smaller piece of the problem. There are three basic rules for developing recursive algorithms.

- Know how to take one step.
- Break each problem down into one step plus a smaller problem.
- Know how and when to stop.

Here is the method for converting and printing the decimal number 100 to a binary number (base 2) that was presented in Chapter 5 of this guide.

    100 / 2 = 50 remainder 0
    50 / 2 = 25 remainder 0
    25 / 2 = 12 remainder 1
    12 / 2 = 6 remainder 0
    6 / 2 = 3 remainder 0
    3 / 2 = 1 remainder 1
    1 / 2 = 0 remainder 1

Reading the remainders in reverse order, we have 1100100 which is the binary representation for the decimal number 100.

Now, let's look at this same problem recursively.

- First, know how to take one step: A step seems to be "Divide by 2; Note the quotient and the remainder."
- Second, break each problem down into one step plus a smaller problem:
  - The quotient is smaller than the original number.
  - The above process can be applied to the quotient.
  - Therefore you have a smaller problem.
- Know how and when to stop: Stop when the quotient is 0. Actually, the recursion stops when the quotient <= 0. Print out the remainders when you reach a quotient of 0. Notice that in the original example from Chapter 4 (*Advanced Topic 4.2*) of your textbook, the remainders were read "from bottom up". The last remainder must be printed first.

Now let's look at code.

Example 15.1

```
// Precondition: decimalNum >= 0
public static void convertToBinary(int decimalNum)
{
   if (decimalNum < 0)
      throw new IllegalArgumentException("number must be >= 0");

   int quotient = decimalNum / 2;
   int remainder = decimalNum % 2;

   if (quotient > 0)
   {
      convertToBinary(quotient);    // Smaller problem
   }

   System.out.print(remainder);    // After all recursive calls
                                   // have been made, last
                                   // remainder printed first

}
```

Divide the decimal number by 2 and remember the remainder. Keep repeating this process with a smaller decimal number (quotient) until the quotient <= 0. Then, print out the remainder for each call. As long as the quotient is > 0, another recursive call is made (no printing occurs yet). When the quotient is <= 0, the `if` statement is not executed and the algorithm continues by executing the `System.out.print` statement. This statement is executed for each recursive call that was made beginning with the last. The "stack" of recursive calls is "unstacked." Thus, the remainders will be printed in the "correct" order. That is, the result on the screen will be the binary representation of the decimal number we started with.

Do you think this solution would work to convert decimal numbers to octal numbers? To hexadecimal numbers?

Section 18.1 in your text presents another simple example using recursion with triangle numbers. This example again demonstrates that a recursive solution solves a problem by using the solution of the same problem with simpler values.

15.2   Permutations

Many gas pumps have displays that spin digits (either analog or digital) while the gas is being pumped into your car's gas tank. The display's digits change to indicate the amount of gas in the tank and the current price.

We'll look at one of these displays and recursively generate the spinning of the digits. Our GasPump class will allow us to create a "gas pump" display with a specified number of display places and will allow us to specify the highest digit in use. We will simplify a gas pump display by using a smaller display of only three digits where the digits are in the limited range of 0–4 inclusive.

Example 15.2

```
// Permutation generator
public class GasPumpDisplay
{
    /*
        Constructor creates a display of digits.
        numberOfPositions is the number of positions displayed
    */
    public GasPumpDisplay(int numberOfPositions)
    {
        digits = numberOfPositions;
        if (digits > 1)
            tail = new GasPumpDisplay(digits - 1);
        else
            tail = null;
        currentDigit = 0;
    }

    // Returns the next permutation display.
    public String nextElement()
    {
        String r = null;
        if (digits == 1)  // filling last position in string
        {
            r = currentDigit + "";
            currentDigit++;
            return r;
        }

        // Permutation not yet complete
        r = currentDigit + tail.nextElement();
```

```
        if (!tail.hasMoreElements())
        {
            currentDigit++;
            tail = new GasPumpDisplay(digits - 1);
        }
        return r;
    }

    // Returns true if there are more elements, false otherwise.
    public boolean hasMoreElements()
    {
        return currentDigit <= MAX_DIGIT;
    }

    private int digits;
    private GasPumpDisplay tail;
    private int currentDigit;
    private static final MAX_DIGIT = 4;
}
```

```
/*
    This program tests the permutation generator.
*/
public class GasPumpTester
{
    public static void main(String[] args)
    {
        GasPumpDisplay d = new GasPumpDisplay(3);   // 3 digits in
                                                    // display
        while (d.hasMoreElements())
            System.out.println(d.nextElement());
    }
}
```

`GasPumpTester` prints the following permutations.

000 001 002 003 004 010 011 012 013 014 020 021 022 023 024 030 031 032 033 034 040 041 042 043 044 100 101 102 103 104 110 111 112 113 114 120 121 122 123 124 130 131 132 133 134 140 141 142 143 144 200 201 202 203 204 210 211 212 213 214 220 221 222 223 224 230 231 232 233 234 240 241 242 243 244 300 301 302 303 304 310 311 312 313 314 320 321 322 323 324 330 331 332 333 334 340 341 342 343 344 400 401 402 403 404 410 411 412 413 414 420 421 422 423 424 430 431 432 433 434 440 441 442 443 444

Section 18.2 of your text demonstrates a `PermutationGenerator` class that generates the permutations of a string using a similar approach.

15.3 Tracing Through Recursive Methods

The AP Exam may include multiple-choice questions that give a recursive algorithm and then ask questions about that algorithm. You need to be able to analyze the algorithm and hand-simulate (trace through) the algorithm. Consider the recursive method below.

Example 15.3

```
public class MysteryMaker
{
   /*
      Constructor
   */
   public MysteryMaker() {. . .}

   /*
      Precondition: x > 0, y > 0
      @return ?????
   */
   public int mystery(int x, int y)
   {
      if (y == 1)
         return x;
      else
         return x * mystery(x, y - 1);
   }
      . . .
}
```

Suppose the statements

```
MysteryMaker magic = new MysteryMaker();
System.out.println(magic.mystery(2, 5));
```

were executed. Examining the method in Example 15.3, we see that our three rules of recursion are satisfied.

- Taking one step is defined in the general case (the `else` clause).
- `y` starts with a positive integer value and each recursive call is made with a smaller `y` (a smaller problem).
- The end condition (base case) occurs when `y == 1`.

Tracing through the program requires us to write down the work done for each recursive call. When the end condition is reached, work backwards, substituting values into the recursive calls.

Figure 15.2

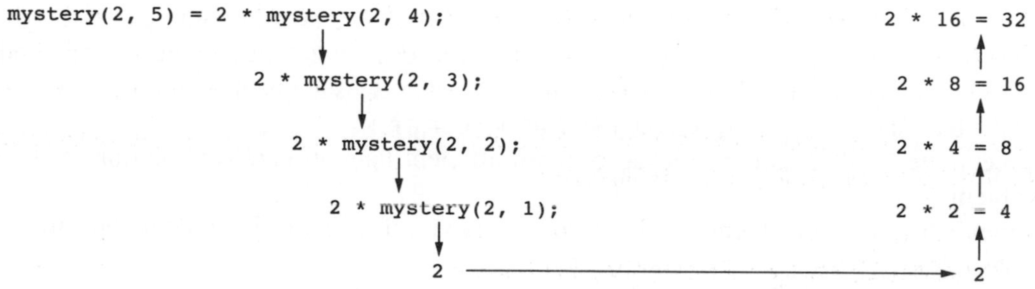

```
mystery(2, 5) = 2 * mystery(2, 4);                          2 * 16 = 32
                                                                 ↑
               2 * mystery(2, 3);                           2 * 8 = 16
                                                                 ↑
                   2 * mystery(2, 2);                       2 * 4 = 8
                                                                 ↑
                       2 * mystery(2, 1);                   2 * 2 = 4
                                                                 ↑
                           2 ───────────────────────────→ 2
```

From Figure 15.2, we can conclude the following:
- The statement `System.out.println(mystery(2, 5))` would print *32*.
- The number of times the call to `mystery` was made, including the original call, is *5*.
- `mystery(x, y)` returns x^y.

15.4 The Efficiency of Recursion

Although recursion is always fun, it's not always the most efficient way to solve a problem. The example of finding the nth Fibonacci number, which is illustrated in Section 18.4 of your text, certainly demonstrates this!

One of the best known recursive functions, Ackerman's Function, is not very useful, but it is very interesting. For *lots* of practice with tracing a recursive function, try tracing this algorithm to evaluate `acker(2, 3)` (or any other call with small numbers). This function grows very fast! By tracing Ackerman's function, you can see that the same method call is executed multiple times.

$$acker(x, y) = \begin{cases} y + 1 & \text{when x = 0} \\ acker(x - 1, 1) & \text{when x != 0, y = 0} \\ acker(x - 1, acker(x, y - 1)) & \text{when x != 0, y != 0} \end{cases}$$

After you try this by hand, test it out by writing a recursive method to solve the problem. If you try to evaluate this function for large values your program will report a "stack fault". *Common Error 18.1* of your text discusses stack faults.

■ Topics That Are Useful But Not Tested

- Section 18.3 of your text demonstrates the use of helper methods to simplify recursive solutions. Section 18.5 discusses mutual recursion. Neither of these topics is specifically listed in the AP CS Topic Outline but both are extensions of recursive solutions. You should read through the examples presented in your text.

■ Things to Remember When Taking the AP Exam

- Recursion is a topic for both AP CS A and AP CS AB. The programming exercises given at the end of Chapter 18 in your text will provide great practice in writing recursive methods.
- It is a common error to use a `while` statement when an `if` statement should be used to check for the base case in a recursive function. Check your work!
- A recursive solution is not necessarily more efficient than an iterative solution to the same problem.
- Remember to include an end condition for recursive solutions. Infinite recursions are usually undesirable.
- Write recursive solutions when the problem statement is defined recursively or when explicitly instructed to do so. Do not use recursion as a substitute for iteration.

■ Key Words

You should understand the terms below. The AP CS Exam questions may include references to these terms. The citations in parentheses next to each term identify the page numbers where it is defined and/or discussed in *Java Concepts*, 4th ed., and *Big Java*, 2nd ed.

infinite recursion (668)   permutation (668)   recursive solution (665)

■ Connecting the Detailed Topic Outline to the Text

The citations in parentheses identify where information in the outline can be located in *Java Concepts*, 4th ed., and *Big Java*, 2nd ed.

*   Thinking Recursively (673–676)
*   Permutations (668–671)
*   Tracing through Recursive Methods (672)
*   The Efficiency of Recursion (678–684)

■ Practice Questions

Multiple Choice

Questions 1 and 2 refer to the following three code segments.

```
I.  public static void mysteryPrint(int n)
    {
        if (n > 0)
        {
            mysteryPrint(n - 1);
        }
        System.out.println(n);
    }

II. public static void mysteryPrint(int n)
    {
        if (n > 0)
        {
            mysteryPrint(n - 1);
            System.out.println(n);
        }
    }

III. public static void mysteryPrint(int n)
     {
         if (n > 0)
         {
             mysteryPrint(n - 1);
         }
         else
         {
             System.out.println(n);
         }
     }
```

1. Assuming that the method `mysteryPrint` is called with a positive integer parameter, which statement about methods I, II, and III above is **true**?

   a. All three methods produce the same output.
   b. Methods I and II produce the same output that is different from the output produced by Method III.
   c. Methods I and III produce the same output that is different from the output produced by Method II.
   d. Methods II and III produce the same output that is different from the output produced by Method I.
   e. All three methods produce different outputs.

2. If the statement

   ```
   mysteryPrint(5);
   ```

   were executed, what output would be produced by code segment II ?

a.	0	b.	1	c.	5	d.	5	e.	0
	1		2		4		4		
	2		3		3		3		
	3		4		2		2		
	4		5		1		1		
	5				0				

3. Which of the following statements is **true** about recursive methods?

   a. Iterative methods are always easier to write than recursive methods.
   b. Recursive solutions to methods are always more efficient than iterative solutions.
   c. For recursion to terminate there must be a special non-recursive case for simple inputs.
   d. If a problem is solved both iteratively and recursively, the solutions will always have the same efficiency.
   e. Recursion is the most elegant and appropriate way to solve all problems.

4. Consider the recursive method whose definition appears below.

   ```java
   public static String mysteryString(String s)
   {
      if (s.length() == 1)
         return s;
      else
         return s.substring(s.length() - 1)
               + mysteryString(s.substring(0, s.length() - 1));
   }
   ```

   What is the result of the following call?

   ```java
   System.out.println(mysteryString("computer"));
   ```

   a. *computer* is printed to the screen.
   b. *retupmoc* is printed to the screen.
   c. *c* is printed to the screen.
   d. A stack fault occurs.
   e. A `StringIndexOutOfBoundsException` is thrown.

Questions 5 and 6 refer to the following recursive method definition.

```
public static int foo(int n)
{
   if (n < 10)
      return 1;
   else
      return 1 + foo(n / 10);
}
```

5. Which of the following statements best describes the value returned by method `foo`?

    a. `foo` returns the sum of the digits in its positive integer parameter.
    b. `foo` returns the sum of the digits in its integer parameter.
    c. `foo` returns the number of digits in its positive integer parameter.
    d. `foo` returns the number of digits in its integer parameter.
    e. `foo` returns the number of 1's in its integer parameter.

6. If the following statement is executed,

    ```
    int n = foo(1234);
    ```

    what is the total number of times the method `foo` is called (including the original call)?

    a. 1
    b. 2
    c. 3
    d. 4
    e. 5

Questions 7–9 refer to the `ArraySearcher` class incompletely defined below.

```
public class ArraySearcher
{
   public ArraySearcher(int[] anArray)
   {
      a = anArray;
   }

   public int searchFor(int n)
   {
      int low = 0;
      int high = a.length - 1;
      return search(low, high, n);
   }

   // Postcondition: Returns the index in the array a where key
   // occurs.
   // Returns -1 if key is not found in a.

   public int search(int low, int high, int key)
   {
      if (low > high)
         return -1;
      else
      {
```

```
                    int mid = (low + high) / 2;
                    if (key == a[mid])
                       return mid;
                    else if (key < a[mid])
                       return search(low, mid - 1, key);
                    else
                       return search(mid + 1, high, key);
                 }
             }

          private int[] a;
      }
```

The recursive method search is intended to locate the value key in array a. The method is to return the index of the first location of key in a and return -1 if key is not found in a.

7. Under which conditions will this work as intended?

    a. search will work as intended only if key is not found in a.
    b. search will work as intended only if key is in position 0.
    c. search will work as intended only if array a is sorted in ascending order.
    d. search will work as intended only if array a is sorted in descending order.
    e. search will never work as intended.

8. Assume that a client program included the following declarations and method calls,

    ```
    int[] a = {1, 21, 32, 45, 58, 61, 72, 80, 99, 100, 101};
    ArraySearcher searcher = new ArraySearcher(a);
    int pos = searcher.searchFor(58);
    ```

    How many times is the method search called before a value is returned?

    a. 1
    b. 2
    c. 3
    d. 4
    e. 5

9. Assume that a client program included the following declarations and method calls,

    ```
    int[] a = {6, 5, 4, 3, 2, 1};
    ArraySearcher searcher = new ArraySearcher(a);
    int pos = searcher.searchFor(5);
    ```

    What value would be assigned to pos?

    a. −1
    b. 0
    c. 1
    d. No value would be assigned. There would be a compile-time error.
    e. No value would be assigned. This would result in infinite recursion.

10. Consider the `Triangle` class defined below.

```
public class Triangle
{
    public Triangle(int aWidth)
    {
        width = aWidth;
    }

    public int getArea()
    {
        if (width <= 0) return 0;
        if (width == 1) return 1;
        Triangle smallerTriangle = new Triangle(width - 1);
        int smallerArea = smallerTriangle.getArea();
        return smallerArea + width;
    }

    private int width;
}
```

Suppose a client program included the following code segment.

```
Triangle t = new Triangle(4);
int area = t.getArea();
```

What value would be assigned to `area`?

a. 1
b. 4
c. 5
d. 10
e. 15

Free Response Questions

1. Euclid's Algorithm can be used to find the greatest common divisor (gcd) of two integers. The algorithm works recursively as illustrated in the example below.

Method Call		Recursive Method Call
gcd(3388, 436)	3388 = 7 * 436 + 336	gcd(3388, 436) = gcd(436, 336)
gcd(436, 336)	436 = 1 * 336 + 100	gcd(436, 336) = gcd(336, 100)
gcd(336, 100)	336 = 3 * 100 + 36	gcd(336, 100) = gcd(100, 36)
gcd(100, 36)	100 = 2 * 36 + 28	gcd(100, 36) = gcd(36, 28)
gcd(36, 28)	36 = 1 * 28 + 8	gcd(36, 28) = gcd(28, 8)
gcd(28, 8)	28 = 3 * 8 + 4	gcd(28, 8) = gcd(8, 4)
gcd(8, 4)	8 = 2 * 4 + 0	gcd(8, 4) = gcd(4, 0)
gcd(4, 0) = 4		

Therefore, gcd(3388, 436) = 4.

You are to implement the recursive method for Euclid's Algorithm. Write your method using the method header below.

```
/*
    Precondition: num1 >= 0, num2 >= 0
    Returns the greatest common divisor of num1 and num2
*/
public static int gcd(int num1, int num2)
```

2. The area of a triangle with corner points $(x1, y1)$, $(x2, y2)$, and $(x3, y3)$ can be computed as:

$$A = \frac{|x1 * y2 + x2 * y3 + x3 * y1 - y1 * x2 - y2 * x3 - y3 * x1|}{2}$$

a. Write the method `triangleArea` that computes the area of its three Point parameters using the above formula. The incomplete `Point` class implementation appears below.

```
public class Point
{
    // Constructor
    Point(double x1, double y1)
    {
        x = x1;
        y = y1;
    }

    // Returns the x-coordinate of this point.
    public double getX() {. . .}

    // Returns the y-coordinate of this point.
    public double getY() {. . .}

    private double x;
    private double y;
}
```

Write your method `triangleArea` using the method header below.

```
public static double triangleArea(Point p1, Point p2, Point p3)
```

b. To compute the area of a polygon with more than three corner points, you can chop off a triangle and recursively compute the area of the remaining polygon (which has one corner point less than the original).

Refer to the incomplete `Polygon` class below.

```
import java.util.ArrayList;

// A polygon with a number of Point corners.
public class Polygon
{
    // Constructs a Polygon object with no corners.
    public Polygon()
    {
        corners = new ArrayList();
    }

    // Adds a point p to the list of Polygon corners.
    // Corners are added in clockwise order.
    public void add(Point p)
    {
        corners.add(p);
    }


    // Returns the area of the triangle with the three vertices
    // p1, p2, and p3.
    public double triangleArea(Point p1, Point p2,
          Point p3) {. . .}

    // Recursively computes and returns the area of a polygon.
    // If this polygon has fewer than 3 vertices, return 0.
    // Otherwise, return the sum of the area of a triangle
    // and the area of a smaller polygon.
    public double getArea()
    {
        // Code goes here
    }

    private ArrayList corners;
}
```

In writing the method `getArea`, you may call the method `triangleArea`. Assume `triangleArea` works as specified regardless of what you wrote for part a. Write `getArea` using the method header below.

```
public double getArea()
```

CHAPTER 16

(Covers *Java Concepts* Chapter 19)

Sorting and Searching

■ Topic Summary

16.1 Selection Sort

The selection sort algorithm orders array elements by inspecting all elements in the array to find the smallest element. This element is exchanged with the first entry in the array. The smallest element is now first. The next step is to inspect the elements to find the second smallest element and exchange this element with the second entry in the array. The smallest two elements in the array are now in the first two positions of the array. This procedure continues until all elements in the array are in sorted order. The complete SelectionSorter class can be found in Section 19.1 of your text. Example 16.1 examines three key methods used in the selection sort.

Example 16.1 sort Method

```
public void sort()
{
    /*
        Loop invariant: Elements a[0]...a[i - 1] are in their final
        positions.
    */
    for (int i = 0; i < a.length - 1; i++)
    {
        int minPos = minimumPosition(i);
        swap(minPos, i);
    }
}
```

The method sort calls the method minimumPosition to return the index of the smallest entry in the tail portion of the array beginning in position i and then calls the method swap to exchange the entries in these two positions of the array. This is the method that puts each element in its final position.

minimumPosition Method

```
private int minimumPosition(int from)
{
    int minPos = from;
    for (int i = from + 1; i < a.length; i++)
        if (a[i] < a[minPos]) minPos = i;
    return minPos;
}
```

The method minimumPosition searches the array for the smallest value beginning in position from. The index of the element with the smallest value in this portion of the array is returned.

swap Method

```
private void swap(int i, int j)
{
    int temp = a[i];
    a[i] = a[j];
    a[j] = temp;
}
```

The method swap has two parameters that represent indices of the array. swap exchanges the entries in these two positions in the array.

Your text uses the ArrayUtil class to fill the array with random values and to print the array values to the screen. The ArrayUtil class is a utility class (similar to the Math class). A utility class has no objects but contains related static methods. These static methods are called by using the class name and passing the appropriate parameters. The statements

```
// Fills a 20 element (first parameter) array with integers in the
// range 0-99 (second parameter) inclusive.
int[] a = ArrayUtil.randomIntArray(20, 100);
```

and

```
    // Prints the contents of the array.
    ArrayUtil.print(a);
```

call static methods of the `ArrayUtil` utility class.

16.1.1 Analyzing the Performance of the Selection Sort Algorithm

We are sometimes asked to analyze the running time of an algorithm or to determine how many comparisons are made in a certain algorithm. Consider the following array:

13	34	1	50	21

Using the selection sort algorithm we have:
- Starting with position 0: 4 comparisons are made to determine that 1 is the smallest value in the array. 1 is swapped with 13.

1	34	13	50	21

1 is in its final position.

- Advancing to position 1: 3 comparisons are made to determine that 13 is the smallest value in the remaining part of the array. 13 is swapped with 34.

1	13	34	50	21

1 and **13** are in their final positions.

- Advancing to position 2: 2 comparisons are made to determine that 21 is the smallest value in the remaining part of the array. 34 is swapped with 21.

1	13	21	50	34

1, 13, and **21** are in their final positions.

- Advancing to position 3: 1 comparison is made to determine that 34 is the smallest value in the remaining part of the array. 34 is swapped with 50.

1	13	21	34	50

All numbers are in their final positions.

The total number of comparisons made during this simulation of the selection sort is

$$4 + 3 + 2 + 1 = 10$$

For 5 elements, the number of comparisons made by the selection sort algorithm is the sum of the first 4 integers. For n elements, the number of comparisons would be the sum of the first $n-1$ integers:

$$(n - 1) + (n - 2) + (n - 3) + \ldots + 3 + 2 + 1.$$

The formula for finding the sum of the first k integers is: $\sum_{i=1}^{k} i = \frac{(k)(k + 1)}{2}$. In our example, the sum of the first 4 integers is $\frac{(4)(5)}{2}$.

The original order of the array elements has no effect on the number of comparisons made by the selection sort algorithm. The nested loop executes the same number of times regardless of the original ordering of the array elements.

For the AP CS A Exam, you should be able to count comparisons (or statement executions) for a given algorithm. For the AB Exam, you need to be able to classify algorithms based on their performance efficiency.

(AB only) As explained above, the number of comparisons made to sort an array with n elements is the sum of the first $n-1$ integers. In general, for an n-element array, this computation evaluates to

$$\frac{n(n-1)}{2} = \frac{n^2}{2} - \frac{n}{2}$$

We classify the selection sort as a *quadratic* sort because it has complexity of the form $y = an^2$, where n is the number of elements being sorted and y is the run-time complexity (in our case, the number of comparisons), and a is some constant. We use the expression $O(n^2)$ (read as "big-Oh of n squared") to represent the complexity of this algorithm. We are generally concerned with what happens to a sorting algorithm's behavior and efficiency as the number of elements, n, gets very large. The curves $y = n^2$, $y = \frac{n^2}{2}$ and $y = \frac{n^2}{2} - \frac{n}{2}$ have the same basic shape and are all classified as $O(n^2)$.

16.2   Insertion Sort

The insertion sort algorithm takes each element of the array and inserts it into an already sorted portion of the array. For each element we look at, the elements to its left are sorted. We look at the first element in the unsorted part of the array. The elements in the sorted part of the array are shifted to make room for this element to be inserted. Insertion sort is outlined below and covered in *Advanced Topic 19.1* in your text.

To sort our original array using insertion sort, position 0 is already sorted.

13	34	1	50	21

- Starting with position 1: Ready to insert 34.

13	34	1	50	21

  34 is compared to 13. Since 13 is not greater than 34, it is not shifted.
  34 is inserted into position 1.

13	34	1	50	21

- Advancing to position 2: Ready to insert 1.

| 13 | 34 | 1 | 50 | 21 |

1 is compared to 34. Since 34 is greater than 1, 34 is shifted.

| 13 | | 34 | 50 | 21 |

1 is compared to 13. Since 13 is greater than 1, 13 is shifted.

1
| | 13 | 34 | 50 | 21 |

1 is inserted into position 0.

| 1 | 13 | 34 | 50 | 21 |

- Advancing to position 3: Ready to insert 50.

| 1 | 13 | 34 | 50 | 21 |

50 is compared to 34. Since 34 is not greater than 50, no entry is shifted.
50 is inserted into position 3.

| 1 | 13 | 34 | 50 | 21 |

- Advancing to position 4: Ready to insert 21.

| 1 | 13 | 34 | 50 | 21 |

21 is compared to 50. Since 50 is greater than 21, 50 is shifted.

21
| 1 | 13 | 34 | | 50 |

21 is compared to 34. Since 34 is greater than 21, 34 is shifted.

21
| 1 | 13 | | 34 | 50 |

21 is compared to 13. Since 13 is not greater than 21, no other entries are shifted. 21 is inserted into position 2.

1	13	21	34	50

The array is now sorted. Example 16.2 shows the `sort` method of the `InsertionSorter` class.

Example 16.2

```
public void sort()
{
    for (int i = 1; i < a.length; i++)
    {
        int temp = a[i];
        int pos = i;
        while (0 < pos && temp < a[pos - 1])
        {
            a[pos] = a[pos - 1];
            pos--;
        }
        a[pos] = temp
    }
}
```

16.2.1 Analyzing the Performance of the Insertion Sort Algorithm

Using insertion sort, we saw that the number of comparisons and the number of shifts made were dependent on the original order of the array. The insertion sort algorithm only compares terms until the correct position of the element to insert is determined. If the original array were in increasing order, there would be only one comparison (and no shifts) for each element we insert. Many more comparisons and shifts are needed if the original array is in decreasing order.

There are different implementations for the insertion sort algorithm but you should recognize the insertion sort regardless of the implementation.

(AB only) For the insertion sort algorithm, the number of comparisons made to sort an array with n elements in the worst case (when the array is in reverse order) will take $(n-1) + (n-2) + ... + 2 + 1$ comparisons (and shifts). This is

$$\frac{n(n-1)}{2} = \frac{n^2}{2} - \frac{n}{2}$$

We see that the insertion sort is also an $O(n^2)$ sorting algorithm. Of course if we start with a sorted array, the complexity is $O(n)$ because only one comparison is made for each of the $n-1$ elements visited. Wouldn't it be nice if all of the arrays we had to sort were already sorted!

16.3 Merge Sort

The merge sort algorithm sorts an array by cutting the array in half, recursively sorting each half, and then merging the sorted halves. Section 19.4 of your text shows the `MergeSorter` class. Let's look at the basic parts of the merge sort algorithm.

Example 16.3   sort Method

```java
public void sort()
{
    if (a.length <= 1) return;
    int[] first = new int[a.length / 2];
    int[] second = new int[a.length - first.length];
    // System.arraycopy(a, 0, first, 0, first.length);
    int j = 0;
    for (int i = 0; i < first.length; i++)
    {
        first[j] = a[i];
        j++;
    }
    // System.arraycopy(a, first.length, second, 0, second.length);
    j = 0;
    for (int i = first.length; i < second.length + first.length;
            i++)
    {
        second[j] = a[i];
        j++;
    }
    MergeSorter firstSorter = new MergeSorter(first);
    MergeSorter secondSorter = new MergeSorter(second);
    firstSorter.sort();    // Recursive call on first half
    secondSorter.sort();   // Recursive call on second half
    merge(first, second);    // Merge two sorted halves
}
```

This sort method contains 2 recursive calls, each calling itself with a smaller array. This process continues with each of the smaller arrays until the array has 1 or 0 elements. Since System.arraycopy is not part of the AP subset, the calls to System.arraycopy have been commented out and replaced by for loops that perform the same task.

Let's look at the merge sort algorithm with a sample array containing 8 elements. One call to sort is made to sort 8 elements

| 12 | 34 | 7 | 2 | 63 | 45 | 17 | 20 |

sort now makes 2 recursive calls to sort 2 smaller arrays, each with 8/2 or 4 elements.

| 12 | 34 | 7 | 2 | | 63 | 45 | 17 | 20 |

And now, 4 recursive calls are made to sort 4 smaller arrays, each with 8/4 or 2 elements.

Finally, 8 recursive calls are made to sort 8 arrays, each of size 1.

| 12 | 34 | 7 | 2 | 63 | 45 | 17 | 20 |

Then the method `merge` is called to merge two adjacent sorted arrays.

Example 16.4   `merge` Method

```
private void merge(int[] first, int[] second)
{
    // Merge both halves into the temporary array
    int iFirst = 0;    // Next element in first half to look at
    int iSecond = 0;    // Next element in second half to look at
    int j = 0;    // Next open position in a

    // Merging the 2 arrays
    while (iFirst < first.length && iSecond < second.length)
    {
        if (first[iFirst] < second[iSecond])
        {
            a[j] = first[iFirst];
            iFirst++;
        }
        else
        {
            a[j] = second[iSecond];
            iSecond++;
        }
        j++;
    }

    // Exactly one of the two following loops will be executed.

    // Copy any remaining entries of the first half
    for (int i = iFirst; i < first.length; i++)
    {
        a[j] = first[i];
        j++;
    }

    // Copy any remaining entries of the second half
    for (int i = iSecond; i < second.length; i++)
    {
        a[j] = second[i];
        j++;
    }
}
```

The `System.arraycopy` statements have again been replaced by equivalent `for` loops.

After recursive calls to `sort` we have

| 12 | 34 | 7 | 2 | 63 | 45 | 17 | 20 |

Now, the `merge` method is called to merge two adjacent sorted arrays.

| 12 | 34 | | 2 | 7 | | 45 | 63 | | 17 | 20 |

We merge two adjacent sorted arrays again,

| 2 | 7 | 12 | 34 | | 17 | 20 | 45 | 63 |

And again.

| 2 | 7 | 12 | 17 | 20 | 34 | 45 | 63 |

16.3.1 Analyzing the Performance of the Merge Sort Algorithm

In almost all cases, merge sort is more efficient than insertion sort and in all cases merge sort is more efficient than selection sort.

(AB only) Suppose that the original size of our array is n where $n = 2^m$. The recursive calls to `sort` create m levels that we must merge.

Each level merges n elements so the complexity of the merge sort algorithm can be informally classified as $O(nm)$. If we apply our rules for logarithms, since $n = 2^m$ we have $m = \log_2(n)$. The shape of logarithm curves is the same regardless of the base. Substituting $\log_2(n)$ for m, we have $O(n \log_2(n))$ and we classify merge sort as an $O(n \log(n))$ algorithm. A more formal analysis of merge sort is in Section 19.5 of your text.

16.4 Quicksort (AB only)

Another $O(n \log(n))$ sort is quicksort. Unlike merge sort, quicksort does not need temporary arrays. The algorithm chooses an element from the array (pivot) and then partitions the array into two smaller arrays so that those elements to the left of the partition are less than or equal to `pivot` and those elements to the right of the partition are greater than or equal to `pivot`. Example 16.5 shows the recursive quicksort `sort` method and the `partition` method.

Example 16.5 sort Method

```
public void sort(int from, int to)
{
   if (from >= to) return;   // There are elements to sort.

   int p = partition(from, to);   // Array partitioned.
   // So that the elements a[from]...a[p] (left partition) are
   // less than or equal to the elements a[p + 1]...a[to]
   // (right partition)

   sort(from, p);   // Sort left partition
   sort(p + 1, to);   // Sort right partition
}
```

sort calls partition to divide the array into two partitions such that all elements in the left partition are less than or equal to pivot and those elements in the right partition are greater than or equal to pivot. The method sort then recursively calls itself to do the same on the left partition and the right partition.

partition **Method**

```
private int partition(int from, int to)
{
    int pivot = a[from];
    int i = from - 1;
    int j = to + 1;
    while (i < j)
    {
        i++;
        while (a[i] < pivot)
            i++;
        j--;
        while (a[j] > pivot)
            j--;
        if (i < j) swap(i, j);
    }
    return j;
}
```

partition returns an index, j, in the array such that the elements a[from]...a[j] are less than or equal to the elements a[j + 1]...a[to].

Consider the array: a = {7 9 1 6 4 8 2 5}

The partition method chooses the first element in the array (7) as pivot.

After the call to partition, the array is partitioned into two smaller arrays.

{5 2 1 6 4}   {8 9 7}

The elements in the left partition are all less than or equal to 7 and the elements in the right partition are all greater than or equal to 7. Then sort is called with each smaller array and each smaller array is partitioned. You are encouraged to trace through this code for the example presented so that you can understand how the partition method and the quicksort algorithm work. *Advanced Topic 19.3* in your text discusses the quicksort algorithm.

16.4.1 *Analyzing the Performance of the Quicksort Algorithm (AB only)*

The most efficient behavior of quicksort occurs when the partition is always found to be in the center of the array (approximately the same number of elements to the left of the partition as there are to the right of the partition). Assume that the number of elements, n, is a power of 2. Then $n = 2^m$. Assume also that the position of the partition is in the exact middle of the subarray.

Table 16.1   Quicksort Comparisons

Number of subarrays	Number of elements in each subarray	Number of comparisons in each subarray	Total number of comparisons
1	n	$n - 1 \approx n$	$1(n)$
2	$\dfrac{n}{2}$	$\dfrac{n}{2} - 1 \approx \dfrac{n}{2}$	$2\left(\dfrac{n}{2}\right)$
4	$\dfrac{n}{4}$	$\dfrac{n}{4} - 1 \approx \dfrac{n}{4}$	$4\left(\dfrac{n}{4}\right)$
8	$\dfrac{n}{8}$	$\dfrac{n}{8} - 1 \approx \dfrac{n}{8}$	$8\left(\dfrac{n}{8}\right)$
...	...	...	...
...	...	...	$n + 2\left(\dfrac{n}{2}\right) + 4\left(\dfrac{n}{4}\right) + \cdots + n\left(\dfrac{n}{n}\right)$

After dividing m times, there are n partitions of size 1.

$$\text{Total comparisons} = n + 2\left(\frac{n}{2}\right) + 4\left(\frac{n}{4}\right) + 8\left(\frac{n}{8}\right) + \cdots + n\left(\frac{n}{n}\right)$$

$$= n + n + n + \cdots + n \ \{m \text{ times}\}$$

$$= nm$$

But, if $n = 2^m$, then $m = \log_2(n)$, so substituting, we have

$$\text{Total comparisons} = n \log_2(n)$$

which classifies the quicksort algorithm as $O(n \log(n))$.

Remember that there are different implementations for the sort algorithm that we present but you should recognize the algorithm regardless of the implementation.

16.5   Comparing $O(n^2)$ and $O(n \log(n))$ (AB only)

We are generally concerned with what happens to a sorting algorithm's behavior and efficiency as the number of elements, n, gets very large. The curves $y = n^2$, $y = n \log(n)$, and $y = n$ are graphed in Figure 16.1 for values of n ranging from 1 to 20. This graph shows that $y = n^2$ increases in value much faster than $y = n \log(n)$.

Figure 16.1   Comparing $y = n^2$, $y = n \log(n)$, and $y = n$

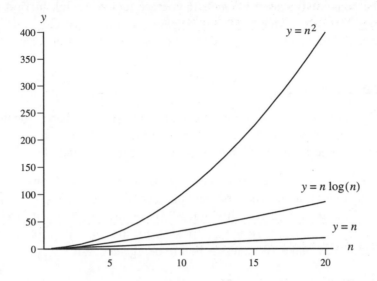

If you look at Table 16.2, you can see that the difference in running times is more pronounced when the number of elements is very large.

Table 16.2   Comparing $O(n^2)$ with $O(n \log(n))$

n	n^2	$n \log(n)$
100	10,000	664
300	90,000	2,468
500	250,000	4,482
800	640,000	7,715
1,000	1,000,000	9,965
10,000	100,000,000	132,877
100,000	10,000,000,000	1,660,964

Table 16.2 uses $\log_2$. Remember that $\log_2(x) = \log_{10}(x) / \log_{10}(2)$. You can calculate the values in Table 16.2 using your calculator and this $\log_2$ relationship.

16.6   Sequential Search

A sequential (or linear) search examines each element in the array until the required match is found or the end of the array is reached. In the best case, the element is found in the first position of the array. In the worst case, the element is not found in the array, so all of the elements in the array are visited. Generally, the sequential search does not depend on any particular ordering of the array elements. If the elements are sorted in increasing order, a sequential search will examine the array elements until the required match is found or until the element being examined is greater than the value being sought (which indicates the required match is not in this sorted array).

16.6.1 Analyzing the Performance of the Sequential Search Algorithm (AB only)
In the worst case, the sequential search is $O(n)$. If you are lucky enough to find the element in position 0 of the array, then the search is $O(1)$. The average number of elements examined with the sequential search is $n/2$ and therefore, the sequential search is classified as an $O(n)$ algorithm.

16.7 Binary Search

The binary search algorithm is used to search a sorted array. Binary search locates a value in a sorted array by determining whether the value occurs in the first half or the second half of the array. This process is repeated in the half where it is expected to be found.

The game of *High-Low* is a game where one person thinks of a number between 1 and 100. The other person is to guess that number. The first person responds "Correct!", "Too high!", or "Too low!" for each guess. What would be your first guess? If you are familiar with the binary search, you can guess the number with no more than 7 tries! A person who attempts to play this game using a sequential search may make 100 guesses before being successful.

16.7.1 Analyzing the Performance of the Binary Search Algorithm
The formal analysis of the binary search is explained in Section 19.7 of your text. Informally, let's assume an array has 8 elements whose values are 11–18. Suppose you are searching for the value 13.

$$a = \{11 \quad 12 \quad 13 \quad 14 \quad 15 \quad 16 \quad 17 \quad 18\}$$

You know how to play this game. You guess 14. The answer is "Too high." You guess 12. The answer is "Too low." You guess 13. If there is no case of "cheating," you will guess the correct value in at most 3 guesses. Notice that $2^3 = 8$.

The maximum number of guesses for *High-Low* is the smallest power of 2 that results in a value greater than or equal to the number of numbers from which we are guessing. For our 1–100 *High-Low* game, the maximum number of guesses is 7 (if you know how to play the game efficiently) because $2^7 > 100$. 7 is the smallest power of 2 that results in a value greater than or equal to 100.

The `BinarySearcher` class is shown in Section 19.7 of your text. Example 16.6 shows the `search` method from `BinarySearcher`. The `search` method returns the index of the value `v` in the array. If `v` is not found in the array, `-1` is returned.

Example 16.6

```
public int search(int v)
{
   int low = 0;
   int high = a.length - 1;
   while (low <= high)
   {
      int mid = (low + high) / 2;
      int diff = a[mid] - v;


      if (diff == 0)    // a[mid] == v
         return mid;
      else if (diff < 0)    // a[mid] < v
         low = mid + 1;
```

```
        else
            high = mid - 1;
    }
    return -1;
}
```

(AB only) If there are n elements in a sorted array, and $n = 2^m$, then $m = \log_2(n)$. The maximum number of visits in the array is $\log(n)$. The binary search is a $O(\log(n))$ algorithm.

16.8   Comparing *O(n)* and *O(log(n))* (AB only)

We are again primarily concerned with what happens to an algorithm's behavior and efficiency as the number of elements, n, gets very large. The curve $y = n$ and $y = \log(n)$ are graphed below for values ranging from 1 to 20. You can see in Figure 16.2 that $y = n$ increases in value much faster than $y = \log(n)$.

Figure 16.2   Comparing *O(n)* and *O(log(n))*

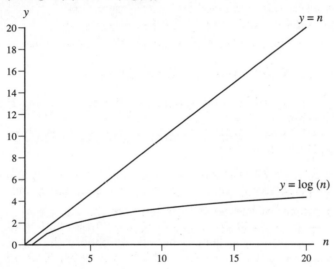

In Table 16.3, you can see that the difference between n and $\log(n)$ is again more pronounced when the number of elements, n, is very large.

Table 16.3

n	$\log(n)$
100	6.64
300	8.22
500	8.97
800	9.64
1000	9.97
10,000	13.28
100,000	16.61

Using a binary search with 100,000 elements will require no more than 17 visits but a sequential search may require 100,000! However, the binary search requires that the array is sorted.

An interesting relationship to remember is that the truncated value of $\log_{10}(n) + 1$ is the number of decimal digits of n, and the truncated value of $\log_2(n) + 1$ is the number of binary digits of n. Thus, $\log_2(n)$ is approximately $(10/3) * \log_{10}(n)$.

■ Topics That Are Useful But Not Tested

- The Java `Arrays` class contains a static `sort` method for sorting arrays of integers and floating-point numbers. This is discussed in Section 19.5 of your text.
- Defining a class that implements the `Comparator` interface is one way to sort objects of a class that we do not own and that does not implement the `Comparable` interface. The `Comparator` interface can also be used to sort objects in a way other than that which is defined in the class. This is explained in *Advanced Topic 19.5* in your text.
- The `Collections` class contains sort methods that can sort array lists. This is presented in Section 19.8 in your text.

■ Things to Remember When Taking the AP Exam

- When given a particular algorithm, you should be able to count the number of times a specific statement is executed.
- The merge sort is more efficient than the insertion sort and selection sort algorithms but requires a temporary array.
- When writing a sorting algorithm, there are many places where off-by-one errors can occur. Be careful when choosing between 0 and 1, < and <=, and `a.length` and `a.length - 1` for loop initializations. Walk through your code carefully.
- When given an algorithm similar to the binary search algorithm and an algorithm similar to the sequential search algorithm, you should be able to choose the algorithm that is more efficient for a specific set of data.
- Remember that an array has to be sorted in order to use binary search.
- Binary search generally is more efficient than sequential search if the array is sorted.
- (**AB only**) Merge sort and quicksort are $O(n \log(n))$ algorithms. Insertion and selection sorts are $O(n^2)$.
- (**AB only**) The worst case for the quicksort algorithm is when the original array is in order or in reverse order. This makes the quicksort running time $O(n^2)$.
- (**AB only**) Algorithms that are $O(n \log(n))$ are more efficient than algorithms that are $O(n^2)$.
- (**AB only**) When given an algorithm, you should be able to classify it as $O(1)$, $O(n)$, $O(\log(n))$, $O(n^2)$, or $O(n \log(n))$.
- (**AB only**) Do not classify an algorithm as $O(2n)$, $O(3)$, or $O(n^2 + 2n + 1)$. These are $O(n)$, $O(1)$, and $O(n^2)$ respectively.
- (**AB only**) Do not simply count loops when determining the big-Oh running time. Consecutive loop algorithms are most often $O(n)$. Nested loop algorithms tend to be $O(n^2)$.

■ Key Words

You should understand the terms below. The AP CS Exam questions may include references to these terms. The citations in parentheses next to each term identify the page numbers where it is defined and/or discussed in *Java Concepts*, 4th ed., and *Big Java*, 2nd ed.

big-Oh notation (712)	merge sort (715)	sequential search (726)
binary search (728)	quicksort (722)	sorting algorithm (704)
insertion sort (713)	selection sort (704)	worst-case runtime
linear search (726)		behavior (723)

■ Connecting the Detailed Topic Outline to the Text

The citations in parentheses identify where information in the outline can be located in *Java Concepts*, 4th ed., and *Big Java*, 2nd ed.

- Selection Sort (704–707)
  - Analyzing the Performance of the Selection Sort Algorithm (711–713)
- Insertion Sort (713–714)
  - Analyzing the Performance of the Insertion Sort Algorithm (714–715)
- Merge Sort (715–718)
  - Analyzing the Performance of the Merge Sort Algorithm (719–722)
- Quicksort (722–723)
  - Analyzing the Performance of the Quicksort Algorithm (723)
- Sequential Search (725–727)
  - Analyzing the Performance of the Sequential Search Algorithm (726)
- Binary Search (728–730)
  - Analyzing the Performance of the Binary Search Algorithm (730)

■ Practice Questions

Multiple Choice

Questions 1 and 2 refer to the incomplete definition of the `SelectionSorter` class below.

```
public class SelectionSorter
{
   public SelectionSorter(int[] anArray)
   {
      a = anArray;
   }

   public void sort()
   {
      for (int i = 0; i < a.length - 1; i++)
      {
         int minPos = minimumPosition(i);
         swap(minPos, i);
      }
```

```
        }

        // Returns the position of the smallest element
        // in a[from]...a[a.length - 1]
        private int minimumPosition(int from){. . .}

        // Exchanges a[i] with a[j]
        swap(int i, int j) {. . .}

        private int[] a;
    }
```

The following segment of code is executed.

```
    SelectionSorter sorter = new SelectionSorter(a);
    sorter.sort();
```

Consider arrays initialized with the values below.

I.   {2, 3, 4, 5, 6}
II. {6, 5, 4, 3, 2}
III. {2, 6, 1, 5, 4}

1. Which of the following statements regarding the number of comparisons made to sort the array is **true**?

   a. I takes fewer comparisons than both II and III.
   b. II takes fewer comparisons than both I and III.
   c. III takes fewer comparisons than both I and II.
   d. I and II require the same number of comparisons, which is different from the number of comparisons required to sort III.
   e. I, II, and III require the same number of comparisons.

2. Consider the `SelectionSorter` method `sort`.

```
    public void sort()
    {
        for (int i = 0; i < a.length - 1; i++)
        {
            int minPos = minimumPosition(i);
            swap(minPos, i);
        }
    }
```

   Which of the following statements is **true** at the beginning of each iteration of the loop?

   I.   For all j, such that 0 <= j < i, 0 <= a[j] <= a[i].
   II. For all j, such that 0 <= j < i, a[j] is in its final position in the sorted array.
   III. For all j, such that 0 <= j < i, a[0]...a[j] is sorted.

   a. I only
   b. II only
   c. III only
   d. II and III only
   e. I, II, and III

3. **(AB only)** Consider the following algorithms to accomplish the task of removing duplicates from an array list `list`.

   I.   For each element in `list` (x_i), look at x_i. Now look at each element in `list` and count how many times x_i occurs in `list`. If the count is larger than 1, remove x_i.

   II. Sort the array list with an efficient sort algorithm. For each x_i in `list`, look at its next neighbor to decide whether it is present more than once. If it is, remove x_i.

   III. Sort the array list, `list`, with an efficient algorithm. Traverse the array list looking at each x_i in `list`. Whenever the element after x_i (if there is one) is strictly larger than x_i, append x_i to a second (initially empty) array list, `list2`. Append the last element to `list2`. Find the difference, `diff`, in the sizes of `list` and `list2`. Beginning with the last element of `list`, delete `diff` elements from `list`. Then, copy the elements of `list2` back into `list`.

   Of the following, which best describes the running time of these algorithms?

   a. I, II, and III are all $O(n^2)$.
   b. I and II are $O(n^2)$, III is $O(n \log(n))$.
   c. I is $O(n^2)$, II and III are $O(n \log(n))$.
   d. I and III are $O(n^2)$, II is $O(n \log(n))$.
   e. I, II, and III are $O(n \log(n))$.

4. The method `removeDupes` is intended to remove duplicates from array `a`, returning `n`, the number of elements in `a` after duplicates have been removed. For example, if array `a` has the values

   ```
   {4, 7, 11, 4, 9, 5, 11, 7, 3, 5}
   ```

   before `removeDupes` is called, then after duplicates are removed, `a` will be

   {4, 7, 11, 5, 9, 3} and 6 will be returned.

   ```java
   public static int removeDupes(int[] a)
   {
       int n = a.length;
       for (int i = 0; i < n; i++)
       {
           int current = a[i];
           int j = i + 1;
           while (j < n)
           {
               if (current == a[j])
               {
                   a[j] = a[n - 1];
                   n--;
               }
               else
                   j++;
           }
       }
       return n;
   }
   ```

How many times is the comparison

```
(current == a[j])
```

executed in removeDupes?

a. 45
b. 42
c. 36
d. 25
e. 21

5. The method removeDupes is intended to remove duplicates from array a, returning n, the number of elements in a after duplicates have been removed. For example, if array a has the values

```
{4, 7, 11, 4, 9, 5, 11, 7, 3, 5}
```

before removeDupes is called, then after duplicates are removed, a will be {4, 7, 11, 5, 9, 3} and 6 will be returned.

Consider the following three implementations of removeDupes.

I.
```
public static int removeDupes(int[] a)
{
    int n = a.length;
    for (int i = 0; i < n; i++)
    {
        int current = a[i];
        int j = i + 1;
        while (j < n)
        {
            if (current == a[j])
            {
                a[j] = a[n - 1];
                n--;
            }
            else
                j++;
        }
    }
    return n;
}
```

II.
```
public static int removeDupes(int[] a)
{
    int n = a.length;
    for (int i = 0; i < n; i++)
    {
        int current = a[i];
        for (int j = 0; j < n; j++)
        {
            if (i != j && current == a[j])
            {
                a[j] = a[n - 1];
                n--;
            }
        }
```

```
        }
        return n;
    }
III. public static int removeDupes(int[] a)
    {
        int n = a.length;
        int count = 0;
        int i = 0;
        while (i < n)
        {
            int j = i + 1;
            boolean found = false;
            while (!found && j < n)
            {
                if (a[i] == a[j])
                {
                    a[j] = a[n - 1];
                    n--;
                    found = true;
                }
                j++;
            }
            if (!found)
                i++;
        }
        return n;
    }
```

Which of the code segments above requires the fewest number of operations?

a. I
b. II
c. III
d. All choices require the same number of operations.
e. It is impossible to determine which segment requires the fewest operations.

6. Which of the following statements about searching is **not** true?

a. The sequential search examines all values in an array until it finds a match or until it reaches the end.
b. A binary search is generally more efficient than a sequential search.
c. A binary search can only be used to search for an item in a sorted array.
d. A sequential search generally takes more comparisons than a binary search.
e. A binary search is always faster than a sequential search.

7. (**AB only**) The quicksort algorithm is to be used to sort an array of integers in decreasing order. Which of the cases below describes the worst case for the quicksort algorithm when the first element is used as the pivot?

I.   The original array is in increasing order.
II. The original array is in decreasing order.
III. The original array is in random order.

    a. I only
    b. II only
    c. III only
    d. I and II only
    e. I, II, and III all take the same number of comparisons.

8. Consider the `search` method (of some class) below which is intended to return the index of the position in array a where `key` is found. If `key` is not in the array a, `-1` is returned.

```java
public int search(int key)
{
    int low = 0;
    int high = a.length - 1;
    while (low <= high)
    {
        int mid = (low + high) / 2;
        int diff = a[mid] - key;

        if (diff == 0)    // a[mid] == key
            return mid;
        else if (diff < 0)   // a[mid] < key
            low = mid + 1;
        else
            high = mid - 1;
    }
    return -1;
}
private int[] a;
```

Suppose:

```
a = {8, 10, 1, 5, 7, 9, 6, 2}
```

What value will `search(2)` return?

    a. 8
    b. 4
    c. 3
    d. −1
    e. No value will be returned. An `ArrayIndexOutOfBoundsException` is thrown.

9. What is the maximum number of elements that will be visited by the binary search algorithm when searching a sorted 45-element array?

    a. 1
    b. 6
    c. 7
    d. 22
    e. 45

10. An array, a, is initialized to contain the following values.

```
a = {1, 23, 44, 56, 77, 81, 88, 90, 99}
```

The following search algorithm is provided.

```java
public int search(int v, int high)
{
    int low = 0;
    while (low <= high)
    {
        int mid = (low + high) / 2;
        int diff = a[mid] - v;

        if (diff == 0)
            return mid;
        else if (diff < 0)
            low = mid + 1;
        else
            high = mid - 1;
    }
    return -low - 1;
}
```

When the call search(60, 9) is invoked, what is returned by this method call?

a. −1
b. −4
c. −5
d. 3
e. 7

Free Response Questions

1. Two words are anagrams if one of the words is made by transposing the letters of the other word. For example, "stop" and "tops" are anagrams. This problem involves reading a dictionary of words, storing the words in a list, and then generating and printing all words in the dictionary that are anagrams of a given word. The problem uses the Word and AnagramList classes whose incomplete implementations are below.

Word Class

```java
/*
    Holds words in two forms: the original word and the word with
    its letters in sorted order.
*/
public class Word
{
    // Constructs a word.
    public Word(String theWord)
    {
        originalWord = theWord;
        sortedWord = sortWord();
    }
```

```
    /*
       Sorts the letters of the word.
       Returns the sorted word.
       Example: if originalWord = "apple", "aelpp" is returned.
    */
    private String sortWord()
    {
        // Code goes here
    }


    // Returns the original word.
    public String getWord() {. . .}

    // Returns the sorted word.
    public String getSortedWord() {. . .}

    private String originalWord;
    private String sortedWord;
}
```

AnagramList Class

```
// Holds a list of Words.
public class AnagramList
{
    // Constructs an empty list.
    public AnagramList()
    {
        wordList = new ArrayList();
    }

    /*
       Adds a Word, whose original order is
       newString, to wordList.
    */
    public void addWord(String newString){. . .}

    /*
       Returns true if aWord and anotherWord have original
       strings that are anagrams (words composed of the same
       letters), otherwise returns false.
    */
    public boolean checkAnagram(Word aWord, Word anotherWord)
    {
        // Code goes here
    }

    // Prints original words of all Words in wordList that
    // are anagrams of key.
    public void printAnagrams(String key)
    {
        // Code goes here
    }

    private ArrayList wordList;
}
```

a. One way to check whether two words are anagrams is to sort the letters of each word and compare the sorted words. If the sorted words contain the same sequence of letters and are the same length, the original words are anagrams.

You are to write the `sortWord` method of the `Word` class. `sortWord` will return a string that contains the letters of `originalWord` in sorted order. For example,

originalWord	sortWord *returns*
cat	act
apple	aelpp
table	abelt

Use the method header below to write `sortWord`.

```
private String sortWord()
```

b. Write the `AnagramList` method `checkAnagram`. `checkAnagram` returns `true` if its two `Word` parameters have original words that are anagrams. If not, `checkAnagram` returns `false`. Use the method header below to write `checkAnagram`. Assume that all `Word` methods work as intended regardless of what you wrote for part a.

```
public boolean checkAnagram(Word aWord, Word anotherWord)
```

c. Write the `AnagramList` method `printAnagrams`. `printAnagrams` prints the original words of all `Words` in `wordList` that are anagrams of `key`. Use the method header below to write `printAnagrams`. Assume that all `Word` methods work as intended regardless of what you wrote for part a. You may call `checkAnagram` in writing `printAnagrams`. Assume that `checkAnagram` works as intended regardless of what you wrote in part b. Use the method header below to write `printAnagrams`.

```
public void printAnagrams(String key)
```

2. An `AddressBook` contains an unknown number of entries. Each entry contains a person's first and last names and an e-mail address. The `Person` class, whose incomplete definition is below, is used to represent an entry.

```
public class Person implements Comparable
{
    /*
        Constructs a person with first name (fName), and last
        name (lName). The e-mail address of the person is set.
    */
    public Person(String fName, String lName)
    {
        firstName = fName;
        lastName = lName;
        emailAddress = makeEmailAddress();
    }

    // Returns an e-mail address based on a person's name
    private String makeEmailAddress(){. . .}
```

```
// Returns name of person in the form 'last, first'.
public String getName(){. . .}

// Returns e-mail address of person.
public String getEmailAddress(){. . .}

/*
    Compares two persons by the alphabetical ordering of
    name (lastName, firstName).
*/
public int compareTo(Object obj)
{
    // Code goes here
}

private String firstName;
private String lastName;
private String emailAddress;
}
```

Some useful public methods in the `AddressBook` class include:

```
addEntry    // Adds entry of type Person to address book.
printEntries   // Prints information in address book.
sortByLastName   // Sorts the information by last name.
sortByEmailAddress   // Sorts the information by e-mail
                     // address.
search    // Returns the e-mail address given the person's name.
```

The incomplete `AddressBook` class appears below.

```
public class AddressBook
{
    // Creates an empty address book of Persons.
    public AddressBook()
    {
        list = new ArrayList();
    }

    // Adds an entry to the address book.
    public void addEntry(Person p) {. . .}

    // Prints the entries in the address book.
    public void printEntries() {. . .}

    /*
        Uses selection sort algorithm to sort the
        address book entries by name (last, first).
    */
    public void sortByLastName()
    {
        for (int i = 0; i < list.size() - 1; i++)
        {
            int minPos = minimumPosition(i);
            swap(minPos, i);
        }
    }
```

```
/*
    Returns the index of smallest element
    in a tail range of the ArrayList.
*/
private int minimumPosition(int from)
{
    // Code goes here
}

// Sorts the address book entries by e-mail address.
public void sortByEmailAddress()
{
    for (int i = 0; i < list.size() - 1; i++)
    {
        int minPos = minimumEmailPosition(i);
        swap(minPos, i);
    }
}

/*
    Returns the index of the element with an e-mail address
    that is alphabetically less than other e-mail addresses
    in a tail range of the array list.
*/
private int minimumEmailPosition(int from)
{
    // Code goes here
}

/*
    Swaps the entry in the ith position of the address
    book with the entry in the jth position of the
    address book.
*/
private void swap(int i, int j){. . .}

private ArrayList list;
}
```

a. `Person` implements `Comparable`. You are to write the method `compareTo` for the `Person` class. `compareTo` for the `Person` class compares two `Person` objects by the alphabetical ordering of their names (last, first). You may call `Person`'s method `getName` in writing `compareTo`. Assume `getName` works as intended.

compareTo	*Summary*
`int compareTo(Object other)`	Returns a value < 0 if this `Person` is less than `other`. Returns 0 if this `Person` is equal to `other`. Returns a value > 0 if this `Person` is greater than `other`.

Use the method header below to write `compareTo`.

```
public int compareTo(Object obj)
```

b. The `AddressBook` class has a method `sortByName` that uses the selection sort algorithm to sort the address book entries by last name. `sortByLastName` calls the method `minimumPosition` that returns the index of the `AddressBook` entry that has the minimum value (the entry whose name (last, first) comes alphabetically before other names in a portion of the `AddressBook`). You are to write the method `minimumPosition`. You may (and should) use the `Person` method `compareTo` when writing your solution. Assume `compareTo` works as specified regardless of what you wrote in part a.

```
private int minimumPosition(int from)
```

c. In order to be able to sort by e-mail address as well as by name, a `Comparator` is used. The `PersonComparator` class is defined below. **(Note: The Comparator interface is not part of the AP subset.)**

```java
public class PersonComparator implements Comparator
{
    public int compare(Object first, Object second)
    {
        Person firstPerson = (Person) first;
        Person secondPerson = (Person) second;
        String firstEmail = firstPerson.getEmailAddress();
        String secondEmail = secondPerson.getEmailAddress();
        return firstEmail.compareTo(secondEmail);
    }
}
```

The `AddressBook` class uses this `PersonComparator` class to sort entries alphabetically by e-mail address. The `AddressBook` class has a method `sortByEmailAddress` that uses the selection sort algorithm to sort the address book entries alphabetically by e-mail addresses. `sortByEmailAddress` calls the method `minimumEmailPosition` that returns the index of the `AddressBook` entry that has the minimum e-mail value (the entry whose e-mail comes alphabetically before other entries in a portion of the `AddressBook`). You are to complete the method `minimumEmailPosition`. You may (and should) use the `PersonComparator` method `compare` (defined above) when writing your solution.

```java
private int minimumEmailPosition(int from)
{
    int minPos = from;
    Comparator comp = new PersonComparator();

    //  Code goes here

    return minPos;
}
```

CHAPTER 17

(Covers *Java Concepts* Chapter 20)

An Introduction to Data Structures
(AB only)

■ Topic Summary

17.1 Using Linked Lists

A linked list is a sequence of elements. Each element stores an object and a reference to the next element.

Figure 17.1

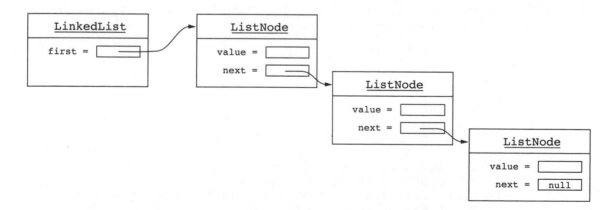

The figures in Section 20.1 of your text illustrate this concept in detail. The Java library provides a `LinkedList` class in the `java.util` package. `LinkedList` implements `java.util.List`.

The `LinkedList` class in the Java 5 `java.util` package is a generic (typed) class, just like the generic `ArrayList` class.

Table 17.1 lists the `List` methods that are currently included in the AP subset and Table 17.2 lists the same methods using the generic `List` interface.

Table 17.1
`java.util.List`

Method	Method Summary
`void add(Object obj)`	Appends the element `obj` to the end of this list.
`Object get(int index)`	Returns the element at position `index` in this list.
`Iterator iterator()`	Returns an iterator for the elements in this list.
`ListIterator listIterator()`	Returns a list iterator for the elements in this list.
`Object set(int index, Object obj)`	Replaces the element at position `index` in this list with the specified element.
`int size()`	Returns the number of elements in the list.

Table 17.2 (Java 5)
`java.util.List<E>`

Method	Method Summary
`void add(E elt)`	Appends the element `elt` to the end of this list.
`E get(int index)`	Returns the element at position `index` in this list.
`Iterator<E> iterator()`	Returns an iterator for the elements in this list.
`ListIterator<E> listIterator()`	Returns a list iterator for the elements in this list.
`E set(int index, E elt)`	Replaces the element at position `index` in this list with the specified element.
`int size()`	Returns the number of elements in the list.

Both the `ArrayList` and the `LinkedList` implement the `List` interface. Example 17.1 illustrates this using untyped lists.

Example 17.1

```
1     import java.util.List;
2     import java.util.ArrayList;
3     // import java.util.LinkedList;
4     import java.util.Iterator;

5     public class ArrayListTester
6     {
7        public static void main(String[] args)
8        {
9           ArrayList staff = new ArrayList();
10             // Construct an empty ArrayList
11          // LinkedList staff = new LinkedList();
12             // Construct an empty LinkedList
13          staff.add("Dick");    // Objects added to end of list
14          staff.add("Harry");
15          staff.add("Romeo");
16          staff.add("Tom");
17          printList(staff);    // Dick Harry Romeo Tom
18          System.out.println(staff.get(2));    // Romeo
```

```
19              staff.set(2, "Karen");    // Dick Harry Karen Tom
20              printList(staff);    // Dick Harry Karen Tom
21          }

22          public static void printList(List staff)
23          {
24              System.out.println();
25              Iterator iter = staff.iterator();
26              while (iter.hasNext())
27                  System.out.println(iter.next());
28          }
29      }
```

Because `ArrayList` and `LinkedList` both implement `List`, the implementation used in Example 17.1 can be changed from an `ArrayList` implementation to a `LinkedList` implementation with two modifications:

- The import statement (Replace line 2 with line 3).
- The declaration (Replace line 9 with line 11).

The `printList` method (line 22) takes a `List` as a parameter and so no changes are necessary.

The only changes that would be necessary when using a generic (typed) `ArrayList` are the declarations:

```
        ArrayList<String> staff = new ArrayList<String>();
```
or
```
        LinkedList<String> staff = new LinkedList<String>();
```

As we will discuss in more detail later, some of these `List` methods are extremely inefficient when used with a `LinkedList` implementation.

The `java.util.LinkedList` class includes the `List` methods as well as some additional methods. The additional methods that are included in the AP subset are listed in Table 17.3.

Table 17.3

class java.util.LinkedList implements java.util.List

Method	Method Summary
`void addFirst(Object obj)`	Inserts the object `obj` at the beginning of this list.
`void addLast(Object obj)`	Appends the object `obj` to the end of this list.
`Object getFirst()`	Returns the first element in this list.
`Object getLast()`	Returns the last element in this list.
`Object removeFirst()`	Removes and returns the first element from this list.
`Object removeLast()`	Removes and returns the last element from this list.

These same methods are provided for the generic `LinkedList` class. The difference, of course, is that a generic (or typed) `LinkedList` returns elements of a specific type rather than of type `Object` and the parameter type for the `add` methods is a specific type, not `Object`.

To access elements in a `LinkedList`, you can use an iterator. Table 17.4 shows the iterator methods that are included in the AP subset. The iterator works in the same way as the `ArrayList` iterator introduced in Chapter 11 of this study guide.

Table 17.4

`java.util.Iterator`

Method	Method Summary
`boolean hasNext()`	Returns `true` if this iterator has more elements when traversing the list in the forward direction.
`Object next()`	Moves the iterator past the next element and returns the traversed element.
`void remove()`	Removes from the list the last element that was returned by `next`.

In addition to the operations `hasNext`, `next`, and `remove` that the `Iterator` interface provides, the `List` interface provides a special iterator, called a `ListIterator` (extending `Iterator`), that allows for element insertion and replacement. The `LinkedList` class provides a method to obtain a list iterator. The statement

```
ListIterator iter = staff.listIterator();
```

calls this method for the `LinkedList staff`. Table 17.5 shows the additional `ListIterator` methods that are included in the AP subset.

Table 17.5

`interface java.util.ListIterator extends java.util.Iterator`

Method	Method Summary
`void add(Object obj)`	Inserts the specified element into the list before the current iterator position and moves the iterator past the inserted element.
`set(Object obj)`	Replaces the last element returned by `next` with `obj`.

Example 17.2 demonstrates the `LinkedList` and `ListIterator` methods included in the AP testable subset. Remember that the iterator position is *between* two list elements.

Example 17.2

```java
import java.util.LinkedList;
import java.util.ListIterator;
/**
    A program that demonstrates the LinkedList methods and
    ListIterator methods in AP subset.
*/
public class LinkedListTester
{
    public static void main(String[] args)
    {
       // Demonstrating LinkedList methods
       LinkedList staff = new LinkedList();   // Construct empty
                                              // list.
       staff.addFirst("Dave");    // Add to front of list, D
       staff.addFirst("Harry");    // H D
       staff.addFirst("Romeo");    // R H D
       staff.addFirst("Tom");    // T R H D
       staff.addLast("Mary");    // Add to end of list, T R H D M
       staff.addLast("Sue");    // T R H D M S
```

```
System.out.println(staff.getFirst());    // Tom
System.out.println(staff.getLast());     // Sue

staff.removeFirst();    // R H D M S
staff.removeLast();     // R H D M
staff.add("George");    // R H D M G

System.out.println(staff.size());    // 5
System.out.println(staff.get(2));    // Dave
staff.set(2, "Kevin");    // R H K M G

// Demonstrating additional ListIterator methods
// # indicates iterator position

ListIterator iter = staff.listIterator(); // # R H K M G

iter.next();    // R # H K M G
iter.next();    // R H # K M G
iter.remove();    // R # K M G
iter.next();    // R K # M G
iter = staff.listIterator();    // Resets iterator # R K M G
iter.next();    //R # K M G

iter.set("Cathy");    // C # K M G

iter = staff.listIterator(); // Resets iterator
iter.next();    // C # K M G
iter.remove();    // # K M G
iter.add("Nina");    // N # K M G

iter = staff.listIterator();  // Resets iterator
while(iter.hasNext())
{
    System.out.print(iter.next() + " ");
        // Nina Kevin Mary George
}
    }
}
```

The `ListIterator` method `remove` removes the last element returned by the iterator. This method can be called only once after a call to `next`.

Example 17.2 includes calls to the methods `get` and `set` because `java.util.LinkedList` implements `java.util.List` and the `List` class includes these methods. However, the `List` methods `get` and `set` are primarily used with the `ArrayList` implementation and *not* with a `LinkedList` implementation. Because array lists allow for random access, the call

```
System.out.println(arrayListName.get(x));
```

gives immediate access to the object whose index is x. This operation is $O(1)$. With a linked list, the list must be traversed to arrive at the element in position x. This operation is $O(n)$. That is, in Example 17.2, Romeo and Harry were visited before Dave with execution of the statement

```
System.out.println(staff.get(2));    // Dave
```

Think about the consequences of the `printList` method when a linked list is passed as the parameter!

```
public static void printList(List staff)
{
    for (int i = 0; i < staff.size(); i++)
        System.out.println((String) staff.get(i));
}
```

Each call to `get` traverses the list. We can see why iterating over the elements in a linked list with an iterator is typically preferable to accessing the elements by indexing through the list!

The same is true for the `List` method `set`. The statement

```
staff.set(2, "Kevin");
```

must traverse the list to arrive at position 2 in order to set the object to "Kevin" (an $O(n)$ operation). In an `ArrayList`, the statement

```
arrayListName.set(2, "Kevin");
```

provides immediate access to the element in position 2 (an $O(1)$ operation).

An iterator should be used to access the elements of a `LinkedList`. Do not use `get` and `set` with linked lists.

Example 17.2 resets the iterator to traverse through the list more than once. You should not use two iterators on the same list at the same time. Resetting the iterator is preferred.

Example 17.3 illustrates some of the same concepts using the generic `LinkedList` class with a generic iterator.

Example 17.3 (Java 5)

```
// Demonstrating LinkedList of strings
LinkedList<String> staff = new LinkedList<String>();
                         // Construct empty list.

staff.addFirst("Dave");     // Add to front of list, D
staff.addFirst("Harry");    // H D
staff.addFirst("Romeo");    // R H D
staff.addFirst("Tom");      // T R H D
staff.addLast("Mary");      // Add to end of list, T R H D M

String first = staff.getFirst();   // no casting is necessary
System.out.println(first);    // Tom

// Generic list iterator to traverse list
ListIterator<String> iter = staff.listIterator();
while(iter.hasNext())
{
    System.out.print (iter.next()+ " ");
                                    // Tom Romeo Harry Dave Mary
}
System.out.println();
```

```
// Enhanced for loop to print items in list
for (String name : staff)
{
    System.out.print(name + " ");
}
System.out.println();
```

The differences between untyped and typed linked lists are the same as the differences between untyped and typed array lists.

17.2   Implementing Linked Lists

Because the implementation of a linked list is a part of the AB course, we will look at pieces of this implementation and discuss how the elements of a linked list are manipulated.

Elements in a linked list are called *nodes*. Nodes are visited in sequential order. Unlike an array, there is no random access in a linked list. Your text uses the Node class to define a node. To facilitate a consistency in the exam questions, the AP Exam uses the ListNode[1] class shown in Example 17.4 to define a node and its methods.

Example 17.4

```
public class ListNode
{
    public ListNode(Object initValue, ListNode initNext)
    {
        value = initValue;
        next = initNext;
    }

    // Returns the value of a List node.
    public Object getValue()
    {
        return value;
    }

    // Returns the next field of a List node.
    public ListNode getNext()
    {
        return next;
    }

    // Sets the value of the list node to theNewValue.
    public void setValue(Object theNewValue)
    {
        value = theNewValue;
    }
```

[1] College Board's AP Computer Science AB: Implementation Classes and Interfaces

```
            // Sets the list node's next field to a new reference.

            public void setNext(ListNode theNewNext)
            {
                next = theNewNext;
            }

            private Object value;
            private ListNode next;
        }
```

A description of the ListNode class will appear at the beginning of the exam booklet. (The comments will not be included!)

Because the ListNode class does not implement equals, if two ListNodes are compared using equals, references are being compared (using the inherited Object equals method). For example, if node1 and node2 are references to ListNodes, the expression

```
        node1.equals(node2)
```

evaluates to true only if node1 and node2 reference the same ListNode.

The implementation of a linked list involves the ListNode and the LList classes. Example 17.5 contains the LList methods that directly involve manipulating the first element in a linked list. These methods are getFirst, addFirst, and removeFirst. The ListNode class is used in this implementation. Your text uses the private inner class Node that implements these same methods. Inner classes are not included in the AP subset.

Example 17.5

```
        public class LList
        {
            // Constructs an empty list.
            public LList()
            {
                first = null;
            }

            // Returns the first object in the list if there is one.
            public Object getFirst()
            {
                if (first == null)
                    throw new NoSuchElementException();
                return first.getValue();
            }

            // Adds an object to the front of the list.
            public void addFirst(Object obj)
            {
                ListNode newNode = new ListNode(obj, first);
                first = newNode;
            }
```

```
/**
    Removes and returns the first object in the list if there
    is one.
*/
public Object removeFirst()
{
    if (first == null)
        throw new NoSuchElementException();
    Object obj = first.getValue();
    first = first.getNext();
    return obj;
}

private ListNode first;
}
```

Figures 4 and 5 in Section 20.2 of your text provide illustrations of adding to and removing from the front of a linked list.

It is also useful to be able to add and remove from the end of a linked list. The Java class library implementation of a linked list provides immediate access to the beginning and the end of the list as illustrated in Figure 17.2.

Figure 17.2

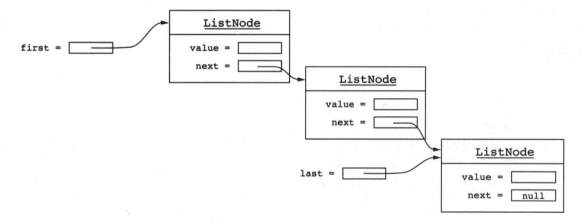

We can write our own linked list implementation with end-of-list access by adding a private instance field that keeps track of the last ListNode in the linked list. Example 17.6 includes the methods that directly manipulate the last element in a linked list. In Section 20.2 of your text, the LinkedList class defines a private inner class LinkedListIterator and its implementation. The iterator is used to traverse the linked list. Example 17.6 traverses the list without the use of an iterator.

Example 17.6

```java
public class LList
{
   // Constructs an empty list.
   public LList()
   {
      first = null;
      last = null;
   }

   // Returns the last object in the list if there is one.
   public Object getLast()
   {
      if (first == null)    // The list is empty.
         throw new NoSuchElementException();
      return last.getValue();
   }

   // Adds an object to the end of the list.
   public void addLast(Object obj)
   {
      ListNode newNode = new ListNode(obj, null);
      if (first == null)    // The list is empty.
      {
         first = newNode;
         last = newNode;
      }
      else
      {
         last.setNext(newNode);
         last = newNode;
      }
   }

   /**
      Removes and returns the last object in the list if there
      is one.
   */
   public Object removeLast()
   {
      if (first == null)    // The list is empty.
         throw new NoSuchElementException();
      Object obj = last.getValue();
      if (first == last)    // Only 1 node in list.
      {
         first = null;
         last = null;
         return obj;
      }
      ListNode temp = first;

      while (temp.getNext() != last)    // More than 1 node in list
      {
         temp = temp.getNext();    // Looking for the node
      }                            // before the last node.
```

```
            Object obj = last.getValue();
            temp.setNext(null);
            last = temp;
            return obj;
        }
    }
```

Now, what happens if you don't have that private instance field, `last`? In order to implement any of the methods above, the list must be traversed. Example 17.7 demonstrates traversing the list to do the same tasks as in Example 17.6.

Example 17.7

```
    public Object getLast()
    {
        if (first == null)    // The list is empty.
            throw new NoSuchElementException();
        ListNode temp = first;    // Must traverse to find the end.
        while (temp.getNext() != null)
            temp = temp.getNext();
        return temp.getValue();
    }

    public void addLast(Object obj)
    {
        ListNode newNode = new ListNode(obj, null);
        ListNode temp = first;    // Must traverse to find the end.
        while (temp.getNext() != null)
            temp = temp.getNext();
        temp.setNext(newNode);
    }

    public Object removeLast()
    {
        if (first == null)    // The list is empty.
            throw new NoSuchElementException();

        if (first.getNext() == null)    // Only 1 node in list.
        {
            Object obj = first.getValue();
            first = null;
            return obj;
        }
        ListNode temp = first;        // Must traverse to find the end
        ListNode follower = temp;    // and the node before the last.
        while (temp.getNext() != null)
        {
            follower = temp;
            temp = temp.getNext();
        }
        follower.setNext(null);
        return temp.getValue();
        }
    }
```

It's a good exercise to trace the implementation above and draw pictures similar to Figure 5 in Section 20.2 of your text as you walk through the code. Try walking through the test program in Example 17.8. Go through each method implementation and sketch your `ListNode` additions and deletions.

Example 17.8

```
public static void main(String[] args)
{
    LList staff = new LList();    // Construct empty list.
    staff.addLast("Dick");        // D
    staff.addFirst("Harry");      // H D
    staff.addLast("Romeo");       // H D R
    staff.addFirst("Tom");        // T H D R
    staff.removeLast();           // T H D
    staff.printList();
    staff.removeFirst();    // H D
    System.out.println(staff.getFirst());    // Harry
    System.out.println(staff.getLast());    // Dick
}
```

Finally, what happens if we want to add to the middle of a linked list? Suppose you have a linked list that maintains its elements in order. How do you insert or delete an element from this list? Let's look at inserting a `ListNode` whose value is a string. We wish to insert the node so that the strings are in alphabetical order. We will use our linked list implementation without the `last` instance field.

Our list is initialized to be empty.

```
ListNode first = null;
```

Our new `ListNode` is created to hold the new string value (name).

```
ListNode newNode = new ListNode(name, null);
```

Now, let's insert. First check to see if we are inserting into an empty list.

```
if (first == null)
{
    first = newNode;
}
```

If the list is not empty, check to see if the new node should be inserted in the front of the list.

```
String firstValue = (String) first.getValue();
String newValue = (String) newNode.getValue();
if (firstValue.compareTo(newValue) >= 0)    // New node goes first
{
    newNode.setNext(first);
    first = newNode;
}
```

If the new node isn't inserted in the front of the list, see if it belongs in the middle or at the end of the list.

```
String newValue = (String) newNode.getValue();
ListNode temp = first;
```

```
ListNode follower = temp;
// Checking for end and for order
while (temp #!= null &&
      newValue.compareTo((String) temp.getValue()) > 0)
{
   follower = temp;
   temp = temp.getNext();
}

// Stopped because end of list OR correct position found in middle
// Does it belong in the middle?
follower.setNext(newNode);
newNode.setNext(temp);
```

Deleting a node from our linked list of `ListNodes` follows a similar coding pattern. You should first make sure that you are not trying to delete a node from an empty list. Then check to see if you are deleting the first node. If so, `first` will have to be adjusted. And finally, consider deleting from the middle or end of the list, setting the `next` fields where required.

When using the Java Library's `LinkedList` class, inserting nodes in order follows a similar pattern.

First, start with an empty list.

```
LinkedList list = new LinkedList();
```

Now, are you adding to an empty list?

```
if (list.size() == 0)
{
   list.addFirst(name);
}
```

If the list is not empty, does the new node belong in the front of the list?

```
String firstValue = (String) list.getFirst();
if (name.compareTo(firstValue) <= 0)
{
   list.addFirst(name);
}
```

If the node doesn't belong in the front of the list, then check to see if it belongs in the middle or at the end of the list.

```
ListIterator iter = list.listIterator();
boolean foundLarger = false;
while (!foundLarger && iter.hasNext())
{
   // Does object belong in the middle?
   if (name.compareTo((String) iter.next()) < 0)
   {
      foundLarger = true;
      iter.previous();   // previous is not tested on the AP Exam
      iter.add(name);
   }
}
```

```
    // Or does it belong at the end?
    if (!iter.hasNext())
        list.addLast(name);
```

The `ListIterator` has a `previous` method that allows us to traverse in reverse. `previous` is very useful when inserting or deleting from the middle or from the end of a `LinkedList`. The use of `previous` will not be tested on the AP Exam.

The preceding code inserts `String` objects into a linked list in lexicographical order. Suppose you wish to keep an ordered linked list of `Integers`, or `Coins`, or `Students`. How could we modify our code so that it can be used by any of these classes? To "order" objects of a class, what must be true of the class (what interface should the class implement)?

Example 17.9 shows an implementation of a generic `ListNode` class and a simplified generic `LinkedList` implementation (includes only a method to add to the front of the list).

Example 17.9 Generic `ListNode` class

```java
public class ListNode<E>
{
    // Constructor
    public ListNode(E initValue, ListNode initNext)
    {
        value = initValue;
        next = initNext;
    }

    // Returns value of list node.
    public E getValue()
    {
        return value;
    }

    // Returns the next field of ListNode.
    public ListNode getNext()
    {
        return next;
    }

    // Sets the value of the list node to theNewValue.
    public void setValue(E theNewValue)
    {
        value = theNewValue;
    }

    // Sets the list node's next field to a new reference.
    void setNext(ListNode theNewNext)
    {
        next = theNewNext;
    }

    private E value;
    private ListNode next;
}
```

Generic Simplified Linked List Implementation

```java
public class LList<E>
{
    public LList()
    {
        first = null;
    }

    public void addFirst(E obj)
    {
        ListNode<E> newNode = new ListNode<E>(obj, first);
        first = newNode;
    }

    public void printList()
    {
        System.out.println();
        ListNode<E> temp = first;
        while (temp != null)
        {
            System.out.println(temp.getValue());
            temp = temp.getNext();
        }
    }

    private ListNode<E> first;
}
```

Test Harness for Generic List and ListNode Classes

```java
public class LLTester
{
    public static void main(String[] args)
    {
        LList<String> staff = new LList<String>();
        staff.addFirst("Ann");
        staff.addFirst("Bob");
        staff.addFirst("Harry");
        staff.addFirst("Dave");
        staff.addFirst("Carol");
        staff.printList();
    }
}
```

Section 22.2 in your text illustrates a generic linked list with Node as an inner class. Implementing generic lists is not difficult and saves you from concerning yourself with casting. A good exercise would be to take the untyped examples in this chapter and convert them to generic lists. Chapter 22 in your text explains generic programming in detail.

17.2.1 Doubly Linked Lists
In addition to linked lists that have a next field referencing the next node in the list, we can have a doubly linked list. In a doubly linked list, the node contains a value, a reference to the next node in the list, and a reference to the previous node in the list.

Figure 17.3

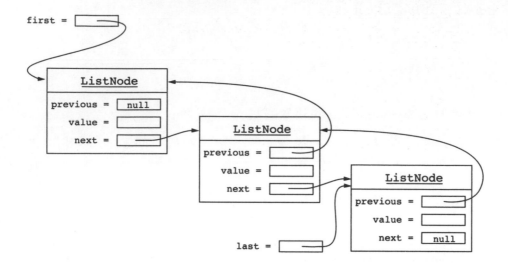

Suppose our ListNode class were modified to be a DLListNode class. Example 17.10 modifies the ListNode constructor for the DLListNode class. A doubly linked list node *is a* linked list node with another instance field.

Example 17.10

```
public DLListNode(DLListNode initPrevious,
        Object initValue, DLListNode initNext)
{
    previous = initPrevious;
    value = initValue;
    next = initNext;
}
```

When adding a node to a doubly linked list, you must make a few more node adjustments! Before writing any code, draw pictures of the intended adjustments. Example 17.11 and Figure 17.4 show adjustments necessary to add a DLListNode to the middle of a doubly linked list.

Example 17.11

```
/*
    Adding a node to middle or end of an ordered doubly linked
    list.
*/
Comparable newValue = (Comparable) newNode.getValue();
DLListNode temp = first;
while (temp.getNext() != null &&
        newValue.compareTo((Comparable) temp.getValue()) > 0)
{
    temp = temp.getNext();
}

if (newValue.compareTo((Comparable) temp.getValue()) <= 0)
{
    // Adding to middle.
    // Four references must be set.
```

```
        DLListNode hold = temp.getPrevious();
        hold.setNext(newNode);
        newNode.setNext(temp);
        newNode.setPrevious(temp.getPrevious());
        temp.setPrevious(newNode);
    }
    else
    {
        // Adding to end.
        // Two references must be set.
        temp.setNext(newNode);
        newNode.setPrevious(temp);
    }
```

Figure 17.4

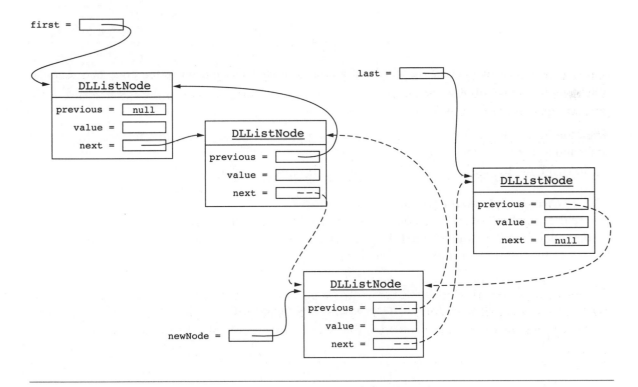

To delete a node from a singly or a doubly linked list, you need to consider the same cases as you do when you insert a node into a linked list. Is the list empty? Is the node that is to be deleted the first node of the list? Is it in the middle? Is it the last node? Is the node to be deleted even in the list? If the node is not in the list, what should happen? If there is more than one node with the same value as the node to be deleted, should only the first occurrence be deleted or all nodes with that value?

To delete from the middle of a doubly linked list, you must adjust two references.

```
        DLListNode hold = temp.getPrevious();
        hold.setNext(temp.getNext());
        DLListNode hold2 = temp.getNext();
        hold2.setPrevious(temp.getPrevious());
```

Figure 17.5

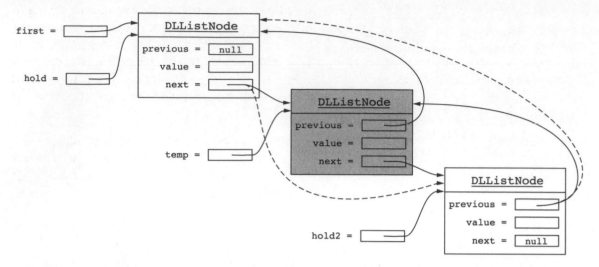

It is a good exercise to draw the nodes of a doubly linked list and write the code necessary to delete the first and last nodes of the list.

The Java `LinkedList` class is implemented using a doubly linked list with references to the first node and to the last node. Operations that index into the list (accessing the *i*th node) will traverse the list from the beginning or the end, whichever is closer to the specified index (*i*).

17.2.2   Circularly Linked Lists

A circularly linked list is a list whose last node references the first node. The implementation works much like the singly linked list implementation except that, when traversing the list with the `temp`, the last node of the list is found when

```
temp.getNext() == first
```

evaluates to `true`. Figure 17.6 illustrates a circularly linked list.

Figure 17.6

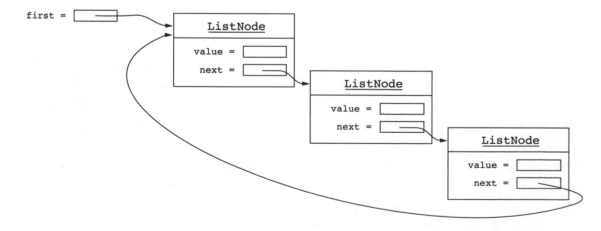

And, if you want to be challenged even more, you can implement a doubly-circularly linked list!

17.2.3 *Header and Trailer Nodes*

When implementing a linked list or a doubly linked list, you considered several cases: adding to the empty list, adding or removing the first node, adding or removing the last node, adding or removing a middle node. A *header* node is a node that comes before all other nodes in the list. A *trailer* node is a node that comes after all of the nodes in the list. If a list has a header node and a trailer node, most of these cases are eliminated. We are left only with adding and deleting from the middle of the list. The header and trailer nodes are not included when printing the list contents or searching the list. They can be considered "dummy" nodes.

The constructor of a linked list implementation that has a header and trailer node would create a list similar to the one illustrated in Figure 17.7. For example, if the list is designed to hold values in increasing order, the value in the header node will be a value smaller than all values in the list and the value in the trailer node will be a value larger than all values in the list.

Figure 17.7

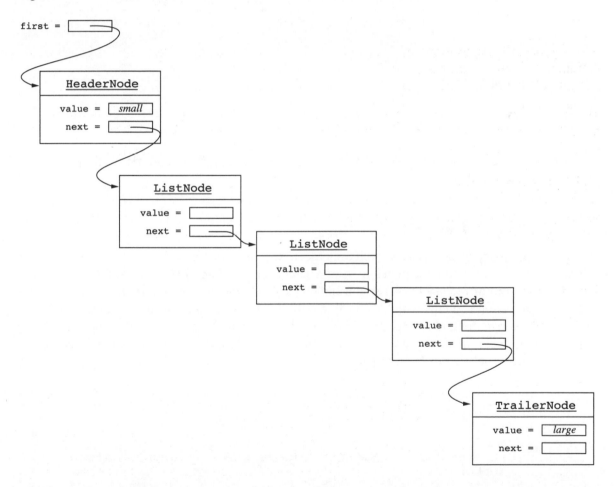

You may see these terms used on the AP Exam but, when implementing linked lists on the free-response questions on the AP Exam, do not use header and trailer nodes unless explicitly told to do so.

17.3 Abstract and Concrete Data Types

An abstract data type defines the fundamental operations on the data but does not specify the implementation. When we refer to a list, we think of an ordered sequence of elements in which an element can be inserted or removed. The concrete representation of a list may be a `LinkedList` or an `ArrayList`. Although the operations performed on both implementations appear to have the same outcome, the performance efficiency of these operations can be quite different. As we discussed in Example 17.1, the implementation of the `List` methods is quite different for the `LinkedList` and the `ArrayList`. The `ArrayList` has random access. The `LinkedList` is accessed sequentially. Figures 8 and 10 in Section 20.3 of your text illustrate the differences. Table 17.5 summarizes the efficiency of some of the more common operations on lists of elements that maintain their order.

Table 17.5

Operation	ArrayList	LinkedList *(Java library class)*
Insert at front	$O(n)$	$O(1)$
Insert at end	$O(1)$	$O(1)$
Remove from front	$O(n)$	$O(1)$
Remove from end	$O(1)$	$O(1)$
Linear Traversal	$O(n)$	$O(n)$
Random Access	$O(1)$	$O(n)$

As you can see, if random access to list elements is important and done frequently, an `ArrayList` may be a better choice than a linked list.

17.4 Stacks and Queues

A stack is an abstract data type to which elements can be added and removed at one end only. Think about a stack of dinner plates in your kitchen cabinet. Each plate you add to the stack is placed on the top of the stack. When you remove a plate, you remove the topmost plate first. A stack is a collection of items with "last in first out" (LIFO) retrieval. The stack's insert method is `push`. The remove method is `pop`. The stack can also "look at" the top element without removing it with the `peekTop` method. To facilitate a consistency in the exam questions, the AP Exam uses the `Stack` interface[2] shown in Example 17.12.

Example 17.12

```
public interface Stack
{
   /**
      Postcondition: Returns true if stack is empty, false
      otherwise.
   */
   boolean isEmpty();
```

---

[2] College Board's AP Computer Science AB: Implementation Classes and Interfaces

```
/**
   Precondition: stack is [e1, e2, ..., en] with n >= 0
   Postcondition: stack is [e1, e2, ..., en, x]
*/
void push(Object x);

/**
   Precondition: stack is [e1, e2, ..., en] with n >= 1
   Postcondition: stack is [e1, e2, ..., e(n - 1)]
   Returns en.
   Throws an unchecked exception if the stack is empty.
*/
Object pop();

/**
   Precondition: stack is [e1, e2, ..., en] with n >= 1
   Postcondition: Returns en
   Throws an unchecked exception if the stack is empty.
*/
Object peekTop();
}
```

A description of this `Stack` interface will appear in the exam booklet.

Now, let's look at the concrete data implementation. Stacks can be implemented using an array, an `ArrayList`, or a linked list. Of course, if the stack were implemented using an array (fixed size), an `isFull` method would be useful. Think about implementing the stack using the Java `LinkedList` class. Implementing the methods in the `Stack` interface defined in Example 17.12 is not complicated at all. Consider the `peekTop` method. Suppose that the stack implementation adds to and removes from the front of the stack. `peekTop` returns the element on the top of the stack without modifying the stack contents.

Example 17.13

```
// Stack implementation using LinkedList.
public Object peekTop()
{
   if (s.isEmpty())
      throw new NoSuchElementException();
   return(s.getFirst());
}
```

Are there any advantages to using the front of the list? `push` and `pop` are $O(1)$. Would this change if we were to implement `push` and `pop` using the back of the list as the top of the stack (`addLast` and `removeLast`)? Does this depend on the linked list implementation used?

You can also use an `ArrayList` implementation for a stack[3]. One such implementation is listed in the *AP Computer Science AB: Implementation Classes and Interfaces* that is available on the College Board Web site. Example 17.14 contains this implementation.

---

[3] College Board's AP Computer Science AB: Implementation Classes and Interfaces

For the `ArrayList` implementation, the top of the stack is the element with the highest index. With this implementation `push` and `pop` are $O(1)$.

Example 17.14

```
public class ArrayStack implements Stack
{
    public ArrayStack()
    {
        array = new ArrayList();
    }

    public void push(Object x)
    {
        array.add(x);
    }

    public Object pop()
    {
        return array.remove(array.size() - 1);
    }

    public Object peekTop()
    {
        return array.get(array.size() - 1);
    }

    public boolean isEmpty()
    {
        return array.size() == 0;
    }

    private ArrayList array;
}
```

Some applications where stacks might be useful include:
- Evaluation of postfix expressions.
- Testing the balancing of nested parentheses (symbols) in an algebraic expression.
  $\{a + (b - [c + d]) / e + (f - g - h)\}$
- Keeping track of variable declarations inside nested { } inside a compiler.

Example 17.15 shows a test program for our `LinkedList` implementation of a stack. If you are providing an array implementation, `ArrayStack`, for the stack, you would only need to change the constructor call.

Example 17.15

```
public class StackTester
{
    public static void main(String[] args)
    {
        Stack s = new ListStack();    // Constructor call
        s.push("Dick");
        s.push("Harry");
```

```
                s.push("Romeo");
                s.push("Tom");

                while (!(s.isEmpty()))
                {
                    System.out.println(s.pop());
                }
            }
        }
```

The resulting output is:

Tom
Romeo
Harry
Dick

A queue is an abstract data type to which you add elements at one end and remove elements from the other end. Think about a queue as being a water fountain line or a cafeteria line. The first person in the line is the first person out of the line. When one is added to the line, he is added to the rear of the line. A queue is a collection of items with "first in first out" (FIFO) retrieval. The insert method that we will use for a queue is enqueue. To remove an element from a queue, we will use the dequeue method. We can "look at" the front element in a queue without removing it with the method peekFront. To facilitate a consistency in the exam questions, the AP Exam uses the Queue interface[4] shown in Example 17.16.

Example 17.16

```
        public interface Queue
        {
            /**
                Postcondition: Returns true if queue is empty, false
                otherwise.
            */
            boolean isEmpty();

            /**
                Precondition: queue is [e1, e2, ..., en] with n >= 0
                Postcondition: queue is [e1, e2, ..., en, x]
            */
            void enqueue(Object x);

            /**
                Precondition: queue is [e1, e2, ..., en] with n >= 1
                Postcondition: queue is [e2, ..., en]
                Returns e1.
                Throws an unchecked exception if the queue is empty.
            */
            Object dequeue();
```

[4] College Board's AP Computer Science AB: Implementation Classes and Interfaces

```
/**
    Precondition: queue is [e1, e2, ..., en] with n >= 1
    Returns e1.
    Throws an unchecked exception if the queue is empty.
*/
Object peekFront();
}
```

A description of the Queue interface will appear in the exam booklet.

One possible implementation of a queue might be a linked list implementation as shown in Example 17.17.

Example 17.17

```java
public class ListQueue implements Queue
{
    // Constructs an empty queue.
    public ListQueue()
    {
        que = new LinkedList();
    }

    //  Adds obj to queue.
    public void enqueue(Object obj)
    {
        que.addLast(obj);
    }

    // The first object is removed from the queue.
    public Object dequeue()
    {
        if (que.isEmpty())
            throw new NoSuchElementException();
        return que.removeFirst();
    }

    // The first object in the queue is returned but not removed.
    public Object peekFront()
    {
        return que.getFirst();
    }

    // Returns true if the queue has no elements, false otherwise.
    public boolean isEmpty()
    {
        return que.size() == 0;
    }

    private LinkedList que;
}
```

Example 17.18 shows a test program for our LinkedList implementation of a queue.

Example 17.18

```java
public class QueueTester
{
    public static void main(String[] args)
    {
        Queue que = new ListQueue();

        que.enqueue("Harry");
        que.enqueue("Romeo");
        que.enqueue("Tom");

        while (!(que.isEmpty()))
        {
            System.out.println(que.dequeue());
        }
    }
}
```

The resulting output is:

Harry
Romeo
Tom

Some applications where queues might be useful include:
- Airport simulation of planes on a runway.
- A printer queue (where your print requests are held while the printer is busy).
- A queue of user interface events (button clicks, keystrokes) that need to be processed.
- Other simulations, e.g., customers waiting in a line at a bank.
- Other requests, e.g., service requests for a web-based application.

■ Expanded Coverage of Material That is Not Found in the Text

- Circularly linked lists are not covered in your text but are explained in Section 17.2.2 of this guide.
- Header and trailer nodes are not covered in your text but are explained in Section 17.2.3 of this guide.

■ Topics That Are Useful But Not Tested

- The `ListIterator` includes the methods `hasPrevious` and `previous`. These methods are used to determine if there is a previous node and to move the iterator position backwards.
- Your text implements a linked list using inner classes for `Node` (a `ListNode` class) and `LinkedListIterator` (the list iterator). Inner classes are very useful here and allow for simpler implementation of the linked list methods. This is demonstrated in Section 20.2 of your text.

■ Java 5 Issues

- Although the AP Exam will not test on generics before 2007, you will not be penalized for using them if appropriate. The generics in this chapter include:
  - `List<E>` interface
  - `LinkedList<E>`
  - `Iterator<E>`
  - `ListIterator<E>`
- The enhanced `for` loop can be used with `java.util.LinkedList`. This is demonstrated in Example 17.3.

■ Things to Remember When Taking the AP Exam

- Inserting and deleting from a `LinkedList` is efficient because these operations do not require shifting the other elements in the list.
- If an application requires many look-ups (searches), use an implementation that provides $O(1)$ access whenever possible. Specifically, use an array when you need random access to individual elements (e.g., sorting algorithms) and use a linked list when you frequently need to insert or remove in the middle of the list (e.g., simulation of cars on a freeway with entrance/exit ramps).
- Be sure to check whether the list data structure is empty before you try to remove an item from it.
- Become familiar with the `ListNode` class, the `Stack` interface, and the `Queue` interface. The AB Quick Reference Guide that you will be given during the AP Exam contains examples similar to Examples 17.4, 17.12, and 17.16 of this guide (minus the comments).
- Be careful when implementing code that adds or removes nodes from a linked list. Ask yourself the following questions:
  - Does this code handle the empty list case?
  - Does this code handle the front of the list case?
  - Does this code handle the end of the list case?
  - Does this code handle the middle of the list case?
  - Does this code handle the list with only one node?
- Use a list iterator to access elements of a `LinkedList`. DO NOT use `get/set/insert`.
- Check for `null` pointers! Whenever calling `p.getNext()`, `p.getData()`, etc., ask yourself "Can `p` be empty? If so, am I checking for it? If not, why not?"
- Stacks are LIFO (last-in, first-out). Queues are FIFO (first-in, first-out).

■ Key Words

You should understand the terms below. The AP CS Exam questions may include references to these terms. The citations in parentheses next to each term identify the page numbers where it is defined and/or discussed in *Java Concepts*, 4th ed., and *Big Java*, 2nd ed.

abstract data type (758)	LIFO (762)	pop (763)
concrete implementation (759)	linked list (742)	push (763)
	links (743)	queue (762)
doubly linked list (745)	list iterator (740)	stack (762)
FIFO (762)	node (742)	stack top (762)

■ Connecting the Detailed Topic Outline to the Text

The citations in parentheses identify where information in the outline can be located in *Java Concepts*, 4th ed., and *Big Java*, 2nd ed.

- Using Linked Lists (742–747)
- Implementing Linked Lists (747–758)
  - Doubly Linked Lists (745)
  - Circularly Linked Lists
  - Header and Trailer Nodes
- Abstract and Concrete Data Types (758–761)
- Stacks and Queues (762–765)

■ Practice Questions

Multiple Choice

1. What is printed to the screen when the following code segment is executed?

```
LinkedList staff = new LinkedList();
staff.addFirst("Mary");
staff.addFirst("Joe");
staff.addLast("Fran");
System.out.print(staff.removeLast() + " ");
System.out.print(staff.removeFirst()+ " ");
System.out.println(staff.removeFirst());
```

   a. *Joe Mary Fran*
   b. *Fran Joe Mary*
   c. *Mary Joe Fran*
   d. *Fran Mary Joe*
   e. *Joe Fran Mary*

2. An application is being written to simulate planes waiting to take off on an airport runway. Which of the following data structures is the best choice for this application?

   a. A fixed-length array
   b. An `ArrayList`
   c. A singly-linked list
   d. A queue
   e. A stack

3. Suppose the following code segment is executed.

```
LinkedList list = new LinkedList();
ListIterator iter = list.listIterator();
iter.add("David");
iter.add("Juliet");
iter.add("Gail");
iter.add("Chris");
iter = list.listIterator();
iter.next();
iter.remove();
iter.add("Mom");
```

What does the linked list, `list`, contain after this code segment is executed?

a. David Mom Gail Chris
b. Mom Gail Juliet David
c. Chris Mom Juliet David
d. Mom Juliet Gail Chris
e. Mom David Gail Chris

4. For the Java library `LinkedList` class, which operations are constant time ($O(1)$) in the worst case?

I. `addFirst`
II. `addLast`
III. `getLast`

a. I only
b. II only
c. III only
d. II and II only
e. I, II, and III

5. A client program wishes to test to see if two `ListNodes`, `node1` and `node2`, have the same `String` values in their value fields. Which of the following conditions properly checks this?

a. `node1 == node2`
b. `node1.equals(node2)`
c. `node1.value == node2.value`
d. `(node1.value).equals(node2.value)`
e. `(node1.getValue()).equals(node2.getValue())`

6. Which of the following conditions tests whether two `ListNodes`, `node1` and `node2`, reference the same node?

I. `node1 == node2`
II. `node1.equals(node2)`
III. `node2.equals(node1)`

a. I only
b. II only
c. III only
d. II and III only
e. I, II, and III

7. Consider a partially-filled array implementation of a stack, stck. Suppose the implementation uses stck[0] as the top of the stack and the last filled position of the array as the bottom of the stack. Which of the following statements about this implementation is **true**?

   a.   push, pop, and peekTop are $O(n)$.
   b.   push, pop, and peekTop are $O(1)$.
   c.   push and pop are $O(1)$; peekTop is $O(n)$.
   d.   push and pop are $O(n)$; peekTop is $O(1)$.
   e.   pop and peekTop are $O(n)$; push is $O(1)$.

8. Consider a partially-filled array implementation of a stack, stck. Suppose the implementation uses stck[0] as the bottom of the stack and the last filled position of the array as the top of the stack. Which of the following statements about this implementation is **true**?

   a.   push, pop, and peekTop are $O(n)$.
   b.   push, pop, and peekTop are $O(1)$.
   c.   push and pop are $O(1)$; peekTop is $O(n)$.
   d.   push and pop are $O(n)$; peekTop is $O(1)$.
   e.   pop and peekTop are $O(n)$; push is $O(1)$.

9. The Integers 1, 2, 3, 4, and 5 are enqueued in a queue (in that order), then dequeued one at a time and pushed on a stack. The stack is popped three times. What element is now on the top of the stack?

   a.   1
   b.   2
   c.   3
   d.   4
   e.   5

10. Which statement is **true** about an abstract data type?

    a.   An abstract data type defines the fundamental operations on the data but does not specify an implementation.
    b.   An abstract data type is an abstract class. It cannot be instantiated.
    c.   An abstract data type defines the implementation choices made.
    d.   An abstract data type is more efficient than a concrete data type.
    e.   An abstract data type is another name for an interface.

11. Suppose you need to organize a collection of phone numbers for a company. There are currently over 6,000 employees. You know the phone system can handle at most 10,000 phone numbers. You expect several hundred lookups against the collection every day. What would be the best choice for a data structure in implementing this simulation?

    a.   array
    b.   linked list
    c.   doubly linked list
    d.   stack
    e.   queue

12. Consider the following.
   - The `Integers` from 1 to 5 inclusive are enqueued into an initially empty queue, `q`, in that order.
   - The `Integers` from 1 to 5 inclusive are pushed onto an initially empty stack, `s`, in that order.

The following code is executed.

```
for (int x = 1; x <= 5; x++)
{
    Integer y, z;
    y = (Integer) q.dequeue();
    if (y.intValue() % 2 == 0)
        s.push(y);
    else
        q.enqueue(y);

    z = (Integer) s.pop();
    if (z.intValue() % 2 == 0)
        s.push(z);
    else
        q.enqueue(z);
}

while (!s.isEmpty())
{
    System.out.print(s.pop() + " ");
}

while (!q.isEmpty())
{
    System.out.print(q.dequeue() + " ");
}
```

What will be printed while evaluating the above expression?

a.   *4 4 3 2 1 5 1 5 3 5*
b.   *1 2 3 4 2 4 1 5 3 5*
c.   *1 2 3 4 2 4 1 5 3 5*
d.   *4 2 4 3 2 1 1 5 3 5*
e.   *4 4 3 2 1 1 5 3 5 5*

13. The following implementations of the method `reverse` are intended to reverse the order of the elements in a `LinkedList`. The `IntStack` class implements the `Stack` interface and the `IntQueue` class implements the `Queue` interface found in Examples 17.12 and 17.16 (or in the *AB Quick Reference Guide*).

I.
```
public static void reverse(LinkedList aList)
{
    LinkedList temp = new LinkedList();
    while (aList.size() > 0)
        temp.addLast(aList.removeFirst());
    while (temp.size() > 0)
        aList.addFirst(temp.removeFirst());
}
```

II.
```
public static void reverse(LinkedList aList)
{
    IntQueue temp = new IntQueue();
    while (aList.size() > 0)
        temp.enqueue(aList.removeFirst());
    while (!temp.isEmpty() )
        aList.addFirst(temp.dequeue());
}
```

III.
```
public static void reverse(LinkedList aList)
{
    IntStack temp = new IntStack();
    while (aList.size() > 0)
        temp.push(aList.removeLast());
    while (!temp.isEmpty() )
        aList.addFirst(temp.pop());
}
```

Which of the choices above perform the intended task successfully?

a. I only
b. II only
c. III only
d. II and III only
e. I, II, and III

Questions 14 and 15 refer to the following problem statement.

Consider the algorithm for determining whether a sequence of parentheses is balanced (has correct nesting). The pseudocode for this algorithm appears below.

> *Initialize a boolean variable* `validExpression` *to true.*
> *while (there are more symbols in the expression)*
> {
>
>   *look at the next* `symbol`
>   *if* `symbol` *is a {, [, or (*
>   *push it on the stack*
>   *if it is a },], or)*
>   {
>   *if the stack is empty then return false*
>   *else pop the stack*

> }
> *if the element popped is not the match for* `symbol` *then return false*
> }
> *if the stack is not empty then return false else return true.*

14. What is the maximum number of symbols that will appear on the stack at any one time for the sequence { [( )] [( )] [( )] }?

    a. 1
    b. 2
    c. 3
    d. 4
    e. 5

15. What sequence of elements is on the stack after processing the input { [( )] [(( ))] { [(? (The top of the stack is to the right.)

    a. { [( )] [(( ))] { [(
    b. { [([(({ [(
    c.)]))]
    d. { { [(
    e. ([{ {

Questions 16 and 17 refer to the postfix problem statement below.

We normally write algebraic expressions with an arithmetic operator between two operands (numbers). A postfix expression is an expression in which the operator is written after the operands. For example, the postfix notation for the expression $2 + 3$ is $2\ 3\ +$.

The following algorithm describes the evaluation of a postfix expression using a stack. The postfix expression is evaluated from left to right. If a number is read, it is pushed on the stack. If an operator is read, two numbers are popped off the stack, the operator is applied to the two popped values and the answer is pushed on the stack. When all has been read from the expression, what's left on the stack is the answer.

16. Using the above algorithm, the postfix expression:

    $3\ 4 + 5 * 3\ 4 * 6 / 8 * +$

evaluates to:

    a. 0
    b. 4
    c. 19
    d. 51
    e. 192

17. What is the maximum number of numbers on the stack at any one time?

    a. 2
    b. 3
    c. 4
    d. 5
    e. 6

18. You are implementing a program for tracking appointments. You have a class `Person` and a class `Appointment`. A person can have multiple appointments. Each appointment has a start time, an end time, and a description. You keep the appointments in order sorted by start time. Which of the following statements are correct?

    I.   If appointments are frequently deleted and inserted, then a linked list of appointments is more efficient than an array.
    II. Using a linked list of appointments makes it efficient to use the binary search algorithm for finding an appointment that falls on a given time.
    III. Appointments should be kept on a stack so that the most important appointment, regardless on start time, is always on the top of the stack.

    a. I only
    b. II only
    c. III only
    d. I and II only
    e. I and III only

19. You are implementing a word processor. You need to find an appropriate data structure to store a sequence of characters. Users will frequently insert and remove characters from the middle of a document. Which of the following statements are **true**?

    I.   Storing all characters in a single array is inefficient, particularly for long documents.
    II. The characters should be stored in a stack so that the most recently inserted character can be immediately deleted when the user hits the "Backspace" key.
    III. A singly linked list of characters is not an appropriate data structure for the document because each node would need to store one character and one link, which uses a lot of storage.

    a. I only
    b. II only
    c. II and III only
    d. I and III only
    e. I, II, and III

20. Suppose we have a stack, `aStack`, implemented using an array list. The methods `push` and `pop` are implemented without causing any shifting of elements in the array list. Also suppose that 5 items are pushed onto this initially empty stack. Now, a new item is pushed onto the stack and 2 items are popped off the stack. In what position of the array list will the next item pushed be placed?

    a. 0
    b. 1
    c. 4
    d. 5
    e. 6

Free Response Questions

1. DLListNode *is a* ListNode with an additional instance field that references the previous node in a doubly linked list. Refer to the ListNode implementation in Example 17.3 or the ListNode class in the *AB Quick Reference Guide* to answer this question.

    a. To convert the ListNode class to a DLListNode class, what do we need to modify?

    b. What additional methods should be added?

    c. Given the class header for DLListNode below,

        ```
        public class DLListNode extends ListNode
        ```

        implement the DLListNode constructor.

    d. Indicate the efficiency of each operation listed in the table below for the doubly linked list of DLListNodes illustrated.

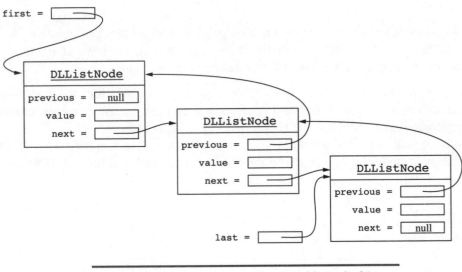

Operation	Doubly Linked List
addFirst	
addLast	
removeLast	
removeFirst	
isEmpty	
Linear Traversal	
Random Access	

Consider the doubly linked list class whose incomplete implementation appears below. This list has two private instance variables, first, that accesses the first node of the list, and last, that accesses the last node of the list. The list does not contain header or trailer nodes.

```
// Invariant: All nodes in the DLList are DLListNodes.
public class DLList
{
```

```
public DLList()     // Constructs an empty list.
{
    first = null;
    last = null;
}

// Inserts a new node containing key in the list.
public void insert(Object key) {. . .}

// Prints the contents of the nodes in the list.
public void printList() {. . .}

// Postcondition: Returns a reference to the first node
// containing key. If key is not found in the list, null is
// returned.
public DLListNode search(Object key)
{
    //  Code goes here
}

// Removes the first node that contains key if that node
// exists.
public void removeOne(Object key)
{
    //  Code goes here
}

// Removes all nodes in the list that contain key.
public void removeAll(Object key)
{
    //  Code goes here
}

    private DLListNode first;
    private DLListNode last;
}
```

e. Implement the method `search` that takes one parameter, `key`, and searches the doubly linked list for the first occurrence of `key` in the list and returns a reference to this node. If `key` is not in the list, `search` returns `null`. Assume that all `DLListNode` methods and constructors work as intended. In writing `search`, use the method header below.

```
public DLListNode search(Object key)
```

f. Implement the method `removeOne`. `removeOne` removes the first node in the list whose value is the same as its one parameter, `key`. You may call `search` in writing `removeOne`. Assume that `search` works as intended regardless of what you wrote in part e. Also assume that all `DLListNode` methods and constructors work as intended. In writing `removeOne`, use the method header below.

```
public void removeOne(Object key)
```

g. Implement the method `removeAll`. `removeAll` removes all nodes in the list whose value is the same as its parameter `key`. You may call `search` and/or `removeOne` in writing `removeAll`. Assume that all methods and constructors written in parts a–f of this problem work as intended regardless of what you wrote. In writing `removeAll`, use the header below.

```
public void removeAll(Object key)
```

2. A stack can be used to convert decimal numbers to binary numbers.

a. You are to write the method `displayBinary` that will convert a decimal number into a binary number using a stack. Assume that `IntStack` is a class that correctly implements the `Stack` interface found in Example 17.12 and in the *AB Quick Reference Guide*. The pseudocode for an algorithm that converts a decimal number to a binary number is given below.

```
public static void displayBinary(int decimalNum)
{
    IntStack stck = new IntStack();
    while decimalNum not equal to 0
    {
        find remainder when decimalNum is divided by 2
        push remainder on the stack
        divide the decimalNum by 2
    }
    while stack isn't empty
        pop num off the stack and display
```

Use the following header in writing your method `displayBinary`.

```
// Precondition: decimalNum > 0
// Displays the binary representation of decimalNum.
public static void displayBinary(int decimalNum)
```

b. Implement a method `displayOtherBase` that will convert a decimal number to a number in any base less than or equal to 16 (hexadecimal numbers). Examples of conversions are given in the table below. Assume that `IntStack` is a class that correctly implements the `Stack` interface found in Example 17.12 and in the *AB Quick Reference Guide*.

Decimal number	Converted to this base	Results in
21	2	10101
100	2	1100100
64	8	100
73	8	111
74	16	4A
447	16	1BF

In writing `displayOtherBase`, use the header given below.

```
// Precondition: num > 0, 0 < base, and base <= 16
// Displays the decimal number converted to base.
public static void displayOtherBase(int num, int base)
```

3. A graphical user interface (GUI) system (such as *Microsoft Windows, Mac OSX,* or an *X Windows* window manager in *Linux*) keeps track of all of the windows on the user's screen. One of the windows is the *top* window. It has a specially marked title bar and is displayed on top of the other windows. The GUI has an operation to *cycle* through the windows, typically with a keystroke such as ALT + TAB. That operation moves the current top window to the bottom and the other windows up by one position. It also has operations to open a new window, which now becomes the top window, and to close the top window, so that the next window under it becomes the top window.

Your task is to implement a class `WindowManager` that manages a collection of objects of type `Window`. Each `Window` has a `Rectangle` indicating its size, and a `String` indicating the message on the title bar. (Real windows would know how to draw their contents, but we will ignore that aspect in this problem.)

The `Rectangle` constructor takes four parameters: *x*- and *y*-coordinates of its top left point, its width, and its height. The `Rectangle` `toString` method returns the `String` representing the `Rectangle` object's coordinate and size values.

Operations of the `WindowManager` are:
- `add`: Adds a new `Window` as the top window.
- `remove`: Removes the top window.
- `cycle`: Moves the current top window to the bottom and the other windows up by one position.
- `print`: Prints the windows from top to bottom. The `toString` method of `Window` returns a "printable" `Window`.

The implementation of `Window` and an incomplete implementation of `WindowManager` are below.

```
public class Window
{
   // Constructs a rectangular Window with title, winTitle.
   public Window(String winTitle, Rectangle winBounds)
   {
      title = winTitle;
      bounds = winBounds;
   }

   // Returns the string representation of the Rectangular window
   // that includes the window title and dimensions.
   public String toString()
   {
      return "Window[title=" + title + ", bounds=" + bounds + "]";
   }

   private String title;
   private Rectangle bounds;
}
```

```
public class WindowManager
{
    // Adds window w. w now becomes the top window.
    public void add(Window w)
    {
        // Code goes here
    }

    // Removes the top window.
    public void remove()
    {
        // Code goes here
    }

    // Moves the current top window to the bottom and the other
    // windows are moved up by one position.
    public void cycle()
    {
        // Code goes here
    }

    // Prints the windows from top to bottom.
    public void print()
    {
        // Code goes here
    }

    // Private stuff here
}
```

A Sample Client Program

```
import java.awt.Rectangle;

public class WindowManagerTester
{
    public static void main(String[] args)
    {
        WindowManager manager = new WindowManager();
        manager.add(new Window("A", new Rectangle(5, 10, 15, 20)));
        manager.add(new Window("B", new Rectangle(15, 20, 15, 20)));
        manager.add(new Window("C", new Rectangle(25, 30, 15, 20)));
        manager.print();
        manager.cycle();
        manager.print();
        manager.remove();
        manager.print();
    }
}
```

The program run is:

```
Window[title=C, bounds=java.awt.Rectangle[x=25,y=30,width=15,height=20]]
Window[title=B, bounds=java.awt.Rectangle[x=15,y=20,width=15,height=20]]
Window[title=A, bounds=java.awt.Rectangle[x=5,y=10,width=15,height=20]]

Window[title=B, bounds=java.awt.Rectangle[x=15,y=20,width=15,height=20]]
Window[title=A, bounds=java.awt.Rectangle[x=5,y=10,width=15,height=20]]
Window[title=C, bounds=java.awt.Rectangle[x=25,y=30,width=15,height=20]]

Window[title=A, bounds=java.awt.Rectangle[x=5,y=10,width=15,height=20]]
Window[title=C, bounds=java.awt.Rectangle[x=25,y=30,width=15,height=20]]
```

a. What data structure is most appropriate for storing the collection of `Window` objects? Choose from an array, a linked list, a stack, and a queue. Justify your choice.

b. Use your chosen data structure to implement the method `add`. Use the method header below when writing `add`.

```
public void add(Window w)
```

c. Use your chosen data structure to implement the method `remove`. Use the method header below when writing `remove`.

```
public void remove()
```

d. Given the incomplete implementation of the `WindowManager` class above, use your chosen data structure to implement the method `cycle`. Use the method header below when writing `cycle`.

```
public void cycle()
```

e. Given the incomplete implementation of the `WindowManager` class above, use your chosen data structure to implement the method `print`. `print` should print the windows from top to bottom. The `toString` method of `Window` returns a "printable" `Window`. If w is a `Window`,

```
System.out.println(w);
```

will print the correct `Window` information in the format displayed in the execution shown above. Use the method header below when writing `print`.

```
public void print()
```

CHAPTER 18

(Covers *Java Concepts* Chapter 21)

Advanced Data Structures (AB only)

■ Topic Summary

18.1 Sets

A *set* is an unordered collection of distinct elements. Unlike linked lists, stacks, and queues, sets contain no duplicate items. Elements can be added to, located in, and removed from a set. The AP subset contains the set methods listed in Table 18.1.

Table 18.1
interface java.util.Set

Method	Method Summary
`boolean add(Object obj)`	Adds the parameter `obj` as an element to this set if it is not already in the set and returns true. If the element is already in the set, returns `false`.
`boolean contains(Object obj)`	Returns `true` if this set contains the element `obj`, otherwise returns `false`.
`boolean remove(Object obj)`	Removes the element `obj` from this set and returns `true` if the `obj` is in this set; if the element is not present, returns `false`.
`int size()`	Returns the number of elements in this set.
`Iterator iterator()`	Returns an `Iterator` that provides access to the elements of this set.

The elements of a set are accessed using a set iterator. Since sets are unordered, the iterator may visit the set elements in a different order from the order in which the elements were added to the set. The set iterator includes the methods listed in Table 18.2.

Table 18.2
`interface java.util.Iterator`

Method	Method Summary
`boolean hasNext()`	Returns `true` if the iteration has more elements.
`Object next()`	Returns the next element in the iteration.
`void remove()`	Removes the last element returned by `next`.

We do not use the `ListIterator` methods `add`, `set`, and `previous` with sets. The list iterator methods `previous` and `add` are dependent on iterating the elements in some order and adding an element to a specific place. This makes no sense with sets because sets are not ordered. The list iterator method `set` allows replacement of an element. Because there are no duplicates in a set, calling a method to replace an element in a set could be dangerous because the replacement may already exist in the set.

Because `Set` is an interface, we cannot instantiate a `Set`. In other words, we can't create an object of type `Set`. Java provides classes that implement the `Set` interface. The AP subset includes two of these classes, `HashSet` and `TreeSet`.

```
class java.util.HashSet implements java.util.Set
class java.util.TreeSet implements java.util.Set
```

These classes enable quick retrievals (searches). To search for a particular element in a linked list, we must search the list sequentially ($O(n)$). To search an ordered array or an ordered `ArrayList` we can use the binary search which improves the retrieval time ($O(\log(n))$). A `HashSet` can be implemented using a hash table which can search in $O(1)$ time and a `TreeSet` can be implemented for searching in $O(\log(n))$ time.

We will look at these data structures in more detail later in this chapter.

With Java 5, the `Set` interface, the `Map` interface, and the Java classes that implement these interfaces are generic. The examples in Section 21.1 in your text instantiate a `HashSet` of `Strings` and demonstrate the use of a generic iterator and an enhanced `for` loop to traverse the items in the `HashSet`.

18.2   Maps

A *map* is a data type that keeps associations between *keys* and *values*. Each *key* in a map is mapped to a unique *value*. But a value may be associated with more than one *key*. Some examples:

- A mapping of names to phone numbers ("Gail Thomas" maps to "212-555-1234").
- A mapping of your college friends to the university that they attend. ("Cay Horstmann" maps to "San Jose State University", "Fran Trees" maps to "Drew University").
- A mapping of animals to animal sounds ("cat" maps to "meow").
- A mapping of a coin name to its value ("Quarter" maps to 0.25).
- A mapping of a car model to its make ("4-Runner" maps to "Toyota").

- A mapping of case numbers of medical patients to the medical technician handling the case.
- A mapping of login IDs to passwords.

Each association has a *key* mapped to a *value*. Figure 3 in Section 21.2 in your text illustrates this mapping relationship. Associations can be put in, changed, and located in a map. The `Map` interface methods that will be tested on the AP CS Exam are listed in Table 18.3.

Table 18.3
`interface java.util.Map`

Method	Method Summary
`Object put(Object key, Object value)`	Associates `value` with `key` in this map so that `get(key)` returns `value`. If the map previously contained a mapping for this key, the old value is replaced by the specified value.
`Object get(Object key)`	Returns the value associated with `key` in this map, or `null` if there is no value associated with `key`.
`Object remove(Object key)`	Removes the mapping for `key` from this map if it is present.
`boolean containsKey(Object key)`	Returns `true` if there is a value associated with `key` in this map, otherwise returns `false`.
`int size()`	Returns the number of keys in this map.
`Set keySet()`	Returns a `Set` of the keys in the map.

Because a `Map` is an interface, we cannot create an object of type `Map`. The AP CS subset includes the Java `HashMap` and `TreeMap` classes that implement `Map`.

```
class java.util.HashMap implements java.util.Map
class java.util.TreeMap implements java.util.Map
```

The `Map` interface requires that the `keySet` method be implemented. The `keySet` method produces a `Set` of keys. We can visit all of the elements of a `HashMap` or `TreeMap` by iterating through the keys in the set that the `keySet` method produces. The `Map` method `get` will return the value associated with a map key. `HashMap` and `TreeMap` differ in implementation. A `HashMap` does not keep the elements ordered. In fact, the order may not even remain the same throughout the implementation. A `TreeMap` keeps the elements in an order (according to the key) from smallest to largest. The choice as to which implementation to use for a given application depends largely on the requirements of that particular application. We will discuss this more as we look at each of the different data structures. Section 21.2 in your text illustrates a generic `HashMap` associates `String` references to `Color` references.

Before we look at the details of a `HashSet` or a `HashMap`, we need to understand what *hashing* is and why it is used. Before we talk about a `TreeSet` and a `TreeMap`, we need to understand binary search trees and their implementation.

18.3   Hash Tables

Hashing is an efficient way to store data for quick insertion and retrieval. Hashing involves the use of a hash function that computes and returns an integer value. This value can be used to determine the place in the hash table where the object will be inserted or can be found. A well constructed hash table allows for quick insertion and quick look-up. Figure 6 in Section 21.3 in your text illustrates a simple example of a hash table that stores names. The hash table illustrated in this example is an array of *buckets* that hold names (String objects). Each bucket holds all the names that produce the hash code that corresponds to the index of the bucket. Figure 18.1 illustrates a small portion of this hash table in your text.

Figure 18.1

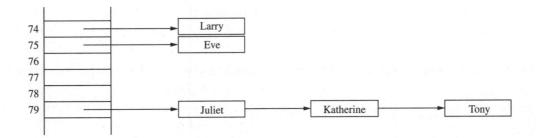

The hash code returned for the name Larry is 74. The names Juliet, Katherine, and Tony return the same hash code, 79. When two objects have the same hash code, a *collision* occurs. The goal of a good hash function is to minimize the number of collisions. If the hash function distributes the elements so that there is one element per bucket (which would be the ideal goal) then searching for a particular name is $O(1)$.

Suppose that a search for the name "Eve" is to be done. First, the hash code for "Eve" is calculated by calling the hashCode method of the String class (because the object is a String). This hash code determines the array index (bucket) in which "Eve" should be found. Searching a hash table is $O(1)$ if the hashCode method uniformly distributes the elements in the hash table. A very bad hash function would put all names in the same bucket. Retrieving an element in this worst case would then be $O(n)$. All objects in that bucket would have to be traversed.

18.3.1   Using HashSet

A hash table can be implemented using a HashSet. A hash set stores an unordered collection of objects. First, we will look at a test program that uses the Java library class HashSet. We will add names (strings) to our hash set.

Example 18.1

```
import java.util.Iterator;
import java.util.Set;
import java.util.HashSet;

/**
    This program tests the HashSet class.
*/
public class HashTester
{
```

```java
public static void main(String[] args)
{
    Set names = new HashSet();
    // Java 5
    // Set<String> names = new HashSet<String>();

    names.add("Mary");
    names.add("Sue");
    names.add("Art");
    names.add("Michael");
    names.add("Paul");
    System.out.println(names.size());

    Iterator iter = names.iterator();
    // Java 5
    // Iterator<String> iter = names.iterator();

    while (iter.hasNext())
    {
        System.out.println(iter.next());
    }

    // Java 5 enhanced for loop
    /*
        for (String i : names)
        {
            System.out.println(i);
        }
    */
}
}
```

The output of the above test program is:

5
Paul
Michael
Mary
Sue
Art

You can see that the iterator does not return the elements in a particular order. The iterator (or the enhanced `for` loop) traverses the hash table by visiting each bucket and sequentially traversing the elements in the bucket. Table 18.4 lists the `HashSet` methods in the AP subset as well as two constructors that can be used to instantiate a `HashSet`. Example 18.1 invoked the `HashSet` default constructor. This created an empty hash table with initial capacity of 16. If the table gets too full, a new table twice the size is created and all the elements are inserted into the new table. The second constructor in Table 18.4 allows the initial capacity to be passed as a parameter. Research shows that the best size for a hash table is a prime number larger than the number of elements your table is expected to hold. An excess of approximately 30% is typical. This means that, if s is the number of slots in the table and e is the number of elements, then

$$s = a\ prime\ number \geq \frac{4}{3} * e$$

Table 18.4
class `java.util.HashSet`

Method	Method Summary
`HashSet()`	Constructs a new, empty hash table with default initial capacity.
`HashSet(int initialSize)`	Constructs a new, empty hash table with an initial capacity of `initialSize`.
`boolean add(Object obj)`	Adds the parameter `obj` as an element to this set if it is not already stored in this set and returns `true`. If the element is already in the set, returns `false`.
`boolean contains(Object obj)`	Returns `true` if this set contains the element `obj`, otherwise returns `false`.
`boolean remove(Object obj)`	Removes the argument `obj` from this set and returns `true` if the argument is in this set; if it is not present, returns `false`.
`int size()`	Returns the number of elements in this set.
`Iterator iterator()`	Returns an `Iterator` that provides access to the elements of this set.

Example 18.2 extends Example 18.1 to show calls to the other `HashSet` methods in Table 18.4.

Example 18.2

```
names.add("Sue");
names.remove("Mary");
System.out.println(names.size());
iter = names.iterator();
while (iter.hasNext())
    System.out.println(iter.next());
if (names.contains("Fran"))
    System.out.println("Fran found.");
else
    System.out.println("Fran NOT found.");
```

The resulting output is:

> *4*
> *Paul*
> *Michael*
> *Sue*
> *Art*
> *Fran NOT found.*

The objects added to and removed from the `HashSet` names in Examples 18.1 and 18.2 were done so using the `HashSet` methods `add` and `remove`. How did the method `add` know in which bucket to insert a given name? How did the method `remove` find the appropriate name to remove? `HashSet add` calls the `hashCode` method of its `Object` parameter. The objects in our example are `String` objects. The `HashSet add` method uses the `String hashCode` method and the table size to determine where to place (or where to look for) the object. Although the `String hashCode` method will not be tested on the AP Exam, it's important to understand how hashing works. It's not magic! Notice in Example 18.2, the name *Sue* is not added a second time. Sets contain no duplicate entries.

When you are using the `HashSet` class to store objects instantiated by your own classes, you need to be careful. You must define an `equals` method and a `hashCode` method for your class. For example, do you wish to store `Student` objects in a hash table according to the student's name, the ID number, the GPA, or a combination of these instance field values? Forgetting to define `hashCode` is an error that is discussed in *Common Error 21.1* in your text. Although implementing the `equals` method and the `hashCode` method will not be tested on the AP Exam, hashing concepts will be tested.

18.3.2 Implementing `HashSet`

Section 21.3 in your text implements the `HashSet` as an array of `Nodes` using the inner classes `Node` and `HashSetIterator`. Our AP implementation implements a hash table as an array of `ListNodes`. This method of hashing is often referred to as *chaining* because a bucket contains a *chain* of `ListNodes` with the same hash value. Example 18.3 demonstrates this implementation.

Example 18.3

```
/**
    A hash set stores an unordered collection of objects, using
    a hash table.
*/
public class HashSet
{
   /**
       Constructs a hash table.
       @param bucketsLength the length of the buckets array
   */
   public HashSet(int bucketsLength)
   {
      buckets = new ListNode[bucketsLength];
      size = 0;
   }

   /**
       Tests for set membership.
       @param x an object to search for
       @return true if x is an element of this set
   */
   public boolean contains(Object x)
   {
      int h = getBucketIndex(x);

      ListNode current = buckets[h];
      while (current != null)
      {
         if ((current.getValue()).equals(x))
            return true;    // x is already in bucket
         current = current.getNext();
      }
      return false;    // x not found in this bucket
   }
```

```java
/**
   Adds an element to this set.
   @param x an object
   @return true if x is a new object, false if x was already in
   the set
*/
public boolean add(Object x)
{
   if (contains(x))
   {
      return false;
   }
   int h = getBucketIndex(x);
   buckets[h] = new ListNode(x, buckets[n]); // Add x to bucket
   size++;
   return true;
}

/**
   Removes an object from this set.
   @param x an object
   @return true if x was removed from this set, false if x was
   not an element of this set
*/
public boolean remove(Object x)
{
   int h = getBucketIndex(x);
   ListNode current = buckets[h];
   ListNode previous = null;
   while (current != null)
   {
      if ((current.getValue()).equals(x))   // Is x in bucket?
      {
         if (previous == null) buckets[h] = current.getNext();
         else previous.setNext(current.getNext());
         size--;
         return true;  // If found, x is removed.
      }
      previous = current;
      current = current.getNext();
   }
   return false;
}

/**
   Gets the number of elements in this set.
   @return the number of elements
*/
public int size()
{
   return size;
}
```

```
/**
   Prints the contents of the HashSet.
*/
public void printHashSet()
{
   for (int i = 0; i < buckets.length; i++)
   {
      ListNode temp = buckets[i];
      while (temp != null)
      {
         System.out.println(temp.getValue());
         temp = temp.getNext();
      }
   }
}

/**
   Determines bucket in which x belongs.
   @param x an object to find bucket for
   @return index (bucket) in which x belongs
*/
private int getBucketIndex(Object x)
{
   int h = x.hashCode();    // Calls String hashCode method
   if (h < 0) h = -h;
   h = h % buckets.length;    // Finding bucket index
   return h;
}

private ListNode[] buckets;    // Array of ListNodes
private int size;
}
```

18.3.3 Using `HashMap`

The `HashMap` class implements the `Map` interface and uses hashing as the technique to store entries. Each entry of a hash map consists of a *key* and a *value*. A `HashMap` stores pairs (key, value) according to the hash code determined by the key. Assuming that the `hashCode` method defined for the key object distributes the entries uniformly in the hash table, searching, insertion, and removal of an entry in the hash map is constant time ($O(1)$). The `HashMap` methods included in the AP subset are listed in Table 18.5.

Table 18.5
`interface java.util.HashMap`

Method	Method Summary
`HashMap()`	Constructs an empty `HashMap` with default size.
`Object put(Object key, Object value)`	Associates `value` with `key` in this map so that `get(key)` returns value. If the map previously contained a mapping for this key, the old value is replaced by the specified value.
`Object get(Object key)`	Returns the value associated with `key` in this map, or `null` if there is no value associated with `key`.
`Object remove(Object key)`	Removes the mapping for `key` from this map if it is present.
`boolean containsKey(Object key)`	Returns `true` if there is a value associated with `key` in this map, otherwise returns `false`.
`int size()`	Returns the number of keys in this map.
`Set keySet()`	Returns a `Set` of the keys in the map.

Example 18.4 demonstrates the `HashMap` methods with the case number for a medical patient mapped to the name of the medical technician handling the case.

Example 18.4

```
import java.util.Iterator;
import java.util.Map;
import java.util.HashMap;
import java.util.Set;

/**
    This program tests the HashMap class.
*/
public class HashMapTester
{
    public static void main(String[] args)
    {
        Map names = new HashMap();  // Constructs an empty HashMap
        names.put(new Integer(1435), "Smith");
        names.put(new Integer(1110), "Thomas");
        names.put(new Integer(1425), "Jones");
        names.put(new Integer(987), "Evans");
        names.put(new Integer(1323), "Murray");

        System.out.println("Number of cases: " + names.size()); // 5

        Integer lookfor = new Integer(1435);
        if (names.containsKey(lookfor))
            System.out.println("Key found.");
        else
            System.out.println("Key NOT found.");
```

```
        Set namesSet = names.keySet();
        Iterator iter = namesSet.iterator();
        while (iter.hasNext())
        {
            Integer caseNumber = (Integer) iter.next();
            System.out.println(caseNumber + " handled by "
                + names.get(caseNumber));
        }
    }
}
```

The resulting output is:

> *Number of cases: 5*
> *Key found*
> *987 handled by Evans*
> *1425 handled by Jones*
> *1323 handled by Murray*
> *1435 handled by Smith*
> *1110 handled by Thomas*

If the statements that insert keys and values into the HashMap were changed to:

```
names.put(new Integer(1435), "Smith");
names.put(new Integer(1110), "Thomas");
names.put(new Integer(1425), "Jones");
names.put(new Integer(987), "Evans");
names.put(new Integer(1323), "Murray");
names.put(new Integer(1323), "Duplicate");
```

The resulting output would be:

> *Number of cases: 5*
> *Key found*
> *987 handled by Evans*
> *1425 handled by Jones*
> *1323 handled by Duplicate*
> *1435 handled by Smith*
> *1110 handled by Thomas*

Notice that case #1323 is handled by Duplicate, not by Murray. If a duplicate key entry is attempted, the original one is replaced.

Section 21.2 in your text includes an example of instantiating a generic HashMap object that implements the generic Map interface.

18.3.4 Implementing HashMap
Our implementation of HashMap would be similar to the implementation for HashSet in Example 18.3. The differences are

- A class MapEntry is defined. MapEntry has a key field, a value field, and the appropriate constructors and accessor methods.
- The ListNode contains a reference to an object, MapEntry.
- When the hashCode method is called on a table entry, it is called on the key field of a MapEntry object.

18.4 Computing Hash Codes

A hash function should be easy and fast to compute and should scatter the data evenly throughout the hash table. Choose a table size that has more space than is actually needed and develop a function to compute the hash address. Remember that a good table size is a prime number greater than or equal to 4/3 times the expected number of elements. You can define `hashCode` methods for your own classes by combining the hash codes for the individual instance variables. Section 21.4 in your text describes how to do this is detail. The implementation of `hashCode` methods is not part of the AP subset but hashing concepts will be tested. You should understand the goal of a good hash function.

18.5 Binary Search Trees

A binary tree consists of nodes, each of which has two child nodes. One of the nodes is the root node; all non-root nodes in the tree can trace their ancestry up the tree to the root. A *leaf* of a binary tree is a node that has no children. A *complete* binary tree is binary tree where each leaf is at the same level and each non-leaf has exactly two children. A complete binary tree is illustrated in Figure 18.2.

Figure 18.2

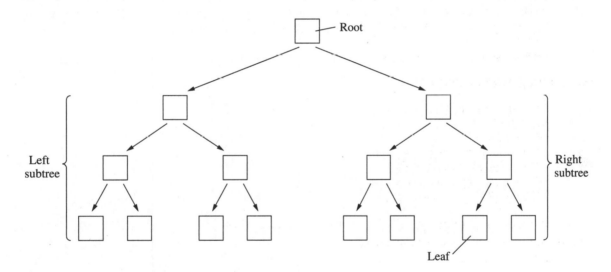

A *binary search tree (BST)* is a binary tree in which the descendants to the left of a node have smaller values than the node value field and the descendants to the right have values that are greater than or equal to the node value field. Figure 18.3 illustrates a binary search tree of `Integers`.

Figure 18.3

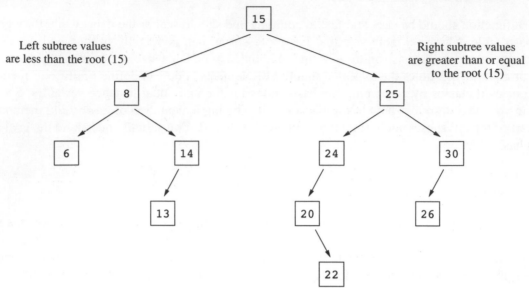

A binary tree is made up of nodes that have a data field and two reference fields. In Figure 18.3, a node is illustrated as a square containing a number (data field) and left and right arrows (reference fields). To facilitate a consistency in the exam questions, the AB exam uses the TreeNode[1] class shown in Example 18.5 to define a node and its methods.

Example 18.5

```
public class TreeNode
{
    public TreeNode(Object initValue,
            TreeNode initLeft, TreeNode initRight)
    {
        value = initValue;
        left = initLeft;
        right = initRight;
    }

    // Returns the value of tree node.
    public Object getValue()
    {
        return value;
    }

    // Returns the left field of tree node.
    public TreeNode getLeft()
    {
        return left;
    }

    // Returns the right field of tree node.
    public TreeNode getRight()
    {
        return right;
```

---

[1] College Board's AP Computer Science AB: Implementation Classes and Interfaces

```
    }

    /**
        Sets the value of the tree node to theNewValue.
        @param theNewValue is the new value of the tree node
    */
    public void setValue(Object theNewValue)
    {
        value = theNewValue;
    }

    /**
        Sets the tree node's left field to a new reference.
        @param theNewLeft is the new reference for the left
        field of the tree node
    */
    public void setLeft(TreeNode theNewLeft)
    {
        left = theNewLeft;
    }

    /**
        Sets the tree node's right field to a new reference.
        @param theNewRight is the new reference for the right
        field of the tree node
    */
    public void setRight(TreeNode theNewRight)
    {
        right = theNewRight;
    }

    private Object value;
    private TreeNode left;
    private TreeNode right;
}
```

A description of the `TreeNode` class will appear at the beginning of the exam booklet.

Figure 7 in Section 21.5 in your text illustrates a binary search tree. Figure 8 illustrates a binary tree that is not a binary search tree. In order to build a binary search tree, we must be able to compare the objects in the value field of the `TreeNode`. This means that the objects that we are inserting into the binary search tree must implement `Comparable` and define `compareTo`. To insert a node into a binary search tree we check first to see if the tree is empty. If it is, then the root of the tree references the new node.

```
    public void insert(Comparable obj)
    {
        Node newNode = new TreeNode(obj, null, null);
        if (root == null) root = newNode;
        else root.insertNode(newNode);
    }
```

If the tree is not empty, the new node must be inserted to the left if the new value is smaller than the present node's value, and to the right if the new node's value is greater than or equal to the value of the current node. An implementation of the binary search tree using the `TreeNode` class appears in Example 18.6.

Example 18.6

```java
/**
    This class implements a binary search tree whose nodes hold
    objects that implement the Comparable interface.
*/
public class Tree
{
    // Constructs an empty tree.
    public Tree()
    {
        root = null;
    }

    /**
        Inserts a new node into the tree.
        @param obj the object to insert
    */
    public void insert(Comparable obj)
    {
        TreeNode newNode = new TreeNode(obj, null, null);
        if (root == null)
            root = newNode;
        else
            insertNode(root, newNode);
    }

    // Prints the contents of the tree in sorted order.
    public void print()
    {
        if (root != null)
            printNodes(root);
    }

    /**
        A TreeNode of a tree stores a data item and references
        to the child TreeNodes to the left and to the right.
    */
    public void insertNode(TreeNode current, TreeNode newNode)
    {
        Comparable newValue = (Comparable) newNode.getValue();
        Comparable currValue = (Comparable) current.getValue();
        if (newValue.compareTo(currValue) < 0)
        {
            if (current.getLeft() == null)
                current.setLeft(newNode);
            else
                insertNode(current.getLeft(), newNode);
        }
        else
        {
            if (current.getRight() == null)
                current.setRight(newNode);
```

```
        else
            insertNode(current.getRight(), newNode);
    }
}

/**
    Prints this TreeNode and all of its descendants
    in sorted order.
*/
public void printNodes(TreeNode current)
{
    if (current != null)
    {
        printNodes(current.getLeft());
        System.out.println(current.getValue());
        printNodes(current.getRight());
    }
}
private TreeNode root;
}
```

Example 18.7 tests this binary search tree implementation for String objects and for Integer objects.

Example 18.7

```
// This program tests the binary search tree class.
public class TreeTester
{
    public static void main(String[] args)
    {
        Tree names = new Tree();
        names.insert("Romeo");
        names.insert("Juliet");
        names.insert("Tom");
        names.insert("Dick");
        names.insert("Harry");
        names.print();    // Dick Harry Juliet Romeo Tom

        // Inserting 15 8 25 6 14 24 20 22 30 13 26
        Tree numbers = new Tree();
        numbers.insert(new Integer(15));
        numbers.insert(new Integer(8));
        numbers.insert(new Integer(25));
        numbers.insert(new Integer(6));
        numbers.insert(new Integer(14));
        numbers.insert(new Integer(24));
        numbers.insert(new Integer(20));
        numbers.insert(new Integer(22));
        numbers.insert(new Integer(30));
        numbers.insert(new Integer(13));
        numbers.insert(new Integer(26));
        numbers.print();    // 6 8 13 14 15 20 22 24 25 26 30
    }
}
```

18.5.1 Searching a Binary Search Tree

Searching a binary search tree follows the same basic algorithm as a binary search of an array. If the key is less than the current value, go left, otherwise go right.

Example 18.8

```java
/**
    Searches for key in the tree.
    @param key is value to search for in tree.
    @return true if key found in tree, false otherwise.
*/
public boolean find(Comparable key)
{
    if (root == null)
        return false;
    else
        return findNode(root, key);
}


/**
    Recursive helper method
    @return true if key is found in tree, false otherwise.
*/
public boolean findNode(TreeNode current, Comparable key)
{
    if (current == null)
        return false;
    else
    {
        Comparable currValue = (Comparable) current.getValue();
        if (key.compareTo(currValue) == 0)
            return true;
        else if (key.compareTo(currValue) < 0)
            return findNode(current.getLeft(), key);
        else
            return findNode(current.getRight(),key);
    }
}
```

A *balanced* tree contains approximately as many children in the left subtree as in the right subtree. As with a binary search on an array, searching for a value in a binary search tree (BST) is $O(\log(n))$. Because inserting an element into a BST follows the same algorithm, and because a BST is a sorted collection of elements, when traversed with an inorder traversal, the binary search tree (when reasonably balanced) is a $O(n \log(n))$ sort. If, however, a BST were created by inserting the Integers 1-10 in that order, a very unbalanced tree would result. The tree, in fact, would be linked as a linked list. The efficiency of searching this tree is $O(n)$. Trace through the insertion algorithm for the numbers 1 to 10 and sketch your resulting tree.

18.5.2 Removing a Node from a Binary Search Tree

Removing a node from a binary search tree is not as intuitive. There are three basic situations: removing a node with no children, removing a node with one child, and removing a node with two children.

To remove a node with no children: set the appropriate field of the parent to `null`. Delete 22.

Figure 18.4

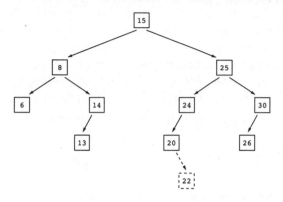

To remove a node with one child, replace the node with its child. Delete 30.

Figure 18.5

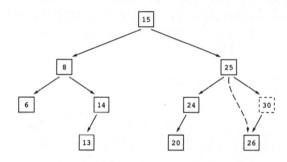

The node containing 30 is replaced with the node containing 26.

To remove a node with two children, go right once then all the way left. The smallest value in the right subtree of the node we are deleting will replace the deleted node. Delete 15.

Figure 18.6

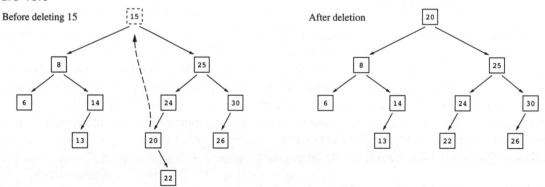

The node containing 15 is replaced by the node containing 20.

Section 21.5 in your text includes the `BinarySearchTree` class implementation. This implementation contains the `remove` method and a non-recursive `find` method using an inner class `Node`. Inner classes will not be tested on the AP Exam.

18.6 Tree Traversal

Notice that the tree node values are printed in order. The print method does an *inorder* traversal of the `TreeNodes`. This means the left subtree is printed, the root value is printed, and then the right subtree is printed. Because the `insert` algorithm inserts nodes with values less than the current node value in the left subtree and nodes with values greater than or equal to the current node value in the right subtree, the inorder traversal results in an ordered printing of the node values. *Preorder* and *postorder* traversals are explained in Section 21.6 in your text. The inorder traversal visits nodes in the order: left, root, right. Preorder traversal visits root, left, right. Postorder traversal visits left, right, root. Consider the binary search tree in Figure 18.3.

- Inorder traversal yields: 6 8 13 14 15 20 22 24 25 26 30
- Preorder traversal yields: 15 8 6 14 13 25 24 20 22 30 26
- Postorder traversal yields: 6 13 14 8 22 20 24 26 30 25 15

The postorder traversal of an expression tree gives a postfix expression. Preorder traversal of an arithmetic expression will result in Lukasiewicz notation (prefix notation). Prefix notation is discussed in *Random Fact 21.1* in your text. The operators precede the operands. Prefix and postfix expressions do not need parentheses. Although prefix and postfix are not topics explicitly listed in the AP CS Topic Outline, they are applications involving binary trees and stacks and questions related to these traversals and applications may appear on the AP Exam.

18.7 Using Tree Sets and Tree Maps

The `TreeSet` class uses a form of a balanced binary tree that guarantees that adding and removing an element takes $O(\log(n))$ time. We know that a good hashing function can give us a retrieval with efficiency $O(1)$ but if we also wanted to be able to list our data in order, a hash table would not be the appropriate choice. Binary search trees, when traversed with an inorder traversal, allow for an efficient search ($O(\log(n))$) and can also be traversed so that elements can be printed in order. The `TreeSet` class implements the `Set` interface. Table 18.6 lists the methods of `TreeSet` that may be tested on the AP Exam.

Table 18.6
class java.util.TreeSet

Method	*Method Summary*
`TreeSet()`	Constructs a new, empty tree set.
`boolean add(Object obj)`	Adds the parameter `obj` as an element if it is not already stored in this set and returns true. If the element is already in the set, returns `false`.
`boolean contains(Object obj)`	Returns `true` if this set contains the element `obj`, otherwise returns `false`.
`boolean remove(Object obj)`	Removes the argument `obj` from this set and returns `true` if the argument is in this set; if it is not present, returns `false`.
`int size()`	Returns the number of elements in this set.
`Iterator iterator()`	Returns an `Iterator` that provides access to elements of this set.

A `TreeSet` requires that its elements be comparable. That means that `compareTo` is defined for the objects placed in the `TreeSet`. This is important because the elements in a tree are ordered (unlike a `HashSet`). For your own classes, you must realize the `Comparable` interface and define `compareTo` or provide a `Comparator` (explained in Section 21.7 in your text; `Comparator` is not tested on the AP Exam) in order to use the `TreeSet`. Because a `TreeSet` implements `Set`, a `TreeSet` contains no duplicates. Example 18.9 demonstrates a test program for `TreeSet`.

Example 18.9

```java
import java.util.Iterator;
import java.util.Set;
import java.util.TreeSet;

// This program tests the tree set class.
public class TreeSetTester
{
    public static void main(String[] args)
    {
        Set names = new TreeSet();
        names.add("Larry");
        names.add("Tony");
        names.add("Katherine");
        names.add("Eve");
        names.add("Juliet");

        System.out.println(names.size());
        Iterator iter = names.iterator();
        while (iter.hasNext())
            System.out.println(iter.next());
        System.out.println();

        names.add("Tony");    // Attempting to add duplicate.
        // Duplicate is not added. (Sets do not contain duplicates.)
        names.remove("Eve");    // Removing name.
        iter = names.iterator();
        while (iter.hasNext())
            System.out.println(iter.next());
        System.out.println();
    }
}
```

The resulting output is:

5
Eve
Juliet
Katherine
Larry
Tony

Juliet
Katherine
Larry
Tony

A `TreeSet` guarantees reasonable search performance ($O(\log(n))$) and allows for visiting the elements of the tree set in order. Because traversing a `TreeSet` with an iterator visits the tree set in order, the first call to the iterator's `next` method takes $O(\log(n))$ time.

A `TreeMap` also requires that the objects belong to a class that realizes the `Comparable` interface and defines `compareTo` for the keys. There is no requirement for the values. The `TreeMap` methods included in the AP subset are listed in Table 18.7 and demonstrated in Example 18.10.

Table 18.7
`interface java.util.TreeMap`

Method	Method Summary
`TreeMap()`	Constructs a new, empty map.
`Object put(Object key, Object value)`	Associates `value` with `key` in this map so that `get(key)` returns value. If the map previously contained a mapping for this key, the old value is replaced by the specified value.
`Object get(Object key)`	Returns the value associated with `key` in this map, or `null` if there is no value associated with `key`.
`Object remove(Object key)`	Removes the mapping for `key` from this map if it is present.
`boolean containsKey(Object key)`	Returns `true` if there is a value associated with `key` in this map, otherwise returns `false`.
`int size()`	Returns the number of keys in this map.
`Set keySet()`	Returns a `Set` of the keys in the map.

Example 18.10

```java
import java.util.Iterator;
import java.util.Map;
import java.util.TreeMap;
import java.util.Set;

// This program tests the TreeMap class.
public class TreeMapTester
{
    public static void main(String[] args)
    {
        Map names = new TreeMap();
        names.put(new Integer(1435), "Smith");
        names.put(new Integer(1110), "Thomas");
        names.put(new Integer(1425), "Jones");
        names.put(new Integer(987), "Evans");
        names.put(new Integer(1323), "Murray");

        System.out.println("Number of cases: " + names.size());

        Integer lookfor = new Integer(1435);
        if (names.containsKey(lookfor))
            System.out.println("Key found");
```

```
        else
            System.out.println("Key NOT found");

        Set namesSet = names.keySet();
        Iterator iter = namesSet.iterator();
        while (iter.hasNext())
        {
            Integer caseNumber = (Integer) iter.next();
            System.out.println(caseNumber + " handled by "
                    + names.get(caseNumber));
        }
    }
}
```

The resulting output is:

> *Number of cases: 5*
> *Key found*
> *987 handled by Evans*
> *1110 handled by Thomas*
> *1323 handled by Murray*
> *1425 handled by Jones*
> *1435 handled by Smith*

Note that the iterator loop casts `caseNumber` to `Integer`. There is no *need* to cast here if you just want to print the value. But if the code is later changed to do anything else with this value, you would then have to go back and change the variable type.

With Java 5, the generic `Map` Interface, `TreeMap` class, and `Iterator` class allows you to specify the type of objects and thus eliminate worry about when to cast and when not to cast!

If the same test program were executed replacing

```
names.put(new Integer(1435), "Smith");
names.put(new Integer(1110), "Thomas");
names.put(new Integer(1425), "Jones");
names.put(new Integer(987), "Evans");
names.put(new Integer(1323), "Murray");
```

with

```
names.put("Smith", new Integer(1435));
names.put("Thomas", new Integer(1110));
names.put("Jones", new Integer(1425));
names.put("Evans", new Integer(987));
names.put("Murray", new Integer(1323));
```

and the iterator code was replaced by

```
while (iter.hasNext())
{
    String who = (String) iter.next();
    System.out.println(who + " handled " + names.get(who));
}
```

the resulting output would be:

> *Number of cases: 5*
> *Evans handled 987*
> *Jones handled 1425*
> *Murray handled 1323*
> *Smith handled 1435*
> *Thomas handled 1110*

In both executions, the nodes are visited in order according to the order dictated by the key's `compareTo` method.

The examples of binary search trees that have been discussed so far contain integer and string values. Recall that a `TreeNode` stores any comparable object. Suppose `Student` objects were to be stored in a binary search tree. The `Student` class must implement the `Comparable` interface. This means `compareTo` must be defined in the `Student` class. The decision is made to compare students by the alphabetical (really lexicographical) ordering of last name, first name, and then ID. Example 18.11 demonstrates this.

Example 18.11

```java
// A student with an ID.
public class Student implements Comparable
{
    /**
        Constructs a Student object.
        @param aFirstName the first name
        @param aLastName the last name
        @param anId the ID
    */
    public Student(String aFirstName, String aLastName, int anId)
    {
        firstName = aFirstName;
        lastName = aLastName;
        id = anId;
    }

    /**
        Gets the student's first name
        @return firstName the first name
    */
    public String getFirstName() { . . .}

    /**
        Gets the student's last name
        @return lastName the last name
    */
    public String getLastName() { . . .}

    /**
        Gets the student's ID
        @return id the ID
    */
    public int getId() { . . .}
```

```
public int compareTo(Object obj)
{
    if (obj == null)
        return -1;
    String thisName = lastName + " " + firstName + " " + id;
    String objName = ((Student) obj).lastName + " " +
        ((Student) obj).firstName + " " + ((Student) obj).id;
    return thisName.compareTo(objName);
}

/**
    Determines if the students are equal.
    @param otherObject the other student
    @return true if the students are equal, false otherwise
*/
public boolean equals(Object otherObject)
{
    return compareTo(otherObject) == 0;
}

/**
    Displays a string representation of the student object.
    @return a string describing the student object.
*/
public String toString() {. . .}

private String firstName;
private String lastName;
private int id;
}
```

The program segment below adds students to a binary search tree and prints the students using an inorder traversal.

```
Tree drewCsiClass = new Tree();
drewCsiClass.insert(new Student("Ann", "Brown", 111));
drewCsiClass.insert(new Student("Alan", "Frazee", 122));
drewCsiClass.insert(new Student("Bob", "Brown", 132));
drewCsiClass.insert(new Student("Ann", "Bergin", 451));
drewCsiClass.insert(new Student("Tim", "Brown", 112));
drewCsiClass.insert(new Student("Tom", "Casper", 171));
drewCsiClass.inOrderPrint();
```

The result is:

Student[First name=Ann,Last name=Bergin,ID=451]
Student[First name=Ann,Last name=Brown,ID=111]
Student[First name=Bob,Last name=Brown,ID=132]
Student[First name=Tim,Last name=Brown,ID=112]
Student[First name=Tom,Last name=Casper,ID=171]
Student[First name=Alan,Last name=Frazee,ID=122]

Because it may also be important to list students by ID number, a Comparator is implemented for Student. Example 18.12 shows this StudentComparator implementation and a test program that stores Student objects in a TreeSet ordered by ID numbers.

Example 18.12

```java
import java.util.Comparator;

public class StudentComparator implements Comparator
{
    public int compare(Object firstObject, Object secondObject)
    {
        Student first = (Student) firstObject;
        Student second = (Student) secondObject;
        if (first.getId() < second.getId())
            return -1;
        else if (first.getId() == second.getId())
            return 0;
        else
            return 1;
    }
}
```

The program segment below adds students to a `TreeSet` using the `StudentComparator` that compares student ID numbers.

```java
Comparator comp = new StudentComparator();
Set studentsByID = new TreeSet(comp);

studentsByID.add(new Student("Ann", "Brown", 111));
studentsByID.add(new Student("Alan", "Frazee", 122));
studentsByID.add(new Student("Bob", "Brown", 132));
studentsByID.add(new Student("Ann", "Bergin", 451));
studentsByID.add(new Student("Tim", "Brown", 112));
studentsByID.add(new Student("Tom", "Casper", 171));

System.out.println();
Iterator iter = studentsByID.iterator();
while (iter.hasNext())
    System.out.println(iter.next());
```

The result is:

Student[First name=Ann,Last name=Brown,ID=111]
Student[First name=Tim,Last name=Brown,ID=112]
Student[First name=Alan,Last name=Frazee,ID=122]
Student[First name=Bob,Last name=Brown,ID=132]
Student[First name=Tom,Last name=Casper,ID=171]
Student[First name=Ann,Last name=Bergin,ID=451]

In Java 5, the `Comparable` interface and the `Comparator` interface are parameterized types. Section 19.8 in your text gives an example of a Java 5 `CoinComparator`. The `Comparator` interface will not be tested on the AP Exam.

18.8 Priority Queues

A priority queue is an abstract data type that has two operations: add an element and remove the element with the highest priority. Unfortunately, the Java class library does not provide a class for a priority queue.

When you send your job to a printer, it is placed in a queue. In some systems, some printing jobs may have a higher priority than other jobs because of their importance. If we assign each of these printing jobs a number to indicate its priority in the queue, then the smaller number is assigned to the most important job indicating that it should be handled first. The AP `PriorityQueue` interface defines a priority queue in which the item with the smallest value is the one with the highest priority and is removed from the priority queue first (similar to the printer queue example).

To facilitate a consistency in the exam questions, the AB exam uses the `PriorityQueue` interface[2] shown in Example 18.13.

Example 18.13

```
/**
    The "highest priority" is defined as the smallest item in this
    priority queue.
*/
public interface PriorityQueue
{
    /**
        Postcondition: returns true if the number of elements in
        the priority queue is 0; otherwise, returns false
    */
    boolean isEmpty();

    /**
        Postcondition: x has been added to the priority queue; the
        number of elements in the priority queue is increased by 1.
    */
    void add(Object x);

    /**
        Postcondition: The smallest item in the priority queue is
        removed and returned; the number of elements in the priority
        queue is decreased by 1. Throws unchecked exception if
        priority queue is empty.
    */
    Object removeMin();

    /**
        Postcondition: The smallest item in the priority queue is
        returned; the priority queue is unchanged. Throws unchecked
        exception if priority queue is empty.
    */
    Object peekMin();
}
```

The AP `PriorityQueue` interface defines the "highest priority" as the smallest item in the priority queue. When the method `removeMin()` is implemented, the item with the smallest value should be returned. Let's consider some options for implementing a priority queue and discuss their limitations.

[2] College Board's AP Computer Science AB: Implementation Classes and Interfaces

- An unsorted array (or `ArrayList`)
  - Adding an element is $O(1)$.
    - Elements will be added to the end of the array.
  - `removeMin` is $O(n)$.
    - In order to delete this element from the array, the smallest value must be found ($O(n)$) and deleted.
- A sorted array (or `ArrayList`)
  - Adding an element is $O(n)$.
    - The array must be searched for the correct place and then elements must be shifted to accommodate the insertion. We should keep the list sorted so that the element with the smallest value is last.
  - `removeMin` is $O(1)$ if this element is stored in last position.
- An unsorted linked list
  - Adding an element is $O(1)$.
    - Elements will be added to the front of the list.
  - `removeMin` is $O(n)$.
    - We must search the linked list to find the element ($O(n)$) and then delete the element.
- A sorted linked list
  - Adding an element is $O(n)$.
    - Must search for the correct place and then insert it. The list will be sorted in ascending order so that the element with the smallest value is first.
  - `removeMin` is $O(1)$ because we are removing the first element of the linked list.
- A tree set
  - Adding an element is $O(\log(n))$.
  - `removeMin` is $O(\log(n))$.

Example 18.14 is an example of the `TreeSet` implementation of `PriorityQueue`.

Example 18.14

```
import java.util.TreeSet;
import java.util.Iterator;

public class TreePriorityQueue implements PriorityQueue
{
    public TreePriorityQueue()
    {
        tree = new TreeSet();
    }

    /**
        Postcondition: returns true if the number of elements
        in the priority queue is 0; otherwise, returns false
    */
    public boolean isEmpty()
    {
        return tree.size() == 0;
    }
```

```
/**
    Postcondition: x has been added to the priority queue; the
    number of elements in the priority queue is increased by 1.
*/
public void add(Object x)
{
    tree.add(x);
}

/**
    Postcondition: The smallest item in the priority queue is
    removed and returned; the number of elements in the priority
    queue is decreased by 1. Throws unchecked exception if
    priority queue is empty.
*/
public Object removeMin()
{
    Iterator iter = tree.iterator();
    Object r = iter.next();
    iter.remove();
    return r;
}

/**
    Postcondition: The smallest item in the priority queue is
    returned; the priority queue is unchanged. Throws unchecked
    exception if priority queue is empty.
*/
public Object peekMin()
{
    Iterator iter = tree.iterator();
    Object r = iter.next();
    return r;
}

private TreeSet tree;
}
```

Now, let's look at another data implementation called a *heap*.

18.9   Heaps

A *min-heap* is a binary tree with the following properties:

1. It is complete or almost complete, which means that every level of the tree is completely filled, except maybe the bottom level. If the bottom level is not filled, the nodes are in the leftmost positions (see Figure 16 in Section 21.9 in your text).

2. The object stored at each node is less than or equal to the values stored in its descendants. Figure 17 in Section 21.9 in your text illustrates this.

These properties are maintained with each addition to the heap. Figure 18.7 illustrates a min-heap.

Figure 18.7

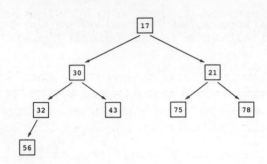

Figure 18.8 below inserts 25 into our heap. When an element is inserted in the heap, it is inserted in a vacant slot at the "end" of the tree representing the heap. After the insertion, the heap is readjusted (by swapping the new element "up" in the heap) so that the heap properties are fulfilled.

Figure 18.8

Insert 25   Heap adjusted

Figures 17 and 18 in Section 21.9 in your text illustrate creating a min-heap and inserting elements into the heap. It is easy to see that the element with the smallest value is the root of the binary tree.

The only element that we will remove from a heap is the root node. To remove the root, we replace the root with the "last" element in the heap and readjust the heap elements so that the min-heap properties are maintained (See Figure 19 in your text for a complete illustration of a node removal from the heap).

Figure 18.9

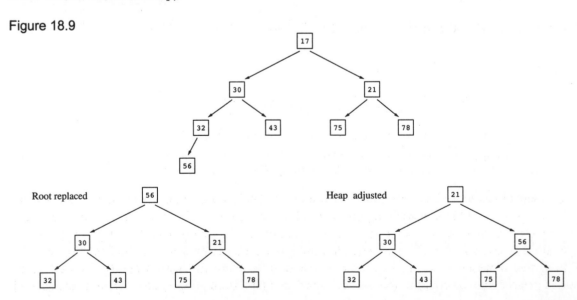

Root replaced   Heap adjusted

With the conclusion of each operation, the properties of a min-heap are satisfied. The algorithms used for insertions into and deletions from a heap are based on a complete binary tree, making each of the operations $O(\log(n))$.

Section 21.9 in your text implements a heap using an `ArrayList`. The elements from the heap are mapped to indices in an array list. The root of the heap is placed in index `1`. The left child of the node in position `x` is placed in index `2x` and the right child is placed in index `2x + 1`. Figure 20 in Section 21.9 in your text illustrates this and the `ArrayList` implementation of the heap follows it.

18.10 The Heapsort Algorithm

Heaps are also used to implement an efficient sorting algorithm, heapsort. This sorting algorithm is $O(n \log(n))$. There are n items in the heap. Each insertion and removal is $O(\log(n))$.

The heapsort inserts elements into a heap and removes them in sorted order. We use an array to store our heap elements. Of course, the original array of values does not represent a heap. To store the elements in the array, we number the heap elements from top to bottom, left to right, starting with 0 at the root. Those values are used as the subscripts into the array. The children of node i can be found at $2 * i + 1$ and $2 * i + 2$.

The idea behind the heapsort algorithm is to first reorder our array elements so that their order represents a heap as defined earlier. We do this by continuously adjusting our array elements until the heap properties are satisfied. Now, we repeatedly remove the root element (replace the last element in the array by the root element) and readjust our heap. This procedure results in our array having the smallest element in the last position. The heapsort algorithm is more easily implemented if we utilize a *max-heap* instead of a *min-heap*. A *max-heap* is a binary tree with the following properties:

1. It is complete or almost complete, which means that every level of the tree is completely filled, except maybe the bottom level. If the bottom level is not filled, the nodes are in the leftmost positions.

2. The object stored at each node is greater than or equal to the values stored in its children.

Let's look at a very simplified description of the heapsort algorithm. Figure 18.10 illustrates this pseudocode.

Start with a max-heap (an array) of size `n`.

```
// Invariant: h[n]. . .h[heapname.size() - 1] is sorted
for (int n = heapName.size() - 1; n > 0; n--)
{
    swap h[n] with root (h[0])
    readjust heap from 1 ... n − 1
}
```

The diagrams in Figure 18.10 illustrate this algorithm. The shaded elements are the sorted portion of the heap (array). The algorithm consists of a `for` loop with two steps. The *swap* step exchanges the values in the root node and the last non-sorted element in the heap (array). After the swap, that last non-sorted array position now joins the sorted portion of the heap (array). The resulting tree representation needs to be readjusted to maintain the heap property that each node value is greater than or equal to the values stored in its children. The *readjust heap* is the second step in the `for` loop. While readjusting to maintain max-heap properties, if we need to demote a node, we swap it with its largest child.

Figure 18.10

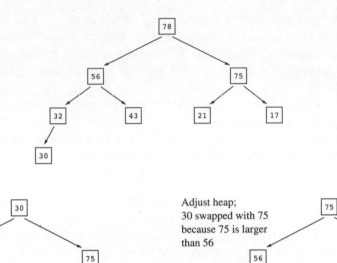

Swap `h[0]` with `h[7]`

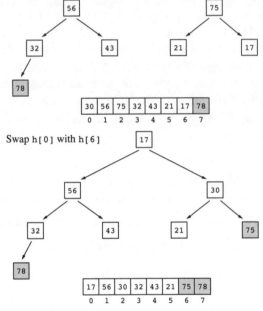

Adjust heap; 30 swapped with 75 because 75 is larger than 56

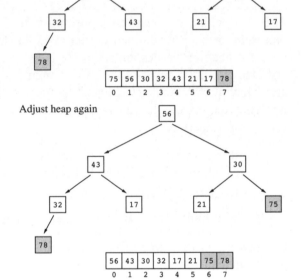

The process continues until...

Swap `h[0]` with `h[1]`

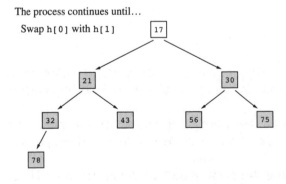

No adjustments necessary

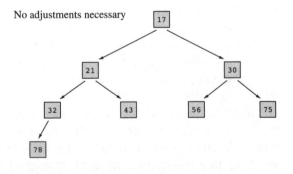

The array implementation for this final heap is: | 17 | 21 | 30 | 32 | 43 | 56 | 75 | 78 |
0 1 2 3 4 5 6 7

When we traverse the array beginning with the first array element, the elements visited are in increasing order. Section 21.10 in your text illustrates the heapsort and implements the heapsort using an array where the root of the heap is in position 0 in the array. The left child of the element in position x is in position 2x + 1 and the right child of the element in position x is in position 2x + 2.

18.11 Choosing a Container

How To 21.1 in your text reviews how to pick the appropriate container (implementation) for your application. The questions you should ask yourself and the possible answers to each question are summarized below. As you read the questions and choose an answer, think about the container that you would use. The comments below the questions discuss possible choices.

Your container choices: array, array list, linked list, set, and map.

1. How will elements be accessed?
   a. The method of accessing doesn't matter in this application.
   b. Accessing elements needs to be by index for immediate retrieval.
   c. The accessing will be done by key (like an ID number or a bank account number).
   d. Accessing is done by an index pair such as a row and column.

2. Does order matter?
   a. Order doesn't matter.
   b. The order of the entries needs to be kept in the order they were entered.
   c. The entries need to be kept in sorted order.

3. Which operations need to be fast?
   a. It doesn't matter.
   b. Adding and/or removing elements needs to be fast.
   c. Finding an element needs to be fast.

- If the answers to all of the questions are "doesn't matter," then use an array list. It's an easy and straightforward implementation.
- If the answer to 1 is b, use an array or array list.
- If the answer to 1 is c, use a map.
- If the answer to 1 is d, use a two-dimensional array.
- If the answer to 2 is b, use an array, an array list, or a linked list.
- If the answer to 2 is c, use a tree set.
- If the answer to 3 is b, use a linked list.
- If the answer to 3 is c, use a set.
- If you need a set or a map, remember
  - To use a `HashSet` and a `HashMap`, the keys/values you are going to store must implement a `hashCode` method. Check to see that the class of your objects implements this method.
  - To use a `TreeSet` or `TreeMap`, the keys/values you are going to store must implement a `compareTo` method. Alternatively, you may provide a `Comparator`, although this method is not included in the AP subset.
- Sets do not contain duplicates. If your application is meant to include duplicates, a set is not your choice.

■ Expanded Coverage of Material That Is Not Found in the Text

- The method we used to implement our hash table involved *chaining*. Another method of storing elements in a hash table is called *linear probing*. With linear probing, each bucket contains at most one element. If an attempt is made to add an element to a bucket that already has an element in it, the new element would be added to the next available (empty) bucket.

■ Topics That Are Useful But Not Tested

- The `String` class, `Double` class and `Integer` class provide a `hashCode` method that returns an integer hash code. When writing your own hash function, you may wish to call these methods. The `Coin` example in Section 21.4 in your text calls the `Double hashCode` method.
- Computing hash codes is covered in Section 21.4 in your text. Implementing `hashCode` will not be tested.

■ Things to Remember When Taking the AP Exam

- Sets do not contain duplicates. If you change an item in a set it may become the same as another item in the set. Moreover, this WILL upset the set data structure because it may change the hash code or the sort order!
- Sets are not ordered, unless they are `TreeSets`.
- Use an iterator to list all elements in a set.
- An iterator for a `HashSet` does not return the elements in any specific order; an iterator for a `TreeSet` returns the elements using an inorder traversal.
- For a `HashSet`, an iterator can iterate through all elements in $O(n)$ time where n is the sum of the `HashSet` instance's size (the number of elements) and the number of buckets.
- You cannot add an element to a set at an iterator position.
- A hash function computes an integer value from an object.
- A good hash function will distribute entries uniformly in a hash table.
- A map associates keys with values.
- In a hash map, only the keys are hashed. In a tree map, only the keys are sorted.
- For `HashSet` and `HashMap`, the operations `add`, `remove`, and `contains` have an expected time of $O(1)$ and are $O(n)$ in the worst case.
- When a class redefines `equals`, it should redefine `hashCode` to be compatible. Implementing these functions is not tested on the AP Exam.
- If a binary search tree is balanced, locating, adding, and removing an element is $O(\log(n))$.
- To use a tree set or a tree map, the elements must be comparable.
- `TreeSets` and `TreeMaps` are implemented as balanced binary trees so the operations `add`, `remove`, and `contains` are $O(\log(n))$.
- For a `TreeSet` iterator, the first call to `next()` takes $O(\log(n))$ time.
- Know the difference between preorder, postorder, and inorder traversals of a binary tree.
- Removing an element from a priority queue will remove the element with the highest priority.
- The heapsort algorithm is $O(n \log(n))$.

■ Key Words

You should understand the terms below. The AP CS Exam questions may include references to these terms. The citations in parentheses next to each term identify the page numbers where it is defined and/or discussed in *Java Concepts*, 4th ed., and *Big Java*, 2nd ed.

balanced binary search
   tree (802)
binary tree (796)
binary search tree (796)
buckets (785)
children (796)
collision (784)
descendant (796)
hash code (783)
hash function (783)

hash map (793)
hash set (778)
hash table (783)
heap (817)
heapsort (827)
inorder (808)
key set (781)
map (781)
postorder (808)

preorder (808)
priority queue (815)
root (796)
set (777)
table size (786)
tree map (811)
tree set (811)
value set (781)

■ Connecting the Detailed Topic Outline to the Text

The citations in parentheses next to each term identify the page numbers where it is defined and/or discussed in *Java Concepts*, 4th ed., and *Big Java*, 2nd ed.

- Sets (776–781)
- Maps (781–783)
- Hash Tables (783–791)
  - Using `HashSet` (778–780)
  - Implementing `HashSet` (786–790)
  - Using `HashMap` (782–783)
- Computing Hash Codes (791–795)
- Binary Search Trees (796–807)
  - Searching a Binary Search Tree (804)
  - Removing a Node from a Binary Search Tree (801–802)
- Tree Traversal (807–811)
- Using Tree Sets and Tree Maps (811–815)
- Priority Queues (815–816)
- Heaps (816–827)
- The Heapsort Algorithm (827–832)
- Choosing a Container (813–814)

■ Practice Questions

Multiple Choice

1. A hash function computes an integer value from an object. The goal of a good hash function is to:

   a. determine the size of the hash table.
   b. provide space for the object that is to be inserted.
   c. provide a method of dealing with collisions.
   d. provide a key for efficiently sorting the objects in the hash table.
   e. provide an integer value for the object so that the objects are uniformly distributed in the hash table.

Questions 2–4 refer to the incomplete binary search tree implementation given below. The class `Tree` is a binary search tree of `TreeNodes`. Refer to the *AB Quick Reference Guide* or Example 18.5 for the `TreeNode` implementation. The `Tree` method `printXxx` calls `xxxPrint` to print the values in the nodes of the binary search tree.

```
/*
    This class implements a binary search tree whose
    nodes are TreeNodes that hold objects that
    implement the Comparable interface.
*/
public class Tree
{
    // Constructs an empty tree.
    public Tree()
    {
        root = null;
    }

    // Other Binary Search Tree methods here

    public void printXxx()
    {
        if (root != null)
            xxxPrint(root);
    }

    public void xxxPrint(TreeNode current)
    {
        ListQueue q = new ListQueue();
        q.enqueue(current);
        while (!q.isEmpty())
        {
            Object temp = q.dequeue();
            current = (TreeNode) temp;
            System.out.print(current.getValue() + " ");
            if (current.getLeft() != null)
                q.enqueue(current.getLeft());
            if (current.getRight() != null)
                q.enqueue(current.getRight());
        }
```

```
        }

        private TreeNode root;
    }
```

The following declaration is made.

```
    Tree numbers = new Tree();
```

The following `Integer` values are inserted, in the order below, into an initially empty binary search tree, `numbers`.

```
    15 8 25 6 14 24 20 22 30 13 26
```

2. What is printed when the statement

    ```
    numbers.printXxx();
    ```

    is executed in a client program of the `Tree` class?

    a. *6 8 13 14 15 20 22 24 25 26 30*
    b. *6 13 14 8 22 20 24 26 30 25 15*
    c. *15 8 6 14 13 25 24 29 22 30 26*
    d. *15 8 25 6 14 24 30 13 20 26 22*
    e. *15 25 8 30 24 14 6 26 20 13 22*

3. Suppose the statements

    ```
    if (current.getLeft() != null)
        q.enqueue(current.getLeft());
    ```

    and

    ```
    if (current.getRight() != null)
        q.enqueue(current.getRight());
    ```

    were exchanged. What would be printed when the statement

    ```
    numbers.printXxx();
    ```

    is executed in a client program of the `Tree` class?

    a. *6 8 13 14 15 20 22 24 25 26 30*
    b. *6 13 14 8 22 20 24 26 30 25 15*
    c. *15 8 6 14 13 25 24 29 22 30 26*
    d. *15 8 25 6 14 24 30 13 20 26 22*
    e. *15 25 8 30 24 14 6 26 20 13 22*

4. Suppose the following methods were added to the `Tree` class above.

    ```
    public int mysterySum(TreeNode current)
    {
        if (current == null)
            return 0;
        else
            return (1 + mysterySum(current.getLeft())
                    + mysterySum(current.getRight()));
    }

    public int mystery()
    ```

```
        {
            return mysterySum(root);
        }
```

The following `Integer` values are inserted, in the order below, into an empty binary search tree, `numbers`.

```
    8 3 10 2 5
```

What would be printed when the statement

```
    System.out.println(numbers.mystery());
```

is executed in a client program of the `Tree` class?

a. *0*
b. *1*
c. *5*
d. *28*
e. Nothing is printed, a run-time error occurs.

5. Which of the following statements about maps **true**?

a. A `HashMap` can have two keys that map to the same value but two values cannot have the same key.
b. A `HashMap` can have two values with the same key but two keys cannot have the same value.
c. Each key in a `HashMap` must have a unique value and each value in a `HashMap` has a unique key.
d. A `HashMap` can have two values with the same key and two keys with the same value.
e. A `HashMap` can have values that do not map to any key.

Questions 6 and 7 refer to the problem statement below.

The following `Integer` values are pushed onto a stack, `s`, that implements the `Stack` interface that is defined in Example 17.12 and in the *AB Quick Reference Guide*. The values are pushed onto `s` in the order that they appear below (left to right).

```
    1 7 4 6 10 9
```

6. Consider a priority queue, `priQue` that is instantiated from a class `PriorityQueueList` implementing the `PriorityQueue` interface defined in Example 18.13 and in the *AB Quick Reference Guide*. The following declarations are made.

```
    PriorityQueue priQue = new PriorityQueueList();
    // PriorityQueueList implements PriorityQueue
```

Values are popped off the stack, `s`, and as each value is popped off the stack, it is inserted into the priority queue, `priQue`. The following code is then executed.

```
    while (!priQue.isEmpty())
    {
        System.out.println(priQue.removeMin())
    }
```

The numbers printed to the screen would be:

a. *1 7 4 6 10 9*
b. *9 10 6 4 7 1*
c. *1 4 6 7 9 10*
d. *10 9 7 6 4 1*
e. *9 6 4 1 7 10*

7. The values are pushed onto stack s in the order that they appear below (left to right).

    1 7 4 6 10 9

The values are then popped off the stack. As each value is popped off the stack, it is inserted into a binary search tree. The values in the tree are printed by visiting the nodes in the tree with a preorder traversal. The numbers printed to the screen would be:

a. *1 7 4 6 10 9*
b. *6 4 9 10 7 1*
c. *1 4 6 7 9 10*
d. *10 9 7 6 4 1*
e. *9 6 4 1 7 10*

8. Which of the following is **not** a fundamental operation for a Set?

a. Adding elements to the set.
b. Removing elements from the set.
c. Listing elements in the set.
d. Testing the set to see if an element is contained in the set.
e. Returning the number of times a given element appears in the set.

9. Which of the following statements is **true**?

a. A set iterator visits the elements in the order in which you inserted them.
b. When adding elements to a set, you should use the add method of the set iterator.
c. Elements can be removed from a set using the iterator method remove or the Set method remove that is defined by the class that implements Set.
d. You should not attempt to add duplicates to a set because an error will occur.
e. To insert an element in a particular place in the set, use the set iterator to find the set position.

10. Which of the following lines of code will add an association of a person and a university in the Map friends?

a. `friends.add("Mary");`
b. `friends.add("Mary", "University of Delaware");`
c. `friends.put("Mary", "University of Delaware");`
d. `friends.addValue("Mary", "University of Delaware");`
e. `friends.putValue("Mary", "University of Delaware");`

11. Which of the following describes how to print all of the keys, with their associated values, of a class that implements `Map`?

    a. Store a value and its associated key in a `TreeNode` and insert the `TreeNode` in a binary search tree. Then, traverse the tree using an inorder traversal.
    b. Store a value and its associated key in a `TreeNode` and insert the `TreeNode` in a binary search tree. Then, use a tree iterator to retrieve the values.
    c. Iterate through the set returned by the class's `keySet` method to retrieve the key and use the class's `get` method to retrieve the value associated with the key.
    d. Iterate through the set returned by the class's `keySet` method to retrieve the value and use the class's `get` method to retrieve the key associated with the value.
    e. Store the elements in an array list and the corresponding values in a set. Iterate through the array list and the set simultaneously to retrieve and print the keys and values.

12. If there are no collisions in the hash table, then locating a hash table element takes

    a. $O(1)$
    b. $O(\log(n))$
    c. $O(n)$
    d. $O(n \log(n))$
    e. $O(n^2)$

13. Consider the following sorting algorithms.

    I. Merge sort
    II. Quicksort
    III. Heapsort

    In the worst case, which of the algorithms is $O(n \log(n))$?

    a. I only
    b. II only
    c. III only
    d. I and III only
    e. I, II, and III

14. The following `Integers` are added to an initially empty min-heap in the order they are listed. The heap properties are maintained with each insertion.

        9 25 32 90 15 4 23

    If the heap is represented by a binary tree and an inorder traversal is done on this binary tree, the resulting order of the visited `Integers` is:

    a. 9 32 15 90 4 25 23
    b. 4 9 15 23 25 32 90
    c. 90 32 25 23 15 9 4
    d. 90 15 25 4 32 9 23
    e. 9 15 32 4 23 25 90

15. Consider the following two methods for sorting a set of strings in descending order.

    Method 1
    - Construct an empty binary search tree.
    - Insert all strings into the binary search tree.
    - Repeatedly get the maximum element (by following the rightmost path) and remove it.

    Method 2
    - Construct an empty heap.
    - Insert all strings into the heap.
    - Repeatedly get the maximum element (stored in the root) and remove it.

    Which of the following statements is **true**?

    a. Method 2 is more efficient than Method 1 if the resulting trees are both balanced after inserting all elements.
    b. Method 1 is more efficient than Method 2 if the input set is already sorted.
    c. Method 1 has $O(n \log(n))$ efficiency in the best case.
    d. Method 2 has $O(n^2)$ efficiency in the worst case.
    e. Method 1 and Method 2 are both less efficient than selection sort.

16. Your job is to choose a data structure to implement polynomials whose coefficients are positive integers, such as $17x^4 + 4x^3 + 0x^2 + 6x^1 + 12x^0$.

    Here are three possible implementations.

    I. As a two-dimensional array of boolean values: coeff[c][i] is true if and only if $c * x^i$ is a term of the polynomial.
    II. As a tree map with `Integer` keys and values. If $c * x^i$ is a term of the polynomial, then we add the following correspondence to the map:

        ```
        coeff.put(new Integer(i), new Integer(c))
        ```

    III. As a hash set of objects of type

        ```
        class Term
        {
           // Based on power
           public int hashcode(){. . .}

           // Based on power
           public boolean equals(Object obj){. . .}

           . . .
           private int coefficient;
           private int power;
        }
        ```

If *n* is the number of terms in the polynomial, which of the following statements is **false**?

a. Implementation I requires more space than implementations II and III.
b. Implementation II makes possible to print the polynomial by decreasing powers in $O(n \log(n))$ time.
c. Implementation II requires $O(\log(n))$ time to find the coefficient of a term with a given power.
d. Implementation III is impossible to carry out because one cannot define a hash code for terms.
e. If the hash code is assumed to run in constant time, implementation III requires $O(1)$ time to find the coefficient of a term with a given power.

17. The principal advantage that heapsort has over the merge sort algorithm is

a. Heapsort is related to priority queues.
b. Heapsort doesn't require a second array for intermediate storage.
c. Heapsort is a $O(n \log(n))$ algorithm.
d. Heapsort uses binary search trees.
e. Heapsort does not require recursion.

18. Consider the following max-heap:

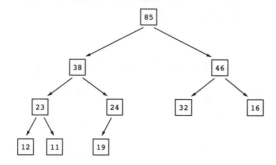

The array representation of this heap is

a. 11 12 16 19 23 24 38 46 85
b. 85 38 46 23 24 32 16 12 11 19
c. 12 11 19 24 24 32 16 38 46 85
d. 85 38 23 12 11 24 19 46 32 16
e. None of the above—the tree doesn't fulfill the max-heap conditions.

19. Consider the following binary trees:

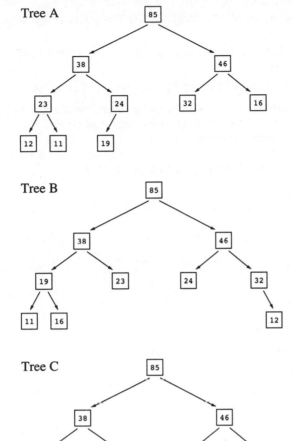

Tree A

Tree B

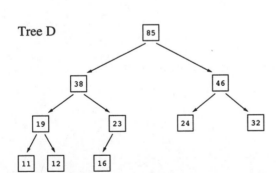

Tree C

Tree D

Which of the binary trees above are max-heaps?

a.   All of the trees above are heaps.
b.   A and B only
c.   C and D only
d.   B and D only
e.   A and D only

20. Consider the following mystery function on a binary tree (not necessarily a binary search tree).

```
public int mystery(TreeNode cur)
{
    if (cur == null)
        return 0;
    else
    {
        int r = mystery(cur.getLeft()) + mystery(cur.getRight());
        if (cur.getLeft() != null && ((Integer) cur.getLeft()
            .getValue()).compareTo(cur.getValue()) > 0) ||
            (cur.getRight() != null && ((Integer) cur.getRight()
            .getValue()).compareTo(cur.getValue()) < 0))
        {
            r++;
        }
        return r;
    }

    public int mystery()
    {
        return mystery(root);
    }
}
```

What is the result of applying the function to the following tree?

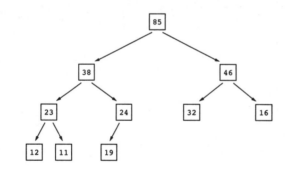

a. 5
b. 4
c. 6
d. 10
e. 306

Free Response Questions

1. The class TreeSetWithOps is a subclass of TreeSet. TreeSetWithOps has functionality that includes the methods setIntersection, setUnion, setDifference, isSubset, and isProperSubset. The incomplete definition of TreeSetWithOps appears below.

```java
import java.util.Set;
import java.util.TreeSet;
import java.util.Iterator;
public class TreeSetWithOps extends TreeSet
{
    /*
        Returns the intersection of this TreeSet with set2.
        set2 is the set with whom the intersection is determined.
    */
    public Set setIntersection(Set set2)
    {
        // Code goes here
    }

    /*
        Returns the union of this TreeSet with set2.
        set2 is a set with whom the set union is determined.
    */
    public Set setUnion(Set set2)
    {
        // Code goes here
    }

    /*
        Returns the difference of this TreeSet with set2.
        set2 is a set with whom the set difference is determined.
    */
    public Set setDifference(Set set2)
    {
        // Code goes here
    }

    /*
        set2 is a set to be evaluated as a subset.
        Returns true if set2 is a subset of this set,
        false otherwise
    */
    public boolean isSubset(Set set2)
    {
        // Code goes here
    }

    /*
        set2 is a set to be evaluated as a proper subset.
        Returns true if set2 is a proper subset of this set,
        false otherwise
    */
    public boolean isProperSubset(Set set2)
    {
        // Code goes here
    }
}
```

a. You are to implement the `TreeSetWithOps` method `setIntersection`. The intersection of two sets is a set whose members are common to both sets. The method `setIntersection` will return the intersection of `this` set with its `Set` parameter. For example, if

    set1 is the set `{"Ginger", "Harry", "Mary", "Thomas"}`

and

    set2 is the set `{"Frank", "Harry", "Kevin", "Mary", "Nancy"}`

and the statement

```
Set set3 = set1.setIntersection(set2);
```

were executed, `set3` would contain `{"Harry", "Mary"}`.

If the two sets have no elements in common, an empty set is returned. Use the method header below to write the method `setIntersection`.

```
public Set setIntersection(Set set2)
```

b. You are to implement the `TreeSetWithOps` method `setUnion`. The union of two sets is a set whose members are in at least one of the sets. The method `setUnion` will return the union of `this` set with its `Set` parameter. For example, if

    set1 is the set `{"Ginger", "Harry", "Mary", "Thomas"}`

and

    set2 is the set `{"Frank", "Harry", "Kevin", "Mary", "Nancy"}`

and the statement

```
Set set3 = set1.setUnion(set2);
```

were executed, `set3` would contain `{"Frank", "Ginger", "Harry", "Kevin", "Mary", "Nancy", "Thomas"}`.

Use the method header below to write the method `setUnion`.

```
public Set setUnion(Set set2)
```

c. You are to implement the `TreeSetWithOps` method `setDifference`. The difference of `set1` minus `set2` is the set whose members are in `set1` but are not in `set2`. The method `setDifference` will return the difference of `this` set with its `Set` parameter. For example, if

    set1 is the set `{"Ginger", "Harry", "Mary", "Thomas"}`

and

    set2 is the set `{"Frank", "Harry", "Kevin", "Mary", "Nancy"}`

and the statement

```
Set set3 = set1.setDifference(set2);
```

were executed, `set3` would contain `{"Ginger", "Thomas"}`.

Use the method header below to write the method setDifference.

```
public Set setDifference(Set set2)
```

d. You are to implement the TreeSetWithOps method isSubset. The method isSubset will return true if every element of set2 is also an element of set1. The set set1 may have exactly the same elements as set2. For example, if

set1	set2	set1.isSubset(set2)
{1,2,3,4,5}	{1,2,3}	true
{1,2,3,4}	{1,2,3,4}	true
{1,2,3,4,5}	{1,2,3,6}	false

Use the method header below to write the method isSubset.

```
public boolean isSubset(Set set2)
```

e. You are to implement the TreeSetWithOps method isProperSubset. The method isProperSubset will return true if every element of set2 is also an element of set1 and set1 has some elements that are not in set2. For example, if

set1	set2	set1.isProperSubset(set2)
{1,2,3,4,5}	{1,2,3}	true
{1,2,3,4}	{1,2,3,4}	false
{1,2,3,4,5}	{1,2,3,6}	false

In writing isProperSubset, you may call the method isSubset described in part d of this problem. Assume isSubset works as intended regardless of what you wrote for part d. Use the method header below to write the method isProperSubset.

```
public boolean isProperSubset(Set set2)
```

2. A concordance is an alphabetical wordlist for a passage of text. Each word in the concordance is mapped to an Integer indicating the frequency of the word's occurrence. The constructor of Concordance has one String parameter that identifies the text file to be read. An incomplete Concordance class is below.

```
public class Concordance
{
    // Constructor
    public Concordance(String nameOfFile)
    {
        concord = new TreeMap();
        createConcordance(nameOfFile);
    }

    // Create and return a TreeMap of words mapped to their
    // Integer frequencies.
    public void createConcordance(String fileName)
    {
        // Code goes here
    }
```

```
        // Prints the alphabetized list of words paired with their
        // frequencies.
        public void printConcordance()
        {
            // Code goes here
        }

        private Map concord;
    }
```

a. The method `createConcordance` will fill `concord`, a `TreeMap` of words mapped to their `Integer` frequencies. Complete the method `createConcordance` below. You may assume that all words in the passage are made up of lowercase letters.

```
    public static TreeMap createConcordance(String fileName)
    {
        // infile(fileName) is open for reading.
        while (!(infile.eof()))
        {
            String word = inFile.readWord();
                  // Reads word from infile
            // More code goes here
        }
    }
```

b. Write the method `printConcordance` that will print the alphabetized list of words paired with their frequencies. If the text file contains the following text:

> *hickory dickory dock*
> *the mouse ran up the clock*
> *the clock struck one*
> *the mouse ran down*
> *hickory dickory dock*

`printConcordance` will print:

> *clock occurs 2 time(s).*
> *dickory occurs 2 time(s).*
> *dock occurs 2 time(s).*
> *down occurs 1 time(s).*
> *hickory occurs 2 time(s).*
> *mouse occurs 2 time(s).*
> *one occurs 1 time(s).*
> *ran occurs 2 time(s).*
> *struck occurs 1 time(s).*
> *the occurs 4 time(s).*
> *up occurs 1 time(s).*

Use the method header below in writing `printConcordance`.

```
    public void printConcordance()
```

c. Suppose, in addition to the method `printConcordance`, you wish to include a method `printByFrequency` that would print the words ordered by frequency. The method `printByFrequency` will print:

> *down occurs 1 time(s).*
> *one occurs 1 time(s).*
> *struck occurs 1 time(s).*
> *up occurs 1 time(s).*
> *clock occurs 2 time(s).*
> *dickory occurs 2 time(s).*
> *dock occurs 2 time(s).*
> *hickory occurs 2 time(s).*
> *mouse occurs 2 time(s).*
> *ran occurs 2 time(s).*
> *the occurs 4 time(s).*

Words with the same frequency can be printed in any order. Describe the data structure(s) and algorithms that you would use to write `printByFrequency`. Comment on the time complexity of your algorithm.

CUMULATIVE REVIEW 3

Chapters 15–18

This review will focus on material in Chapters 15–18 but may include questions on the material in previous chapters. You should consider this a mini-practice for the AP Exam. Look over the material in these chapters and read over the section *Things to Remember When Taking the AP Exam* below. Have available the Quick Reference Guide or the Exam Reference Materials for the AP Exam that you will be taking. Because you will have reference materials available to you during the exam, you should become familiar with them now.

■ Things to Remember When Taking the AP Exam

General Guidelines
- It is a common error to use a `while` statement when an `if` statement should be used to check for the base case in a recursive function. Check your work!
- A recursive solution is not necessarily more efficient than an iterative solution to the same problem. For many problems, a recursive solution is shorter and/or clearer and thus a more efficient use of the programmer's time writing and testing the solution.
- Include an end condition for recursive solutions. Infinite recursions are usually undesirable.
- Write recursive solutions when the problem statement is defined recursively or when explicitly instructed to do so. Do not use recursion as a substitute for iteration.
- When given a particular algorithm, you should be able to count the number of times a specific statement is executed.
- The merge sort is more efficient than the insertion sort and selection sort algorithms but requires a temporary array.
- When given an algorithm similar to the binary search algorithm and an algorithm similar to the sequential search algorithm, you should be able to choose the algorithm that is more efficient for a specific set of data.
- Remember that an array has to be sorted in order to use binary search.
- Binary search generally is more efficient than sequential search if the array is sorted.
- When writing a sorting algorithm, there are many places where off-by-one errors can occur. Be careful when choosing between 0 and 1, < and <=, and `a.length` and `a.length - 1` for loop initializations. Walk through your code carefully.
- The worst case for the quicksort algorithm occurs when the original array is in order or in reverse order.
- Be sure to check whether an array or an array list is empty before you try to remove an item from it.

AB Topics

- You should be able to throw the unchecked `IllegalStateException` and `NoSuchElement-Exception` in your own methods.

- Merge sort, quicksort, and heapsort are $O(n \log(n))$ algorithms. Insertion and selection sorts are $O(n^2)$.

- When the quicksort algorithm is performed on an array that is originally in order or in reverse order, running time is $O(n^2)$.

- Algorithms that are $O(n \log(n))$ are more efficient than algorithms that are $O(n^2)$.

- When given an algorithm, you should be able to classify it as $O(1)$, $O(n)$, $O(\log(n))$, $O(n^2)$, or $O(n \log(n))$.

- Algorithms are not classified as $O(2n)$, $O(3)$, or $O(n^2 + 2n + 1)$. These are $O(n)$, $O(1)$, and $O(n^2)$ respectively.

- Do not simply count loops when determining the big-Oh running time. Consecutive loop algorithms are most often $O(n)$. Nested loop algorithms tend to be $O(n^2)$.

- Inserting and deleting from a `LinkedList` is efficient because these operations do not require shifting the other elements in the list.

- Stacks are LIFO (last-in, first-out). Queues are FIFO (first-in, first-out).

- If an application requires many look-ups (searches), use an implementation that provides $O(1)$ access whenever possible. Specifically, use an array when you need random access to individual elements (e.g., sorting algorithms) and use a linked list when you frequently need to insert or remove in the middle of the list (e.g., simulation of cars on a freeway with entrance/exit ramps).

- Be sure to check whether the list data structure is empty before you try to remove an item from it.

- Become familiar with the `ListNode` class, the `Stack` interface, and the `Queue` interface. The *AB Quick Reference Guide* that you will be given during the AP Exam contains examples similar to Examples 17.4, 17.12, and 17.16 of this guide (minus the comments).

- Be careful when implementing code that adds or removes nodes from a linked list. Ask yourself the following questions:
  - Does this code handle the empty list case?
  - Does this code handle the front of the list case?
  - Does this code handle the end of the list case?
  - Does this code handle the middle of the list case?
  - Does this code handle the list with only one node?

- Use a list iterator to access elements of a `LinkedList`. DO NOT use `get/set/insert`.

- Check for `null` references! Whenever calling `p.next`, `p.data`, etc., ask yourself "Can p be empty? If so, am I checking for it? If not, why not?"

- Sets do not contain duplicates. If you change an item in a set it may become the same as another item in the set. Moreover, this WILL upset the set data structure because it may change the hash code or the sort order!

- Sets are not ordered except for `TreeSet`.

- Use an iterator to list all elements in a set.

- An iterator for a `HashSet` does not return the elements in any specific order.

- For a `HashSet`, an iterator can iterate through all elements in $O(n)$ time where n is the sum of the `HashSet` instance's size (the number of elements) and the number of buckets.

- You cannot add an element to a set at an iterator position.

- A hash function computes an integer value from an object.

- A good hash function will distribute entries uniformly in a hash table.

- A map associates keys with values.

- In a hash map, only the keys are hashed. In a tree map, only the keys are sorted.

- For `HashSet` and `HashMap`, the operations `add`, `remove`, and `contains` have an expected time of $O(1)$ and are $O(n)$ in the worst case.

- When a class redefines `equals`, it should redefine `hashCode` to be compatible. Implementing these functions is not tested on the AP Exam.

- If a binary search tree is balanced, locating, adding, and removing an element is $O(\log(n))$.

- To use a tree set or a tree map, the elements must be comparable.
- `TreeSets` and `TreeMaps` are implemented as balanced binary trees so the operations `add`, `remove`, and `contains` are $O(\log(n))$.
- For a `TreeSet` iterator, the first call to `next()` takes $O(\log(n))$ time.
- Know the difference between preorder, postorder, and inorder traversals of a binary tree.
- Removing an element from a priority queue will remove the element with the highest priority.

■ Practice Questions

Multiple Choice

Questions 1 and 2 refer to the method `design`, given below. The method prints a design of `*`'s.

```
public static void design(int n)
{
    for (int i = n; i >= 1; i--)
    {
        for (int j = 1; j <= i; j++)
        {
            System.out.print("*");
        }
        System.out.println();
    }
}
```

1. In order for the method `design` to be guaranteed to print some `*`'s, which of the following is a correct precondition?

    a. $n \neq 0$
    b. $n < 0$
    c. $n \leq 0$
    d. $n > 0$
    e. $n \geq 0$

2. Which of the following methods will result in the same output as the method `design`?

    a.
    ```
    public static void design(int n)
    {
        System.out.println();
        if (n >= 1)
        {
            design(n - 1);
        }
        else
        {
            System.out.print("*");
        }
    }
    ```

b.
```java
public static void design(int n)
{
    if (n == 1)
    {
        System.out.println("*");
    }
    else
    {
        System.out.println();
        for (int j = 1; j <= n; j++)
        {
            System.out.print("*");
        }
        design(n - 1);
    }
}
```

c.
```java
public static void design(int n)
{
    if (n == 1)
    {
        System.out.println("*");
    }
    else
    {
        for (int j = 1; j <= n; j++)
        {
            System.out.print("*");
        }
        System.out.println();
        design(n - 1);
    }
}
```

d.
```java
public static void design(int n)
{
    if (n == 1)
    {
        System.out.println("*");
    }
    else
        for (int j = 1; j <= n; j++)
        {
            design(n - 1);
            System.out.print("*");
        }
}
```

e.
```java
public static void design(int n)
{
    if (n == 1)
    {
        System.out.println("*");
    }
    else
        for (int j = 1; j <= n; j++)
        {
            System.out.print("*");
            design(n - 1);
        }
}
```

3. The following code segments are intended to eliminate duplicates from an `ArrayList` of `Integers`.

   I.
   ```
   for (int i = 0; i < arr.size() - 1; i++)
   {
       if (arr.get(i).equals(arr.get(i + 1)))
       {
           arr.remove(i);
       }
   }
   ```

   II.
   ```
   int i = 0;
   while (i < arr.size() - 1)
   {
       if (arr.get(i).equals(arr.get(i + 1)))
       {
           arr.remove(i);
       }
       else
       {
           i++;
       }
   }
   ```

   a. Choices I and II work as intended for all `ArrayLists` of `Integers`.
   b. Choices I and II work as intended for `ArrayLists` of `Integers` that are sorted.
   c. Choices I and II work as intended for all non-empty `ArrayLists` of `Integers`.
   d. Choice I works as intended for `ArrayLists` of `Integers` that are sorted but Choice II does not.
   e. Choice II works as intended for `ArrayLists` of `Integers` that are sorted but Choice I does not.

4. **(AB)** (Java 5) The following code segment is intended to eliminate duplicates from an `ArrayList` of `Integers`.

   ```
   Iterator<Integer> iter = arr.iterator();
   Integer num = iter.next();
   while (iter.hasNext())
   {
       Integer num2 = iter.next();
       if (num.equals(num2))
       {
           iter.remove();
       }
       else
       {
           num = num2;
       }
   }
   ```

   Which statement about the code segment is **true**?

   a. This code segment works as intended for all `ArrayLists` of `Integers`.
   b. This code segment works as intended for all `ArrayLists` of `Integers` that are sorted.
   c. This code segment works as intended for all non-empty `ArrayLists` of `Integers`.
   d. This code segment works as intended for all non-empty `ArrayLists` of `Integers` that are sorted.
   e. This code segment eliminates only those values that are duplicates of the first value in the `ArrayList`.

5. **(AB)** Suppose it takes x milliseconds to sort a set of data using the selection sort algorithm. Approximately how long will it take to sort a data set that is four times as large?

   a. x milliseconds
   b. $4x$ milliseconds
   c. $16x$ milliseconds
   d. x^2 milliseconds
   e. There is no way to determine the answer.

Questions 6 and 7 refer to the following algorithm for sorting values in an array.

```
public class Orderer
{
    public Orderer(int[] anArray)
    {
        a = anArray;
    }

    public void order()
    {
        for (int i = 0; i < a.length - 1; i++)
        {
            int position = findPosition(i);
            swap(position, i);
        }
    }

    private int findPosition(int from)
    {
        int pos = from;
        for (int i = from + 1; i < a.length; i++)
            if (a[i] < a[pos])
            {
                pos = i;
            }
        return pos;
    }

    private void swap(int i, int j)
    {
        int temp = a[i];
        a[i] = a[j];
        a[j] = temp;
    }

    private int[] a;
}
```

6. Which of the following statements is **true** about the `Orderer` method `order` above?

    a. This algorithm closely resembles the selection sort algorithm.
    b. This algorithm closely resembles the insertion sort algorithm.
    c. This algorithm closely resembles the merge sort algorithm.
    d. This algorithm reverses the order of the data in the array.
    e. This sort algorithm randomly reorders elements in the array.

7. If the array a contains the numbers 5, 2, 12, 6, and 72, how many times is the comparison

    `a[i] < a[pos]`

    made?

    a. 1
    b. 5
    c. 10
    d. 25
    e. 50

8. Which of the following statements about classes and interfaces are **true**?

    I.   Abstract classes can contain constructors.
    II. Interfaces can contain constructors.
    III. Classes that have no abstract methods can contain constructors.

a. III only
b. I and II only
c. II and III only
d. I and III only
e. I, II, and III

9. Consider the `NumberGenerator` class defined below.

```java
public class NumberGenerator
{
    public NumberGenerator(int numberOfPositions, int startNum)
    {
        digits = numberOfPositions;
        currentDigit = startNum;
        if (digits > 1)
        {
            tail = new NumberGenerator(digits - 1, currentDigit + 1);
        }
        else
        {
            tail = null;
        }
    }

    public String nextElement()
    {
        String r = "";
        if (digits == 1)
        {
            r = currentDigit + "";
            currentDigit++;
            return r;
        }
        r = currentDigit + tail.nextElement();
        if (!tail.hasMoreElements())
        {
            currentDigit++;
            tail = new NumberGenerator(digits - 1, currentDigit + 1);
        }
        return r;
    }

    public boolean hasMoreElements()
    {
        return (currentDigit <= MAXDIGITS)
                && (digits <= MAXDIGITS - currentDigit + 1);
    }

    private int digits;
    private NumberGenerator tail;
    private int currentDigit;
    private final int MAXDIGITS = 4;
}
```

What is the result of the following code segment?

```java
NumberGenerator combs = new NumberGenerator(3, 0);
int count = 1;
while (combs.hasMoreElements() && count <= 5) // only printing 5
{
    System.out.print(combs.nextElement() + " ");
    count++;
}
```

a. 012 013 014 023 024
b. 000 001 002 003 004
c. 010 012 013 014 020
d. 000 111 222 333 444
e. 011 012 013 014 022

(Java 5) For Questions 10 and 11, assume that the following declarations

```
LinkedList<Integer> aList = new LinkedList<Integer>();
SomePriorityQueue pq = new SomePriorityQueue();
StackList s = new StackList();
QueueList q = new QueueList();
```

where

SomePriorityQueue implements PriorityQueue
StackList implements Stack
QueueList implements Queue

10. **(AB)** Suppose the following segment of code is executed.

```
aList.add(1);
aList.add(2);
aList.add(3);
aList.add(4);
aList.add(5);

ListIterator<Integer> iter = aList.listIterator();
while (iter.hasNext())
{
    Integer item = iter.next();
    s.push(item);
    q.enqueue(item);
}
System.out.print("Queue: ");
while (!q.isEmpty())
{
    System.out.print(q.dequeue());
}
System.out.println();
System.out.print("Stack: ");
while (!s.isEmpty())
{
    System.out.print(s.pop());
}
```

What would be printed?

a. Queue: 12345
    Stack: 54321

b. Queue: 12345
    Stack: 12345

c. Queue: 54321
    Stack: 12345

d. Queue: 54321
    Stack: 54321

e. Queue:
    Stack:

11. **(AB)** Suppose the following segment of code is executed.

```
pq.add(new Integer(5));
pq.add(new Integer(9));
pq.add(new Integer(6));
pq.add(new Integer(4));
pq.add(new Integer(1));
pq.add(new Integer(7));

while (!(pq.isEmpty()))
{
    Integer num = (Integer) pq.peekMin();
    if (num % 2 == 0)
    {
        s.push(pq.removeMin());
    }
    else
    {
        q.enqueue(pq.removeMin());
    }
}
System.out.print("Queue: ");
while (!q.isEmpty())
{
    System.out.print(q.dequeue());
}
System.out.println();
System.out.print("Stack: ");
while (!s.isEmpty())
{
    System.out.print(s.pop());
}
```

What would be printed?

a. Queue: 5917
    Stack: 64

b. Queue: 1579
    Stack: 64

c. Queue: 5917
    Stack: 46

d. Queue: 1579
    Stack: 46

e. Queue: 596417
    Stack:

For Questions 12 and 13: Suppose that the implementation of `add` in the `SomePriorityQueue` class is

```
public void add(Object x)
{
    someDataImplementation.add(x);
}
```

and that the elements are added to this priority queue in random order.

12. **(AB)** Which choice for a data structure for `someDataImplementation` would yield the fastest retrieval time for the `SomePriorityQueue` method `peekMin`?

    a. `java.util.LinkedList`
    b. `java.util.ArrayList`
    c. `java.util.HashSet`
    d. `java.util.TreeSet`
    e. `java.util.TreeMap`

13. **(AB)** Assuming that the choice of data type for `someDataImplementation` yields the fastest retrieval time for `peekMin`, the big-Oh efficiency for `peekMin` is

    a. $O(1)$
    b. $O(n)$
    c. $O(\log(n))$
    d. $O(n \log(n))$
    e. $O(n^2)$

14. **(AB)** Suppose that the `Integers` 9, 5, 3, 7, 1 are added, in the order given, to an initially empty queue, `q`, and that the `Integers` 2, 4, 6, and 8 are added, in the order given, to an initially empty stack, `s`. Also suppose that `hp` is an initially empty min-heap and that the min-heap method `addToHeap` adds an element to the min-heap using the standard algorithm for inserting into a heap thus maintaining the min-heap properties after each insertion into the heap. After the following code is executed,

```
while (!q.isempty())
{
    hp.addToHeap(q.dequeue());
}
while (!s.isempty())
{
    hp.addToHeap(s.pop());
}
```

which of the following min-heaps is a representation of `hp`?

a.

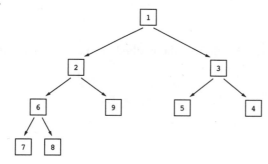

b.

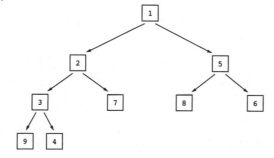

c.

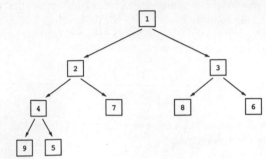

d.

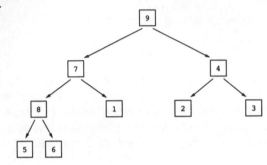

e.

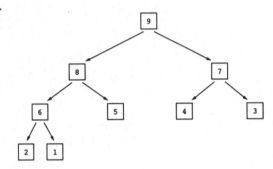

15. **(AB)** The linked list class, `java.util.LinkedList`, defines the method `addLast()`. The run-time efficiency of this `addLast` method is:

a. $O(1)$
b. $O(\log(n))$
c. $O(n)$
d. $O(n \log(n))$
e. $O(n^2)$

Questions 16 and 17 refer to the following partial class declaration.

```
public class LList
{
   public LList()
   {
      first = null;
   }

   public void addLast(Object obj)
   {
      ListNode newNode = new ListNode(obj, null);
      if (first == null)
      {
         first = newNode();
```

```
        }
        else
        {
            ListNode temp = first;
            while (temp.getNext() != null)
            {
                temp = temp.getNext();
            }
            temp.setNext(newNode);
        }
    }

    public void addLastRecursive(Object obj)
    {
        first = addLastHelper(first, obj);
    }

    private ListNode addLastHelper(ListNode list, Object obj)
    {
        // Code goes here
    }

    // ... Other methods and data not shown
    private ListNode first;
}
```

16. **(AB)** The linked list class, `LList`, defines the method `addLast()`. The run-time efficiency of this `addLast` method is:

 a. $O(1)$
 b. $O(\log(n))$
 c. $O(n)$
 d. $O(n \log(n))$
 e. $O(n^2)$

17. **(AB)** The `LList` method `addLastRecursive`, with its helper method `addLastHelper`, is intended to have the same result as the `LList` method `addLast` defined above. Which of the following is a correct implementation of `addLastHelper`?

 a.
```
    private ListNode addLastHelper(ListNode list, Object obj)
    {
        if (list == null)
        {
            return new ListNode(obj, null);
        }
        else
        {
            addLastHelper(list.getNext(), obj);
            return list;
        }
    }
```

 b.
```
    private ListNode addLastHelper(ListNode list, Object obj)
    {
        if (list == null)
        {
            list = new ListNode(obj, null);
        }
        else
        {
            list = (addLastHelper(list.getNext(), obj));
        }
        return list;
```

```
        }
    c.  private ListNode addLastHelper(ListNode list, Object obj)
        {
            if (list == null)
            {
                return new ListNode(obj, null);
            }
            else
            {
                return addLastHelper(list.getNext(), obj);
            }
        }
    d.  private ListNode addLastHelper(ListNode list, Object obj)
        {
            if (list == null)
            {
                return new ListNode(obj, null);
            }
            else
            {
                list.setNext(addLastHelper(list.getNext(), obj));
                return list;
            }
        }
    e.  private ListNode addLastHelper(ListNode list, Object obj)
        {
            if (list == null)
            {
                return new ListNode(obj, null);
            }
            else
            {
                list.setNext(addLastHelper(new ListNode(obj, null), obj));
                return list;
            }
        }
```

18. **(AB)** Which of the following statements about the LList methods addLast and addLastRecursive is **true**?

    a. addLastRecursive is always more efficient than addLast.
    b. addLast is always more efficient than addLastRecursive.
    c. For small lists, there is no significant difference in efficiencies between addLast and addLastRecursive.
    d. addLast is only more efficient than addLastRecursive if the elements are added to the list in increasing order.
    e. addLast is only more efficient than addLastRecursive if the elements are added to the list in decreasing order.

19. You have been asked to write a program that will serve as a Spanish-English dictionary of commonly used words and phrases. If the input to your program is a word or phrase in English, your program should output the equivalent word or phrase in Spanish. Which of the following data structures would be the best choice if you will be adding information to your dictionary and doing many look-ups in the dictionary?

a. An array list of maps where each key is a string representing the English word or phrase and each value is the corresponding Spanish word or phrase.

b. A `HashMap` where each key is a string representing the English word or phrase and each value is the corresponding Spanish word or phrase.

c. A `TreeMap` where each key is a string representing the English word or phrase and each value is the corresponding Spanish word or phrase.

d. An unordered linked list of `Words` where a `Word` object has an accessor method that can return the Spanish form of the English word.

e. An ordered linked list of `Words` where a `Word` object that has an accessor method that can return the Spanish form of the English word.

20. Consider the incomplete `BinaryTree` class below.

```
/*
    This class implements a binary tree whose nodes hold objects that
    implement the Comparable interface.
*/
public class BinaryTree
{
    // Constructs an empty tree.
    public BinaryTree() {. . .}

    // Returns true if root == null, false otherwise.
    public boolean isEmpty() {. . .}

    /*
        Inserts a new node into the tree in order using the Binary
        Search Tree insert algorithm. obj is the object to insert
    */
    public void insert(Comparable obj) {. . .}

    // Prints the TreeNode values using an in-order traversal order.
    public void inOrder() {. . .}

    public void swapBigAndSmall()
    {
        // Code goes here
    }

    private TreeNode root;
}
```

The `BinaryTree` method `swapBigAndSmall` is intended to exchange the largest and smallest values in the tree. For example, suppose the integers 15, 8, 25, 6, 14, 24, 20, 22, 30, 13, 26, were inserted into a tree in the order given. An inorder traversal of the tree would print:

6 8 13 14 15 20 22 24 25 26 30

After a call to `swapBigAndSmall`, an inorder traversal of the same tree would print

30 8 13 14 15 20 22 24 25 26 6

Which of the following code segments could be the body of `swapBigAndSmall` so that the intended task is completed?

```
I.  TreeNode temp = root;
    TreeNode temp2 = root;
    while (temp.getLeft() != null)
    {
        temp2 = temp;
        temp = temp.getLeft();
    }
    TreeNode almostSmall = temp2;
    temp = root;
    temp2 = root;
```

```
        while (temp.getRight() != null)
        {
            temp2 = temp;
            temp = temp.getRight();
        }
        TreeNode almostBig = temp2;
        temp = almostSmall.getLeft();
        almostSmall.setLeft(almostBig.getRight());
        almostBig.setRight(temp);

II. TreeNode temp = root;
        TreeNode temp2 = root;
        while (temp.getLeft() != null)
        {
            temp2 = temp;
            temp = temp.getLeft();
        }
        TreeNode small = temp;
        temp = root;
        temp2 = root;
        while (temp.getRight() != null)
        {
            temp2 = temp;
            temp = temp.getRight();
        }
        TreeNode big = temp;
        Object tempValue = small.getValue();
        small.setValue(big.getValue());
        big.setValue(tempValue);

III. TreeNode temp = root;
        TreeNode temp2 = root;
        while (temp.getLeft() != null)
        {
            temp2 = temp;
            temp = temp.getLeft();
        }
        TreeNode almostSmall = temp2;
        temp = root;
        temp2 = root;
        while (temp.getRight() != null)
        {
            temp2 = temp;
            temp = temp.getRight();
        }
        TreeNode almostBig = temp2;
        almostSmall.setLeft(almostBig.getRight());
        almostBig.setRight(almostSmall.getLeft());
```

a. I only
b. II only
c. III only
d. I and II only
e. I, II, and III

Free Response

1. (Java 5) A combination can be thought of as an unordered list of elements. For example, consider individuals: Tom, Dick, Harry, and Romeo. To form a committee of three individuals from this group of four, we look at combinations. There are four such combinations: [Tom, Dick, Harry], [Tom, Dick, Romeo], [Tom, Harry, Romeo], and [Dick, Harry, Romeo]. The ordering of the members of the

committee doesn't matter. The committee [Dick, Harry, Romeo] is the same committee as [Romeo, Dick, Harry] and so both orders would not be included in a list of all combinations.

The `CombinationGenerator` class generates all combinations that can be formed with a given set of integers. The incomplete `CombinationGenerator` class is below.

```
public class CombinationGenerator
{
    /*
        Constructor creates a display of digits.
        numberOfPositions is the number of positions diplayed
        startNum is the lowest number appearing in the combination
        endNum is the highest number appearing in the combination
    */
    public CombinationGenerator(int numberOfPositions,
            int startNum, int endNum) {. . .}

    // Returns the next combination display.
    public ArrayList<Integer> nextElement() {...}

    // Returns true if there are more combinations, false otherwise.
    public boolean hasMoreElements() {. . .}

    // Private instance fields declared here
}
```

The program segment

```
CombinationGenerator combs = new CombinationGenerator(3, 0, 4);
while (combs.hasMoreElements())
{
    System.out.println(combs.nextElement() + " ");
}
```

would print array lists of size 3, containing combinations of integer values from 0 to 4 inclusive:

[0, 1, 2] [0, 1, 3] [0, 1, 4] [0, 2, 3] [0, 2, 4] [0, 3, 4] [1, 2, 3] [1, 2, 4] [1, 3, 4] [2, 3, 4]

A high school wishes to use this program to generate combinations of players for the starting line-ups for its teams. For example, suppose there is a total of 8 members of the basketball team. A starting line-up consists of 5 players. The coach wants to generate all possible 5-player starting line-ups formed from the 8 members of the basketball team. For example, if the players are stored as a team in the array list as [James, John, Bob, Larry, Henry, Tom, Michael, Norman] then the combination generator

```
CombinationGenerator combs = new CombinationGenerator(5, 0, 7);
```

would generate all possible team combinations and the combination [0, 1, 2, 3, 7] would represent the team consisting of the players [James, John, Bob, Larry, Norman] (array list positions in the team). The incomplete definitions for the `Player` class and the abstract `Team` class are given below.

Player Class

```
public class Player
{
    // Constructor
    public Player(String firstName, String lastName, int jerseyNumber,
        String position) {. . .}

    // Returns player name.
    public String getName() {. . .}

    // Returns player's jersey number.
    public int getJersey() {. . .}
```

```
                  // Returns player's position.
                  public String getPosition() {. . .}

                  // Returns string representation of this player.
                  public String toString() {. . .}

                  // Other methods here
                  // Private instance fields here
          }
```

Team Class

```
        public abstract class Team
        {
            public Team(String fileName, String ratingFile, int number)
            {
                myTeam = new ArrayList<Player>();
                getTeamInfo(fileName);
                ratings = setRatingInfo(ratingFile);
                numberOnLineUp = number;
                startingLineUps = null;
            }

            // Fills myTeam with player information from fileName.
            private void getTeamInfo(String fileName) {. . .}

            // Returns string representation of all players on myTeam.
            public String toString() {. . .}

            // Prints player information of particular ArrayList of players.
            public void printLineUpInfo(ArrayList<Player> p) {. . .}

            // Returns the number of total members on team.
            public int getTeamSize() {. . .}

            // Returns rating of thisTeam.
            public int getLineUpRating(ArrayList<Player> thisTeam)
            {
                // Code goes here
            }

            // Reads player rating information from file and stores in SomeDataType.
            private SomeDataType setRatingInfo(String fileName)
            {
                // Code goes here
                return playerRatings;
            }

            /*
                Returns ArrayList of Players given player positions in
                ArrayList of Integers.
            */
            public ArrayList<Player> getPlayersInLineUp(ArrayList<Integer> bb)
            {
                // Code goes here
            }

            // Prints all valid starting lineups.
            public void printValidStartingTeams()
            {
                // Code goes here
            }
```

```
    // Returns the valid lineup that has the highest rating.
    public ArrayList<Player> getBestTeam()
    {
        // Code goes here
    }

    // Returns true if this lineup of players is valid, false otherwise.
    public abstract boolean isLineUpValid(ArrayList<Player> p);

    private ArrayList<Player> myTeam;
    private SomeDataType ratings;
    private CombinationGenerator startingLineUps;
    private int numberOnLineUp;
}
```

A basketball team is a team with 5 players in its starting line-up. An incomplete class definition for `BbTeam` is given below.

BbTeam Class

```
public class BbTeam extends Team
{
    public BbTeam(String fileName, String ratingFileName, int number)
    {
        super(fileName, ratingFileName, number);
    }

    /*
        Returns true if this lineup has exactly 2 guards, 2 forwards,
        and 1 center, otherwise returns false.
    */
    public boolean isLineUpValid(ArrayList<Player> lineup)
    {
        // Code goes here
    }
}
```

a. Write the implementation of the `Team` method `getPlayersInLineUp` that will return the `ArrayList<Player>` chosen from `myTeam` that corresponds to its parameter, an `ArrayList<Integer>` that was generated by the `CombinationGenerator`. For example, if `myTeam` contains [James, John, Bob, Larry, Henry, Tom, Michael, Norman] and lineup contains [1, 2, 4, 5, 7] then `getPlayersInLineUp` would return [John, Bob, Henry, Tom, Norman]. Use the header below in writing `getPlayersInLineUp`.

```
public ArrayList<Player> getPlayersInLineUp(ArrayList<Integer> bb)
```

b. Write the implementation of the `BbTeam` method `isLineUpValid` that returns true if the line-up is a valid starting line-up and false otherwise. A valid starting line-up for a Basketball team must have 2 forwards, 2 guards, and 1 center. Player positions returned by `Player` method `getPosition` will be one of the `String` values `"center"`, `"guard"`, or `"forward"`. Use the header below in writing `isLineUpValid`.

```
public boolean isLineUpValid(ArrayList<Player> lineup)
```

c. A coach wishes to list all possible valid line-ups for a basketball team. The following code segment is intended to do that task.

```
BbTeam bb = new BbTeam("PlayerFileName", "RatingFileName", 5);
bb.printValidStartingTeams();
```

Write the implementation of the `Team` method `printValidStartingTeams` that will print the valid starting lineups for the basketball team.

d. Explain why the class `Team` is an abstract class.

e. **(AB only)** Player ratings are recorded in a text file in the following format:

0 55 7
52 11 3

where the first two integers on a line represent the jersey numbers of two players and the last integer on the line represents the rating (on a scale from 1 to 10 inclusive) of how well the two players play together. Jersey numbers are in the range 0 to 99 inclusive. If a pair of players is not listed in the file, they are assigned a default rating of 5. The `Team` method `setRatingInfo` reads the file information and fills some data structure with this rating information. An incomplete implementation of `setRatingInfo` is below.

```
private SomeDataType setRatingInfo(String fileName)
{
    final int defaultRating = 5;

    // Code goes here: Declare and initialize playerRatings here

    // fileName is open for reading
    while //  (there is still information to read in the file)
    {
        readFromFile(jersey1);
        readFromFile(jersey2);
        readFromFile(pairRating);
        // Code goes here
    }
    return playerRatings;
}
```

In determining the rating for a team, the sum of the ratings of all possible players on the team is calculated. Describe a data structure that you would use to store this rating information that would allow for quick retrieval of pair ratings.

f. **(AB only)** Using the data structure chosen in part d, declare and initialize `playerRatings`.

g. **(AB only)** Write the code that would replace the comment // *Code goes here* and fill `playerRatings`.

h. **(AB only)** Based on the data structure chosen in part d, write the implementation of the `Team` method `getLineUpRating` that will return the integer rating of its parameter `thisTeam`. This rating is found by calculating the sum of the ratings of all possible players on `thisTeam`. You may assume that method `setRatingInfo` works as intended regardless of what you wrote for parts f and g.

```
public int getLineUpRating(ArrayList<Player> thisTeam)
```

i. Write the implementation of the `Team` method `getBestTeam` that returns the valid lineup with the highest rating. You may assume that the methods written in previous parts of this problem work as intended. Use the header below in writing `getBestTeam`.

```
public ArrayList<Player> getBestTeam()
```

2. (Java 5) **(AB only)** A polynomial is stored as a tree map with `Integer` keys and values. If $c * x^i$ is a term of the polynomial, then we add the following correspondence to the map:

```
poly.put(new Integer(i), new Integer(c))
```

The incomplete `Polynomial` class is below.

Polynomial Class

```
public class Polynomial
{
    // Constructs an empty polynomial.
    public Polynomial()
    {
        poly = new TreeMap<Integer, Integer>();
    }

    // Adds a term to this polynomial.
    public void addTerm(Integer exponent, Integer coefficient)
    {
        poly.put(exponent, coefficient);
    }

    /*
        Returns the String representation of this polynomial with the
        term having the largest exponent being first.
    */
    public String toString()
    {
        // Code goes here
    }

    // Returns the value of the polynomial for x.
    public double evaluatePolynomial(double x)
    {
        // Code goes here
    }

    // Returns a polynomial that is the sum of this polynomial and other.
    public Polynomial add(Polynomial other)
    {
        // Code goes here
    }

    // Returns a polynomial that is the product of this polynomial and
    // other.
    public Polynomial multiply(Polynomial other)
    {
        // Code goes here
    }

    private TreeMap<Integer, Integer> poly;
}
```

a.   Write the `Polynomial` method `toString` that returns the string representation of the polynomial. The representation is such that the term with the largest exponent is first and the other terms appear in decreasing exponent order. For example, 2x^5 + 4x^3 + 6x^2 + 7x + 8 is one such string representation. Use the header below in writing `toString`.

```
public String toString()
```

b.   Write the `Polynomial` method `evaluatePolynomial` that will return the value of the polynomial found by substituting its `double` parameter into the polynomial. For example, if `p1` is the `Polynomial` representing $2x^5 + 4x^3 + 6x^2 + 7x + 8$, `p1.evaluatePolynomial(1)` would return 27. Use the header below in writing `evaluatePolynomial`.

```
public double evaluatePolynomial(double x)
```

c. Write the `Polynomial` method `add` that returns the sum of this `Polynomial` and its `Polynomial` parameter. For example, if $p1 = 2x^5 + 4x^3 + 6x^2 + 7x + 8$ and $p2 = 3x^2 + 4x + 7$ then `p1.add(p2)` would return the `Polynomial` representing $2x^5 + 4x^3 + 9x^2 + 11x + 15$. Use the header below in writing `add`.

```
public Polynomial add(Polynomial other)
```

d. Write the `Polynomial` method `multiply` that returns the product of this `Polynomial` and its `Polynomial` parameter. For example, if $p1 = 3x + 1$ and $p2 = 2x + 3$ then `p1.multiply(p2)` would return the `Polynomial` representing $6x^2 + 11x + 3$. Use the header below in writing `multiply`.

```
public Polynomial multiply(Polynomial other)
```

CHAPTER 19

The AP Exam Case Study

■ Topic Summary

19.1   What Is a Case Study?

A case study is a document that includes a problem statement, a program that solves the problem, and a narrative discussing the steps taken and the decisions made in developing the problem solution. Case studies have been used for years to teach law, medicine, business, and science. Case studies were added to the AP Computer Science curriculum in 1994. The AP CS Case Study contains a large program, written by experts, that is meant to serve as a good programming example. The narrative discusses the development of this program. Within the narrative there are exercises and analysis questions. Through these questions and the questions posed within the narrative, development options are explored as they would be before development decisions are made. This enables you, the student, to act as an apprentice in the programming situation. You will be learning from the experts as you work through the program. The case study narrative makes it clear that having a program that just "works" should never be the focus of a software system — the process of arriving at a solution is just as important as the final product itself. In Chapter 14 we discussed the software life cycle. This cycle consists of five distinct processes.

- Analysis
- Design
- Implementation
- Testing
- Deployment

The focus of the case study is to become familiar with each of these five processes as they relate to the particular case study problem. You will be able to study the different alternatives to a problem solution and you will understand why certain choices were made in each step of the software life cycle.

The exercises and analysis questions guide you through the software life cycle for the case study problem. Do not skip these questions and do not "leave them for later." Completing the questions as you go through the case study document allows for an understanding of the complete development process.

19.2   Why Are Case Studies Included in AP CS?

The AP CS Exam consists of 40 multiple-choice questions and 4 free-response questions. Answering these types of questions would not necessarily indicate that you have ever worked with a program of any size. Since AP Computer Science parallels the first semester or two of university-level computer science courses, and since universities generally require the development and completion of larger programs, the case study offers a method for ensuring that AP CS students have some experience with a large program. This case study program requires you to read a very large program written by someone else. By working with the case study, you will gain experience modifying and extending a large program, and you will be exposed to a good programming example written by experts. The exercises throughout the case study deal with all stages of development and encourage you think through design and implementation tradeoffs.

19.3   How Do I Use the Case Study During the School Year?

The case study will help develop critical thinking skills. You should begin reading the case study very early in the year. It is important that you become familiar with the current case study documents. If possible, you should visit the case study several times throughout the AP CS course. Do not wait until two weeks before the exam to look at the document for the first time. The case study will help you learn computer science concepts. Studying the case study will improve your performance throughout the course, not just on the case study exam questions. Complete all of the exercises and analysis questions as you go through the case study. These questions will help you understand the design decisions and programming alternatives. Research has indicated that the more time spent on the case study, the better the mastery of all AP CS material.

19.4   How Do I Prepare for the Case Study Questions on the AP Exam?

Familiarize yourself with the goal of the case study. Review the exercises and analysis questions before the exam. There may be different requirements for the A and AB Exams. Be aware of the material that is covered on the AP Exam that you will be taking. You can find this information on the College Board Web site listed at the end of this chapter.

You will be given certain documents during the AP CS Exam. You may use these documents throughout the multiple-choice and free-response parts of the exam. These documents include the AP CS A or AB Quick Reference Guide and portions of the case study document. The case study materials will include the source code for the visible classes, a summary of class documentation for the black box classes (the classes whose code you are not responsible for knowing), and an index for the source code. All of these documents are available to you during the school year and are found in the case study narrative document. Become familiar with these resources.

Be familiar with the classes that are included in the case study. Understand the constructors, accessor methods, and modifier methods for each class. Know the class dependencies and inheritance hierarchies. Be able to modify and extend the existing classes. You should have quite a bit of experience with this already if you have been faithfully completing the questions and exercises and implementing these changes in the case study.

Remember that there will be 5–10 multiple-choice questions and one free-response question directly related to the case study. These questions may include tasks such as:
- Extend the case study code by writing a new method, class, or subclass.
- Give a different design for a class.
- Design an entirely new class.
- Design a set of interacting classes. **(AB only)**
- Give an alternative choice of data structure.
- Implement a given method using an alternative data structure or approach.
- Develop test data for a particular implementation.
- Explain the interaction and dependencies among classes.
- Analyze given code, explaining how it might be made more efficient.
- Give the big-Oh analysis for a particular algorithm. **(AB only)**
- Modify classes based on an alternative problem description.

Do not wait until the exam to look at the case study resources! Time is very valuable during the exam period. Read the exam questions carefully. They may be simple modifications of problems that you have already done.

19.5   Where Do I Get the Case Study?

The case study consists of several parts. The required material is available for you to download from the College Board Web site. Important College Board links are listed below.

Information on the current case study:

http://www.collegeboard.com/student/testing/ap/compsci_a/case.html?compscia

You can access general information about the Advanced Placement Program at:

http://www.collegeboard.com/student/testing/ap/about.html

Current information about AP Computer Science:

AP CS A: http://www.collegeboard.com/student/testing/ap/sub_compscia.html?compscia

AP CS AB: http://www.collegeboard.com/student/testing/ap/sub_compsciab.html?compscia

APPENDIX A

Exercise Solutions

■ Chapter 2

Answers to Multiple Choice Questions

1.	a	5.	c	9.	d
2.	b	6.	e	10.	d
3.	e	7.	e		
4.	b	8.	e		

Notes on Answers

6. The entire body of the `void` method is a comment. There is no error but nothing is printed.

■ Chapter 3

Answers to Multiple Choice Questions

1.	b	5.	e	9.	e
2.	c	6.	a	10.	d
3.	a	7.	c		
4.	a	8.	d		

Notes on Answers

9. Modifiers change the state of the object. I, II, and III all change the attributes (or state) of the `Rectangle` object. The correct anwer is e.
10. Accessors do not change the state of an object. The methods `getY` and `getHeight` return information about the object without changing the state. The correct answer is d.

■ Chapter 4

Answers to Multiple Choice Questions

1. c   5. e   9. a
2. d   6. e   10. b
3. d   7. e
4. a   8. d

Notes on Answers

5. b1 and b2 are BankAccount objects.

```
b1.deposit(b2.getBalance());    // deposits 500 in b1
                                // b1 balance now 1000
                                // b2 balance now 500
b2.deposit(b1.getBalance());    // deposits 1000 in b2
                                // b1 balance now 1000
                                // b2 balance now 1500
```

6. b2 and b1 reference the same BankAccount object.

```
BankAccount b1 = new BankAccount(500);
BankAccount b2 = b1;    // balance of b1 and b2 is 500
b1.deposit(b2.getBalance());    // balance of b1 and b2 is 1000
b2.deposit(b1.getBalance());    // balance of b1 and b2 is 2000
```

Answers to Free Response

1a.
```
public Employee(String firstName, String lastName, double moneyEarned)
{
    myFirstName = myfirstName;
    myLastName = mylastName;
    salary = moneyEarned;
}
```

1b.
```
public void raiseSalary(double byPercent)
{
    double amountOfRaise = byPercent / 100 * salary;
    salary = salary + amountOfRaise;
}
```

1c.
```
public double calculateBonusAmount(double byPercent)
{
    return (salary * byPercent / 100);
}
```

2a.
```
public Book(String name, String writer, double cost)
{
    title = name;
    author = writer;
    price = cost;
}
```

2b.
```
public void giveDiscount(double byPercent)
{
    double amountOfDiscount = byPercent / 100 * price;
    double newPrice = price - amountOfDiscount;
    price = newPrice;
}
```

■ Chapter 5

Answers to Multiple Choice Questions

1. c	4. d	7. a	10. e
2. c	5. a	8. e	
3. c	6. b	9. d	

Answers to Free Response

1a.
```
public double findGasUsed(double numMiles)
{
    return numMiles / mpg;
}
```

1b.
```
public void drive(double numMiles)
{
    mileage += numMiles;
    double gas = findGasUsed(numMiles);
    gasInTank -= gas;
}
```

2a.
```
public int totalInPennies()
{
    return (int) (PENNIES_PER_DOLLAR * getTotal())
}
```

2b.
```
public int getDollars()
{
    int amount = totalInPennies();
    return amount / PENNIES_PER_DOLLAR;
}
```

2c.
```
public int getCents()
{
    int amount = totalInPennies();
    return amount % PENNIES_PER_DOLLAR;
}
```

■ Chapter 6

Answers to Multiple Choice Questions

1. d	5. d	9. e
2. b	6. d	10. c
3. e	7. e	
4. a	8. c	

Notes on Answers

1. This is an example of a *dangling-else*. The else goes with the closest if regardless of the indentation. Indentation does not control the flow of the program execution. The answer is d.

```
x = 6;
y = 19;
z = 2;    // x = 6, y = 19, z = 2
if (x > y)    // x is not greater than y so this if-else is not executed.
    if (z > x)
        z++;
    else
        z -= 5;
y += x;    // x = 6, y = 19 + 6 = 25, z = 2
```

4. The answer is a.

```
foo = word.substring(1, 3) = "om"
hoo = word.substring(4) = "ute"
if (foo.compareTo(hoo) < 0)   // true
{
    hoo += foo;   // hoo is now "uteom", foo is "om".
}
else
{
    foo += hoo;
}
```

7. The correct answer is e.

```
string2 = string1;   // string2 now references "Hello"
string1 += "There!";   // A new string is created. The variable string1
                       // references this new string ("HelloThere") and
                       // string2 still references "Hello".
```

8. Choice I is incorrect because a client program is trying to access private instance fields. Choice II is incorrect because `equals` is not specifically defined for the `Point` class and so the call to `equals` would return `true` if and only if `p1` and `p2` are reference the same object but `p1` and `p2` can have the same *x*- and *y*- coordinates and be referencing different objects. The correct answer is c.

9. Choices I and III are both correct because a class can access its private variables. Choice II is not correct because `equals` is not used with primitive types.

10. De Morgan's Law. The correct answer is c.

Answers to Free Response

1a.
```
public double gasNeeded(double numMiles)
{
    return numMiles / mpg;
}
```

1b.
```
public boolean enoughGas(double numMiles)
{
    return gasNeeded(numMiles) <= gasInTank;
}
```

1c.
```
public void getGas()
{
    if (gasInTank < 0.5 * tankCapacity)
    gasInTank = tankCapacity;
}
```

1d.
```
public void drive(double numMiles)
{
    if (enoughGas(numMiles))
    {
        mileage += numMiles;
        gasInTank -= gasNeeded(numMiles);
    }
    else
    {
        double milesToGo = gasInTank * mpg;
        mileage += milesToGo;
        gasInTank = 0;
    }
}
```

```
2a. public double getDistanceFromOrigin()
    {
        double d = Math.sqrt(x * x + y * y);
        return d;
    }

2b. public static Point findFarPoint(Point p1, Point p2, Point p3)
    {
        double d1 = p1.getDistanceFromOrigin();
        double d2 = p2.getDistanceFromOrigin();
        double d3 = p3.getDistanceFromOrigin();

        double longest = d1;
        Point far = p1;
        if (d2 > longest)
        {
            longest = d2;
            far = p2;
        }
        if (d3 > longest)
        {
            longest = d3;
            far = p3;
        }
        return far;
    }
```

■ Chapter 7

Answers to Multiple Choice Questions

1.	c	6.	a	11.	c
2.	e	7.	c	12.	c
3.	d	8.	c	13.	c
4.	e	9.	e	14.	b
5.	c	10.	d	15.	c

Notes on Answers

4. All loops result in the desired output. The values of the loop control variables appear in the first two columns of each table. The third column shows the printed result at the completion of each execution of the outer loop.

Choice I

i	j	*Prints the value of i for each j*
4	1	4
3	2, 1	33
2	3, 2, 1	222
1	4, 3, 2, 1	1111

Choice II

i	j	Prints 4 − i + 1 for each j
1	1	4
2	1, 2	33
3	1, 2, 3	222
4	1, 2, 3, 4	1111

Choice III

i	j	Prints 4 − i + 1 for each j
1	4	4
2	4, 3	33
3	4, 3, 2	222
4	4, 3, 2, 1	1111

5. The answer is c. For each execution of the `while` loop, a's value is increased by the last digit of the current value of n (n % 10 gives you the last digit of n). Then n is divided by 10 so that the new value of n is the old value of n without the last digit. This process continues until n <= 0.

9. Choice I checks each letter of the string `"aeiou"` for an occurrence in `word`. If that letter occurs (no matter how many times) `count` is incremented by 1. For example. if `word` = `level`, `count` would return 1. This choice is incorrect. The correct answer is e.

10. A loop invariant is a statement that is true before the loop is executed, at the beginning of each execution of the loop and after the loop terminates. In this problem, `p` and `i` are initialized to 1 and n is a positive integer.

```
while (i <= n)
{
   p = p * i;
   i++;
}
```

Clearly, the code calculates *n* factorial (*n!*). Eliminate choice e (the code is not calculating *n* to a power). Since *n* could begin with the value 1, choices a and b are incorrect. When the loop terminates, *i* = *n* + 1 so choice c is not correct. Choice d is the correct answer.

14. Assuming that the original number is a positive integer, the loop continuously divides by 2 (incrementing x each time this division is done) until the quotient is 0. When the loop terminates, number of divisions-by-2 made is x. Therefore, x is the smallest power of 2 such that $2^x \geq n$. The correct answer is b.

15. From the explanation of 14 above, 5 is the smallest power of 2 that is greater than or equal to 32. The correct answer is c.

Answers to Free Response

```
1a. public void waitForYears(int y)
    {
       for (int i = 1; i <= y; i++)
       {
          double interest = balance * rate / 100;
          balance += interest;
       }
    }
```

1b.
```
public void compoundTheInterest(int y, int n)
{
    for (int year = 1; year <= y; year++)
    {
        for (int numTimes = 1; numTimes <= n; numTimes++)
        {
            double interest = balance * rate / 100 / n;
            balance += interest;
        }
    }
}
```

2a.
```
public Game()
{
    myWheel = new Spinner(4);
}
```

2b.
```
public int spinTheWheel()
{
    int number = myWheel.spin();
    if (number >= 2)
        return number;
    else return 0;
}
```

2c.
```
public double playRoulette(Purse myPurse)
{
    double myMoney = myPurse.getTotal();
    double myEndMoney = 2 * myMoney;
    Coin aCoin;

    while (myPurse.coinCount() > 0 && myPurse.getTotal() < myEndMoney)
    // Comparing the int coinCount to 0 rather than
    // worrying about precision errors when comparing doubles
    {
        aCoin = myPurse.removeCoin();
        int r = spinTheWheel();    // Value of r is 0, 2, or 3
        for (int i = 1; i <= r; i++)
        {
            myPurse.add(new Coin(aCoin.getValue(), aCoin.getName()));
            // Actually add new coins to myPurse--not
            // references to the same coin!
        }
    }
    return myPurse.getTotal();
}
```

■ Cumulative Review 1

Answers to Multiple Choice Questions

1. a	8. d	15. d
2. e	9. d	16. e
3. e	10. d	17. d
4. d	11. d	18. d
5. b	12. e	19. d
6. c	13. c	20. b
7. b	14. d	

16. The loop is executed 11 times. `vowels.substring(0)` evaluates to `"aeiou"`. Because the string `"aeiou"` is not found in `"mathematics"`, `-1` is added to `number` 11 times and the resulting value of `number` is `-11`. The correct answer is e.

17. One 6-sided die is rolled and its value is stored in `rand`. Four more dice are rolled. If the value on the rolled die is not equal to `rand`, `false` is returned. The method returns `true` only if all five dice result with the same value, `rand`.

Answers to Free Response Questions

1a.
```java
public int numDigits()
{
    int num = myNum;
    int digits = 0;
    while (num > 0)
    {
        num = (num / 10);
        digits++;
    }
    return digits;
}
```

Alternate Solution

```java
public int numDigits()
{
    String s = "" + myNum;
    return s.length();
}
```

Alternate Solution 2

```java
public int numDigits()
{
    return toString.length();
}
```

1b.
```java
public int sumDigits()
{
    int temp = myNum;
    int sum = 0;
    while (temp > 0)
    {
        sum += temp % 10;
        temp = temp / 10;
    }
    return sum;
}
```

1c.
```java
public boolean isPerfect()
{
    int sum = 0;
    for (int i = 1; i < myNum / 2; i++)
    {
        if (myNum % i == 0)
        {
            sum += i;
        }
    }
    return (sum == myNum);
}
```

1d.
```java
public FunNumber reverseNum()
{
    int rev = 0;
    int pow = 0
    int digits = 0;
    int temp = myNum;
    while (temp > 0)
    {
        digits = temp % 10;
        rev = 10 * rev + digits;
        temp = temp / 10;
    }
    FunNumber reversedNumber = new FunNumber(rev);
    return reversedNumber;
}
```

Alternate Solution

```java
public FunNumber reverseNum()
{
    String s = toString();
    String newString = "";
    for (int i = s.length() - 1; i >= 0; i--)
        newString += s.substring(i, i + 1);
    FunNumber reversedNumber = new FunNumber(newString);
    return reversedNumber;
}
```

Alternate Solution 2

```java
public FunNumber reverseNum()
{
    String s = "";
    int temp = myNum;
    while (temp > 0)
    {
        s = (temp % 10) + s;
        temp = temp / 10;
    }
    return s;
}
```

2a.
```java
public String getSuit()
{
    if (mySuit.equals("H"))
        return "Hearts";
    else if (mySuit.equals("C"))
        return "Clubs";
    else if (mySuit.equals("D"))
        return "Diamonds";
    else return "Spades";
}
```

2b.
```java
public String getDenomination()
{
    String temp = "";
    if (myValue < 11 && myValue > 1)
        temp = "" + myValue;
    else if (myDenom.equals("J"))
        temp = "Jack";
    else if (myDenom.equals("Q"))
        temp = "Queen";
    else if (myDenom.equals("K"))
        temp = "King";
```

```
            else if (myDenom.equals("A"))
                temp = "Ace";
            return temp;
        }
```

2c. `public int getValue()`

```
    {
        String values = "00234567890JQKA";

        if (myDenom.equals("10"))
            return 10;
        else
            return values.indexOf(myDenom);
    }
```

Alternate Solution

```
public int getvalue()
{
    if (myDenom.equals("10"))
        return 10;
    else if (myDenom.equals("J"))
        return 11;
    else if (myDenom.equals("Q"))
        return 12;
    else if (myDenom.equals("K"))
        return 13;
    else if (myDenom.equals("A"))
        return 14;
    else
    {
        Integer num = new Integer(myDenom);
        return num.intValue();
    }
}
```

2d. `public String toString()`

```
    {
        return getDenomination() + " of " + getSuit();
    }
```

3a. `public boolean isPair()`

```
    {
        return (card1.getValue() == card2.getValue());
    }
```

3b. `public boolean sameSuit()`

```
    {
        return (card1.getSuit().equals(card2.getSuit()));
    }
```

3c. `public boolean sameColor()`

```
    {
        String temp1 = card1.getSuit();
        String temp2 = card2.getSuit();
        if ((temp1.equals("Spades") || temp1.equals("Clubs"))
                && ((temp2.equals("Spades") || temp2.equals("Clubs"))))
        {
            return true;
        }
        if ((temp1.equals("Hearts") || temp1.equals("Diamonds"))
                && (temp2.equals("Hearts") || temp2.equals("Diamonds")))
        {
            return true;
        }
```

```
        else
        {
            return false;
        }
    }
3d. public int getTotal()
    {
        int temp = card1.getValue();
        if (temp > 10)
        {
            if (temp == 14)
            {
                temp = 11;
            }
            else
            {
                temp = 10;
            }
        }
        int temp2 = card2.getValue();
        if (temp2 > 10)
        {
            if (temp == 14)
            {
                temp = 11;
            }
            else
            {
                temp = 10;
            }
        }
        return temp + temp2;
    }
```

■ Chapter 8

Answers to Multiple Choice Questions

1. d	6. a	11. d
2. d	7. b	12. b
3. e	8. e	13. d
4. b	9. b	14. d
5. b	10. d	15. c

Notes on Answers

2. This is an untyped ArrayList of Objects. The method getName must be invoked on a Coin, not an Object or a String.
4. This method returns the number that has the longest sequence of consecutive repeated values in the array.
5. The statement B = A results in B referencing the same array that A references. When a change is made in B, the change also occurs in A.
8. In Java versions prior to Java 5, the parameter would be an untyped array and casting would be necessary.
9. Choice I checks references. To check if arrays have equal values, each element must be checked.

Answers to Free Response

1a.
```java
// Java 5
public FooList(int numLetters)
{
    fooLength = numLetters;
    possibleFoos = new ArrayList<String>();
}
```

Alternate Solution: Versions Prior to Java 5

```java
public FooList(int numLetters)   // Versions prior to Java 5
{
    fooLength = numLetters;
    possibleFoos = new ArrayList();
}
```

1b.
```java
// Java 5
public boolean found(String key)
{
    for (int i = 0; i < possibleFoos.size(); i++)
    {
        String temp = possibleFoos.get(i);
        // Prior versions of Java would need to cast
        // String temp = (String) possibleFoos.get(i);

        if (temp.equals(key))
            return true;
    }
    return false;
}
```

Alternate Iterator Solution Java 5 **(AB)**

```java
public boolean found(String key)
{
    Iterator<String> iter = possibleFoos.iterator();
    while (iter.hasNext())
    {
        String temp = iter.next();
        if (temp.equals(key))
            return true;
    }
    return false;
}
```

1c.
```java
public void addFoo(String entry)
{
    if (entry.length() == fooLength && !found(entry))
    {
        possibleFoos.add(entry);
    }
}
```

1d.
```java
// Java 5
public String removeRandomFoo()
{
    int choice = generator.nextInt(possibleFoos.size());
    String temp = possibleFoos.remove(choice);
    // Prior versions of Java would have to cast
    // String temp = (String) possibleFoos.remove(choice);
    return temp;
}
```

2a.
```java
// Java 5
private void fillBoard()
{
    for (int i = 0; i < size / 2; i++)
    {
        String word = possibleTileValues.removeRandomFoo();
        // Need to cast for versions prior to Java 5
        // String word = (String) possibleTileValues.removeRandomFoo();
        for (int j = 0; j < 2; j++)
        {
            int place = generator.nextInt(size);
            while (gameBoard[place] != null)
            {
                place = generator.nextInt(size);
            }
            gameBoard[place] = new Tile(word);
        }
    }
}
```

2b.
```java
public void lookAtTile(int p)
{
    gameBoard[p].turnFaceUp();
}
```

2c.
```java
public void checkMatch(int pos1, int pos2)
{
    if (gameBoard[pos1].equals(gameBoard[pos2]))
    {
        numberOfTilesFaceUp += 2;
    }
    else
    {
        gameBoard[pos1].turnFaceDown();
        gameBoard[pos2].turnFaceDown();
    }
}
```

2d.
```java
public void printBoard()
{
    final int PADDING = 3;    // spacing of tiles
    int spacing = possibleTileValues.getFooLength() + PADDING;
    for (int i = 0; i < size; i++)
    {
        if (gameBoard[i].isFaceUp())
        {
            String temp = gameBoard[i].showFace();
            System.out.print(format(temp, spacing));
        }
        else
        {
            System.out.print(format(i, spacing));
        }
        if (i % rowLength == rowLength - 1)
            System.out.println("\n");
    }
}
```

```
3a. // Java 5
    private void fillBoard()
    {
       for (int i = 0; i < size / 2; i++)
       {
          String word = possibleTileValues.removeRandomFoo();
          // Need to cast for versions prior to Java 5
          // String word = (String) possibleTileValues.removeRandomFoo();

          for (int j = 0; j < 2; j++)
          {
             int row = generator.nextInt(rowLength);
             int col = generator.nextInt(rowLength);
             while (gameBoard[row][col] != null)
             {
                row = generator.nextInt(rowLength);
                col = generator.nextInt(rowLength);
             }
             gameBoard[row][col] = new Tile(word);
          }
       }
    }

3b. public void printBoard()
    {
       final int PADDING = 8;    // for proper spacing of tiles
       int spaces = possibleTileValues.getFooLength() + PADDING;
       for (int row = 0; row < rowLength; row++)
       {
          for (int col = 0; col < rowLength; col++)
          {
             if (gameBoard[row][col].isFaceUp())
             {
                String temp = gameBoard[row][col].showFace();
                System.out.print(format(temp, spaces));
             }
             else
             {
                String temp = "[" + row + "][" + col + "]";
                System.out.print(format(temp, spaces));
             }
          }
          System.out.println();
       }
    }
```

■ Chapter 9

Answers to Multiple Choice Questions

1. c	5. d	9. c
2. c	6. c	10. c
3. d	7. a	
4. e	8. e	

Notes on Answers

4. Perimeter is not a behavior of a point.

7. `change1` attempts to reassign the parameter reference inside the method body. Parameters to methods cannot change. The method `change2` actually changes the state of the object, not the object reference.

The order of parameters can also be confusing. `student3` is passed to the first parameter `stdt1` of `change2` and `student1` is passed to the second parameter `stdt2` of `change2`.

Answers to Free Response

1a.
```
public class Book
{
    /*
        Constructor
        Precondition: cost > 0
        Postcondition: Book object created
    */
    public Book(String name, String writer, double cost) {. . .}

    // Postcondition: Returns the identification number of the book
    public double getIdentificationNumber() {. . .}

    // Postcondition: Returns author's name
    public String getAuthor() {. . .}

    /*
        Precondition: newPrice > 0
        Postcondition: Book price is updated and now equals newPrice
    */
    public void setPrice(double newPrice) {. . .}

    // Postcondition: Returns price of book
    public double getPrice() {. . .}
}
```

1b.
```
private String title;
private String author;
private double price;
private int idNum;
private static int identification = 0;
```

1c.
```
/*
    Precondition: cost > 0
    Postcondition: Book object created
*/
public Book(String name, String writer, double cost)
{
    if (cost <= 0) throw new IllegalArgumentException();    // AB only
    title = name;
    author = writer;
    price = cost;
    identification++;
    idNum = identification;
}
```

1d. Alternative 1: Throw an exception if the precondition is not met. The advantage is that control will be transferred to the exception handler and if there isn't an exception handler, the program stops. There will be no data corruption. The disadvantage is that the program may stop prematurely.

Alternative 2: Assume the precondition is always satisfied. The advantage is that there is no extra work on the programmer's part. It is the responsibility of the calling method to check the precondition, not the method's responsibility. The disadvantage is that there may be data corruption or other failures that occur that will be the result of the caller's failure to satisfy the precondition.

2a.
```
public class Client
{
    // Constructor
    public Client(String who, int inches, int lbs, String gender) {. . .}
```

```
      // Postcondition: returns client name
      public String getName() {. . .}

      // Postcondition: returns client gender
      public String getGender() {. . .}

      // Postcondition: returns client height
      public int getHeight() {. . .}

      // Postcondition: returns client weight
      public int getWeight() {. . .}

      // setRecommendedCalories omitted

      // Postcondition: returns suggested calorie intake per day
      public int getRecommendedCalories() {...}
   }
```

2b.
```
   private String name;
   private int weight;
   private int height;
   private String gender;
   private int caloriesPerDay;
```

2c.
```
   public void setRecommendedCalories(WeightCalculator plan)
   {
      final int CALORIES_TO_CUT = 500;

      int idealWeight = plan.getIdealWeight(gender, height);
      int calories = plan.getCalorieIntake(gender, height);
      if (idealWeight < weight)
      {
         calories -= CALORIES_TO_CUT;
      }
      caloriesPerDay = calories;
   }
```

■ Chapter 10

Answers to Multiple Choice Questions

1. b	5. a	9. d
2. a	6. e	10. d
3. d	7. d	
4. c	8. a	

Notes on Answers

3. The variable n is initialized before it is used. This initialization occurs when a value is read from the file. Choice I is OK.
   If the file is empty, the while loop is not executed and there is an attempt to calculate the average. However, this calculation fails because count = 0 and there is an attempt to divide by 0. In this case, Choice II causes a runtime error.
   If the file is not empty, when the average is calculated, an integer is divided by an integer and a truncated result may result. For example, if the sum is 10 and count is 4, average will be calculated to be 10 / 4 = 2.0. The average *should be* 2.5. In this case, choice III causes a logic error.
5. According to the precondition, the first parameter to the method weeklyPay must be between 0 and 168 inclusive. All three choices satisfy this precondition. The second parameter to this method must be greater than 0. Choice I is the only choice that violates this. The correct answer is a.

Answers to Free Response Questions

1a. `// Precondition: 0 < amount and amount <= balance`

1b.
```
public void withdraw(double amount)
{
    if (amount > balance)    // (AB students)
    {
        throw new IllegalArgumentException();
    }
    double newBalance = balance - amount;
    balance = newBalance;
}
```

1c. Test cases would include typical values, boundary values, and degenerate values. For the specific example given, test values would include:
- typical test values: 1, 499
- boundary values: 0, 500
- degenerate test values : −1, 501

Specific numerical answers may vary.

■ Chapter 11

Answers to Multiple Choice Questions

1. d   5. c   9. b
2. b   6. c   10. c
3. c   7. a
4. e   8. d

Notes on Answers

2. You cannot instantiate an interface. The correct answer is b.
3. `skyRider2` is a `Flier` and a `Flier` is not an `Athlete` and does not implement the `Athlete` interface. The correct answer is c.
4. `Athlete` does not have a `fly` method. The compiler will complain. The correct answer is e.
5. When converting from an interface type to a class type, you must cast.
   `s = a;` will cause the compiler to complain.
   `s = (SkiJumper) a;` would be OK.
7. Recall the `Flier` interface and the `SkiJumper` class from Examples 11.1 and 11.2 in this guide.
```
Flier f;
Skijumper sj1 = new SkiJumper();
f = sj1;    // This is OK.
sj1 = f;    // This causes a compile time error.
sj1 = (SkiJumper) f;    // This is OK.
```

Answers to Free Response

1a. `public class SkiJumper implements Flier, Athlete, Comparable`

1b.
```
public int compareTo(Object obj)
{
    SkiJumper temp = (SkiJumper) obj;
    if (myNumberOfJumps < temp.myNumberOfJumps)
        return -1;
    if (myNumberOfJumps == temp.myNumberOfJumps)
        return 0;
    return 1;
}
```

Alternate Solution

```java
public int compareTo(Object obj)
{
    SkiJumper temp = (SkiJumper) obj;
    return myNumberOfJumps - temp.myNumberOfJumps;
}
```

2.
```java
public int compareTo(Object obj)
{
    Purse temp = (Purse) obj;
    if (getTotal() < temp.getTotal())
        return -1;
    if (getTotal() > temp.getTotal())
        return 1;
    return 0;
}
```

3a.
```java
public interface Instrument
{
    void setSeatAssignment(String seat);
    String getSeatAssignment();
    void tune();
}
```

3b.
```java
public class BrassInstrument implements Instrument
{
    public BrassInstrument(String theSeat)
    {
        mySeat = theSeat;
    }

    public String getSeatAssignment()
    {
        return mySeat;
    }

    public void setSeatAssignment(String seat)
    {
        mySeat = seat;
    }

    public void tune()
    {
        System.out.println("Tuning middle G");
    }

    private String mySeat;
}
```

■ Chapter 12

Answers to Multiple Choice Questions

1. c	5. e	9. b
2. d	6. a	10. e
3. d	7. e	
4. d	8. e	

Notes on Answers

4. Think of the IS-A relationship. "An `Employee` IS-A `Manager`" is a *false* statement. The correct answer is d.

5. When using the IS-A relationship statement, all choices are OK.

6. The actual type of the object referenced by `employ1` is `Manager` and the actual type of the object referenced to `employ3` is `Manager`. The `work` method called is that of the actual type of the variables, not the reference type.

8. The first statement in the subclass constructor should be a call to the superclass constructor. If it isn't, then the superclass default constructor (if it exists) will be executed before executing code in the subclass constructor.

Answers to Free Response

1a.
```
public Person(String firstName, String lastName)
{
    myFirstName = firstName;
    myLastName = lastName;
    myEmailAddress = myFirstName.substring(0, 1);
    if (myLastName.length() >= 5)
    {
        myEmailAddress += myLastName.substring(0, 5);
        // Substring expression would throw a StringIndexOutOfBoundsException
        // if the length of myLastName is less than 5.
    }
    else
    {
        myEmailAddress += myLastName;
    }
    myEmailAddress += "@jc.com";
}
```

Alternate Solution

```
public Person(String firstName, String lastName)
{
    myFirstName = firstName;
    myLastName = lastName;
    myEmailAddress = myFirstName.substring(0, 1);
    int n = myLastName.length();
    if (n > 5) n = 5;
    myEmailAddress += myLastName.substring(0, n);
}
```

1b.
```
public String toString()
{
    return ("name = " + myFirstName+ " " + myLastName
        + "\nemail address = " + myEmailAddress);
}
```

1c. `public class Student extends Person implements Comparable`

```
1d. public Student(String firstName, String lastName)
    {
        super(firstName, lastName);
        myGpa = 0;
        myNumberOfCredits = 0;
        lastIdAssigned++;
        myStudentId = lastIdAssigned;
    }

1e. public String toString()
    {
        String s = super.toString();
        return s + "\nGPA = " + myGpa + "\nnumber of credits = "
            + myNumberOfCredits + "\nid = " + myStudentId;
    }

1f. public int compareTo (Object other)
    {
        Student temp = (Student) other;
        if (myGpa < temp.myGpa) return -1;
        if (myGpa > temp.myGpa) return 1;
        return 0;
    }

2.  public class Marathoner extends Runner
    {
        public Marathoner(String firstName, String lastName)
        {
            super(firstName, lastName);
        }

        public void race(double raceLength)
        {
            final int minimumRaceLength = 10;
            final double minutesPerMile = 8.5;
            final int minutesPerHour = 60;

            if (raceLength > minimumRaceLength)
            {
                super.race(raceLength);
            }
            else
            {
                double trainingTime = minutesPerMile * raceLength / minutesPerHour;
                train(trainingTime);
            }
        }
    }

3a. Course HAS-A ClassRoster
    Course HAS-A Teacher
    ClassRoster HAS-A Student
    Person HAS-A HomeAddress
```

3b. Hierarchy Diagram

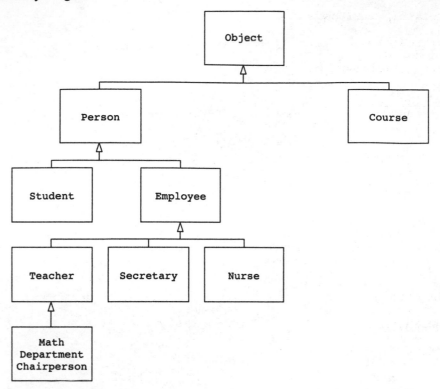

Note: Math Department Chairperson may be subclass of `Employee`. `Nurse` may be subclass of Teacher.

■ Chapter 13

Answers to Multiple Choice Questions

1. b	5. d	9. a
2. a	6. e	10. b
3. d	7. b	
4. c	8. c	

Notes on Answers

2.   There is a division by 0 error at runtime. The answer is a.

3.   `myLastName.substring(0,5)` will cause a `StringIndexOutOfBoundsException` when called on a last name that has fewer than 5 characters. The answer is d.

4.   `"Tote"` has fewer than 5 characters. The answer is c.

5.   Since `"John"` is not found in positions 0, 1, 2, or 3, `count` is incremented in the loop and there is an attempt to check the next (non-existent) element in this array list.

7.   `workers.get(1)` is not a `Manager` object. It was instantiated and added to the array list as an `Employee` object.

8.   Choice II causes a `ClassCastException` and Choice IV causes an `IndexOutOfBounds-Exception`.

10. `IOException` is a checked exception.

Answers to Free Response Questions

1.
```java
public class Teacher extends Person
{
    public Teacher(String first, String last, double money)
    {
        super(first, last);
        if (money <= 0)
        {
            throw new IllegalStateException("Salary must be a
                positive number.");
        }
        salary = money;
    }

    public void getRaise(double more)
    {
        if (more <= 0)
        {
            throw new IllegalArgumentException("Raise must be a
                positive number.");
        }
        salary += more;
    }

    private double salary;
}
```

2a.
```java
private int tossesRemaining;
private Random generator;
```

2b.
```java
public CoinTosser()
{
    generator = new Random();
    tossesRemaining = generator.nextInt(21);
}
```

2c.
```java
public boolean hasMoreTosses()
{
    return (tossesRemaining > 0);
}
```

2d.
```java
public String nextToss()
{
    if (hasMoreTosses())
    {
        tossesRemaining--;
        int toss = generator.nextInt(2);
        if (toss == 1)
            return "HEADS";
        else
            return "TAILS";
    }
    else   // (AB only)
        throw new NoSuchElementException("No tosses remaining.");
}
```

■ Chapter 14

Multiple Choice Questions

1.	a	5.	e	9.	b
2.	c	6.	e	10.	a
3.	a	7.	a		
4.	d	8.	d		

Notes on Answers

6. The best way to attack this problem is to dissect the various parts. The two parts described in the problem are Food Item and Drink Item. They both have a name and a price. Drink Item has a size. Based on this, we should be able to conclude that we need a `FoodItem` class and a `DrinkItem` class. We eliminate choice a. Because `FoodItem` and `DrinkItem` have common elements (name, price), they can inherit from `Item`. We now have to choose between c and e. Hamburgers and hot dogs differ only in name. They should not be separate classes so e is the best choice.

9. "Check trip" is the responsibility of `Trip`. The Trip class holds the responsibility of the trip as a whole. The `Ticket` class is responsible only for knowing about the ticket (whatever it is: airline, boat, etc). `HotelReservation` is responsible for knowing only about the hotel information.

10. Whole trips consist of transportation ticket, hotel reservations, car rentals, etc. These are represented by objects of different classes. There is an unknown number of these objects that constitute a trip. This indicates an array list (number of *objects* in trip list is *not fixed* so choice III is eliminated.). There may be various `CarRental` objects that are part of this trip so choice II is eliminated. Choice I is the only correct answer.

Answers to Free Response

```
1a. public class Car
    {
        public Car(String carMake, int yearMade, double miles)
        {
            make = carMake;
            year = yearMade;
            mileage = miles;
            price = 0;
        }

        public void setPrice(double howMuch)
        {
            price = howMuch;
        }

        public void addMiles(double milesDriven)
        {
            mileage += milesDriven;
        }

        public double getPrice()
        {
            return price;
        }

        public String getMake()
        {
            return make;
        }
```

```
        public int getYear()
        {
           return year;
        }

        public double getMiles()
        {
           return mileage;
        }

        public String toString()
        {
           String s = getYear() + " " + getMake()
                   + "\nMileage: " + getMiles() + " miles"
                   + "\ncosts $" + getPrice() + "\n";
           return s;
        }

        private String make;
        private int year;
        private double price;
        private double mileage;
     }
```

1b.
```
     public void addCar(Car aNewCar)
     {
        if (numberOfCars < MAX_CARS)
        {
           lot[numberOfCars] = aNewCar;
           numberOfCars++;
        }
        else    // AB students
        {
           throw new IllegalStateException("No room in lot.");
        }
     }
```

1c.
```
     public void printCarsInLot()
     {
        for (int i = 0; i < numberOfCars; i++)
        {
           System.out.println(lot[i]);
        }
     }
```

1d.
```
     private ArrayList findMatchingCars(int year, String make)
     {
        ArrayList wantedCars = new ArrayList();
        for (int i = 0; i < numberOfCars; i++)
        {
           Car c = lot[i];
           if (c.getYear()== year && make.equals(c.getMake()))
              wantedCars.add(c);
        }
        return wantedCars;
     }
```

The generic `ArrayList` implementation would be the same except for the `ArrayList` declarations.

```
     private ArrayList<Car> findMatchingCars(int year, String make)
     {
        ArrayList<Car> wantedCars = new ArrayList<Car>();
        . . .
     }
```

1e.
```
public void printMatchingCars(int year, String make)
{
    ArrayList carList = findMatchingCars(year, make);
    if (carList.size() == 0)
       System.out.println("No cars with your specifications are available.");
    else
    {
       System.out.println("Your requested list of available cars:");
       for (int i = 0; i < carList.size(); i++)
       {
           System.out.println(carList.get(i));
       }
    }
}
```

Alternative loop using `Iterators` (can replace the `for` loop):

```
Iterator iter = carList.iterator();
while (iter.hasNext())
{
    System.out.println(iter.next());
}
```

The generic `ArrayList` implementation would be the same except for the `ArrayList` declarations and the optional enhanced `for` loop.

```
public void printMatchingCars(int year, String make)
{
    ArrayList<Car> carList = findMatchingCars(year, make);
    . . .
    for (Car i : carList)
    {
        System.out.println(i);
    }
}
```

2a. (Note: Variable and method names may be different but should be descriptive.)

```
Class name: Employee
Methods:
    // Constructor
    public Employee(String firstName, String lastName)

    public String getName()    // Needed to return name of employee
                               // with highest total sales
    public double getCommission()
    public double getTotalSales()   // Needed to find employee with
                                    // highest total sales
    public int getId()    // Needed to remove employee from company
    public void addSale(double money)

Instance fields:
    private String myFirstName;
    private String myLastName;
    private int idNumber;
    private double totalSales;

Static variables:
    int nextAvailableId;
```

```
Class name: Company
Methods:
   public Company()    // Constructor
   public void addEmployee(Employee worker)
   public ArrayList getEmployeeList()
   public void removeEmployee(int idNum)
   public Employee getHighestSeller()

Instance fields:
   private ArrayList realEstateCompany;    // No static variables needed
```

2b. (Note: Variable names may be different but should be descriptive and consistent with part a.)

```
public class Employee
{
   private static int nextAvailableId = 0;

   Employee(String firstName, String lastName)
   {
      myFirstName = firstName;
      myLastName = lastName;
      nextAvailableId++;
      idNumber = nextAvailableId;
      totalSales = 0;
   }
}
```

2c. (Note: Variable names may be different but should be descriptive and consistent with part a.)

```
public class Company
{
   public Company()
   {
      employeeList = new ArrayList();
   }

   private ArrayList employeeList;
}

public class Company    // Java 5
{
   public Company()
   {
      employeeList = new ArrayList<Employee>();
   }

   private ArrayList<Employee> employeeList;
}
```

3a. SmartPlayer *is-a* Player
    HumanPlayer *is-a* Player
    NimGame *has-a* HumanPlayer
    NimGame *has-a* SmartPlayer
    NimGame *has-a* NimPile

3b. NimGame class

```
public class NimGame
{
    // Constructs game. Creates players and pile of marbles.
    public NimGame(int low, int high) {. . .}
    // Plays game.
    public void playNim() {. . .}

    private HumanPlayer human;
    private NimPile pile;
    private Player computer;
}
```

NimPile class

```
public class NimPile
{
    // Constructs marble pile for Nim with a random number of
    // marbles between a (inclusive) and b (exclusive).
    public NimPile(int a, int b) {. . .}

    // Returns number of marbles in pile.
    public int getMarbles() {. . .}

    // n <= numMarblesInPile
    public void takeMarbles(int n) {. . .}

    private int numMarblesInPile;
}
```

Player class

```
public class Player
{
    // Constructor
    public Player(String aName) {. . .}

    // Generic turn ... stupid player's strategy.
    public int takeTurn(NimPile pile) {. . .}

    // Returns name
    public String getName() {. . .}

    private String name;
}
```

SmartPlayer class

```
public class SmartPlayer extends Player
{
    public SmartPlayer(String n) {. . .}

    // Takes marbles using "smart" algorithm.
    public int takeTurn(NimPile pile) {. . .}
}
```

HumanPlayer class

```java
public class HumanPlayer extends Player
{
    public HumanPlayer(String n) {. . .}

    // Human decides the number of marbles to take.
    public int takeTurn(NimPile pile) {. . .}
}
```

3c. NimGame class

```java
public class NimGame
{
    // Constructs game. Creates players and pile of marbles.
    public NimGame(int low, int high)
    {
        System.out.print("What is the human player's name?");
        String nm = Utilities.readWord();
        human = new HumanPlayer(nm);
        boolean isStupid = (Utilities.getRandNumber(0, 1) == 1);
        String computerName = "ROBO COMPUTER";
        if (isStupid)
            computer = new Player(computerName);
        else
            computer = new SmartPlayer(computerName);
        pile = new NimPile(low, high);
    }

    // Plays game.
    public void playNim()
    {
        boolean computerHasTurn = (Utilities.getRandNumber(0, 1) == 1);
        if (computerHasTurn)
            System.out.println(computer.getName() + " goes first!");
        else
            System.out.println(human.getName() + " goes first!");
        while (pile.getMarbles() > 1)
        {
            System.out.println("\nMarbles in pile: " + pile.getMarbles());
            if (computerHasTurn)
            {
                int n = computer.takeTurn(pile);
                System.out.println(computer.getName() + " takes " + n
                        + " marbles");
            }
            else
            {
                human.takeTurn(pile);
            }
            computerHasTurn = !computerHasTurn;
        }
        if (computerHasTurn)
            System.out.println("Congratulations! You won!");
        else
            System.out.println("Sorry, you lost.");
    }

    private HumanPlayer human;
    private NimPile pile;
    private Player computer;
}
```

NimPile class

```java
public class NimPile
{
    // Constructs marble pile for Nim.
    public NimPile(int a, int b)
    {
        numMarblesInPile = Utilities.getRandNumber(a, b);
    }

    // Returns number of marbles in pile.
    public int getMarbles()
    {
        return numMarblesInPile;
    }

    // n <= numMarblesInPile / 2
    public void takeMarbles(int n)
    {
        numMarblesInPile -= n;
    }

    private int numMarblesInPile;
}
```

Player class

```java
public class Player
{
    // Constructor.
    public Player(String aName)
    {
        name = aName;
    }

    // Generic turn...stupid player's strategy.
    public int takeTurn(NimPile pile)
    {
        int n = Utilities.getRandNumber(1, pile.getMarbles() / 2);
        pile.takeMarbles(n);
        return n;
    }

    // Returns name.
    public String getName()
    {
        return name;
    }

    private String name;
}
```

SmartPlayer class

```java
import java.util.Random;
public class SmartPlayer extends Player
{
    public SmartPlayer(String n)
    {
        super(n);
    }
```

```
          // Takes marbles using "smart" algorithm.
          public int takeTurn(NimPile pile)
          {
              int marbles = pile.getMarbles();
              int n = 0;
              if (Utilities.isPowerOfTwoMinusOne(marbles));
                  n = Utilities.getRandNumber(1, marbles / 2);
              else
              {
                  int p = Utilities.largestPowerOfTwoMinusOneBelow(marbles);
                  n = marbles - p;
              }
              pile.takeMarbles(n);
              return n;
          }
      }
```

HumanPlayer class

```
      public class HumanPlayer extends Player
      {
          public HumanPlayer(String n)
          {
              super(n);
          }

          public int takeTurn(NimPile pile)
          {
              int n;
              do
              {
                  System.out.println("How many marbles do you take?");
                  n = Utilities.readInt();
              }
              while (n <= 0 || n > pile.getMarbles() / 2);
              pile.takeMarbles(n);
              return n;
          }
      }
```

■ Cumulative Review 2

Answers to Multiple Choice Questions

1. d	8. a	15. a
2. e	9. d	16. d
3. a	10. c	17. c
4. c	11. b	18. e
5. c	12. e	19. d
6. c	13. c	20. d
7. b	14. c	

Notes on Answers

1. We start with `i` = 1. Mary is in position 1, so Joe is deleted. Now `i` = 3. Because Joe has been deleted, Harry is in position 3 and David is deleted. The size of the list is now 5. When `i` is increased to 5, the loop is not executed. The correct answer is d.

2. An array of size 31 would store the number of samples having 0, 1, 2, 3, ..., 30 left-handed people. `arr[0]` is the number of the 500 samples having 0 lefties; `arr[1]` is the number of the 500 samples that have 1 leftie, etc. The correct answer is e.

9. $n(n-1)/2$ is $O(n^2)$. Expanding the algebraic expression gives a quadratic expression. As n gets very large, the constants can be ignored. We classify this by the largest power of n. The correct answer is d.

14. When `getWorkDetail` is called, it is called from the `Person` method `work`. The implicit type of `this` in the `Person` class is `Person`. Therfore, the parameter type for `getWorkDetail` is `Person` and the correct answer is c.

15. The correct answer is a.

    `e2.printSalary(e2);`   e2 is instantiated as a `Manager`. Even though e2's type is `Employee`, dynamic binding applies when determining whether the `Employee printSalary` or `Manager printSalary` method is called. Because e2 references a `Manager` object, the `Manager printSalary` method is called.

    `e1.printSalary(e1);`   e1 is of type `Employee` and therefore the `printSalary` method (there is only one) of `Employee` is executed.

    `m1.printSalary(m1);`   m1 is of type `Manager` and therefore the `Manager printSalary` method that has a parameter of type `Manager` is executed.

    `e1.printSalary(m1);`   e1 is of type `Employee` and therefore the `printSalary` method (there is only one) of `Employee` is executed. Since m1 is of type `Manager`, which is a subclass of `Employee`, a `Manager` object can be passed to a parameter of type `Employee`.

Answers to Free Response Questions

1a.
```java
public Hand(int numCards)
{
    myHand = new Card[numCards];
    cardsInHand = 0;
}
```

1b.
```java
public void addCard(Card c)
{
    if (!isHandFull())
    {
        myHand[cardsInHand] = c;
        cardsInHand++;
    }
}
```

1c. Java 5
```java
public void printHand()
{
    for (Card i : myHand)
        System.out.println(i);
}
```

1d.
```java
public boolean isFlush()
{
    Card[] myCards = getHand();
    String suit = myCards[0].getSuit();
    for (int i = 1; i < MAX_CARDS; i++)
    {
        String cardSuit = myCards[i].getSuit();
        if (!(suit.equals(cardSuit)))
            return false;
    }
    return true;
}
```

1e.
```java
public boolean isStraight()
{
    sortCards();
    Card[] myCards = getHand();
    for (int i = 1; i < MAX_CARDS; i++)
    {
```

```
            if (myCards[i].getValue() - myCards[i - 1].getValue() != 1)
                return false;
        }
        return true;
    }
```

1f. `public boolean isStraightFlush()`

```
    {
        return isFlush() && isStraight();
    }
```

1g. `public boolean isRoyalFlush()`

```
    {
        // Must call sortCards() if it was not called in isStraight.
        Card[] myCards = getHand();
        return isFlush() && isStraight()
            && ("Ace".equals(myCards[4].getDenomination()));
    }
```

1h. `public boolean isFullHouse()`

```
    {
        int countVal = 0; int countVal2 = 0;
        sortCards();
        Card[] myCards = getHand();
        int val = myCards[0].getValue();
        int val2 = myCards[MAX_CARDS - 1].getValue();

        for (int i = 0; i < MAX_CARDS; i++)
        {
            if (myCards[i].getValue() == val) countVal++;
            if (myCards[i].getValue() == val2) countVal2++;
        }
        return (countVal == 2
                && countVal2 == 3
                || countVal == 3
                && countVal2 == 2)
    }
```

2a. Java 5
    `public static double mean(int[] sampleData)`

```
    {
        int sum = 0;
        for (int i : sampleData)
        {
            sum += i;
        }
        double avg = (double) sum / sampleData.length;
        return avg;
    }
```

2b. Java 5
    `public static double variance(int[] sampleData)`

```
    {
        int sum = 0;
        double avg = mean(sampleData);

        for (int i : sampleData)
        {
            double diff = (i - avg);
            sum += diff * diff;
        }
        return sum / (sampleData.length - 1);
    }
```

```java
2c. public static double standardDeviation(int[] sampleData)
    {
        return Math.sqrt(variance(sampleData));
    }

2d. public static int mode(int[] sampleData)
    {
        int[] b = new int[101];
        for (int i = 0; i < sampleData.length; i++)
        {
            b[sampleData[i]]++;
        }

        int large = b[0];
        int value = 0;
        for (int i = 1; i < b.length; i++)
        {
            if (b[i] > large)
            {
                large = b[i];
                value = i;
            }
        }
        return value;
    }

2e. public static double median(int[] sampleData)
    {
        int[] arr = sortValues(sampleData);
        int len = arr.length;
        if (len % 2 == 0)
            return ( arr[len / 2] + arr[len / 2 - 1]) / 2.0;
        else
            return (arr[len / 2]);
    }

2f. public static void stemAndLeafPlot(int[] sampleData)
    {
        int[] arr = sortValues(sampleData);
        int j = 0;
        for (int i = 0; i <= 10; i++)
        {
            int stem = i;
            System.out.print(stem);
            if (stem < 10)
                System.out.print("   | ");
            else
                System.out.print(" | ");
            while (j < arr.length && stem == arr[j] / 10)
            {
                int leaf = arr[j] % 10;
                System.out.print(leaf + " ");
                j++;
            }
            System.out.println();
        }
    }
```

3. Solutions will vary.

EMT class

```java
import java.util.ArrayList;

public class Emt
{
    public Emt(String emtLastName, String emtFirstName, String emtSs)
    {
        lastName = emtLastName;
        firstName = emtFirstName;
        ssNumber = emtSs;
        ceuCourses = new ArrayList<Course>();
    }

    public String getSsNumber()
    {
        return ssNumber;
    }

    public String getName()
    {
        return firstName + " " + lastName;
    }

    public int getRequiredCredits()
    {
        int totalRequired = 0;
        for (Course i : ceuCourses)
        {
            if (i.getIsRequired())
                totalRequired += i.getNumCeus();
        }
        return totalRequired;
    }

    public int getElectiveCredits()
    {
        int totalElectives = 0;
        for (Course i : ceuCourses)
        {
            if (!i.getIsRequired())
                totalElectives += i.getNumCeus();
        }
        return totalElectives;
    }

    public void addCourse(Course c)
    {
        ceuCourses.add(c);
    }

    public boolean completeRequirements()
    {
        return getRequiredCredits() >= CREDITS_NEEDED
                && getElectiveCredits() >= CREDITS_NEEDED;
    }

    public String toString()
    {
        String s = getName() + "\nSS#: " + getSsNumber() + "\n";
```

```
        for (Course c : ceuCourses)
            s += c.toString();
        return s;
    }

    private String ssNumber;
    private String firstName;
    private String lastName;
    private ArrayList<Course> ceuCourses;
    private static final int CREDITS_NEEDED = 48;
}
```

Course class

```
public class Course
{
    public Course(String name, int credits, String required)
    {
        courseName = name;
        numCeus = credits;
        isRequired = required.equals("required");
    }

    public boolean getIsRequired()
    {
        return isRequired;
    }

    public String getCourseName()
    {
        return courseName;
    }

    public int getNumCeus()
    {
        return numCeus;
    }

    public String toString()
    {
        String s = getCourseName() + " " + getNumCeus();
        if (isRequired)
            s += " required\n";
        else
            s += " elective\n";
        return s;
    }

    private String courseName;
    private int numCeus;
    private boolean isRequired;
}
```

■ Chapter 15

Answers to Multiple Choice Questions

1. e	5. c	9. a
2. b	6. d	10. d
3. c	7. c	
4. b	8. d	

Notes on Answers

1. Each method results in a different output.

Method I	Method II	Method III
0	1	0
1	2	
2	3	
3	4	
4	5	
5		

4. The argument to the recursive method is the string minus its last character. The `return` statement returns the last character plus the result of the recursive call. This basically creates a string that is the reverse of the original string.

7-9. The `ArraySearcher` method `searchFor` is a *helper* method called by the client program. The recursive method is the method `search`. Helper methods are explained in Section 18.3 of your text. The method `search` is recursively called with half of the array, the lower half if `key` is less than `a[mid]` and the upper half if `key` is greater than `a[mid]`. The recursion ends when `key` is found (`a[mid] == key`) or there are no more values to check (`low >= high`). If `key` is not found, `-1` is returned. This method will work as intended only if the original array is in ascending order.

10. This is based on the triangle number problem explained in Section 18.1 in your text.

Answers to Free Response

```
1. public static int gcd(int num1, int  num2)
   {
      if (num2 == 0)
         return num1;
      else
         return gcd(num2, num1 % num2);
   }

2a. /*
      Can be static because a Polygon object does not need to be
      created to determine the area of a triangle formed by the three
      points that are passed as parameters.
   */
   public static double triangleArea(Point p1, Point p2, Point p3)
   {
      double x1 = p1.getX();
      double y1 = p1.getY();
      double x2 = p2.getX();
      double y2 = p2.getY();
      double x3 = p3.getX();
      double y3 = p3.getY();
```

```
        double area = Math.abs((x1 * y2)
              + (x2 * y3)
              + (x3 * y1)
              - (y1 * x2)
              - (y2 * x3)
              - (y3 * x1))
              / 2;
      return area;
   }
```

2b.
```
public double getArea()
{
    if (corners.size() < 3) return 0;

    Point p1 = (Point) corners.get(0);    // in diagram: p1 = c(0)
    Point p2 = (Point) corners.get(1);    // in diagram: p2 = c(1)
    Point p3 = (Point) corners.get(2);    // in diagram: p3 = c(2)
    double area = triangleArea(p1, p2, p3);    // Ax = area of xth triangle

    Polygon remainder = new Polygon();
    remainder.add(p3);    // r(0)
    for (int i = 3; i < corners.size(); i++)
        remainder.add((Point) corners.get(i));
    remainder.add(p1);    // r(r.size() - 1)
    return area + remainder.getArea();
}
```

2b. Illustrated calls to area of polygon:

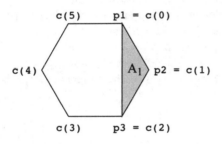

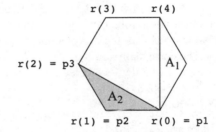

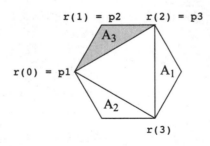

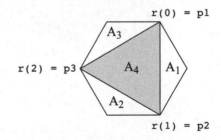

Chapter 16

Answers to Multiple Choice Questions

1. e	5. a	9. b
2. d	6. e	10. c
3. b	7. d	
4. d	8. d	

Notes on Answers

1. The number of comparisons made by the selection sort is based on the number of elements in the array, not the order of the values. The correct answer is e.

2. Choice I is incorrect because it assumes that the elements in the array are all non-negative values.

3. The correct answer is b.

   Choice I. For each element in `list` (x_i), look at x_i. Now look at each element in `list` and count how many times x_i occurs in `list` (n comparisons for each of n elements). So far this is $O(n^2)$. If the count is larger than 1, remove x_i. Removal may require shifting ($O(n$ for each element removed)). Total $= n^2 + n^2 = O(n^2)$

   Choice II. Sort the array list with an efficient sort algorithm.($n \log(n)$). For each x_i in `list`, look at its next neighbor to decide whether it is present more than once. If it is, remove x_i. If we detect adjacent duplicates, we must shift the remainder of the array down, which is $O(n^2)$ in the worst case. So, this gives us a total of $O(n \log(n) + n^2) = O(n^2)$ algorithm.

   Choice III. Sort the array list, `list`, with an efficient algorithm ($n\log(n)$). Traverse the array list looking at each x_i in `list`. Whenever the element after x_i is strictly larger than x_i, append x_i to a second (initially empty) array list, `list2`. Find the difference, `diff`, in the sizes of `list` and `list2`. Beginning with the last element of `list`, delete `diff` elements from `list`. Then, copy the elements of `list2` back into `list`. Total $= n \log(n) + 3n = O(n \log(n))$.

8. This is a binary search but the array is not ordered so it does not work as is intended. The value 2 is never found. The correct answer is d.

9. The smallest power of 2 that is greater than or equal to 45 is 6 ($2^6 = 64$). The correct answer is b.

Answers to Free Response

```
1a. private String sortWord()
    {
        String s = "";
        for (int i = 0; i < originalWord.length(); i++)
        {
            int pos = i - 1;
            String wordLetter = originalWord.substring(i, i + 1);
            while (pos >= 0 && wordLetter.compareTo(s.substring(
                pos, pos + 1)) < 0)
            {
                pos--;
            }
            s = s.substring(0, pos + 1) + wordLetter + s.substring(pos + 1);
        }
        return s;
    }
```

Alternate solution for 1a (outside AP subset)

```
    private String sortWord()
    {
        String s = "";
        int len = originalWord.length();
        char[] a = new char[len];
```

```java
        for (int i = 0; i < len; i++)
        {
            a[i] = originalWord.charAt(i);
        }
        Arrays.sort(a);
        for (int i = 0; i < len; i++)
        {
            s += a[i];
        }
        return s;
    }
```

1b. `public boolean checkAnagram(Word aWord, Word anotherWord)`

```java
    {
        return (anotherWord.getSorted().equals(aWord.getSorted()));
    }
```

1c. `public void printAnagrams(String key)`

```java
    {
        Word newWord = new Word(key);
        for (int i = 0; i < wordList.size(); i++)
        {
            Word temp = (Word) wordList.get(i);
            if (checkAnagram(newWord, temp))
            {
                System.out.println(temp.getWord());
            }
        }
    }
```

2a. `public int compareTo(Object obj)`

```java
    {
        String fullName = getName();
        Person other = (Person) obj;
        String otherFullName = other.getName();
        return fullName.compareTo(otherFullName);
    }
```

2b. `private int minimumPosition(int from)`

```java
    {
        int minPos = from;
        for (int i = from + 1; i < list.size(); i++)
        {
            Person ithPerson = (Person) (list.get(i));
            Person minPerson = (Person) (list.get(minPos));
            if (ithPerson.compareTo(minPerson) < 0)
                minPos = i;
        }
        return minPos;
    }
```

2c. `private int minimumEmailPosition(int from)`

```java
    {
        int minPos = from;
        Comparator comp = new PersonComparator();
        for (int i = from + 1; i < list.size(); i++)
        {
            Person ithPerson = (Person) (list.get(i));
            Person minPerson = (Person) (list.get(minPos));
            if (comp.compare(ithPerson, minPerson) < 0)
                minPos = i;
        }
        return minPos;
    }
```

■ Chapter 17

Answers to Multiple Choice Questions

1.	b	8.	b	15.	d
2.	d	9.	b	16.	d
3.	d	10.	a	17.	b
4.	e	11.	a	18.	a
5.	e	12.	d	19.	d
6.	e	13.	e	20.	c
7.	d	14.	c		

Notes on Answers

6. When `equals` is not defined for a class, the class inherits `Object`'s `equals` method and will return `true` if and only if `node1` and `node2` reference the same object.

11. Lookups need to have a quick retrieval time. The array provides this. In order to retrieve a value from a linked list, the list must be traversed. The stack and queue can not return a specific element, they can access only one element (the top or front element).

Answers to Free Response

1a. Add another instance field and modify the constructor.

1b.
```
public DLListNode getPrevious();
public void setPrevious(DLListNode theNewPrevious);
```

1c.
```
public DLListNode(Object initValue, DLListNode initNext,
       DLListNode initPrev)
{
    super(initValue, initNext);
    previous = initPrev;
}
```

1d.

Operation	Doubly Linked List
addFirst	$O(1)$
addLast	$O(1)$
removeLast	$O(1)$
removeFirst	$O(1)$
isEmpty	$O(1)$
Linear Traversal	$O(n)$
Random Access	$O(n)$

1e.
```
public DLListNode search(Object key)
{
    DLListNode temp = first;
    while (temp != null && !temp.getValue()).equals(key))
    {
        temp = (DLListNode) temp.getNext();
    }
    return temp;
}
```

```
1f. public void removeOne(Object key)
    {
        DLListNode temp = search(key);
        if (temp == null)    // Key isn't in list.
          return;
        if (temp == first)    // Is it the first node?
        {
          if (temp == last)    // Is it the only node?
            last = null;
          first = (DLListNode) first.getNext();  // first.getNext() returns a
                                                 // ListNode so we need to cast
          if (first != null)
            first.setPrevious(null);
          return;
        }

        if (temp.getNext() == null)    // Deleting last node.
        {
          DLListNode hold = temp.getPrevious();
          hold.setNext(null);
          return;
        }

        // Deleting a middle node.
        DLListNode hold = temp.getPrevious();
        hold.setNext(temp.getNext());
        hold = (DLListNode) temp.getNext();
        hold.setPrevious(temp.getPrevious());
        return;
    }

1g. public void removeAll(Object key)
    {
        while (search(key) != null)
        {
          removeOne(key);
        }
    }

2a. public static void displayBinary(int decimalNum)
    {
        final int BASE = 2;
        IntStack stck = new IntStack();

        while (decimalNum != 0)
        {
          int remainder = decimalNum % BASE;
          stck.push(new Integer(remainder));
          decimalNum /= BASE;
        }
        while (!stck.isEmpty())
        {
          Integer num = (Integer) stck.pop();
          System.out.print(num);
        }
    }
```

2b.
```java
public static void displayOtherBase(int num, int base)
{
    IntStack stck = new IntStack();

    while (num != 0)
    {
        int remainder = num % base;
        stck.push(new Integer(remainder));
        num /= base;
    }

    while (!stck.isEmpty())
    {
        Integer number = (Integer) stck.pop();
        int numValue = number.intValue();
        String alpha = "ABCDEF";
        if (numValue >= 10)
        {
            int converted = numValue % 10;
            System.out.print(alpha.substring(converted, converted + 1));
        }
        else
        {
            System.out.print(numValue);
        }
    }
}
```

3a. The appropriate data structure is a linked list. Arrays are not a good choice because the actual number of windows is not known. Array lists are inefficient because of the insertions and deletions to the top. Quite a bit of shifting would be necessary. Stacks add and delete from one end so `cycle` would not be an appropriate operation for a stack. Queues add to one end and delete from the other end. The `WindowManager` operation of `add` and `remove` both refer to the same end. Therefore a queue is not an appropriate choice.

3b.
```java
public void add(Window w)
{
    windows.addFirst(w);
}
```

3c.
```java
public void remove()
{
    windows.removeFirst();
}
```

3d.
```java
public void cycle()
{
    if (windows.size() == 0) return;
    Window w = (Window) windows.removeFirst();
    windows.addLast(w);
}
```

3e.
```java
public void print()
{
    Iterator iter = windows.iterator();
    while (iter.hasNext())
        System.out.println(iter.next());
    System.out.println();
}
```

Note: Knowledge of `java.util.awt.Rectangle` is not tested on the AP Exam.

■ Chapter 18

Answers to Multiple Choice Questions

1.	e	8.	e	15.	c
2.	d	9.	c	16.	d
3.	e	10.	c	17.	b
4.	c	11.	c	18.	b
5.	a	12.	a	19.	e
6.	c	13.	d	20.	b
7.	e	14.	d		

Notes on Answers

4. This method returns the number of nodes in a binary tree. The answer is c.

14. After insertion of all values, the binary tree is:

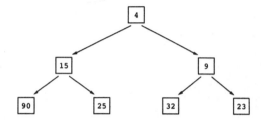

Answers to Free Response

```
1a. public Set setIntersection(Set set2)
    {
        Set set3 = new TreeSet();
        Iterator iter = iterator();
        while (iter.hasNext())
        {
            Object temp = iter.next();
            if (set2.contains(temp))
            {
                set3.add(temp);
            }
        }
        return set3;
    }

1b. public Set setUnion(Set set2)
    {
        Set set3 = new TreeSet();
        Iterator iter = iterator();
        while (iter.hasNext())
        {
            set3.add(iter.next());
        }
        iter = set2.iterator();
        while (iter.hasNext())
        {
            set3.add(iter.next());
        }
        return set3;
    }
```

```
1c. public Set setDifference(Set set2)
    {
        Set set3 = new TreeSet();
        Iterator iter = iterator();
        while (iter.hasNext())
        {
            Object temp = iter.next();
            if (!(set2.contains(temp)))
                set3.add(temp);
        }
        return set3;
    }

1d. public boolean isSubset(Set set2)
    {
        Iterator iter = set2.iterator();
        while (iter.hasNext())
        {
            if (!(contains(iter.next())))
                return false;
        }
        return true;
    }
```

Alternate Solution

```
public boolean isSubset(Set set2)
{
    return setUnion(set2).size() == size()
           && setIntersection(set2).size() == set2.size();
}

1e. public boolean isProperSubset(Set set2)
    {
        if (!(isSubset(set2)))
            return false;
        else if (size() != set2.size())
            return true;
        else
            return false;
    }
```

Alternate Solution

```
public boolean isProperSubset(Set set2)
{
    return (isSubset(set2) && size() != set2.size());
}
```

2a.
```java
public void createConcordance(String fileName)
{
    // infile(fileName) is open for reading
    while ( !(inFile.eof()))
    {
        String word = inFile.readWord();    // Reads word from infile
        Integer temp = (Integer) concord.get(word);
        if (temp == null)
        {
            concord.put(word, new Integer(1));
        }
        else
        {
            int value = temp.intValue();
            value++;
            concord.put(word, new Integer(value));
        }
    }
}
```

2b.
```java
public void printConcordance()
{
    Set concordSet = concord.keySet();
    Iterator iter = concordSet.iterator();
    while (iter.hasNext())
    {
        Object word = iter.next();
        System.out.print(word + " ");
        System.out.println("occurs " +  concord.get(word) + " time(s).");
    }
}
```

2c. A method similar to `printConcordance` would have the iterator traverse the set created by the `TreeMap`'s `keySet` method to obtain the word and its frequency. A `WordFreq` class would be defined to have instance fields that hold word-frequency pairs. With each move of the iterator, a new `WordFreq` object would be instantiated and its two instance fields would be set. The `WordFreq` objects would then be inserted into one of the following data structures.

- A binary search tree implemented so that duplicates are possible according to the frequency. An inorder traversal would give the required results. Insertion of n `WordFrequency` objects is $O(n \log(n))$. Traversal is $O(n)$.
- A priority queue implemented so that duplicates are possible and where the priority is the frequency. Executing `removeMin` repeatedly would give the desired results. Insertion is $O(n \log(n))$. Traversal is $O(n)$.
- An ordered linked list of nodes whose information field is the `WordFreq` object. Nodes would be inserted in order according to the frequency. A linear traversal of the linked list would give the required results. Insertion is $O(n^2)$ ($O(n)$ for each of n elements). Traversal is $O(n)$.
- An ordered `ArrayList` of `WordFreq` objects ordered by frequency. Insertion is $O(n^2)$. Traversal is $O(n)$.

The ones that won't work:
- A stack cannot maintain frequency order.
- A queue cannot maintain frequency order.
- A hash set does not maintain order.
- A hash map does not maintain order.
- A tree set cannot have duplicate values.
- A tree map cannot have duplicate keys.

■ Cumulative Review 3

Answers to Multiple Choice Questions

1. d	8. d	15. a
2. c	9. a	16. c
3. e	10. a	17. d
4. d	11. b	18. c
5. c	12. d	19. b
6. a	13. c	20. b
7. c	14. b	

Answers to Free Response Questions

```java
1a. public ArrayList<Player> getPlayersInLineUp(ArrayList<Integer> bb)
    {
        ArrayList<Player> someTeam = new ArrayList<Player>();
        for (Integer i : bb)
        {
            Player p = myTeam.get(i);
            someTeam.add(p);
        }
        return someTeam;
    }

1b. public boolean isLineUpValid(ArrayList<Player> lineup)
    {
        int numForwards = 0;
        int numGuards = 0;
        int numCenters = 0;
        for (Player i : lineup)
        {
            if (i.getPosition().equals("guard")) numGuards++;
            if (i.getPosition().equals("center")) numCenters++;
            if (i.getPosition().equals("forward")) numForwards++;
        }
        return numGuards == 2 && numForwards == 2 && numCenters == 1;
    }

1c. public void printValidStartingTeams()
    {
        bbLineUps = new CombinationGenerator(numberOnLineUp, 0,
                getTeamSize() - 1);
        while (bbLineUps.hasMoreElements())
        {
            ArrayList<Integer> list = bbLineUps.nextElement();
            ArrayList<Player> p = getPlayersInLineUp(list);
            if (isLineUpValid(p))
            {
                System.out.println(p);
            }
        }
    }
```

1d. The method `isLineUpValid` is defined differently for each type of team and each type of team has requirements for a starting line-up. All other methods are the same.

1e. `int [][] = new int [100][100]` would allow immediate access to a player pair rating.

1f.
```
final int defaultRating = 5;
final int numRow = 100;
final int numCol = 100;
int[][] playerRatings = new int[numRow][numCol];
for (int row = 0; row < numRow; row++)
{
    for (int col = 0; col < numCol; col++)
    {
        playerRatings[row][col] = defaultRating;
    }
}
```

1g.
```
playerRatings[jersey1][jersey2] = pairRating;
playerRatings[jersey2][jersey1] = pairRating;
```

1h.
```
public int getLineUpRating(ArrayList<Player> thisTeam)
{
    int total = 0;
    for (int i = 0; i < thisTeam.size(); i++)
    {
        for (int j = i + 1; j < thisTeam.size(); j++)
        {
            total += ratings[thisTeam.get(i).getJersey()]
                    [(thisTeam.get(j)).getJersey()];
        }
    }
    return total;
}
```

1i.
```
public ArrayList<Player> getBestTeam()
{
    ArrayList bestTeam = new ArrayList<Player>();
    CombinationGenerator lineUps
            = new CombinationGenerator(numberOnLineUp, 0, getTeamSize() - 1);
    int maxRating = 0;
    while (lineUps.hasMoreElements())
    {
        ArrayList<Integer> list = lineUps.nextElement();
        ArrayList<Player> p = getPlayersInLineUp(list);
        if (isLineUpValid(p))
        {
            int rating = getLineUpRating(p);
            if (rating > maxRating)
            {
                bestTeam = p;
                maxRating = rating;
            }
        }
    }
    return bestTeam;
}
```

```
2a. public String toString()
    {
        Set<Integer> st = poly.keySet();
        Iterator<Integer> iter = st.iterator();
        String s = "";
        while (iter.hasNext())
        {
            Integer exponent = iter.next();
            Integer coef = poly.get(exponent);
            if (exponent > 0)
            {
                if (s != "")
                    s = coef + "x^" + exponent + " + " + s;
                else
                    s = coef + "x^" + exponent;
            }
            else
            {
                s = coef + "";
            }
        }
        return s;
    }

2b. public double evaluatePolynomial(double x)
    {
        double answer = 0;
        Set<Integer> s = poly.keySet();
        Iterator<Integer> iter = s.iterator();
        while (iter.hasNext())
        {
            Integer p = iter.next();
            Integer coef = poly.get(p);
            answer += Math.pow(x, p) * coef;
        }
        return answer;
    }

2c. public Polynomial add2(Polynomial other)
    {
        Polynomial theSumPolynomial = new Polynomial();
        TreeMap<Integer, Integer> poly3 = theSumPolynomial.poly;
        Set<Integer> s1 = poly.keySet();
        Iterator<Integer> iter1 = s1.iterator();

        TreeMap<Integer, Integer> poly2 = other.poly;
        Set<Integer> s2 = poly2.keySet();
        Iterator<Integer> iter2 = s2.iterator();

        while (iter1.hasNext())    // Get terms with common exponents
        {
            Integer exponent = iter1.next();
            if (poly2.containsKey(exponent))
            {
                theSumPolynomial.add(exponent, poly.get(exponent)
                    + poly2.get(exponent));
            }
            else
            {
                theSumPolynomial.add(exponent, poly.get(exponent));
            }
        }
```

```
        while (iter2.hasNext())
        {
            Integer exponent = iter2.next();
            if (!poly3.containsKey(exponent))
            {
                theSumPolynomial.add(exponent, poly2.get(exponent));
            }
        }
        return theSumPolynomial;
    }
```

2d. ```
    public Polynomial multiply(Polynomial other)
    {
        Polynomial theProductPolynomial = new Polynomial();
        TreeMap<Integer, Integer> poly3 = theProductPolynomial.poly;
        Set<Integer> s1 = poly.keySet();
        Iterator<Integer> iter1 = s1.iterator();
        TreeMap<Integer, Integer> poly2 = other.poly;
        Set<Integer> s2 = poly2.keySet();
        Iterator<Integer> iter2 = s2.iterator();

        while (iter1.hasNext())
        {
            Integer exponent1 = iter1.next();
            Integer coef1 = poly.get(exponent1);
            iter2 = s2.iterator();
            while (iter2.hasNext())
            {
                Integer exponent2 = iter2.next();
                Integer coef2 = poly2.get(exponent2);
                Integer prodExponent = exponent1 + exponent2;
                Integer prodCoef = coef1 * coef2;
                if (poly3.containsKey(prodExponent))
                {
                    prodCoef += poly3.get(prodExponent);
                }
                theProductPolynomial.add(prodExponent, prodCoef);
            }
        }
        return theProductPolynomial;
    }
```
```